AF712199

The Force of Logic

Using Formal Logic as a Tool in the Craft of Legal Argument

The Force of Logic

Using Formal Logic as a Tool in the Craft of Legal Argument

Stephen M. Rice

NITA®
National Institute for Trial Advocacy

© 2017 National Institute for Trial Advocacy

No part of this work may be reproduced or transmitted in any form or by any means, electronic or mechanical, including photocopying and recording, or by any information storage or retrieval system without the prior written approval of the National Institute for Trial Advocacy unless such copying is expressly permitted by federal copyright law.

Address inquiries to:

Reprint Permission
National Institute for Trial Advocacy
1685 38th Street, Suite 200
Boulder, CO 80301-2735
Phone: (800) 225-6482
Fax: (720) 890-7069
E-mail: permissions@nita.org

ISBN 978-1-60156-609-6
eISBN 978-1-60156-610-2
FBA 1609

Library of Congress Cataloging-in-Publication Data

Names: Rice, Stephen M. (Stephen Matthew), 1969- author.

Title: The force of logic : using formal logic as a tool in the craft of legal argument / Stephen M. Rice.

Description: Boulder, CO : National Institute for Trial Advocacy, 2017. | Includes index.

Identifiers: LCCN 2016057899 (print) | LCCN 2016058192 (ebook) | ISBN 9781601566096 (alk. paper) | ISBN 9781601566102

Subjects: LCSH: Law--Methodology. | Logic. | Trial practice--United States.

Classification: LCC K213 .R53 2017 (print) | LCC K213 (ebook) | DDC 347/.075--dc23

LC record available at https://lccn.loc.gov/2016057899

ASPEN PUBLISHING

Official co-publisher of NITA.
aspenpublishing.com/NITA

Dedication

To my family.

Contents

Appendices: Exercises: Solutions and Discussions

Preface

I love the practice of law, and particularly the role of lawyers in the litigation process. You fall in love with things that fascinate and challenge you through their complexity, unpredictability, and beauty. There are a handful of things in my life that I have found so beautifully complex and unpredictable that I have sought after them for decades and have full confidence that I will continue to pursue them, but never master them, to the end of my life. Things worthy of such pursuit inspire us to a rich, sustained, patient, and humble path toward understanding the thing pursued, and self-improvement. This book is, in a sense, a reflection of my own walk down that path toward understanding something about legal argument. I hope, whether you are a student curious about how lawyers design, deliver, and respond to legal argument, or an experienced trial lawyer or judge seeking some deeper or different understanding or advantage over the arguments you make, respond to, or evaluate every day, that this book will inspire you to love legal argument, and appreciate its complexity, unpredictability, and beauty in a new way.

Studying logic as an undergraduate student was what inspired me to pursue a career as a lawyer, and later, to transition from a practitioner of law to a teacher of law. As a practitioner, I had the great privilege of working with and against lawyers who made great arguments, and delivered them brilliantly. I remember listening to lawyers' courtroom arguments and thinking, "Wow, that was really good." As important as the practice of law is, it has not developed many objective tools for assessing the difference between good legal argument and bad legal argument. That assessment has been left to the subjective tastes of juries, judges, and appellate tribunals, and the silent declarations of opposing counsel thinking, "Wow, that was really good."

The study of logic provides some tools for assessing legal argument for making legal argument and making it better. Logic provides specific and practical tools for making and evaluating arguments. One of those tools is the ability to recognize a *formal logical fallacy*—a defined argumentative pattern that appears to be logical but is not. The formal logical fallacies that result from failing to comply with specific, ancient rules of formal logic are the focus of this book. At the very least, good legal argument should not be logically fallacious. Formal logical fallacies can be efficiently identified by their patterns in legal argument. Learning the rules of formal logic helps law students, lawyers, and judges be attentive to something that exists at the foundation of every legal argument: a logical structure that has the potential to be persuasive, or unpersuasive. Moreover, developing attentiveness to the logical structure of argument presents opportunities for lawyers to improve their skills at designing, delivering, and defending against arguments.

This book will not suggest that all legal argument is entirely controlled by the rules of formal logic. Instead, it reasons that formal logic is one useful tool in the unpredictable and beautiful complexity of legal argument. Pursuing a deeper understanding of that complexity is personally satisfying and deepens a lawyer's ability, understanding, and love for practical legal argument. Understanding and using better logic in legal argument facilitates better arguments, better evaluation, and better results in the pursuit of justice.

One of the best tools for understanding and using better logic is studying case examples that explicitly employ rules of formal logic. Fortunately, many published decisions involving diverse legal and procedural issues also focus on rules of formal logic. These cases provide examples of lawyers and judges communicating about rules of logic and applying them in legal argument. I base my discussion of these cases on my reading and interpretation of the facts and arguments as revealed in the decisions of the courts. I have no personal knowledge of any case discussed in this book beyond my own reading and interpretation of those judicial opinions. This book uses those cases and examples of argument for understanding how lawyers use logic in argument, and not as an effort to report on the parties, their arguments, or the facts of their cases. Better perspectives on those matters can be found in the opinions themselves, reviewing the records of those cases, and speaking directly with the witnesses, parties, and their attorneys. Further, judicial opinions do not always accurately reflect the arguments intended by the litigants, and regularly omit the context, details, and entirety of the arguments offered by their counsel. As you will see from the book, lawyers are not always provided with cases that lend themselves to strict compliance with the rules of formal logic, and sometimes what courts have described as logically fallacious arguments are simply lawyers' best arguments available to them under the circumstances. Accordingly, one should not draw any conclusions about the lawyers or quality of their advocacy from the case discussions in this book.

Similarly, the sample arguments and case documents referred to and provided throughout the book provide additional examples of logic in legal argument, and are not intended to report or reflect any actual legal dispute. The names of the parties and facts in those examples are fiction, and are not designed to resemble any actual lawsuit, party, or events; they should not be relied upon as such.

Additionally, the ancient rules of formal logic and formal logical fallacies at the center of this book are nothing new. They are not the invention of this author. They have been written about by countless authors and studied by philosophers and students of philosophy for more than two thousand years. However, the practical value of formal logic in legal argument has received limited attention. My hope is that this book will encourage you to ask hard questions about how you design legal arguments, your standards for evaluating arguments, and the value of considering formal logic's role in legal argument. I hope you will be inspired to take something very old and apply it fruitfully in the contemporary, complex, unpredictable system of legal argument.

Acknowledgments

First, I am grateful to the National Institute for Trial Advocacy (NITA) for its steadfast commitment to legal advocacy skills training and its willingness to pursue the development of the place of formal logic in trial advocacy by publishing this book. NITA has supported a diverse catalog of publications providing different perspectives on the art and science of trial advocacy, and I am grateful that this topic and title would be among them.

I also extend my thanks to the colleagues at Liberty University School of Law who encouraged my interest in developing the practical application of formal logic in legal argument during my tenure at that institution. However, I write here in my individual capacity and not on behalf of Liberty University. I am particularly grateful to many of my students over the years who have encouraged me to write a book like this, some of whom, now practitioners, have provided thoughtful guidance as I have worked to make this text accessible and useful to both students and practitioners. Many of the concepts developed in this book began as topics of law review articles, and I thank the past editors at *Akron Law Review, Mississippi Law Journal, Willamette Law Review, Pace Law Review, Barry Law Review*, and *Oklahoma City Law Review* for providing a forum and support for my interest in developing the topic of formal logic in legal advocacy.

I am grateful to the lawyers and judges I was privileged to practice with and against before leaving full-time practice to teach law. The rigor of trial practice presents extraordinary opportunities to grow and to regress, be inspired and become cynical, develop good habits and bad ones. Lawyers sometimes undeservedly find themselves practicing alongside and against others who are good lawyers, good teachers, and good people. I admit to enjoying such undeserved opportunities, and to the extent I have experienced any growth, inspiration, and good habits as a lawyer, I am indebted to the professionals who surrounded me.

Last, my wife and children also surrounded me, and extended much grace to me, as I wrote about this topic, talked with them about logic and legal argument, and was distracted from them by this book. I am grateful for their support as I pursued logic's place in legal argument.

Chapter One

Ancient Rules of Logic and a New Perspective on Argument

Important, and sometimes mysterious, rules of logical thinking play a crucial, frequently unnoticed role in the way lawyers design and deliver legal arguments. This book begins by challenging you to consider some questions about what legal argument is, how lawyers think about and design legal arguments, what is meant by a "logical" argument, and why logical arguments are persuasive. The questions are applicable to people interested in legal argument, whether they are learning about legal argument for the first time or are courtroom veterans. As you read this chapter, consider the following questions:

- If you had to explain how legal argument is different from other kinds of argument, how would you explain that difference?
- What criteria would you use to distinguish a good legal argument from a poor one?
- Do you know someone who demonstrates logical thinking in the way they speak or write? Do you find them credible or persuasive because of their logicality?
- Have you ever heard someone make an argument that was unpersuasive or simply nonsensical, but you struggled to articulate why?
- Think for a moment about the various kinds of legal arguments lawyers make, whether they take the form of an opening statement at trial, arguing a legal issue during a motion hearing, discussing a persuasive line of cases in an appellate brief, or in the organization of a civil complaint. How much thought do you think you would give to the logical structure and organization of those various kinds of argument? If you would give a lot of attention, why? If you give a little, why?
- When a legal argument is logically compelling, what words do you use to describe it?
- What does it mean to say that a legal argument is "logical" or "illogical"?
- When a legal argument is illogical, what words do you use to describe it?

1.1 A New Way of Thinking about Jazz—and Legal Argument

At 2:30 p.m. on March 2, 1959, Miles Davis, Julian "Cannonball" Adderley, John Coltrane, Winton Kelly, Bill Evans, Paul Chambers, and Jimmy Cobb assembled at Columbia Records' 30th Street Studio in Manhattan.[1] That afternoon, this extraordinary group of musicians created *Kind of Blue*, the bestselling traditional jazz album in history.[2] *Kind of Blue*, sometimes referred to simply as *Blue*, is an extraordinary piece of music for many reasons: the virtuosic artists who assembled to create it, the role of the incomparable jazz virtuoso Miles Davis in its creation and performance, and the impact and perseverance *Blue* has had in jazz for more than fifty years. But to me, *Blue* is more than just a classic jazz album. Discovering *Blue* caused me, like countless others, to fall in love with midcentury jazz. *Blue*'s impact went beyond changing the way I would listen to and think about music. *Blue* unexpectedly transformed the way I thought about how lawyers design legal argument and the role theories of logic play in the work of crafting persuasive legal argument.

This transformation transpired not simply from hearing the music Miles Davis made on March 2, 1959. It transpired from learning something about why the music carried such impact. *Blue* begins with a song called "So What." After hearing it for the first time, the first few measures of "So What" replayed in my head for weeks before I asked a musician friend about both the song and album. As he explained something about music generally and jazz specifically, I could tell that he thought about music from a different perspective than I did—and it changed the way I think about music, and other things. He explained something about jazz music theory, the rules of music, and what it means to improvise as a jazz musician. His explanation revealed how six immensely talented, creative musicians, huddled together in the studio at 30th Street in Manhattan with very little preconceived, detailed direction on how to play "So What,"[3] could create such a beautiful, enduring piece of music. My friend focused his explanation on what jazz theorists call *modal jazz*. Modal jazz is one method of jazz improvisation, where the musicians' improvisations are organized around selected musical scales or modes.[4] Traditional jazz forms prior to modal jazz had organized improvisation around chords, groups of three or four notes

1. Ashlay Kahn, Kind of Blue: The Making of the Miles Davis Masterpiece 94–102 (2001).
2. Bambarger, Bradley, *Miles Davis' True "Blue,"* Billboard (Aug. 1999), at 7 (describing the album as "the all-time most popular traditional jazz album at well more than 3 million copies sold worldwide according to label reports").
3. "'*Kind of Blue*' is perhaps the ultimate testament to spontaneity, even in a genre fueled by improvisation. Without rehearsal, the collective created finished music spontaneously from sketches Davis brought fresh into the studio." *Id.*
4. Barrett, Samuel. *"Kind of Blue" and the Economy of Modal Jazz*, 25 Popular Music 185, 188 (2006) (including this definition among others, as modal jazz has been "defined in a number of different ways extending from improvisation based (however loosely) on selected scales, to playing over static harmonic backgrounds, to any harmonic organization that is not straightforwardly diatonic.").

played simultaneously. In 1959, modal jazz organized improvisation around scales or modes, groups of eight notes played in ordered succession.[5]

As it relates to *Blue*,[6] the modal jazz structure was an organizational tool that accomplished at least three important things that lend some perspective on the role of logic in legal argument. First, the common organizational structure provided the musicians with a set of "rules" that brought order, predictability, and coherence to the music. Second, this structure provided a frame of reference for the musicians to understand one another's respective musical efforts and communicate, both verbally and musically, about the music and its performance. Third, modal jazz allowed musicians freedom to exercise their own creative powers within a common structure. The power to discipline creativity is used by musicians who leverage rules of modal jazz to make music that their audiences love. The logic of modal jazz is what took six musicians' otherwise disparate voices in 1959, and empowered their assembly in a way that expressed the creativity of each artist in a form that makes sense to their audiences. At least to my ears, modal jazz took what might otherwise sound like voices from unorganized instruments and turned them into something orchestrated, carefully executed, and beautiful. Understanding something about the fundamental organization of the music helped me appreciate why it was extraordinarily appealing and persuasive to me. It also made me think about the musician's craft and how similar it was to other types of creative processes. Since I was a lawyer and not a musician, this revelation caused me to think critically about the things that organize legal argument and make legal argument persuasive.

1.2 Persuasive Music, Logical Order, and Compelling Legal Argument

Learning about the rules of modal jazz might help you better appreciate the influences that rules have in music. The power of rules is also at work in legal argument. Doubtless, substantive rules of law play a large role in legal argument. Similarly, procedural rules play an important role in litigation. However, these rules of substantive and procedural law are not the only ones at work in legal argument. The most fundamental rules of legal argument are rules of logic—and they can make legal arguments more appealing and persuasive.

5. This is a simplified definition of a more complex concept. Keith Waters offers a more complete summary of the elements of modal jazz: 1) "modal scales for improvisation," 2) "slow harmonic rhythm," 3) "pedal point harmonies," 4) "absence or limited use of functional harmonic progressions . . . in accompaniment or improvisation," 5) "harmonies characteristic of jazz after 1959," and 6) "prominent use of melodic and/or harmonic perfect fourths." Keith Waters, The Studio Recordings of the Miles Davis Quintet, 1965–68, 41–46 (2011).

6. There is some difference of opinion regarding whether some or all of the songs on *Blue* are modal in nature. *Id.*

First, understanding something about modal jazz and how that music theory held the improvisation of the artists together seems directly applicable to legal argument. The modal jazz form organizes the musicians' improvisation and makes the music appealing. Similarly, good, logically ordered, thoroughly organized argument is pleasing to the ear, easy to follow, and makes the audience want to hear more.

The most fundamental rules of legal argument are rules of logic — and they can make legal arguments more appealing and persuasive.

Second, understanding some of the language and theory of modal jazz helps even neophytes talk about what they like and dislike about the music they hear. Communicating about jazz, understanding the passion of the artists, learning about the social and musical background of the music they played all help to develop a more complete understanding of and appreciation for jazz. In the same way, learning about logic, its role in argument generally and legal argument specifically, provides a powerful tool for evaluating and communicating what is appealing about a good argument and what might seem misguided and unpersuasive about another argument.

Finally, learning something about the theory behind the music changes the way one thinks about and listens to music. Although I am by no means an expert on jazz, I became more curious and thoughtful about why I listen to music, how I invest my time into learning about jazz and the musicians who perform it, and why jazz is appealing to me. Learning about logic, studying its place in legal argument, and developing some knowledge of the language of logic empowers you to communicate about logic in legal argument. It develops appreciation of something new about legal argument by encouraging thoughtfulness regarding when and how you make an argument. Further, it promotes intentionality about listening to and objectively, thoughtfully evaluating the components, organization, and details of argument, legal and otherwise.

This is a book about a concept philosophers call "philosophical logic,"[7] without being a philosophy book. It argues that the philosophy of formal logic, developed over thousands of years, is an important and practical tool for making, evaluating, and communicating effective legal argument. However, the focus and the vehicle for making this argument circumvent much of the philosophical writing on logic. Further, this book will not retread the substantial philosophical debate regarding logic's role in jurisprudence. Instead, it focuses on the simple, but important, truths gleaned from the philosophy of logic and how they can become powerful, practical tools for those interested in the integrity and efficacy of legal argument. The purpose in this approach is twofold. First, the author is a lawyer, not a logician or philosopher. My experience has been in developing and studying logic's role in convincing arguments rather than studying philosophy. Others have written more

7. *See, e.g.*, Dale Jacquette, Philosophy of Logic 1 (2007).

expertly and extensively on the philosophy of logic and the nature of legal reasoning from a jurisprudential perspective. The philosophical history of logic and the jurisprudential place of formal logic are topics better left to other authors and other forums. Second, you, the reader, are likely not a professional philosopher either. Contemporary lawyers, judges, and law students rarely have a formal education in philosophy—and yet, the philosophy of logic has an important practical role to play in legal argument.

Modern lawyers, judges, and law students are all engaged in argument in some capacity. The arguments take different forms, and are delivered in different contexts, in oral argument and in written briefs, in the courtroom and in the boardroom, to judges, to jurors, at trial or on appeal, and beyond. What is common to all lawyers, civil and criminal, trial and transactional, is that we must communicate and convince daily. Convincing is an eminently practical skill. Rules of philosophical logic are important practical tools when you develop and execute strategies for using legal arguments to convince.

While this is a book about using logical rules as a foundational tool for communicating and convincing, it takes a tighter focus on one among the several topics and methods traditionally taught in law schools and continuing legal education courses on advocacy. Modern trial advocacy teaching frequently focuses on the important topics of utilizing rhetorical devices at trial, relating to jurors, developing storytelling techniques, fostering and maintaining credibility in the courtroom, and effectively cross-examining and impeaching witnesses. These important topics are essential to effective trial advocacy. At times, however, they are presented as topics distinct from the design and structure of the arguments they communicate or support. Further, these advocacy topics often receive more prominence and emphasis than the structure of argument or the process for designing argument. If a lawyer in a negligence case knows he has a strong argument on liability, he might decide to focus on the favorable liability facts in his closing argument, rather than the more problematic facts relating to damages. He might decide to begin and end his closing argument discussing the most persuasive liability facts he developed during trial. His decision to do so might very well be an important and beneficial choice supporting his argument. Similarly, a lawyer making an argument on appeal might focus on a favorable standard of review to support her client's position. She might spend most of her oral argument reminding the tribunal that it cannot review the facts of the case *de novo* but instead, must defer to the credibility assessment made by the trier of fact. Such a decision to spend more time focused on the favorable standard of review might be an essential decision, important to delivering a good argument. However, students and practitioners of legal argument frequently focus more time on how to *deliver* the argument than on how to *design* the argument.

This book focuses on the methods for designing legal argument itself, rather that the methods for delivery of argument. Further, it focuses on what makes argument's design sound and compelling. It considers whether legal arguments can be stripped of their rhetorical façades, masonry cladding, and cornices and be reduced simply to a concrete foundation and steel framing. The subject of this book is this most basic structure of legal argument. One author has described it as the "architecture of argument."[8] The argument's supportive skeleton is in many ways essential to a successful argument. However, while lawyers have many tools to explain to a judge or jurors how opposing counsel's argument is misleading, ignores important facts, or mischaracterizes a case holding, lawyers are typically equipped with comparatively few tools to explain what is wrong with the logical architecture of opposing counsel's argument.

The modest goal of this book is to show you a few of those tools, explain their names and how they work, provide some examples of how they have been used by lawyers and judges in the past, and show how they can be used by lawyers and judges in the future. For new lawyers or law students, focusing on the logical form of legal argument for a few chapters may help you discover something important about legal argument. It might help you to learn a couple lessons that experienced lawyers learn after a few years in practice: that not all arguments are good, and that some are helplessly logically flawed and should be abandoned entirely. For experienced lawyers, this book might convince you that opposing counsel, or the lawyers in your conference room or on your conference call, have been pulling the proverbial "fast one" on you, sometimes without even realizing what they were doing. Focusing on the logical rules described in the next chapters may help you to think more intentionally about something lawyers frequently assume: that lawyers always make *logical* arguments in every case. You will see here that lawyers sometimes make necessarily *illogical* arguments, dressed in a logical argument's clothing, and because neither their adversary nor their judge is trained in logic or knows how to describe the logical errors of the argument, the unsupportive skeleton of their argument goes unnoticed.

Many undergraduate students take an introductory logic course. If you took a basic class that explored the philosophy of logic, you likely learned at least two things. First, logic is persuasive and useful. Logic is at work in many important tasks, like solving a mathematical equation and making an argument. Second, knowing even something limited about logic is beneficial in many disciplines, including law. That is, you do not have to be a professional logician, or devote several hundred hours to the study of logic, to find a few things that help you think about how you reason and argue, and how to think and argue better. Studying logic might help you to better understand the things that you took for granted when, for example, you solved a geometric proof, wrote computer code, organized an essay, or presented an argument. Further, if you took a basic logic course and knew nothing about law school or the practice of law, it might have sparked an interest in argument, even the kind of professional arguments that lawyers learn about in law school and deliver in briefs and courtrooms.

8. This apt description for formal logic as the "architecture of argument" is found in James C. Raymond, *The Architecture of Argument*, 7 Jud. Rev. J. Jud. Comm'n New S. Wales 39 (2004).

However, if you then assumed lawyers thought about argument the same way logicians do, you would be disappointed to find this is not so. Some law students decide to pursue a legal career based on the assumption that because, from a philosophical perspective, logic seems useful in making, testing, and challenging arguments, they could go to law school and spend more time continuing to study about the logical rules they were exposed to as undergraduates and then apply those rules to what they would learn about the substantive law.[9] But with few exceptions, formal philosophical logic is not ordinarily taught in law school.[10] It is occasionally mentioned in first-year "legal methods" classes, but for the most part, new lawyers are taught legal reasoning in a way that presupposes that they have fundamental

---

9. *See, e.g.*, Kristen K. Tiscione, *How the Disappearance of Classical Rhetoric and the Decision to Teach Law as "Science" Severed Theory from Practice in Legal Education*, 51 Wake Forest L. Rev. 385, 400 (2016) ("I believe our students crave what rhetoric provides. It is what they expect to learn when they arrive for their first year of law school. Teaching rhetoric today would mean teaching epistemology, the philosophy of law, classical and contemporary theories of persuasion, the canons of rhetoric, modes of reasoning (induction, deduction, analogy, narrative, and inferential), argumentation theory, the psychology of human behavior, and the ethics of persuasion.").

10. The absence of substantial systematic teaching of the process and logic of legal reasoning has been described elsewhere in more detail. For example, one report is that:

> Viewing their law school experience in its entirety, most students do receive some exposure to each method of legal reasoning that is used in law practice. Most students, however, do not participate in a systematic and in-depth study of each method's operation, potential uses, and conceptual bases. Further, the reductionist approach created by the case method, coupled with the lack of practical, large-scale problem solving, means that law students are not exposed to, and do not intuitively perceive, legal reasoning in a comprehensive, synthetic manner. They often do not understand that legal reasoning is a dynamic, iterative process which must be adapted to the needs of a particular legal problem. They often do not understand that legal reasoning involves the structured manipulation and utilization of information, not the information itself.
>
> Law students carry this lack of understanding into the practice of law. As a result, new attorneys often treat cases and statutes as discrete entities that are to be analyzed separately. Their memoranda reflect this narrow orientation and often contain long discussions of rules of law, but little synthesis and analysis. Their memoranda often are disjointed, reflecting a lack of flow or direction due to the writer's inability to link the various forms of, and steps in, legal reasoning so as to create a seamless whole.

Kevin H. Smith, *Practical Jurisprudence: Deconstructing and Synthesizing the Art and Science of Thinking Like a Lawyer*, 29 U. Mem. L. Rev. 1, 2–3 (1998) (citations omitted); *see also* Kristen K. Tiscione, *How the Disappearance of Classical Rhetoric and the Decision to Teach Law as "Science" Severed Theory From Practice in Legal Education*, 51 Wake Forest L. Rev. 385 (2016) (discussing the history of classical rhetoric, including the place of teaching logic, in legal education); Ruggero J. Aldisert et al., *Logic for Law Students: How to Think Like a Lawyer*, 69 U. Pitt. L. Rev. 1, 2 (2007) ("Notwithstanding the emphasis on logical reasoning in the legal profession, our law schools do not give students an orientation in the principles of logic."); Jon M. Garon, *Legal Education in Disruption: The Headwinds and Tailwinds of Technology*, 45 Conn. L. Rev. 1165 (2013) ("The casebooks and materials provided to the students in these MBE-tested courses do not include any formal training on logic or reason."); Kristen K. Robbins, *Paradigm Lost: Recapturing Classical Rhetoric to Validate Legal Reasoning*, 27 Vt. L. Rev. 483 (2003) ("Many students enter law school thinking that they will receive formal training in either logic or rhetoric, but very few law schools even teach classes in these subjects.").

knowledge of how to think logically and that they can spot an illogical argument intuitively. Legal education may be entirely right to make this determination: the LSAT records prospective law students' performances on logical tasks. For the most part, law students can learn to make and respond to arguments without resorting to any of the tools of formal logic. Understanding formal logic takes time, time that law students are using to learn the case method, substantive law, procedural law, and the practical skills of lawyering. As a result, few law schools have made space in their curricula for courses focused on logic in legal argument.[11]

Lawyers trained in some of the foundational rules of argument may see legal argument differently from their colleagues who are not. Studying logic encourages one to think carefully about designing arguments before spending a lot of time planning how to deliver them. Conversely, an understanding that argument has to play by logical rules causes a lawyer to think more deliberately than he might otherwise have when evaluating the logical form of opposing counsels' arguments. The logical force (or failure) of an argument's architecture will reveal itself, even when it is heavily decorated with bricks and mortar. Identifying those logical strengths and weaknesses requires some knowledge of logical rules and vigilance in identifying arguments that fail to comply with them.

The lawyer's job, when confronted by an argument with an errant logical structure, is to focus on the architecture of the argument. Herein lies the problem: many lawyers are not trained in formal logic enough to spot these logical errors. Even when they do sense the errors, they do not have requisite language tools to talk about them. We should not expect them to. Most have never been taught the language of formal logic. They learn the case method, legal reasoning, substantive and procedural law, and basic lawyering skills. They know how to adorn their own arguments with compelling stories and analogies. Confronted with seemingly robust presentation of opposing counsel's argument, they might take a deep breath, and repeat their own argument with a little more volume or vehemence. They might suggest their case is more compelling. They might

11. Some have suggested that teaching logic occupy a larger space in the law school curriculum. *See, e.g.*, LARRY ALEXANDER & EMILY SHERWIN, DEMYSTIFYING LEGAL REASONING 234 (2008) ("We do not mean to suggest that legal training is pointless, although our analysis may imply that law schools should spend more time than they currently do teaching logic and empirical methods."); *see also* Tiscione, *supra* note 10, at 400–01.

"pound on the facts"[12] of their case. They might "pound on the law" in their favor. If all else fails they might "pound on the table" a bit. However, all this pounding might be misplaced. The problem with an argument with an errant logical structure is neither a fact problem nor a law problem. Instead, it is a logic problem and many lawyers are not well armed to talk about logic. They never learned about it. It was assumed that they understood basic logic: what logic is, what logic's role is in legal argument, and importantly, how to describe and talk about problems of logical form.[13] My hope is that this book will help you think about logic differently, use logic more intentionally, and practice more successfully, by developing better logical tools for making, evaluating and discussing legal arguments.

1.3 A Focus on One Logical Tool: Formal Logic

The next chapter describes several logical tools at the disposal of lawyers engaged in the craft of legal argument. However, the focus of this book is on just one category of these tools, something logicians call *formal logic*. Formal logic is described

12. It is an aphorism among trial lawyers that "if the facts are on your side, pound on the facts. If the law is on your side, pound on the law. If neither is on your side, pound on the table." *See, e.g.*, Findley v. Jones Motor Freight, Div. Allegheny Corp., 639 F.2d 953, 960 (3d Cir. 1981); State ex rel. Owners Ins. Co. v. McGraw, 233 W. Va. 776, 788, n. 1 (2014); Titlow v. Burt, No. 07-CV-13614, 2010 U.S. Dist. LEXIS 111459, at *56 (E.D. Mich. Oct. 19, 2010) *rev'd*, 680 F.3d 577 (6th Cir. 2012) *rev'd*, 134 S. Ct. 10, 187 L. Ed. 2d 348 (2013); Magin v. Solitude Homeowner's Inc., 255 P.3d 920, 935 (Wyo. 2011) ("'When you have compelling facts, pound on those facts. When the law is agreeable to your position, pound on the law. When you have neither favorable facts nor law, pound the table. It is less amusing than unsettling.'") (quoting Hatch v. State Farm Fire & Cas. Co., 930 P.2d 382, 398 (Wyo. 1997), O'Brien, J., concurring); Hendricks v. State, 640 S.W.2d 932, 936 (Tex. Crim. App. 1982); *see also* Grant Dorfman, *The Founders' Legal Case: "No taxation without Representation" Versus Taxation No Tyranny*, 44 Hous. L. Rev. 1377, 1412 (2008) (quoting one version of this saying and attributing its original source to Carl Sandburg, The People, Yes 181 (1936)).

13. *See, e.g.*, James M. Boland, *Legal Writing Programs and Professionalism: Legal Writing Professors Can Join the Academic Club*, 18 St. Thomas L. Rev. 711, 722 (2006) ("I can attest from personal experience that many attorneys and even law professors are not quite sure how the syllogism fits into legal argument . . . . In fact, even after I completed law school and passed the bar, I had no idea that the basis of my writing should be grounded in syllogistic logic. It was not until I began teaching legal writing and contemplating and researching the pedagogy of legal analysis, that the importance of thinking in terms of making legal arguments as opposed to rigidly applying IRAC, became clear.").

generally as set of rules for disciplined thinking.[14] These rules are also useful in designing convincing argument. They are rules that are applicable when we take an ordinary argument and organize it into a common argumentative framework and test that framework against the rules of formal deductive logic. We frequently organize arguments, or at least think about them this way intuitively. For example, the following argument takes a familiar form:

> If Plaintiff has failed to state a claim upon which relief can be granted, then its complaint must be dismissed. Plaintiff has failed to state a claim upon which relief can be granted. Therefore, its complaint must be dismissed.

This argumentative structure, comprised of two *premises* and a *conclusion*, is called a *syllogism*.[15]

While lawyers can readily break arguments down simple arguments into their basic components, it would be incorrect to say that formal logic is the only tool lawyers use to design persuasive argument or solve legal problems. To say that legal reasoning or legal argument is entirely based on formal logic would be incorrect. However, formal logic is foundational to making and evaluating legal arguments.

To say that legal reasoning or legal argument is entirely based on formal logic would be incorrect. However, formal logic is foundational to making and evaluating legal arguments.

Formal logic is a particularly well-suited tool, since legal argument is frequently about classification or categorization of behavior or status, and concepts of formal logic are readily applicable to these kinds of tasks. Laws or contracts define the categories. For example, persons who have committed larceny, parties who have earned a contractual performance, businesses that have obtained trademark protection, persons who have undertaken a fiduciary obligation, persons who are agents, persons who have violated the terms of probation, and plaintiffs who have plead fraud with requisite particularity are all categories of behavior or status defined by

14. Formal logic has been defined in several different ways. However a sample of alternative definitions exemplifies how the concept of "formal logic" is used to distinguish it from other definitions of logic or reasoning. *See, e.g.*, ARNOLD VANDER NAT, SIMPLE FORMAL LOGIC: WITH COMMON-SENSE SYMBOLIC TECHNIQUES 2 (2010) ("the methods and the principles . . . of correct argumentation, as these methods and principles are part of a formal system."); J. LACY O'BYRNE CROKE, LOGIC 3 (1906) ("Pure or Formal Logic is the science of the necessary laws of thought. It has thought rather than language for its adequate object-matter; for though it must express itself in language, and is very much concerned with it, language comes in only as the minister of thought. It is a science;—a science rather than an art.") (footnote omitted); W. R. BOYCE GIBSON, THE PROBLEM OF LOGIC 157 (1908) (". . . Formal Logic is a propaedeutic which is abstractly concerned with consistency of reasoning without any reference to the truth or the falsehood of the accepted premises, or to the knowledge or the ignorance of the reasoner.").
15. The *syllogism* will be described and discussed further in Chapters Two and Three.

a legal rule. Lawyers argue about whether a party fits into the category. As Chapter Three describes, this process of putting concepts in categories and drawing inferences from them is, foundationally, a process governed by rules of formal logic. The process does not end there, since lawyers use other tools to advocate for whether a party fits into the category. For example, they might use analogy to make their argument, claiming that the facts of the case are similar to another case, in which the court determined the party did not fall within the category.

There is a basic kind of thinking, sometimes called *formal logic* or *deductive logic*, which has a place at the foundation of most legal arguments. Frequently, this formal logic lurking in the background of a legal argument is uncontested, and the lawyers in the case give virtually no thought to its role in legal argument. Sometimes this is a mistake. Formal logic plays by certain rules. The rules are simple, but powerful. One consequence of their simplicity is that it is easy for logical errors in argument to go undetected. When an argument breaks a rule of logic, it commits a logical fallacy. Identifying those formal logical fallacies is the heart of this book, its approach to understanding legal argument, and honing argumentative skills. If lawyers learn about formal logic and learn how to spot flawed formal logic at the foundation of legal arguments, they gain substantial advantages in seeing these logically false arguments and explaining why they are unpersuasive. This book endeavors to leverage the logical fallacy as an efficient way to evaluate and respond to the logical form of legal arguments. Arguments that have a fallacious logical form fit into patterns—and once you identify and label those patterns, it provides an efficient and effective method for using formal logic in legal argument.

1.4 Formal Logic's Pervasive, Practical Advantage in Litigation

The first substantial advantage of harnessing the power of formal logic is its pervasive application in the various and diverse phases of litigation. The litigation process involves a lot of different legal tasks but logic is involved in all of them. When you are determining what claims to include in a civil complaint; considering how to plead each claim; drafting an answer to a complaint or affirmative defenses; drafting interrogatories, requests to produce documents, or requests for admission; asking a series of questions in a deposition designed to discover new facts; drafting a motion to compel answers to discovery; drafting a dispositive motion; arguing a motion in court; designing a line of questioning for voir dire; organizing a closing argument; drafting proposed jury instructions; or organizing an appellate brief, you are engaged in tasks with a logical foundation. Understanding the rules of formal logic unlocks your potential to be more cogent and convincing at each of these phases of litigation.

A second advantage to developing knowledge of formal logic and using it in legal argument is that attention to logic distinguishes legal argument. Logic is consistent, credible, and convincing. Logic's structure and rules ensure consistent application of law to similar facts and parties. Logic requires justification of conclusions, and an advocate who insists on sound logic better communicates even complicated concepts with clarity and efficiency. Last, the goal of argument is to convince; few will genuinely embrace the value, effectiveness, or propriety of knowingly pitching illogical arguments to judges, jurors, or opposing counsel. One of the benefits of studying formal logic is its capacity to help you identify and categorize illogical, or fallacious, argument patterns and justify why they must be rejected as unpersuasive.

Understanding the rules of formal logic unlocks your potential to be more cogent and convincing at each of these phases of litigation.

The third benefit of studying and using the rules of formal logic in making and evaluating legal argument is a subtle but important one. If the rules of formal logic are about ensuring the foundational integrity of legal argument, lawyers who build their argumentative habits on sound logic ensure that they have designed arguments that are built on rock rather than sand. The sound logical foundation of the argument provides a comfortable framework for the lawyer to argue from—something like organization structure of modal jazz that Miles Davis and his sextet used in 1959 to make *Kind of Blue*. When we think about logic, particularly formal logic, our thoughts might turn to mathematics and science, computer programs, and "mechanical jurisprudence."[16] However, another perspective is that that our thoughts should instead be drawn to great music. In the same way that the Miles Davis sextet put modal jazz theory to work as a foundation for making a complex system of improvised sound into artistic genius, formal logic can be put to work by lawyers to make creative, persuasive arguments. Modal jazz was a logical organizational framework that allowed the musicians to exercise creativity in a way that created music.

Davis once said: "Do not fear mistakes. There are none."[17] Lawyers live in a world where they spend most of their professional time obsessing about mistakes and working to ensure they don't make them when they represent their clients. They are not alone. Mistakes make people feel incompetent and embarrassed. Mistakes cost lawyers cases and clients. Most lawyers would disagree with Davis's quote entirely—or at least claim that it is inapplicable to the practice of law. His quote, it seems, suggests a mindset of a musician who enjoyed unqualified confidence in his ability to improvise. Confronted with something that had the potential to sound

16. The term "mechanical jurisprudence" is most frequently associated with former Harvard Law School Dean Roscoe Pound. Dean Pound used the term "in a pejorative sense in contrast to the way in which classical jurists themselves understood that term—that largely ignored the factual context of cases in favor of a formal, almost reflexive adherence to legal precedent." Samuel R. Olken, *The Decline of Legal Classicism and the Evolution of New Deal Constitutionalism*, 89 NOTRE DAME L. REV. 2051, 2070 (2014) (citations omitted).

17. *See, e.g.*, Michael Humphreys et al., *Sensemaking and Sensegivng of Jazz Leadership*, HUMAN RELATIONS, (Jan. 2012), at 49.

like a "mistake" in his performance, Davis would, working consistently within the framework of the music, respond in a way that would accommodate, even embrace, the "mistake" into the work itself. Miles Davis made mistakes into music, empowered by his mastery of his instrument and the musical framework in which he performed.

Lawyers cannot plan for every contingency, whether in deposition, trial, appellate argument, or around the negotiating table, because litigation is not a closed, predictable system with a mathematical solution. While competent planning is essential, at some point, every lawyer is required to improvise. When we have to improvise, we fall back on our experience, knowledge of the law, knowledge of the facts, and our own abilities to "think on our feet" and communicate with clarity and passion for our clients. A lawyer with mastery of the logical foundation for argument is in a better place to improvise than one with no knowledge of logic's most basic principles. In fact, when an unexpected question is tendered from the bench during appellate argument, or defense counsel's closing argument takes a wildly unexpected turn, you will have to respond, and in a way that will make you feel a little bit like Paul Chambers, the extraordinary bassist playing with Miles Davis on March 2, 1959. You might respond by listening to the sounds around you and delivering an argument on rebuttal that turns what might be a mistake into something appealing and convincing. A firm foundation in formal logic better equips a lawyer to turn what might otherwise be a mistake into something like music.

1.5 An Overview of this Book, Its Approach, Method, and Chapters

The first goal of this book is to make formal logic accessible to lawyers who deal with legal argument but have limited or no formal training in philosophical logic. The second goal is to make formal logic useful in learning about and refining legal argumentation at every phase of trial practice. The third goal is to serve as a resource for lawyers and judges, confronted with logic problems in legal argument, by providing a collection of cases to draw upon for solving problems of formal logic and as authority for the use of formal logic in legal decision making.

The goals of this book are to make formal logic accessible to lawyers, to make logic useful in trial practice, and to serve as a resource for solving logic problems in legal argument.

The first goal is necessitated by the nature of a litigation practice. Most lawyers are busy people. They have clients to communicate with, hearings and trials to attend, briefs to write, and exhibits to organize. Even lawyers who would like to spend a week studying philosophy do not have time to do that. The philosophy of formal logic is extensive and voluminous and can seem esoteric and impractical to some. Much has been written about formal logic from a philosophical and jurisprudential perspective. That is not the perspective of this book. Rather, by focusing on the simple rules of logic and the patterns of argument that typically result from violating them, it demonstrates and discusses the most practical concepts of formal logic in a way that is accessible to non-philosophers. By defining and illustrating these patterns and demonstrating how courts have used them to solve legal problems, you will have an "off the shelf" solution to logic problems in legal argument—one you can put to use without having to exhaustively study and understand the details of philosophical logic.

The second goal is to demonstrate how practical these lessons of formal logic are. We will not spend much time revisiting the philosophy of logic, alternative logical frameworks, or even the jurisprudential perspectives on logic in legal reasoning. Instead, we will focus on formal logic as a practical tool. The book provides examples from real cases of lawyers and judges using the rules of formal logic in litigation. Additionally, each of the chapters on formal logical fallacies will include a practice example—a motion for partial summary judgment, a motion for sanctions, a deposition transcript, a complaint, a brief in support of a new trial, and a jury instruction special interrogatory—each designed not only to help you exercise your ability to take each chapter's lesson of logic and use it in practice, but also to demonstrate the utility of formal logic has in legal argument generally.

The third goal—providing a resource for lawyers and judges looking for authorities and guidance on how to apply logic to law—is accomplished by collecting cases that confront problems of formal logic in legal argument. Logic problems are nothing new to American jurisprudence. Courts have confronted problems with faulty logical architecture before and described their analytical processes for solving those problems. These descriptions provide a model for lawyers and judges seeking solutions to similar logic problems in legal argument. This book organizes those cases based on the category of the logic problem confronted by the court, rather than by the areas of law in which they appear, and describes and explains how the courts used rules of formal logic to reach their legal conclusions.

This approach begins in Chapter Two, which describes the process of legal argument and the role of different logical tools within that process. It opens with a brief review of the role of formal logic in jurisprudence, and then describes three common logical tools lawyers regularly use to solve legal problems and make legal argument: deduction, induction, and analogy.

Chapter Three details more precisely what is meant by "formal logic" by describing its role in legal argument and distinguishes it from the roles played by other kinds of logic. It also previews an important concept, a device called the *logical fallacy*, which will be an important focus of the balance of the book. Finally, it explains why you do not need to master the philosophy of logic to make use of logical fallacies; rather, you simply need a general understanding of what formal logic is, why it is important, and what the patterns of logical fallacies look like.

Philosophy has explored, defined, and refined the philosophy of formal logic into simple rules. Chapter Four describes those rules and explains their relationship to logical fallacies. The chapter goes on to explain something important about the nature of arguments that commit logical fallacies and why they are sometimes accepted, despite their logical failings. A description of each of the various fallacies and their treatment by courts is the subject of each of the next six chapters.

The first formal logical fallacy is introduced in Chapter Five: the fallacy of affirming the consequent. This fallacy applies to hypothetical syllogisms, a common form of argument that includes an "if . . . then" proposition. To be valid, hypothetical syllogisms must take one of two forms. One form results in the fallacy of affirming the consequent. The chapter describes the fallacy, describes some real examples of courts using the fallacy to evaluate legal arguments, and explains how you can use the fallacy to make better arguments and examine your opponent's arguments.

Chapter Six describes the second form, the fallacy of denying the antecedent. Like the fallacy of affirming the consequent, arguments that do not comport with the requirements for hypothetical syllogisms commit logical fallacies.

Chapter Seven moves to a different kind of formal logical fallacy, applicable to a different kind of syllogism. The fallacy of the undistributed middle term is the first of three fallacies that apply to categorical syllogisms. It is a fallacy of *distribution*, meaning that the fallacy occurs when an argument is not disciplined about the difference between referring to a universal category rather than a more limited one (for example, the difference between referring to "all" of something instead of "some" of something). The concept of distribution is important in logic and is more fully described in Chapter Four.

Chapter Eight introduces a logical fallacy that is, like the fallacy of the undistributed middle term, another fallacy of distribution. This kind of false argument takes a slightly different form and is called the fallacy of the illicit process. The chapter describes this fallacy and how it occurs in legal argument, then provides examples of courts' uses of the fallacy to evaluate legal arguments. It also explains how you can avoid this fallacy to make better arguments and use your knowledge to examine your opponent's arguments.

Chapter Nine addresses the fallacy of the negative premise—or reaching an affirmative conclusion based on a negative premise. In a sense, it is the problem with arguments that suggest a conclusion about what something *is* based on evidence of what it *is not*. This fallacy is simple to identify and provides a straightforward tool for dealing with a common error in legal argument.

Chapter Ten discusses a fallacy that results from the ambiguity in the simple word "or" and its logical consequence, referred to in logic as a disjunction. When a disjunctive argument does not follow the rule that governs disjunctive arguments, it commits the fallacy of affirming a disjunct. The chapter discusses the often overlooked logical ambiguity in disjunction; considers some of the problems lawyers and judges have encountered as a result of disjunction's logical ambiguity; and how rules of logic, like the rules of disjunction, discipline lawyers' use and interpretation of disjunctive statements, legal rules, and arguments.

Chapter Eleven describes how the patterns of formal logical fallacies can been seen in legal argument, evaluating the various patterns seen in Chapters Five through Ten together, as a set of patterns of fallacious legal argument. The chapter discusses how lawyers and judges can use logical fallacies to understand the process of legal argument and persuasion, craft written or oral arguments, respond to fallacious written or oral arguments, and write legal opinions. It reviews the fallacies described in the previous chapters and considers them in the practical context of legal argument.

Last, in Chapter Twelve, the book concludes with a discussion of the importance of formal logic in the practical and theoretical business of legal argument. Legal argument's persuasive role in the practice of law and the integrity of the legal process depends on legal argument being a discipline and being disciplined. This final chapter explores some of the contemporary challenges to formal logic's place in legal reasoning and concludes that understanding and using formal logic is necessary to a principled legal system, is valuable to lawyers and judges who want to distinguish their legal argument and analytical skills, is a platform for more dynamic and creative legal argumentation, and is important to legal educators and students who want to communicate and comprehend something foundational to the process of legal reasoning and argument.

As the analogy to improvisational jazz suggests, the place of formal logic in legal argument is importantly, but merely, foundational. It is a starting point, but not an ending point, for understanding legal argument. The objective of this book is not to suggest that all legal argument must take the form of a syllogism, nor is it to suggest that it is effective or practicable to painstakingly reduce every legal argument into syllogistic form. There are other logical tools necessary to complete the assortment of components that make up "legal logic." However, legal arguments that are logically fallacious as a matter of formal logic should be unpersuasive. Lawyers should not knowingly advance these fallacious arguments and courts should not find them persuasive. This is not a book that suggests that legal reasoning and argument can be reduced to rules of formal logic; they cannot. However, the rules of logic are a powerful force for making and evaluating argument and have important practical value to litigators and judges.

1.6 Chapter One in Review

This chapter introduced the topic of formal logic in legal argument, explained the benefits of studying logic for the practice of law, and given an overview of the rest of this book. As you move to the next chapter, which will discuss logic and its role in legal argument more specifically, consider the following review points and whether this chapter has made you think about the benefit of studying logic more carefully.

- Lawyers know a lot about logic, but do not usually devote the same time to analyzing the role of logic in legal argument as they might to researching the law or discovering the facts relevant to their cases.
- Logic has an important role to play in legal argument, but most lawyers lack understanding of logic concepts or logic vocabulary to evaluate and communicate logical strengths and weaknesses of a legal argument.
- Formal logic is one of several tools that lawyers use in solving legal problems and communicating legal arguments. Those tools are discussed further in the next chapter.
- Lawyers are busy; they do not always have time to break down the legal arguments they encounter in briefs or the courtroom into their logical components. However, they can use the rules of logic to quickly spot patterns of argument that commit logical fallacies.
- Studying formal logic provides a new foundational perspective for understanding legal argument. It helps lawyers to become more disciplined and efficient legal thinkers, empowers them to more effectively design their legal arguments, and improvise legal argument when they do not have time to plan a response.

Chapter Two

Logic and the Tools of Disciplined, Creative Legal Argument

Leveraging formal logic's role in legal argument begins with considering what it means to design a legal argument and what roles logic, generally, and formal logic, specifically, play in designing legal argument. Lawyers use different processes to design arguments. They use different kinds of logic in the practice of law. This book will focus on one kind of logic, formal logic, and its role as a tool in legal argument. There are other logical tools that lawyers use as well. Understanding how to define and distinguish those other logical tools from formal logic will help you to develop a new perspective for thinking about legal argument, understanding the logical context of legal argument, and appreciating the important role of formal logic within that context. As you read Chapter Two, consider the following questions:

- What are the intellectual tools of the practice of law? Knowledge of the law; perception of distinct but related legal issues; understanding the process of legal practice; and skill in analyzing, writing, and communicating about the law likely might come to mind. Are there other intellectual tools that lawyers use to practice law effectively? Do you think logical thinking is one of those intellectual tools?
- What logical tools do lawyers use when designing a legal argument?
- Think of some of the legal arguments you may have made in the past or heard in the courtroom. If you were to put those arguments into categories, would your first instinct be to categorize them in terms of their substantive legal category (for example, negligence, causation, contract, self-defense, damages) or their procedural legal category (a dispositive motion argument, an evidentiary argument, an argument in a closing statement, an argument on appeal) or some other means of categorization?
- If you had to describe or categorize a legal argument based not on its substantive legal basis or procedural posture but, instead, on the nature of the argument's pattern or technique, would you be able to do that? What categories would you use?

2.1 Logic and the Craft of Making Legal Argument

The word "logic" might evoke mental images of formulae written on chalkboards, geometric proofs scrawled on graph paper, and lines of computer code scrolling across a monitor. However, logic has just as much a place in the seemingly unmathematical craft of legal argument as it does in the physical and mathematical sciences.

Logic has just as much a place in the seemingly unmathematical craft of legal argument as it does in the physical and mathematical sciences.

Some do not think of the role of a lawyer planning a legal argument as being very much like an engineer using equations to calculate the proper size of a steel girder to support the roof structure of a building. That engineer might begin with some assumptions about the size and weight of the roof structure, some limitations in the available materials and dimensions available for an appropriate girder, and some formulae necessary to calculate the forces at work in assembling and maintaining the structure. The engineer could use these assumptions and formulae to reach a conclusion about the sufficient geometry of the girder necessary to do the job. She might even make something that looks like an "argument" to her supervisor that her calculations are accurate, her assumptions are reasonable and justifiable, and her design choices are economically feasible.

This description of an engineer's work does not sound very much like what lawyers do when they design argument. However, lawyers and engineers use some of the same kinds of tools and processes. Lawyers make assumptions, justify their reasonableness, use rules, and are disciplined in applying known and assumed facts to legal rules to argue for a certain result. However, the role of logic in a lawyer's process for designing an argument does not always yield the same certain results that an engineer's process for calculating the geometry and materials of a roof support girder does. In legal disputes, there is frequently indeterminacy in the proffered meanings of the legal rules at issue or the litigants' competing perceptions of the facts, which makes the process of designing and evaluating legal argument different from making mathematical calculations or drawing scientific conclusions. Instead, logic's role in legal argument might compare to the role mathematics plays in the work of a mandolin luthier, who creates an instrument using wood, metal, varnish, geometric shapes and patterns, and the proper space between and among the components to design a musical instrument that is at once beautiful, durable, and functional. However, without some understanding of the physics of the material they are using and the acoustical properties and science of vibration and sound waves, their end product might look like any other mandolin, but sound terrible. These logical concepts are just a few among the several tools the luthier uses to create something that looks and sounds compelling.

Thinking about logic as a tool of legal argument puts the practice of designing and evaluating legal argument in a different setting than is typically thought of. Because lawyers use tools to make arguments, their work is sometimes be described as "craft." Describing the practice of law as "craft" has been ably justified by some legal scholars:

> Craftsmanship involves the skillful use of tools. Tools serve specific purposes; one does not use a hammer when one wants to cut. Even good tools will work poorly if they are used on tasks for which they were not intended, or in inappropriate ways. A single tool is not fit for every job. And a tool that serves one purpose well may be unsuited for other jobs.[1]

If lawyers craft arguments like the Miles Davis sextet crafted *Kind of Blue*, or an engineer designs a roof support girder, or a luthier plans and finishes the distinctive wood curvature of an f-style mandolin, those arguments will use "tools of the trade" in the same ways musicians, engineers, or luthiers do. The methods of logic we lawyers use to create, design, and evaluate arguments are among many tools we can use. Don't merely employ these logical tools occasionally; use them throughout the spectrum of skills necessary to successfully practice law. Learning about these tools and how to master them results in a more refined, consistent, and valuable end product. Considering logic as a tool for legal argument might raise questions. What do we mean when we say "logic?" What are the different kinds of logical tools? How do these tools play a role in legal argument? This chapter considers those questions.

2.2 Logic as a Tool of the Craft of Legal Argument

The study of logic is a study of philosophy. Philosophy has designed many different frameworks and classifications of logic—too many to usefully describe comprehensively in this book—but three frameworks in particular are frequently used in legal argument: deduction, induction, and analogy.[2]

---

1. Brett G. Scharffs, *Law as Craft*, 54 Vand. L. Rev. 2245, 2292 (2001). *See also* Larry Alexander & Emily Sherwin, Demystifying Legal Reasoning 2 (collecting sources describing legal reasoning as "craft" and stating "[l]egal decision making is frequently described as a "craft" involving special forms of reasoning that are accessible only to those with long experience in applying law."); *see also* Larry O. Natt Gantt, II, *Deconstructing Thinking Like a Lawyer: Analyzing the Cognitive Components of the Analytical Mind*, 29 Campbell L. Rev. 413, 445 (2007) ("The importance of crafting arguments thus must factor into the overall structure of legal thinking."); Jack L. Sammons, *Traditionalists, Technicians, and Legal Education*, 38 Gonz. L. Rev. 237 (2003).

2. This is not to suggest that these are the only kinds of logic. Logicians have described and categorized logic in many different ways, and many of those categories of logic have application to legal argument and legal reasoning. One logician organizes logic into two main categories: formal logic and informal logic. Arnold Vander Nat, Simple Formal Logic: With Common-Sense Symbolic Techniques 5 (2010). Subcategories of logic appear within these two categories. Within formal logic five categories can be found: traditional logic, propositional logic, modal logic, quantification logic, and mathematical logic. Within formal logic are the categories of critical thinking and inductive logic. *Id.* at 5–6. This is not the only way to describe various logic systems. *See, e.g.,* Patrick J. Hurley, A Concise Introduction to Logic (2015) (dividing logic into informal logic, formal logic, and inductive logic, and placing analogy in the category of inductive logic).

This chapter also introduces two categories of arguments that occur when the logical frameworks are used improperly: formal logical fallacies and informal logical fallacies.

2.2.1 Deductive Logic

The first of these tools is *deductive logic*, or simply *deduction*. Deduction is the process of reasoning from a general rule to a particular outcome.[3] Every time you apply a rule of law to a set of particular case facts in order to predict an outcome or legal result, you use deductive logic.[4]

Three frameworks in particular are frequently used in legal argument: deduction, induction, and analogy.

Deduction is useful in many different legal arguments. It is especially common, and useful, where an argument can be crafted from a stipulated or uncontroverted proposition of law or fact or even an assumed or legally presumed proposition of fact. Further, deduction even works when there are disputes about the applicable rule of law and about the facts, because it provides a framework for assessing the consequence of a legal dispute about the law or the facts once that dispute is resolved. Accordingly, deduction can, and does, play a role in arguing about what the correct legal rule is, what the facts are, and how a rule of law is applied to facts of a case. Reasoning deductively requires adherence to some formal rules. Accordingly, deductive reasoning requires some degree of formality and is sometimes referred to as *formal deductive logic*, or simply *formal logic*.[5] Formal logic requires that, for a moment, we set aside the truth or falsity of the premises and focus instead on the logical form of the argument.[6] While lawyers use deduction frequently, formal logic's focus on the logical form or structure of an argument, is less familiar territory. Formal logic represents a fairly significant shift in focus for lawyers, who are generally more concerned with the truth or falsity of the law or facts in an argument than its logical form. Appreciating and using logical form requires that you, for a moment, stop thinking about what the law is, stop thinking about what the facts

---

3. *See, e.g.*, Neil MacCormick, *Legal Deduction, Legal Predicates and Expert Systems*, 5 International Journal for the Semiotics of Law 181, 182 (1992) (describing deductive legal reasoning as "a form of deductive inference, or, if you like, deductive/subsumptive reasoning; you postulate a general hypothetical rule, you establish facts in a particular case subsumable within the rule's hypothesis, and you draw the logical conclusion for the particular case from the rule plus facts.").

4. *Id.*

5. *See, e.g.*, Ralph H. Johnson, *The Relation between Formal and Informal Logic*, Argumentation 13:265–74 (1999).

6. This presents an opportunity for the respondent, restrained by advocated, accepted, assumed, or undeniable premises to still salvage a viable argument, not based on the law or the facts, but instead, based on the logical form of the argument respondent is faced with.

are, and narrow your focus on the organization and interrelationships of those components. Appreciating and using formal logic requires you to learn about the proper form of a deductive argument. To start, you must arrange arguments, which are normally articulated in nonstandard, casual, forms,[7] into a standardized, simplified form that allows you to distinguish the terms that are the subjects of each premise, their relationship to one another, and their relationship to the conclusion.[8] You know this form[9] as a *syllogism*:[10] an argumentative structure made up of two distinct but related premises and a conclusion.[11] For example:

> All valid corporations are legal entities with at least one shareholder.
>
> Excavation Solutions, Inc. is a valid corporation.
>
> Therefore, Excavations Solutions, Inc. is a legal entity with at least one shareholder.

Figure 1. *An example of a syllogism.*

This syllogism in Figure 1 is made up of three sentences, each of which is called a *proposition.* Each proposition corresponds with the three components of a syllogism: the first two propositions are called *premises* and the third is called a *conclusion.* The syllogism is important because it is the argumentative structure upon which the rules of formal logic are centered. It is a common, intuitive method of organizing argumentative components and has been studied and utilized by rhetoricians and philosophers for centuries. Further, the structure of the syllogism has endured and is used in briefs and courtrooms around the world today.

7. Irving M. Copi & Carl Cohen, Introduction to Logic 267 (13th ed. 2008) ("In ordinary discourse the argument we encounter rarely appear as neatly packaged, standard-form categorical syllogisms. So the syllogistic arguments that arise in everyday speech cannot always be readily tested. They can be tested, however, if we put them into standard form—and we can generally do that by reformulating their constituent propositions. The terms syllogistic argument refers to any argument that either is a standard-form categorical syllogism or that can be reformulated as a standard-form categorical syllogism without any loss or change of meaning.").

8. The syllogism, different forms of syllogisms, and the place of syllogistic logic in legal argument will be discussed in more detail in Chapter Three.

9. "Now, to put an argument in syllogistic form is to strip it bare for logical inspection. We can see whether its weak points must lie, if it has any, and consider whether there is reason to believe that it is actually (i.e., materially) weak at those points." F. C. S. Schiller, Formal Logic, A Scientific and Social Problem 221 (1912).

10. *Id.*

11. *See, e.g.*, Alexander Bain, Logic: Deductive and Inductive 134 (1870); Elliot D. Cohen, Critical Thinking Unleashed 25 (2009); Copi & Cohen, *supra* note 7, at 224.

While the details of the syllogism and the rules of deductive reasoning are explored in more detail in the next chapter, consider the simple example in Figure 1. First, the goal of the sample syllogism in Figure 1 is to reach a conclusion that Excavation Solutions, Inc. is a legal entity with at least one shareholder. That is found in the final proposition in the syllogism, the *conclusion* of the argument. The arguer seeks to justify this conclusion by introducing two sentences, called *premises*. The first premise states a general rule about corporations and shareholders, while the second premise introduces a statement about Excavation Solutions, Inc. and its status as a corporation. The value of a syllogism is its ability to justify an inference, revealed as the conclusion, from two true premises. That value is ensured by (1) the truth of the premises and (2) the form of the syllogistic structure of the argument and its compliance with rules of deductive logic. If the syllogism complies with the rules, then an arguer can do something significant with two true premises: justify a third proposition, the conclusion, simply because of the relationship between the two premises. This explains why we are so comfortable with syllogistic reasoning that we can take for granted the power of deductive inference and make syllogistic arguments—frequently without even knowing what a syllogism is or why it is persuasive.

Importantly the rules of formal logic, and the power derived from using them are focused on the relationship between the premises and conclusion—the *form* of the argument. When this book refers to formal logic, it means the rules of deductive logic that ensure the integrity of these syllogistic arguments. Different species, or patterns, of syllogistic arguments have to conform to certain rules. If the argument fits into a specific syllogistic pattern that does not conform to the rules of logic, then there is something wrong with the argument's form. An argument that fails to conform is called a *logical fallacy*. In fact, each rule of logic that is violated has a corresponding logical fallacy that describes what is wrong with the argument. These fallacies are powerful tools for evaluating, explaining, and defeating fallacious argumentative patterns that should be unreliable and unpersuasive.

2.2.2 Inductive Logic

Of course, deductive logic and its formal rules are not the only logical tools in the lawyer's argumentative toolbox. We frequently use another tool, *inductive logic*, or simply *induction*, in legal argument.

Lawyers frequently use inductive logic, reasoning from particular truths to a generalized principle, in legal argument.

While deduction is reasoning from general principles to particular instances, induction is the inverse: reasoning from particular instances to general principles.[12] Both lawyers and non-lawyers alike make inductive judgments and arguments daily. For example, if I conclude that the bus will arrive at 6:15 p.m. on Friday because it arrived at 6:15 p.m. on Monday, Tuesday, Wednesday, and Thursday, I have arrived at that conclusion inductively: I have reached a general conclusion because of my observation of several specific instances. Lawyers use inductive logic frequently, particularly in cases where deduction is not the right tool. For example, where there is not a certain rule of law that applies to a particular case, deduction might seem like a weak argument since the truth of at least one premise will be dubious. Instead, your goal is to resolve the indeterminacy in the law and argue what, based on a sufficient sampling of cases, the rule of law should be.[13] You might argue that three or four specific case holdings can be synthesized into a single generalized rule statement. Similarly, where there is a general rule that might apply, but because of some ambiguity regarding the rule's scope or meaning its application to your facts creates uncertainty, deduction might not be your best or only tool. Further, where two general rules might apply to the facts, each yielding a different conclusion, you might turn from deduction to induction to solve the legal problem and resolve this ambiguity.

Your skill at using induction is essential to your value as a practitioner. Lawyers frequently use induction to predict or argue what rule a court will apply (and how it applies to the facts of the case), in cases where the law is uncertain. We examine the universe of relevant cases to engage in a predictive analysis of what the court

12. Kevin H. Smith, *Practical Jurisprudence: Deconstructing and Synthesizing the Art and Science of Thinking Like a Lawyer*, 29 U. MEM. L. REV. 1, 40 (1998) (citing ALEXANDER BIRD, PHILOSOPHY OF SCIENCE (1998) ("Synthesis involves inductive reasoning, the creation of general propositions from the results of specific cases.")); *see also* Dan Hunter, *Teaching and Using Analogy in Law*, 2 J. ASS'N LEGAL WRITING DIRECTORS 151, 153–54 (2004) ("Induction is, generally, the process of taking a number of specific cases or instances, classifying them into categories according to relevant attributes and outcomes, and generalizing an inclusory rule from them. That is, we take a number of isolated experiences and attempt to explain them by a general rule that covers the instances examined. Within law, we can find numerous examples of this: the ability of attorneys to say from experience what particular judges' decisions are likely to be, their ability to fit multiple precedents into a coherent framework of rules and principles, and so on."); Edwin W. Patterson, *Logic in the Law*, 90 PENN L. REV. 884 (1942); IRVING M. COPI & CARL COHEN, INTRODUCTION TO LOGIC (13th ed. 2008), at 26–28. Sometimes induction is not so narrowly defined and is defined more broadly to encompass any kind of logical inference that results in an uncertain conclusion; *see, e.g.*, PAUL THAGARD, *Abductive Inference: From Philosophical analysis to Neutral Mechanism, in* INDUCTIVE REASONING: EXPERIMENTAL, DEVELOPMENTAL AND COMPUTATIONAL APPROACHES 226 (2007).

13. *See, e.g.*, KARL N. LLEWELLYN, THE BRAMBLE BUSH: OUR LAW AND ITS STUDY 71–73 (2012).

will do.[14] But because we cannot always examine the entirety of the universe of relevant cases and sometimes judgment is required to determine the scope of the universe of relevant cases, we must, at least to some extent, exercise "logical intuition"[15] to predict what rule of law the court will apply in a certain case. Your ability to accurately make these judgment calls is a valuable skill, because the success or failure of a legal position is frequently a consequence of which legal rule controls a particular case when the proper rule is uncertain.

Lawyers make inductive arguments for other purposes as well.[16] For example, when arguing that a seller knew of the defective condition of commercial equipment but did not disclose it at the time of sale, you might use evidence of the seller's knowledge at times other than the moment the equipment was sold. For example, you could focus on the facts that the seller knew about the performance problems the week before the sale, knew about unperformed equipment maintenance a month before the sale, gotten complaints about the equipment's inefficiency two weeks before the sale, and admitted to knowing about a defect two days after the sale. By relating these specific instances showing what the buyer knew, you advance a conclusion for the proposition that the seller probably knew of the defect at the time of sale. While deductive arguments can claim that if their premises are true

---

14. *See, e.g.*, Jane Kent Gionfriddo, *Thinking Like a Lawyer: The Heuristics of Case Synthesis*, 40 TEX. TECH L. REV. 1, 4 (2007) ("In the law, this idea of synthesis comes into play as lawyers, in their many roles, analyze groups of legal authority to determine reasonable interpretations of law. . . . Lawyers begin this process of synthesis by first identifying the pieces of authority relevant to a legal issue and then fitting these pieces together to determine the overall analytical framework they reasonably support.") (citing KENNETH J. VANDEVELDE, THINKING LIKE A LAWYER: AN INTRODUCTION TO LEGAL REASONING 39 (1996), and Paul T. Wangerin, *Skills Training in "Legal Analysis": A Systematic Approach*, 40 U. MIAMI L. REV. 409, 442-43 (1986), but observing, at note 72, that "'hypothesizing and testing back' is a more useful way to describe the process of working with implicit ideas in a group of cases than the more prevalent phrase of "deductive and inductive reasoning."); *see also* ALEKSANDER PECZENIK & JAAP HAGE, ON LAW AND REASON 141 ("Legal dogmatics is filled with examples of generalizing the statutory provision and other norms of established law via the so-called 'legal induction.'") (emphasis added).

15. Edwin W. Patterson, *Logic in the Law*, 90 PENN L. REV. 884 (1942) ("The 'logical intuition' of the experienced counselor is an expert's hunch.").

16. *See, e.g.*, DAVID CRUMP ET AL., CRIMINAL LAW: CASES, MATERIALS, AND LAWYERING STRATEGIES 235 (2013) ("Induction in law is used in several ways. Sometimes it is applied to the evidence: we know from experience that the guilty sometimes flee, and so evidence of flight is often admitted before juries considering criminal cases. Sometimes induction helps a judge or lawyer reading a series of cases to infer a rule that is hidden in them. 'In all reported cases in this state where the defendant's car has struck another car from behind, the court has upheld a finding of negligence; therefore, perhaps the courts should recognize an inference of negligence where there is a collision from behind.").

their conclusion is necessarily true, inductive arguments merely make the claim that the conclusion is probable, not conclusive.[17]

Discovery is an important phase in litigation and one that frequently requires you to use inductive logic as you prepare for trial. When you design a discovery plan, you must think inductively to determine what interrogatories, requests for production of documents, request for admissions, and deposition questions you must raise. Induction allows you to predict the universe of specific facts you must investigate to reach a general conclusion. For example, if I believe that a plaintiff claiming breach of an employment agreement has failed to mitigate her damages,[18] I will design a discovery plan that gathers the specific information necessary to justify a generalized conclusion that she failed to mitigate her damages and accordingly is barred from claiming them. I do that by using my knowledge of the law and the general facts relating to how a party in the plaintiff's circumstances might reasonably mitigate their damages. Next, I ask questions about whether the plaintiff did those things and I use the answers to infer a generalization about her actions.

Induction is useful in many phases of litigation. Importantly, as will be discussed later, induction often supplies a premise in a subsequent deductive argument. Accordingly, the inductive and deductive processes work in concert in legal reasoning and elsewhere.[19]

---

17. Jens S. Allwood et al., Logic in Linguistics 16 (1977) ("One of the most important aspects of logic is the study of valid inference and sentences that are necessarily true. There are two main types of inference: those that are necessarily valid and those that are valid only with greater or lesser degree of probability. Each type of inference is correlated with a special type of logical study. The study of necessarily valid inferences is pursued within deductive logic, while inferences that are valid with some degree of probability are studied within inductive logic."). One logician describes the difference between induction and deduction this way: "If we claim that the connection is a logical connection, then the argument is a *deductive argument,* and if we claim that the connection is an empirical connection, then the argument is an *inductive argument.*" Arnold Vander Nat, Simple Formal Logic: With Common-Sense Symbolic Techniques 14 (2010) (emphasis in original).

18. "As a general rule, a party cannot recover damages for loss that he could have avoided by reasonable efforts. Once a party has reason to know that performance by the other party will not be forthcoming, he is ordinarily expected to stop his own performance to avoid further expenditure." Restatement (Second) of Contracts § 350 cmt. b. (Am. Law Inst. 1981).

19. *See, e.g.*, Karl N. Llewellyn, The Bramble Bush: Our Law and Its Study 71 (2012), at 73 (discussing the interplay between induction and deduction in developing legal argument); Ralph H. Johnson, *The Relation between Formal and Informal Logic*, Argumentation 13:265–74 (1999) (concluding that "In sum, informal logic and formal logic differ in their in their subject matter. [Formal logic] studies the entailment relationship between propositions; informal logic is about argumentation. They likewise differ in their approaches: formal as against informal, as explained above. Hence informal logic and FDL are complementary rather than oppositional."). *See also* Anita Schnee, *Logical Reasoning "Obviously,"* 3 Legal Writing: J. Legal Writing Inst. 105, 106 (1997) ("Deductive reasoning, however, is not the whole story. It has a near-mirror image, which is the inductive process. The two work in unison, to create the singular tongue of advocacy."); Jane Kent Gionfriddo, *Thinking Like a Lawyer: The Heuristics of Case Synthesis*, 40 Tex. Tech L. Rev. 1 (2007), at 36 ("For instance, hypothesizing an explanation from the facts and results of a group of cases requires inductive reasoning-inducing from the specific facts and results of a group of cases and coming up with a possible general explanation or explanations. Testing this hypothesis back, then, is deductive reasoning-deducing whether the synthesized explanation does, in fact, explain the facts and results of all relevant cases and is consistent with any relevant explicit ideas in the cases.").

2.2.3 Analogy

Analogical reasoning is a third,[20] and often used,[21] tool in legal argument. Analogy is "a non-identical or non-literal similarity comparison between two things, with a resulting predictive or explanatory effect."[22]

Lawyers frequently use the logical tool of analogy in legal argument, arguing that because the facts or legal issues of one case are similar to another case, the conclusion in one case should be similar the other.

On your first day of law school, you were probably exposed to the most common analogical reasoning used in practicing law: analogizing the facts of one case to the facts of another to conclude that both cases should be resolved similarly, when faced with some uncertainty about which rule controls the outcome.[23] Conversely, you also argue analogically when you distinguish the facts of one case from another to conclude that the second case is so factually different that comparison is inappropriate, and that thus a different rule must apply or a different outcome is required.[24] The persuasiveness of analogical reasoning is a function of the similarity of the case(s) used for comparison. While similar cases might be strong analogical bases for reaching similar results, dissimilar cases, sharing limited or irrelevant common characteristics, provide little authority for reaching the same result.[25]

---

20. There is some lack of agreement among logicians as to analogical reasoning's place within or without deduction and induction. *See, e.g.*, Fabrizio Macagno & Douglas Walton, *Argument from Analogy in Law, the Classic Tradition, and Recent Theories*, 42 Philosophy & Rhetoric 154, 155 (2009).

21. *Id.* at 154 ("Analogy is one of the most common forms of reasoning in law."); David Crump et al., Criminal Law: Cases, Materials, and Lawyering Strategies 235 (2013) ("Legal reasoning also includes heavy use of analogy.").

22. Dan Hunter, *Teaching and Using Analogy in Law*, 2 J. Ass'n Legal Writing Directors 151, 152 (2004) (crediting the definition as an adaptation from another by Dedre Gentner et al., *Viewing Metaphor as Analogy, in* Analogical Reasoning: Perspectives of Artificial Intelligence, Cognitive Science, and Philosophy 171 (Daniel H. Helman ed., 1988)). *See also* Wilson Huhn, *The Stages of Legal Reasoning: Formalism, Analogy, and Realism*, 48 Vill. L. Rev. 305, 312 (2003) ("Reasoning by analogy . . . is the application of a rule of law to a case because the facts of the case are similar to the terms of the rule. While formalism is scientific and grounded in logic, analogical reasoning is an art that is grounded in rhetoric.") (citations omitted).

23. *See, e.g.*, Fabrizio Macagno & Douglas Walton, *Argument from Analogy in Law, the Classic Tradition, and Recent Theories*, 42 Philosophy & Rhetoric 154, 155 (2009) ("This form of argument is widely used to fill "the gap between facts and rule." In other words, analogy is used to apply general legal rules to cases not directly falling under the classifications of the rule.") (citation omitted).

24. *See, e.g.*, Edwin W. Patterson, *Logic in the Law*, 90 Penn L. Rev. 884, 877 (1942).

25. *See, e.g.*, Lloyd L. Weinreb, Legal Reason, The Use of Analogy in Legal Argument 32 (2005) ("All accounts of analogical argument agree that an analogy is successful and justifies its conclusion only if the observed similarity between the sources and the target is relevant to the further similarity that is in question."). More comprehensive jurisprudential studies of the role of analogy in legal reasoning can be found in Scott Brewer, *Exemplary Reasoning: Semantics, Pragmatics, and the Rational Force of Legal Argument by Analogy*, 109 Harv. L. Rev. 925 (1996).

Although deductive logic is disciplined by rules of logical form and inductive logic's persuasiveness is tied to the quality and quantity of specific instances used to arrive at a generalization, analogy itself is relatively unconstrained by formality. Unlike deduction, an analogy can be crafted without limits on what characteristics of the specific instances are relevant for making a useful analogy. Generally, you can often find some kind of analogical argument to make—but that does not mean analogies are always good arguments, or persuasive. As one commentator recognized: "The analogy has a seductive charm for the imaginative jurisprudent . . . ."[26] Further, while proper deductive argument requires its conclusion be true, analogy only proffers a conclusion that is, at best, probably true. In fact, analogical arguments might be made that provide a very weak justification for their proffered conclusion. The persuasiveness of the analogical argument is a function of the quality of the analogy.

2.3 Logical Fallacies as Tools of the Craft of Legal Argument

Logical fallacies are a tool distinguished from deduction, induction, and analogy. While deduction, induction and analogy are logical frameworks, logical fallacies are used to classify and describe logical failures in arguments. You might describe logical fallacies as a tool for policing the logical integrity of legal argument.

Logical fallacies are used to classify and describe logical failures in arguments.

As discussed in connection with deduction, above, being able to identify an argument that commits a logical fallacy is important. The logical fallacy's value to argument is something like the names given to penalties in football. In football, certain players are tasked with blocking other players from tackling a ball carrier. While one player is running with or passing the ball, other players are responsible for protecting them. They do this by blocking players on the other team, who have been tasked with tackling the player attempting to run or pass the ball. Blockers have certain rules they have to obey. For example, while blocking another player, the blocker is not allowed to grab the other players' body, pads, or uniform—and if they do, they get a penalty, aptly called "holding." The team that commits holding is penalized by moving its position on the field ten yards back from the goal—what is called a ten-yard holding. While there are other rules in football, the term "holding" describes the violation of just that one rule. The referee does not explain the rule, nor does he describe the violation. In some leagues, he does not even identify the player who committed it. The power of the referee's explanation is in the rule

26. Edwin W. Patterson, *Logic in the Law*, 90 Penn L. Rev. 884, 877 (1942).

and the name given to violations of the rule. The word "holding" is powerful in the game of football.

In evaluating argument, the word "fallacy" is of similar importance to the word "holding" in football. If an argument violates a rule of logic, then it commits a fallacy. The fallacy has a name that indicates, like "holding," the nature of the rule violation. Importantly, by definition, a deductive argument that commits a fallacy has a significant consequence (more significant than the ten-yard penalty in football). Logic divides fallacies into two categories: *informal fallacies* and *formal fallacies*.

Many of the logical weaknesses in legal arguments are not related strictly to the form of the argument and its failure to comply with the strict rules of deductive logic. Instead, arguments sometimes present with an *informal* weakness. These informal critiques of arguments are called *informal fallacies*.[27] Like formal fallacies, the name of each type of informally fallacious argument describes the nature of what is wrong with the argument. For example, straw man,[28] *ad hominem*,[29] and slippery slope[30] are all descriptions of arguments that commit informal logical fallacies. Informal fallacies identify a weakness in the argument, but the argument might still have some persuasive value.[31]

Formal fallacies are distinguishable from informal fallacies. First, formal fallacies apply only to deductive argument—that category of argument that takes a strict, syllogistic form. Formal fallacies require that the proffered conclusion cannot be supported by the argument as composed, and the argument must fail. Accordingly, in a deductive argument where the premises are true and the form of the argument complies with the rule, then the conclusion is necessarily true. But when the

27. Logicians disagree about the description and categorization of fallacies. Arnold vander Nat, Simple Formal Logic: With Common-Sense Symbolic Techniques 228 (2010). Another way of distinguishing formal and informal fallacies is that, in informal fallacies, there is something merely persuasive about the premise, but the argument has the "psychological power to fool the audience into accepting the conclusion anyway." *Id.* (and explaining that not all informal fallacies are invalid). Another logician describes informal fallacies as those detectible only by examining their argumentative content, rather than simply by examining the form of the argument. Patrick J. Hurley, A Concise Introduction to Logic 122–23 (2015).

28. A straw man fallacy is committed when a party mischaracterizes another's argument into another, weaker, form in order to more effectively criticize the weaker, mischaracterized argument. *See, e.g.*, Douglas Walton, Informal Logic 22–23 (2nd ed. 2008).

29. An *ad hominem* argument is one that is focused on criticizing the opponent making an argument rather than criticizing the argument itself. *Id.* at 170–71.

30. A slippery slope argument is one where a party is led to acknowledge an inconsequential concession in their argument, and then is led to make further similarly inconsequential concessions. *Id.* at 315. This is a common trial cross-examination technique. Logicians describe slippery slope arguments as committing an informal fallacy, but recognize this method of argument is sometimes legitimate and effective. *Id.* at 316.

31. *See, e.g.*, *id.* ("[t]he traditional category of informal fallacy has been stretched too widely in traditional accounts, including not only arguments that are weak or incomplete, but even instances of argument that are basically correct and reasonable as mechanisms of argument in persuasion dialogue.").

premises are true but the form does not comply with the rules, the argument commits a fallacy and it is not merely weak but unreliable entirely.[32]

When an argument is formally fallacious, there is an illogical and unreliable relationship between the premises and its conclusion, so the conclusion must be rejected for another argument that is, at least, logically coherent. Logicians recognize a distinction between an argument that is logically *valid* and an argument that is *true*. Logical validity is a consequence of conforming to the rules of deductive logic: if the rules are followed, then the form of the argument is logically valid. However, an argument's valid form does not necessarily mean the argument's conclusion is true. Truth (or falsity) is an attribute of the individual propositions that appear within an argument. Accordingly, the logical form of an argument is *either* valid or invalid. The *form* is *neither* true nor false. Conversely, the *premises* of an argument are *either* true or false. They are *neither* valid nor invalid. However, these distinct concepts of truth and falsity, validity and invalidity work together. When the logical form of an argument is valid and its premises are true, then the argument requires that the conclusion be true.[33] If either a premise is false or the form is invalid, the conclusion necessarily cannot be true.[34]

Lawyers engaged in legal argument have several kinds of logical tools at their disposal: deduction, induction, analogy, and logical fallacies.[35] Deductive logic is important, and learning about formal logic can be valuable in legal argument. Because the typical legal standards of proof require something less than conclusiveness,[36] the rigor of deductive logic may not seem necessary in legal argument—and yet, lawyers

32. Conversely, arguments that commit informal fallacies may merely be weak argument.

33. "When an argument is valid, if its premises are true then its conclusion must (necessarily) be true." JEROME E. BICKENBACH & JACQUELINE M. DAVIES, GOOD REASONS FOR BETTER ARGUMENTS 237 (1996); *see also* PATRICK J. HURLEY, A CONCISE INTRODUCTION TO LOGIC 46 (2015) (noting that "validity is something that is determined from the *relationship* between premise and conclusion" and further that "[t]he question is not whether the premises and conclusion are true and false, but whether the premises *support* the conclusion.") (emphasis in original); *see also* TRUDY GOVIER, A PRACTICAL STUDY OF ARGUMENT 108 (1985) ("In formal logic, a sound argument is one in which all the premises are *true* and they provide logically conclusive support for the conclusion because they deductively entail it.") (emphasis in original omitted); *see also* Hurley, *id.*, at 35. ("A valid deductive argument is an argument in which it is impossible for the conclusion to be false given that the premises are true."); *see also* WILLIAM J. KILGORE, AN INTRODUCTORY LOGIC 509 (2d ed. 1979) (noting that deductive logic "is the analysis of arguments whose form requires that in all cases in which the conclusion is false at least one premise is also false"). In the context of legal proof, it has been said that "[i]nference is the essence of proof; proof is good or bad according to the quality and number of inferences drawn from facts to conclusion." J. S. COVINGTON, JR., THE STRUCTURE OF LEGAL ARGUMENT AND PROOF, CASES, MATERIALS AND ANALYSES 2 (2d ed. 2006).

34. IRVING M. COPI & CARL COHEN, INTRODUCTION TO LOGIC 30–34 (13th ed. 2008).

35. Lawyers use other logical tools as well, like abduction, but these are the most commonly deployed logic tools in legal argument.

36. Examples of the typical standards of proof in cases include "a preponderance of the evidence," "by clear and convincing evidence," and "beyond a reasonable doubt." *See, e.g.*, MICHAEL H. GRAHAM, 2 HANDBOOK OF FED. EVID. § 301:5 (7th ed.) (2011).

still frequently use deductive arguments. Legal logic is complex, multifaceted, sometimes communicated in ways that do not fit neatly into a deductive framework, and used by lawyers and judges who are often unfamiliar with the details of the rules of formal logic and their application to legal argument. Deduction seems the best starting place for learning the lessons of logic and applying them to legal argument. An argument couched in the form of deduction but does not comply with the rules of logic should always be rejected. That is, at the very least, deductively fallacious arguments are not good tools for legal argument, and need to be identified and rejected for either better argumentative tools or different conclusions. Furthermore, studying deductive logic alone as a single tool of legal argument can yield practical results for the law student and practitioner. The next chapter explains deduction's role in legal argument in more detail and why deduction is so foundational to making and evaluating legal argument.

Before the focus of this book narrows on deductive logic, formal logical fallacies, and the role they play in legal argument, a *caveat* is necessary. Our focus on formal logic does not suggest that it is the only logical tool that lawyers use, nor should it suggest that the other logical tools are necessarily inferior to deduction. Legal reasoning and legal argument are not exclusively deductive processes. Instead, the focus on formal logic here is an effort to do something useful in just one of the places where legal argument and philosophical logic intersect, and with enough depth and examples to help you to progress in your understanding of formal logic and its place in legal argument, adding value to your ability to evaluate and make legal argument.

2.4 Chapter Two in Review

This chapter started the process of describing formal logic's role in legal argument, explored some of the logical tools lawyers use, and explained why this book is limited to just one kind of logical tool—formal logic. Understanding what the study of logic is, what roles it has in legal argument, and how different logical tools serve different roles in making and evaluating argument is an important step in using formal logic as a tool in crafting legal argument. Think about whether you agree with the following points after having read this chapter.

- Lawyers use different kinds of logical tools in making and evaluating legal argument.
- While legal arguments are sometimes described in terms of their subject matter or whether they are substantive or procedural arguments, they can also be described in terms of their logic, as being deductive, inductive, or analogical arguments.

- There are significant differences between deductive logic and inductive logic. Deduction argues from a general principle to a specific conclusion. Induction argues from a collection of specific observations to reach a general conclusion.
- Both deduction and induction have important roles to play in legal argument. You should be able to provide an example of a deductive legal argument. You should be able to provide an example of an inductive legal argument.
- Analogical arguments are also common in legal argument. Analogical arguments claim that similar characteristics between two specific examples suggest a conclusion about other characteristics in the examples. You should be able to provide an example of an argument by analogy in legal argument.
- If a conclusion can be supported by a valid deductive argument, a valid inductive argument, or a valid analogical argument, which tool do you think would be the most convincing? Why?
- A deductive argument that fails to comply with the rules of deductive logic commits a formal logical fallacy. A logically fallacious argument cannot support its conclusion.
- Legal argument frequently takes a deductive form. However, deduction is not the only logical tool that lawyers use. The focus of this book is on deductive argument and the formal logical fallacies that follow from failing to comply with the rules of formal logic.

Chapter Three

Formal Logic and Its Role in Litigation

Think about the kinds of arguments you hear made outside of the practice of law: a college basketball coach questioning an official's call, two policy advocates taking opposing views on a televised news segment, a letter to the editor in a local newspaper, an undergraduate economics student disputing a poor grade on his group project. The form and format of those arguments are different from that of arguments made in court. When you generally consider the differences between arguments made in court and other kinds of argument, what role does logic play in those differences? How is logic's role different in legal argument compared to the role it plays in other argument forms? While Chapter Two introduced three logical tools—deduction, induction and analogy—this chapter focuses on the role deduction (or formal logic) plays in legal argument. As you read, consider the following questions, some of which might be challenging to answer.

- How is legal argument different from the kinds of arguments you might experience outside of litigation?
- If someone told you that legal argument is more disciplined than other kinds of argument, would you agree? If so, can you explain how?
- Now that you have had a chance to think about the different logical tools discussed in Chapter Two, how are those logical tools used in legal argument?
- When you were first introduced to legal reasoning, did you learn to make and analyze argument in a strict, formal fashion? Do you still take a strict formal approach to making and evaluating legal argument? If so, how would you describe your process? If not, can you describe your process?
- Do you think you can improve on your process for making and evaluating legal argument? How?

3.1 A Practical View of Formal Logic's Role in Litigation

Deductive formal logic is the process of reasoning from a general statement to a particular one. It is common logical tool, both within and without the practice of law. Law students are frequently introduced to the method of legal analysis through the acronym IRAC: Issue, Rule, Application and Conclusion.[1] The IRAC pattern of legal analysis is consistent with deductive logic's role in making and evaluating legal argument. *Issue* spotting is the process of identifying the relevant rule that applies in the case. The *rule* statement is the rule that governs the outcome of the analysis and justifies the conclusion. The *application* is the process of identifying the particular case facts relevant to the applicable general rule and filtering them through the rule to justify a *conclusion*. The IRAC process of applying general rules to specific facts to reveal a conclusion is much like the deductive process of reasoning from general principles to conclusions applicable to specific facts.[2]

Formal logic's role in litigation is not merely limited to applying general rules of law to specific case facts, however. Lawyers use deductive reasoning in many other litigation contexts. In fact, once you understand what formal logic "looks like" in practice and begin searching for formal logic in the design of legal argument, you start to "see" it everywhere. In legal argument, reasoning from general principles to specific outcomes typically begins with legal rules. Legal rules from case holdings,

1. "The IRAC acronym stands for Issue, Rule, Application, and Conclusion. It is probably the most widely known of the acronyms describing conventions for organizing a legal analysis. Many books or popular courses on law school exam-taking tips suggest that using the acronym will increase performance on law school exams." Terrill Pollman, *Building a Tower of Babel or Building a Discipline? Talking about Legal Writing*, 85 MARQ. L. REV. 887 n. 50 (2002). *See also* James Ottavio Castagnera, *Why the Nation Needs More Lawyers*, 22 T. MARSHALL L. REV. 19, 26 (1996) ("IRAC is to legal analysis what 'Force = Mass x Velocity' is to Newtonian physics"); J. Christopher Rideout & Jill J. Ramsfield, *Legal Writing: A Revised View*, 69 WASH. L. REV. 35, 99 (1994) ("This acronym stands for Issue, Rule, Application, and Conclusion, an oversimplified version of deductive reasoning useful in some legal writing contexts as an introduction, but not in others."). Variations on the IRAC theme are sometimes used. For example, CREAC is another acronym representing five stages in legal writing and analysis. The letters in the acronym represent Conclusion, Rule, Elaboration, Application, and a restatement of the Conclusion. *See, e.g.*, JOHN DELANEY, HOW TO DO YOUR BEST ON LAW SCHOOL EXAMS 78 (1988) ("[L]egal writing teachers and texts have offered alternatives like CRAC (Conclusion, Rule, Application, Conclusion) or FORAC (Facts of precedent case, Outcome of precedent case, Rule, Application, Conclusion.)"); BRYAN A. GARNER, GARNER ON LANGUAGE AND WRITING 403 (2009). Another example is CIRI(P), an acronym representing five stages in legal writing and analysis: Conclusion, Issue, Rule (or principle), Interweaving, and Policy; Terrill Pollman, *Building a Tower of Babel or Building a Discipline? Talking about Legal Writing*, 85 MARQ. L. REV. 887 (2002). *See also* Susan E. Provenzano & Lesley S. Kagan, *Teaching in Reverse: a Positive Approach to Analytical Errors in 1L Writing*, 39 LOY. U. CHI. L.J. 123 (describing IRAC, as a "'positive' teaching tool and recognizing that [t]hrough positive teaching tools, 1Ls learn the many different ways that legal analysis can go right, but see fewer contrasting varieties of how their own legal analysis is likely to go wrong."); Gerald Lebovits, *Cracking the Code to Writing Legal Arguments: From Irac to Crarc to Combinations in Between*, N.Y. ST. B.J., July/August 2010, at 64 (discussing IRAC and collecting a number of "IRAC variants.").

2. *See* James M. Boland, *Legal Writing Programs and Professionalism: Legal Writing Professors Can Join the Academic Club*, 18 ST. THOMAS L. REV. 711, 724 (2006) ("The IRAC model, while helpful in providing a superficial template for legal analysis, is simply not enough. Legal analysis and argument must be grounded in the legal syllogism, and IRAC placed within the syllogistic context. If students understand the syllogism, then all possible forms of IRAC can be placed within that context, so that the syllogism becomes a roadmap to guide the students through the analytical process."); Anita Schnee, *Logical Reasoning "Obviously,"* 3 LEGAL WRITING: J. LEGAL WRITING INST. 105, 106 (1997) ("'IRAC' is just another way of saying 'the deductive syllogistic process.'").

statutes or other authority are the general principles lawyers use to make argument. The following hypothetical demonstrates formal logic's role in legal analysis.

Your client has just been served with a lawsuit naming him as the defendant. The complaint alleges that your client agreed with the plaintiff to sell an undeveloped residential lot among several in a parcel your client is planning to develop. No written agreement is alleged in the complaint, nor is one attached to the complaint. When asked, your client tells you that there was never any written agreement to sell the property to the plaintiff. The only discussions regarding the sale were preliminary and no promise to sell the property was ever made by your client, either verbally or in writing. You know that the Statute of Frauds[3] provides that contracts for the sale of real property must be in writing to be enforceable. When your client asks what his best defense is, your advice and justification for that advice could be described this way:

> All enforceable contracts for the sale of real property[4] are contracts that are in writing.
>
> The contract for the sale of real property that is the subject of the lawsuit is not a contract that is in writing.
>
> Therefore, the contract for the sale of real property that is the subject of the lawsuit is not an enforceable contract.

Figure 2. *An example of a syllogism.*

The form of this argument in Figure 2 is a *syllogism*,[5] the most basic structure of formal logic. It is comprised of three sentences, each called a *proposition*. The first two propositions are called *premises*. The first premise is the *major premise*,[6] the second the *minor premise*.[7] The third proposition in the syllogism is a *conclusion*. When you make this argument, you know (or at least assume) that so long as your

3. Ordinarily contracts are enforceable regardless of whether they are in writing. However, the Statute of Frauds makes exceptions to this rule for certain categories of contracts. Where a contract fits the criteria for one or more of those categories enumerated in the Statute of Frauds, the contract generally is required to be in writing to be enforceable. Where a contract meets the criteria of one or more of these categories, it is said to be "within" the Statute of Frauds. RESTATEMENT (SECOND) OF CONTRACTS § 110 cmts. a, b (Am. Law Inst. 1981).

4. Contracts for the sale of real property are one of the categories of contracts that are said to be "within" the Statute of Frauds and require a written agreement to be enforceable. RESTATEMENT (SECOND) OF CONTRACTS § 125(1) (Am. Law Inst. 1981) ("A promise to transfer to any person any interest in land is within the Statute of Frauds"). There are some exceptions to this requirement. *See, e.g.*, RESTATEMENT (SECOND) OF CONTRACTS § 129 (Am. Law Inst. 1981).

5. More specifically, this example is a categorical syllogism. There are other kinds of syllogisms that will be described later in this chapter.

6. IRVING M. COPI & CARL COHEN, INTRODUCTION TO LOGIC 225 (13th ed. 2008); *see also* PATRICK J. HURLEY, A CONCISE INTRODUCTION TO LOGIC 44 (2015).

7. *Id.* Categorical syllogisms, and their components, including the subject terms and predicate terms, are more completely described in Chapter Four.

client has provided all relevant information and that it is accurate, the conclusion is true. In fact, if both premises are true and the logical form of the syllogism is valid, the principles of formal logic require that the conclusion must be true.[8]

For lawyers introduced to basic legal reasoning through IRAC or another method of applying general legal rules to specific case facts, the place of deduction in legal reasoning might be obvious. Typically, legal rules provide the major premise in a deductive syllogism and case facts provide the minor premise. Again, in deduction, where the premises are true and the form the syllogism is valid, the conclusion must be true. Accordingly, correctly identifying the legal rules and operative facts is essential to the power of deductive argument.

There are three principal types of deductive syllogisms: the hypothetical syllogism, the categorical syllogism, and the disjunctive syllogism.[9] All three are found in legal argument. In a hypothetical syllogism, the conclusion follows from the relationship between the propositions in the premises. It begins with a hypothetical proposition—an "if . . . then" statement—affirming that if one of its terms is true, then the other is true as well.[10] For example:

> If a person is a partner in a general partnership, then he or she is personally liable for the partnership's liabilities.[11]
>
> Jennifer is a partner in a general partnership.
>
> Therefore, Jennifer is personally liable for the partnership's liabilities.

Figure 3. *An example of a hypothetical syllogism.*

In a categorical syllogism, the conclusion follows from the relationship between the concepts in the premises and their membership in certain categories.[12] Categorical propositions about classes of objects are described by relation of their subject and predicate terms.[13] For example, like the syllogism in Figure 2, the following example argues for a conclusion based on the relationship of categories:

---

8. *Id.* at 26.

9. *Id.* at 301. *See also* Patrick J. Hurley, A Concise Introduction to Logic 36 (2015).

10. *Id.*

11. A general partnership is a business association between at least two people who are called partners. The partners in a general partnership have ownership rights and management rights in the partnership.

12. "A *categorical syllogism* is defined as a form of argument consisting of three categorical propositions which contain between them three and only three terms. Two of the propositions are premises, the third is the conclusion." Morris R. Cohen & Ernest Nagel, An Introduction to Logic and Scientific Method 77 (1934); *see also* J. S. Covington, Jr., The Structure of Legal Argument and Proof, Cases, Materials and Analyses 437 (2d ed. 2006). (defining categorical syllogism as "[a] form of argument in which the antecedent and the consequent of the major proposition places subjects in categories, such as all A are B").

13. Irving M. Copi & Carl Cohen, Introduction to Logic 181–82 (13th ed. 2008).

All valid corporations are legal entities with at least one shareholder. Excavation Solutions, Incorporated is a valid corporation. Therefore, Excavation Solutions, Incorporated is a legal entity with at least one shareholder.

Figure 4. *An example of a categorical syllogism.*

Because analysis often involves placing legal labels on (or categorizing) status or conduct, many arguments fit neatly into a categorical syllogism. In Figure 3, the premises are focused on categorizing "all valid corporations" and legal entities with "at least one shareholder" and the business called "Excavation Solutions, Inc." If there is a question about whether Excavation Solutions, Inc. has a shareholder, it can be resolved by establishing that Excavation Solutions, Inc. is a valid corporation.

A disjunctive syllogism begins with a disjunctive or alternative premise—a statement asserting that the truth is one thing or it is another thing—followed by a categorical premise that asserts one of the alternatives in the disjunctive premise is false.[14] For example:

Limited Liability Companies are either member-managed or manager-managed.[15] Redundant Technologies, LLC is not manager-managed. Therefore, Redundant Technologies, LLC is member-managed.

Figure 5. *An example of a disjunctive syllogism.*

Whether the deductive argument takes the form of a categorical, hypothetical, or disjunctive syllogism, spotting the logical issue in an argument is the first step toward analyzing the argument's logical form. Once you have a general understanding of these common syllogisms, you can identify arguments by their logical structure. The "if . . . then" arguments lawyers so often confront are hypothetical syllogisms. The arguments about labels, definitions, and categories common in legal argument are typically categorical syllogisms. The "or" statements we sometimes confront litigating matters of statutory and contract interpretation are often disjunctive syllogisms.

14. *Id.*

15. A limited liability company (LLC) is a business association. A limited liability company has one or more members, who own the company. The members may also manage the company. If the members elect to do that, the LLC is considered a member-managed LLC. Alternatively, members may elect to simply be owners of the company, without rights to manage it beyond appointing the managers and limited other rights. If the members elect to limit their interests to ownership and delegate management of the company to one or more managers, the LLC is considered a manager-managed LLC.

3.2 The Pervasive Role of Formal Logic in Legal Argument

Ordinarily, when two parties have a legal dispute, there are two sides to the story. Formal logic's value in arranging argument into a syllogism is important, because its role pervades how lawyers design claims and defenses. However, even when either party's particular argument takes a syllogistic form, each party's argument only presents one of the two competing arguments. For example, if we return to the hypothetical of the Statute of Frauds defense in Figure 2, we can see how formal logic informs the positions you and opposing counsel will take in the case. Assume your client takes the following position as an affirmative defense[16] to the plaintiff's breach of contract claim:

> All enforceable contracts for the sale of real property are contracts that are in writing.
>
> The contract for the sale of real property that is the subject of the lawsuit is not a contract that is in writing.
>
> Therefore, the contract for the sale of real property that is the subject of the lawsuit is not an enforceable contract.

Figure 6. *An example of a syllogistic legal argument.*

This is just one argument that will be introduced in this case—the defendant's argument. Plaintiff's counsel will have to respond to this affirmative defense. Just as formal logic is at work in the design of defendant's argument, it is also at work in the plaintiff's response. Formal logic provides that if the plaintiff does not confront this syllogism, he must lose the case because the conclusion ("the contract for the sale of real property that is the subject of the lawsuit is not an enforceable contract") will be true and provide a complete defense to the plaintiff's claim; that is the nature of deduction.

This characteristic of deduction is as important for the plaintiff, however, as it is for your client, the defendant. The plaintiff might attack the major premise of your syllogism ("All enforceable contracts for the sale of real property are contracts that are in writing."). If there is an exception to the rule that contracts for the sale of real property must be in writing, then your syllogism is founded on the wrong rule[17]—that is, the major premise of your syllogism is not true, and a false premise in a

16. An affirmative defense is a defense to a complaint that endeavors to avoid liability by making "allegations of excuse, justification, or other negating matter" rather than by contradicting the allegations of the complaint. *See* Hon. Amy St. Eve & Michael A. Zuckerman, *The Forgotten Pleading*, 7 Fed. Cts. L. Rev. 152, 161 (2013) (quoting *Riemer v. Chase Bank USA*, N.A., 274 F.R.D. 637 (N.D. Ill. 2011) and citing *Donohue v. Am. Isuzu Motors*, Inc., 155 F.R.D. 515, 519 (M.D. Pa. 1994)). The argument that a contract is unenforceable because it does not comply with the Statute of Frauds is typically raised as an affirmative defense.

17. In fact, there are some exceptions to this rule. In limited circumstances, a contract to sell real property will be enforced even when it is not in writing.

deductive syllogism ensures the failure of the argument. Even if the form of your argument is valid, the falsity of the premise is fatal. Remember, formal logic recognizes a distinction between an argument that is logically *valid* and an argument that is *true*. Logical validity is conformity with the rules of deductive logic. If the rules are followed, then the form of the argument is valid and the argument is logically valid. However, an argument's valid form does not necessarily ensure the truth of the conclusion. Truth (or falsity) is an attribute of the individual propositions that appear within an argument. Accordingly, the logical form of an argument is *either* valid or invalid. The *form* is *neither* true nor false. Conversely, the *premises* of an argument are *either* true or false. They are *neither* valid nor invalid. These distinct concepts of truth and falsity, validity and invalidity work together. When the logical form of an argument is valid and its premises are true, *then* the argument requires that the conclusion be true.[18] If either a premise is false or the form is invalid, the conclusion necessarily cannot be true.[19] While formal logic is at work in designing a legal argument, it is at work in responding to a legal argument as well—even if the essence of the response is to suggest that there are other logical tools, like induction or analogy, better suited to solving this legal disagreement.

Even beyond the strategic decisions of what claims to assert and what elements to allege in a plaintiff's complaint, or what defenses to raise in the defendant's response, the tactical decisions imbedded in drafting pleadings, motions, and responses are also infused with principles of formal logic. Articulating legal elements and claims in a complaint or motion should take a deductively valid structure, and other logical tools, like induction and analogy, are not ordinarily the best tools for these legal tasks. For example, a lawyer drafting a complaint would never construct the following allegations in his complaint:

12. Plaintiff was injured when Defendant's car collided with Plaintiff while Plaintiff was riding a bicycle on the shoulder of Seven Mile Road.
13. Other plaintiffs who have been injured while riding their bicycles on the shoulders of roads have been injured by the negligence of car drivers.
14. Therefore plaintiff was probably injured by Defendant's negligence.

Figure 7. *An excerpt from a complaint taking a syllogistic form.*

Lawyers rarely design inductive arguments at the pleading stage—and even when they do, they do not couch them in the explicit language of induction. Instead, legal arguments, especially at the pleading stage, are typically described, specifically and explicitly, in the form of a deductive argument. Universally, complaints are written in a way that argues that the plaintiff's demand for relief is required by law, the

18. *See, e.g.*, PATRICK J. HURLEY, A CONCISE INTRODUCTION TO LOGIC 44 (2015).
19. IRVING M. COPI & CARL COHEN, INTRODUCTION TO LOGIC 30–34 (13th ed. 2008).

language of deduction. They do not merely suggest that relief is potential or probable, like the language in paragraph 13 in Figure 7—the language of inductive or analogical argument.

Formal logic's role in litigation is not limited to lawyers' processes for performing legal analysis and formulating claims and defenses. Indeed, it is prolific in litigation. Examples can be found in the written discovery process, in depositions, at trial, in instructing the jurors, and elsewhere. When you prepare requests for admissions,[20] you make strategic decisions about what facts, opinions, or mixed questions of law and fact for which you seek admission. Logically speaking, what benefit would it be to you to obtain an admission of a fact in a case? If the fact is relevant to the dispute, then it likely has a place in a syllogistic argument in your case. Obtaining a formal admission of the truth or falsity of the fact may ensure that the minor premise in the argument will succeed or fail and, potentially, the persuasive power of the syllogism along with it.

Formal logic's role in litigation is not limited to performing legal analysis and formulating claims and defenses. Indeed, it is prolific in litigation.

For example, litigators spend a lot of time in discovery and at trial attacking premises. In the deposition of an expert witness, securing the expert's admission that one of the premises of the expert's opinion is based on false or unjustified assumption of fact is an important concession. In terms of logic, it is important because it defeats a premise necessary to ensure a conclusion in an opinion that might otherwise take the form of a valid syllogism. At trial, if a fact witness lacks credibility, a trial lawyer must be skilled at impeaching that credibility on cross-examination and elsewhere. This is important because, logically speaking, defeating a premise is a powerful tool in defusing a legal argument. Lawyers do this every day; many do it very well, even if they do not know what a syllogism is or understand the difference between a major and a minor premise. Lawyers who skillfully attack premises without knowing the rules of formal logic are able to do this because the rules of formal logic are at work in their argument and tactics without them even realizing it.

Another common example of formal logic at work in trial advocacy is the use of jury instructions. Jury instructions and special interrogatories do not engage jurors in an inductive process where they are provided universe of legal rules to choose from for the rule they will apply; instead, jury instructions provide the rule for the

20. Requests for admissions are documentary requests served on the opposing party asking that party to admit certain facts, applications of law to facts, or opinions. If an admission is made in response to such a request, the admission is conclusive for purposes of the litigation, unless the court grants leave to withdraw or amend the admission. *See, e.g.*, FED. R. CIV. P. 36.

jurors to apply.[21] The jurors, then, find that either the rule encompasses the facts of the case or it does not. Typically, this is a purely deductive process. An example can be found in this sample jury instruction on agency:

> Agency: Apparent Agency
>
> The plaintiff claims that a man wearing a uniform indicative of employment by the defendant University (the "Uniformed Man") was acting as the University's agent. The actions of the Uniformed Man are binding on the University if all three of the following elements are established by plaintiff's evidence:
>
> (1) the University put the Uniformed Man in such a situation that a reasonable person familiar with the University's practices would be justified in believing the Uniformed Man had the authority to act on the University's behalf,
>
> (2) the plaintiff actually believed the Uniformed Man had the authority to act on the University's behalf, and
>
> (3) the plaintiff was justified in believing that the Uniformed Man had the authority to act on the University's behalf.

This instruction would be provided to the jurors at the conclusion of the trial. The form of the logical relationship among the rule, the facts, and the jury verdict is that of a deductive syllogism. In a case involving a dispute about whether a principal would be bound because of the apparent agency of another person, the lawyers' closing arguments might well review the structure of the rule contained in this instruction and suggest the application of the legal rules to the jurors. The lawyers' arguments and the jurors' process for utilizing the rule would take a deductive pattern, with the legal rule as the major premise in a deductive syllogism and the facts established by the evidence as the minor premise.

Lawyers often make arguments that have nothing to do with what the law is, but instead, are limited to what the facts are, or what facts are more credible, or whether a witness is credible, or whether an expert's opinion is based on a false assumption, or any other manner of fact disputes that litigators deal with daily. Frequently, these arguments about fact disputes fit into a deductive pattern. Of course, IRAC is not an effective tool for designing arguments about fact disputes, even when made in a legal context. For example, if a lawyer has to argue about which of two witnesses had a better perspective from which to identify a criminal defendant, the IRAC

21. At the end of a jury trial and prior to their deliberations and decision, jurors are generally provided with a set of instructions on the law. The language of the instructions is frequently agreed to by the lawyers and ruled upon by the judge prior to being communicated to the jurors. Many common legal issues are addressed by published "model" or "pattern" jury instructions. Other instructions are drafted to meet the specific issues and evidence in the particular case at issue.

framework offers no assistance. The argument might be important, even essential to a successful case, but the technique for designing a convincing argument here is one rarely understood with any specific and developed methodology. In a factual argument, other rules are sometimes substituted in lieu of legal rules in the major premise of a syllogism. Rules like "the person closest to the scene of the accident is the most reliable witness," or "when you are telling the truth, your story always stays the same," or "a car traveling less than fifty-five miles per hour requires 205 feet of stopping distance," can be just as persuasive a logical basis for deductive legal argument as those arguments premised on legal rules. Further, when deduction is not the right tool for resolving fact disputes, fact-based arguments that reach a conclusion by way of induction or analogy generally fit into a broader deductive context, providing a minor premise in another deductive syllogism. Stated otherwise, these fact-based arguments might use non-deductive logic tools to reach conclusions, but those conclusions typically find an eventual place in a broader legal argument that takes a syllogistic form.

3.3 The "Formal" in Formal Logic, and How it Helps Support and Attack Legal Argument

Formal logic is an appropriate tool at different points in the litigation process, and for different purposes in the litigation process—especially when disputes about what the law or facts are in the case have been resolved by the court, legal presumptions, or admissions. Disputes about the law and facts are frequently resolved or suspended by procedural presumptions or admissions. For example, in a breach of contract claim, the plaintiff's complaint might allege that a certain contractual obligation was performed by the defendant in a way that did not comply with the requirements of the contract. The defendant might disagree with the plaintiff's factual characterization of the defendant's contractual performance and seek to have the complaint dismissed. However, a judge ruling on a defendant's motion to dismiss a complaint "must accept as true all of the factual allegations contained in the complaint."[22] That is, for procedural reasons, this important, potentially disputed fact is assumed to be true for the limited purposes of arguing a motion to dismiss. This procedural presumption makes this a good candidate for a deductive argument, because the factual premise is required to be assumed as true. Similarly, other times arguments can be made based on proffered assumptions that a fact in a legal dispute will be resolved in a certain way. Because formal logic recognizes that the *truth* of the argument and the logical *validity* of the argument's form are both essential to argument, impeaching the *validity* of the logical *form* is just as powerful as proving the premises false are.

22. *Bell Atl. Corp. v. Twombly*, 550 U.S. 544, 572 (2007) (citing *Swierkiewicz v. Sorema N.A.*, 534 U.S. 506, 508, n. 1 (2002)).

This presents an important opportunity for a party responding to an argument—who may be restrained by stipulated, advocated, presumed facts, unfavorable and unassailable legal precedents, or other undeniable premises—to still make a convincing argument. This argument rests on neither the facts nor the law, but the logical form of the argument faced by the respondent. However, unlike attacks on an argument's syllogistic premises, which are intuitive even to lawyers unfamiliar with the rules of logic or form of syllogisms, attacks on a syllogism's validity require some understanding of the formal structure, concepts, language, and rules of formal deductive logic.

Because formal logic recognizes that the truth of the argument and the logical validity of the argument's form are both essential to argument, impeaching the validity of the logical form is just as powerful proving the premises false.

3.4 Learning the Tools of Formal Logic

Deduction is regarded as the most persuasive logical tools.[23] If successfully attacking a potential persuasive legal argument's deductive form is just as powerful as successfully attacking its premises, then lawyers can benefit from learning the concepts, rules, and language tools necessary to understand and evaluate formal logic. The understanding begins with dissecting and labeling legal argument in its syllogistic form.

Understanding formal logic's influence on a legal argument begins with dissecting and labeling legal argument in its syllogistic form.

Dissecting and labeling an argument's syllogistic form begins with subdividing the argument into components and assembling them into a syllogism.[24] Instead of using all of the precise words contained in an argument, it is simpler and just as effective to

23. "Arguments consist of inferences to conclusions from sets of premises. The degree of reliability of an argument is the extent to which one may rely on the truth of the conclusion based on the assumed truth of the premises. In these terms, 'rational force' means the degree of reliability the argument form has at its most reliable. By this definition, valid deductive arguments—the most reliable type of deductive argument—have the highest degree of rational force. Well framed (and thus highly probable) inductive arguments probably have the next highest degree; well framed abductive arguments, though they are deductively invalid, may have as much rational force as well framed inductive arguments." Scott Brewer, *Exemplary Reasoning: Semantics, Pragmatics, and the Rational Force of Legal Argument by Analogy*, 109 Harv. L. Rev. 925, 950–51 (1996) (citations omitted).

24. "Now, to put an argument in syllogistic form is to strip it bare for logical inspection. We can see whether its weak points must lie, if it has any, and consider whether there is reason to believe that it is actually (i.e., materially) weak at those points." F. C. S. Schiller, Formal Logic, A Scientific and Social Problem 221 (1912).

eliminate and paraphrase some of the words in the argument before arranging them in the syllogism.[25] It may even be possible to further simplify the argument by reducing some of those words to symbols.[26] Furthermore, sometimes it is appropriate to add implied words into the framework of the syllogism to ensure consistency in the intended meaning of the terms of the argument. Ultimately, this process reduces the argument to a series of phrases, letters, or symbols that accurately represent the essential components of the argument and the relationships between and among those components. Translating legal argument into syllogistic form can be easy, but when arguments contain ambiguities and implied terms, that translation can be burdensome. This is especially true given that the infirmities and ambiguities of language make up so much of the problems practitioners deal with in the practice of law.[27]

As explained earlier, the form of a syllogism consists of two premises and a conclusion.[28] A premise is a proposition[29] that is used to support the truth of a conclusion. Each premise consists of *terms*.

A first type of syllogism, common in legal argument, is a hypothetical syllogism. It contains at least one hypothetical proposition, affirming that if one of its terms (the antecedent term) is true, then the other of its terms (the consequent term) is true.[30] Legal arguments frequently employ hypothetical syllogisms,[31] the most commonly encountered of which is the mixed hypothetical syllogism. It contains

25. *See* Irving M. Copi & Carl Cohen, Introduction to Logic 267–93 (13th ed. 2008) (describing in detail the process of converting arguments into standard syllogistic form).

26. One commentator illustratively referred to this process of arranging legal language into syllogistic form as "systematic pulverization." Layman E. Allen, *Symbolic Logic: A Razor-Edged Tool for Drafting and Interpreting Legal Documents*, 66 Yale L. J. 833, 835 (1957).

27. "[S]yllogisms, as they occur in ordinary spoken and written expression, are seldom phrased according to the precise norms of the standard-form syllogism. Sometimes quantifiers, premises, or conclusions are left unexpressed, chains of syllogisms are strung together into single arguments, and terms are mixed together with their negations in a single argument." Patrick J. Hurley, A Concise Introduction to Logic 264 (2015).

28. "Legal argument generally has three sources of major premises: a text (constitution, statute, regulation, ordinance, or contract), precedent (case law, etc.), and policy (i.e., consequences of the decision). Often that major premises is self evident and acknowledged by both sides. The minor premises, meanwhile, is derived from the facts of the case. There is much to be said for the proposition that 'legal reasoning revolves mainly around the establishment of the minor premise.'" Justice Antonin Scalia & Brian Garner, Making Your Case: The Art of Persuading Judges 42 (2008) (quoting O.C. Jensen, The Nature of Legal Argument 20 (1957)).

29. A proposition is an assertion that something is the case, or that it is not the case. Copi & Cohen, *supra* note 25, at 5. Logicians sometimes use the term "statement" in place of the term "proposition." *Id.*

30. Copi & Cohen, *supra* note 25, at 301. Hypothetical propositions are sometimes referred to as conditional propositions. *Id. See also* Elliot D. Cohen, Critical Thinking Unleashed 33 (2009).

31. *See, e.g.*, *Iams v. DiamlerChrysler*, 883 N.E.2d 466 (Ohio. App. 2007); *Edwards v. Riverdale Sch. Dist.*, 188 P.3d 317 (Or. App. 2008); *Crouse-Hinds Co. v. Internorth, Inc.* 634 F.2d 690, 703 (2nd Cir. N.Y. 1980); *Zinpro Corp. v. Ridenour*, No. 07-96-0008-CV, 1996 Tex.App. LEXIS 3380 (Tex. Amarillo Aug. 1, 1996).

a hypothetical premise and a categorical premise.[32] The hallmark of a hypothetical syllogism is the "if . . . then" relationship that is the center of the argument. For example:

> If the subject of a contract is the sale of an interest in land, then the contract is within the Statute of Frauds.[33]
>
> The contract is a contract for the sale of an interest in land.
>
> Therefore, the contract is within the Statute of Frauds.[34]

Figure 8. *An example of a legal argument taking the form of a hypothetical syllogism.*

While "if . . . then" language is commonly associated with hypothetical syllogisms, other words also suggest arguments that fit into a hypothetical syllogism structure. For example, "on condition that," "in the event that," "when," "wherever," "assuming that," and other words[35] suggest a logical relationship that can be described in a hypothetical syllogism.

A hypothetical syllogism has two premises. The hypothetical premise[36] contains two terms. The first term in the hypothetical premise is the *antecedent* term. The second term is the *consequent* term. The second premise in a mixed hypothetical syllogism is a categorical premise[37] that will either affirm or deny one of the terms in the hypothetical premise. The third proposition in a hypothetical syllogism is a conclusion. In the argument described in Figure 8, the first proposition ("If the subject of a contract is the sale of an interest in land, then the contract is within the Statute of Frauds") is the hypothetical premise. It is the proposition that makes a

32. Copi & Cohen, *supra* note 25, at 299. The mixed hypothetical syllogism is "mixed" because it contains only one hypothetical premise. The other premise is a categorical one. Therefore, it is a mixed hypothetical syllogism. This type is contrasted with a pure hypothetical syllogism, which would include two hypothetical premises. See *infra* note 9 in Chapter Four.

33. *See, e.g.*, Restatement (Second) of Contracts, § 125(1) (Am. Law Inst. 1981) ("A promise to transfer to any person any interest in land is within the Statute of Frauds.").

34. Once again, in this example, the structure of the syllogism is more readily apparent if we reduce its components to symbols. If we assign the term "transfer of an interest in land" the letter "A" and assign "within the statute of frauds" the letter "B" the syllogism takes this form:

If A then B.

A.

Therefore B.

35. *See* Elliot D. Cohen, Critical Thinking Unleashed 34 (2009) (providing further examples of statement that indicate a hypothetical syllogism, and discussing the process of translating them into the standard form of a hypothetical syllogism).

36. In a mixed hypothetical syllogism, the major premise is the hypothetical premise—i.e., the "if . . . then" premises.

37. *See, e.g.*, Copi & Cohen, *supra* note 25, at 298–99.

hypothetical or conditional statement. It includes an antecedent term ("the subject of a contract is the sale of an interest in land") and a consequent term ("the contract is within the Statute of Frauds"). The second sentence ("The contract is a contract for the sale of an interest in land") is a categorical premise. The third sentence ("Therefore, the contract is within the Statute of Frauds") is the conclusion.

Understanding the components of hypothetical syllogisms provides some new language tools for describing and analyzing hypothetical syllogisms.

- Hypothetical syllogism
- Hypothetical premise
- Antecedent term
- Consequent term
- Categorical premise
- Conclusion

A second kind of syllogism, the categorical syllogism, is designed to reach an inference by putting concepts in categories. For example, one might begin to argue, "All prosecutors are lawyers." This *categorical premise* has two terms: "[persons who are] prosecutors" and "[persons who are] lawyers." If we add a second premise, "No public defenders are prosecutors," we see that it also contains two terms "[persons who are] public defenders" and "[persons who are] prosecutors." To complete the syllogism, we might attempt to add the following conclusion: "Therefore, no public defenders are lawyers."[38] We could then arrange these two premises and the conclusion this way:

All prosecutors are lawyers. No public defenders are prosecutors. Therefore, no public defenders are lawyers.

Figure 9. *An example of a legal argument taking the form of a categorical syllogism.*

Accordingly, we have crafted a syllogism with three terms: "prosecutors," "lawyers" and "public defenders." Each of the three propositions includes two terms. Each of three propositions also includes some other components. First, each sentence includes a *qualifier*.[39] Qualifiers are typically the words "all," "some," or "no." So, when you see the term "public defenders" in the conclusion, it is qualified by

38. Of course this conclusion is factually incorrect. The conclusion is also the result of a logically invalid argument. We will understand why the argument is logically invalid after exploring the fallacies of the illicit minor and major term in Chapter Six.

39. *See, e.g.*, Arnold vander Nat, Simple Formal Logic: With Common-Sense Symbolic Techniques 150–51 (2010).

the term "no." Additionally, logic also provides a name for the word or words that relate the two terms in a proposition; the word or words that connects the terms, like "is," "are," "is not," or "are not," are the *copula*.[40] The conclusion, like the other two propositions in a categorical syllogism, contains two terms: a *subject* term ("public defenders") and a *predicate* term ("lawyers"). The subject term is labeled as such because, when the proposition is affirmative, it is the term that is included in the predicate term and when the proposition is negative, it is excluded from the predicate term.[41] The conclusion provides: "no public defenders are lawyers." Accordingly, the conclusion asserts that no members of the class "public defenders" is included in the class "lawyers."[42] Of course, that is not a true statement. As we will see in the next chapter, the reason the conclusion is not true is explained by rules of formal logic. However, formal logic's explanation requires that we first put the argument in syllogistic form. Formal logic then provides tools that identify all of the syllogistic components, including the subject and predicate terms of the conclusion. This structure and these tools allow us to identify the remaining components with more specificity.

That additional specificity allows us to distinctly name each of the premises and each of the terms in the various premises. In a valid categorical syllogism, there must be a common term that appears in both of the premises. This common term is called the *middle term.* [43] In this example syllogism in Figure 9, the term "prosecutors" is the middle term, since it appears in both premises. Additionally, formal logic provides names for the remaining two terms. The term that is the predicate of the conclusion is the *major term.*[44] The premise that contains the major term is the *major premise.* The term that is the subject of the conclusion is the *minor term.*[45] The premise that contains the minor term is the *minor premise.* Accordingly, the conclusion, "no public defenders are lawyers" identifies the predicate term, "lawyers," as the major term. The conclusion also identifies the subject term, "public defenders," as the minor term. With the following language tools we can describe and discuss any argument that fits into a categorical syllogistic form:

- Categorical syllogism
- Categorical premise
- Subject term
- Predicate term
- Quantifier

40. *Id.*; *see also* PATRICK J. HURLEY, A CONCISE INTRODUCTION TO LOGIC 201 (2015).
41. *See, e.g.*, ROBERT COGAN, CRITICAL THINKING: STEP BY STEP 84 (1998).
42. *Id.*
43. Copi & Cohen, *supra note* 25, at 225.
44. *Id.*
45. *Id.*

- Copula
- Major premise
- Minor premise
- Major term
- Minor term
- Middle term

The third category of syllogism is the disjunctive syllogism. A disjunctive syllogism uses the logical operator "or" providing two alternatives in one of its premises. Like hypothetical and categorical syllogisms, a disjunctive syllogism contains two premises and a conclusion. The first premise is a disjunctive proposition. A disjunctive proposition contains two terms separated by a *disjunct*, typically represented by the word "or." A second proposition, a *categorical premise*, follows this disjunctive proposition and affirms or denies one of the disjuncts.[46] The last proposition of a disjunctive syllogism is a conclusion.[47] The terminology common to disjunctive syllogisms adds just three more language tools to our list:

- Disjunctive syllogism
- Disjunctive premise
- Disjunct

Understanding the structure of a syllogism and naming the components of the syllogism unlock an opportunity for you to talk about the logical form of legal argument. Without these tools, you are limited in your ability to evaluate the logic of legal argument and communicate about it. Without these tools, you can only talk about the truth or falsity of the premises. If you sense something is wrong with the logical structure of the argument, you are without sufficient tools to describe or justify what is logically wrong. Frequently, all you can do is, in conclusory fashion, label the argument as "illogical." Conversely, understanding the syllogistic structure and terminology of formal logic allows you to do something more than conclusory analysis of the argument's logical structure. Knowledge of formal logic allows for an understanding of the rules of formal logic, the logical fallacies that follow from failure to follow the rules, and language tools effective to describe and justify the logical failings of logically fallacious legal arguments.

46. Copi & Cohen, *supra* note 25, at 298–99.
47. *Id.* at 298.

3.5 Using the Language of Formal Logic to Reveal a Legal Argument's Logical Form

Armed with knowledge of some of the concepts and language of formal logic, you can employ it in legal argument. The process of reducing legal argument in its natural form down to its syllogistic framework can be time-consuming and impracticable. Reducing every legal argument to a syllogism is unnecessary. Even reducing a difficult logical argument, or an important logical argument, to a syllogism might not be necessary. The real value of the syllogism is that it is the embodiment of the logical substructure of deductive argument, providing a formal frame of reference for evaluating that logical substructure. This revelation is at the heart formal logic. The key to leveraging knowledge of logic in legal argument as a practical tool in litigation is efficiently exposing logical form.

The key to leveraging knowledge of logic in legal argument as a practical tool in litigation is efficiently exposing logical form.

There is more than one way to do that. One method is to rearrange the argument as presented in court or a brief into a formal syllogism, as described above. A second method is to spot some of the patterns of argument and associate them with either a valid or invalid argument type, without comprehensively arranging an entire argument into a syllogism.

The first method is the traditional one, requiring translation of the language generally used in argument. For example, assume that a defendant makes the following argument in a brief in support of a motion to dismiss.

> Plaintiff's allegations, which, for purposes of this motion must be accepted as true, fail to state a claim upon which relief can be granted. Plaintiff alleges that the breach of contract took place seven years prior to the filing of the complaint. The statute of limitations for breach of contract in this state is six years. Accordingly, if it is assumed that, as Plaintiff's own Complaint concedes, any cause of action for breach of contract accrued over six years ago, the Plaintiff's claim for breach of contract must be barred by the statute of limitations.

Figure 10. *An excerpt from a legal argument not yet in the standard form of a syllogism.*

The initial challenge is to take this legal argument and convert it to a syllogism. One approach to that is to find the logical core of the legal argument in Figure 10:

> Accordingly, if it assumed that, as Plaintiff's own Complaint concedes, any cause of action for breach of contract accrued over

> six years ago, the Plaintiff's claim for breach of contract must be barred by the statute of limitations.

This proposition takes the form of a hypothetical syllogism. The word "if" is a hallmark of such arguments. The next step is to identify the premises and conclusion of the argument. The conclusion is pretty simple to identify: "Plaintiff's claim for breach of contract is barred by the statute of limitations." The premises are the propositions that support this conclusion. The argument takes an "if . . . then" approach to justify the conclusion, the hallmark of the hypothetical syllogism. The hypothetical premise of a hypothetical syllogism might be stated this way:

> If a claim for breach of contract accrues more than six years prior to the date of filing of the complaint, then the claim is barred by the statute of limitations.

As discussed above, the hypothetical premise in a hypothetical syllogism is often a general rule of law. This premise is phrased in terms of a hypothetical proposition and contains two terms. The categorical premise in a hypothetical syllogism follows, and in legal argument, the categorical premise is frequently a statement of fact from the case. The categorical premise might be stated this way: "The claim for breach of contract accrued seven years prior to the date of filing the complaint." The conclusion might be stated: "The claim is barred by the statute of limitations."

Having identified the conclusion and both premises, we can see the syllogistic structure of the argument in Figure 10 by putting the hypothetical premise, the categorical premise, and the conclusion together, in that order in Figure 11, below. Note that some of the language from the argument has been refined to provide clarity and consistency in the syllogism below.

> If a claim for breach of contract accrues more than six years prior to the date of filing of the complaint, then the claim is barred by the statute of limitations.
>
> The claim accrued more than six years prior to the date of filing the complaint.
>
> Therefore, Plaintiff's claim for breach of contract is barred by the statute of limitations.

Figure 11. *An example of a legal argument in the form of a hypothetical syllogism.*

The details and relationships among of the components of a hypothetical syllogism are described in more fully in Chapter Four.

The second method is to identify the pattern of errant reasoning in an argument without first translating the argument into syllogistic form. Courts sometimes write opinions that seem to fit into this abbreviated, or at least unrevealed, pattern. In such cases, the court simply identifies the logical fallacy the argument commits, without explicitly separating the argument into premises and conclusion. This sort of fallacy-based perspective on legal argument is the subject of Chapter Eleven. This methodology will be more apparent once you have read about the rules of formal logic in Chapter Four and the fallacies that follow from failure to follow the rules in Chapters Five through Ten. However, the essence of the methodology is spotting specific patterns of illogical argument, identifying the logical fallacy suggested by the pattern, and explaining why the illogical pattern of argument cannot support the argument's conclusion. This frequently can be done without breaking an argument down into all of its syllogistic components.

The rules of syllogistic logic that are introduced in the next chapter are named and described in terms of the language of formal logic. Accordingly, knowledge of foundational concepts of formal logic—for example, what is a *middle term*, what is an *antecedent term*, and what is a *consequent term*—becomes a powerful tool for legal argument. The descriptions of logical rules and the fallacies that result from failing to comply with them are the key to using logic to evaluate legal argument. Furthermore, seeing the deductive pattern of an argument—its syllogistic architecture—empowers you to evaluate the validity and persuasiveness of the argument using the rules of logic explored in Chapter Four.

3.6 Chapter Three in Review

- Legal argument differs from the kinds of arguments made outside of the practice of law. One difference is the emphasis on the structure and formality of legal arguments.
- The structure of legal argument often takes the form of the basic framework of deductive logic: the syllogism.
- Some legal arguments take the logical form of a hypothetical, categorical, or disjunctive syllogism.
- Hypothetical syllogisms make conditional "if . . . then" arguments.
- Categorical syllogisms reach conclusions based on the relationships between categories.
- Disjunctive syllogisms make "or" arguments.
- Evaluating the logic of legal argument requires knowing something of the terminology of logic. Knowing the language of logic enables you to describe and evaluate the logical form of legal arguments.
- Lawyers can reduce a legal argument to its logical framework by identifying the essential terms in an argument and arranging those terms into a syllogism.

- The syllogistic structure can be tested against the rules of logic to determine whether the argument complies, or fails to comply, with the rules.
- If a deductive legal argument fails to comply with the rules of logic, it is logically fallacious.
- Lawyers frequently attack the persuasive value of deductive legal arguments by proving that the premises of the arguments are false. However, lawyers armed with an understanding for formal logic and its role in legal argument can also attack the persuasive value of these arguments by proving they are logically fallacious.

CHAPTER FOUR

THE RULES OF FORMAL LOGIC AND THE LOGICAL FALLACY

Lawyers who have not studied formal logic or its role in legal argument might be surprised that formal logic, and frequently legal argument, plays by a short list of specific, logical rules. When we perceive or declare that an argument is logical or illogical we frequently do so based on an intuitive sense of what a logical argument looks or sounds like. The rules of logic provide a way to test our intuition. Conversely, when an argument appears to be illogical, the rules provide a way to prove, objectively and definitively, that the argument is illogical and explain why that is so. As you read through this chapter consider the following points:

- You have just finished learning about three kinds of deductive arguments: hypothetical, categorical, and disjunctive syllogisms. Consider how proper categorization of an argument makes it easier to determine which rules have to be applied to the argument.
- You have just learned some of the terminology of formal logic. As you read through the descriptions of the rules of formal logic in this chapter, consider how understanding the terminology of logic empowers you to understand and discuss logical form.
- Each of the logical rules discussed in this chapter is designed to ensure the truth of an argument's conclusion. Consider how each rule works to ensure the truth of an argument's conclusion.
- As you read about the rules of logic and their application, you can begin to see some patterns of valid argument and invalid argument. Chapters Five through Eleven will discuss that in more detail, but look for some of the patterns and think about how spotting those patterns might help you use logic in legal argument efficiently.

4.1 RULES, LAWS, AND LEGAL ARGUMENT

Rules have a special place in the work of lawyers, permeating the work they do. Rules govern the place for filing a lawsuit, the allegations required in the complaint, the amount of the filing fee, and the font size and spacing of each line of the text of a complaint. Rules establish the beginning and end of the time to complete discovery. Rules limit the time to depose a witness, the scope of questions the witness can be subject to, and how far the witness can be made to travel to appear for their deposition. Rules specify the number of jurors who will hear the trial, where the prosecuting attorney will be seated in the courtroom, and where the defense lawyers will sit. Rules control when an appeal must be filed, the page limits on the appellate brief, and sometimes even the color of the cover of the appellate brief submitted.

As familiar as lawyers are with rules and their consequences in the practice of law, many are surprised to learn that the arguments they encounter and deliver every day are governed by a set of rules they have probably never heard of: the rules of logic.

Many lawyers are surprised to learn that the arguments they encounter and deliver every day are governed by a set of rules they have probably never heard of: the rules of logic.

Arguments that can be arranged into syllogistic form can be tested by rules of logic. The rules are simple, yet powerful, as violating a single rule of logic has a significant consequence, just as would violating a court rule. In logic, an argument that violates a rule is said to be fallacious. A fallacious argument is invalid and cannot support its conclusion. Arguments that follow the rules are reliable and persuasive. Arguments that do not follow the rules are unreliable and unpersuasive.

That consequence should not surprise us. On my way to the office, I stop my car at several intersections. The stop light positioned above one intersection might be red. A stop light is sort of a rule machine. It tells me what the rule is and the rule is either "stop" or "go." When the light is red, a rule is in effect that I cannot cross the intersection with my car. When the light is green, a rule is in effect that I can cross the intersection. When the light is yellow, the light is putting me on notice that the light is about to change from green to red and that I should ensure that I follow the new rule. The rules of the traffic light are simple but powerful. If I understand and follow them, something pretty extraordinary happens. Hundreds of cars can pass through an intersection at high, even dangerous, rates of speed, in close proximity and nobody gets hurt. The rules of the traffic light ensure the integrity of the intersection, and so long as everybody follows all of the rules, every time, I can be confident that I will safely traverse the intersection whenever the light is green. Conversely, it only takes one person who disregards the rules to make the intersection unpredictable, unreliable, and dangerous. The rules ensure the integrity of the safety of the intersection, and it is because of this integrity that we pass through busy intersections every day with complete confidence in our safety.

Similarly, the rules of logic ensure the integrity of deductive argument. Remember, deduction makes an extraordinary claim. If the premises are true and the syllogistic form is valid, then the conclusion must be true. This is why formal logic has been recognized as having such persuasive force.[1] To ensure that bold claim, deduction has high standards for logical form. Those standards are enforced by important rules. If the rules are observed, then the form of the argument ensures the conclusion in the same way the rules of the traffic light, when observed, ensure the safety of the drivers passing through an intersection at fifty-five miles per hour. Conversely, an argument that fails to adhere to just one of the rules of logic fails entirely. In the same way you would not feel comfortable crossing an intersection if I told you that just one of a dozen speeding cars on a roadway was not going to observe the rules of the stoplight, you cannot rely on an argument that fails one or more of the rules of logic. Spotting the failure to comply with a rule of logic is a pretty powerful skill, because even an argument with true premises that violates one rule of logic can be called fallacious, and should be unpersuasive. Herein lays the power and persuasive force of formal logic. The syllogism provides a standard, objective framework for evaluating argument and inference.[2]

4.2 Rules of Formal Logic

The focus of this book is on the rules of formal logic, the fallacies that result when our arguments do not comply with the rules, and how lawyers and judges use logical fallacies in legal argument. Accordingly, understanding these rules is foundational to this process. This chapter begins by introducing a set of rules of logic commonly implicated in legal argument and explaining why each rule ensures the power of deductive argument. The remaining chapters consider each of the fallacies that follow

---

1. Justice Antonin Scalia and Bryan Garner have suggested that lawyers "think syllogistically" and observe that "[t]he most rigorous form of logic and hence the most persuasive is the [basic form of formal logical analysis called the] syllogism." Justice Antonin Scalia & Brian Garner, Making Your Case: The Art of Persuading Judges 41 (2008); *see also* James A. Gardner, Legal Argument: The Structure and Language of Effective Advocacy 8 (1993) ("The power of syllogistic argument leads to the only significant rule about crafting legal arguments: *every good legal argument is cast in the form of a syllogism.*") (emphasis in original); J. S. Covington, Jr., The Structure of Legal Argument and Proof, Cases, Materials and Analyses 199 (2d ed. 2006) ("The enticing thing about the syllogism is that it yields a necessary conclusion, which means that if the listener accepts the premises, then the listener must accept the conclusion or contradict himself. The early European intellectual prized the power of the syllogism to the point that much of medieval university training was about intricate points in disputation based on the syllogism."); Richard A. Posner, *The Jurisprudence of Skepticism*, 86 Mich. L. Rev. 827, 831 (1988) ("So compelling and familiar is syllogistic reasoning that lawyers and judges try hard to make legal reasoning seem syllogistic. And often they exceed. A legal rule has the form of the major premise of a syllogism, as in the example 'No contract is enforceable without consideration; the contract in suit has no consideration; therefore, the contract is not enforceable.' Judges extract rules from statutes and previous decisions (the extraction itself is not a deductive process, as well shall see) and then use the rule to determine the outcome of the case. The overuse of the syllogism, and its cousin the enthymeme (a syllogism one of whose premises is understood), is the principal defining characteristic of legal 'formalism' when used in a pejorative sense. Used nonpejoratively, legal formalism just means—or should just mean—logical reasoning in law.").

2. *See, e.g.*, Vernon J. Edwards, *Arguing Syllogistically: Finding the Logic in Acquisition*, Contract Management (June 2015) ("The beauty of the syllogism is that it provides a framework for critical thinking, which is self-evaluative thinking.").

from disregarding the rules and how courts have used each rule of logic to solve legal problems and evaluate legal arguments.

The focus of this book is on the rules of logic, the fallacies that result from not complying with the rules and how lawyers and judges use logical fallacies in legal argument.

The rules of logic can be divided up based on the kind of syllogism they apply to. Chapter Three described three main types of deductive arguments common to legal argument: hypothetical syllogisms, categorical syllogisms, and disjunctive syllogisms. Each type has its own set of logical rules that ensure the integrity of the argument and guarantee that formal logic compels the truth of the conclusion. Now, we will consider six rules of logic.[3]

The first rule applies to hypothetical syllogisms:

1) A hypothetical syllogism must take one of two forms. First, a hypothetical syllogism is valid where the categorical premise affirms the truth of the antecedent of the hypothetical premise and the consequent of the hypothetical premise is the conclusion. Alternatively, a hypothetical syllogism is valid where the categorical premise affirms the falsity of the consequent of the hypothetical premise, and the conclusion asserts the falsity of the antecedent of that hypothetical premise.[4]

The next four rules only apply to categorical syllogisms:

2) A categorical syllogism can only have three terms and three propositions.

---

3. The concept of rules of formal logic is not a new one; it has been the subject of discussion and debate by logicians for centuries. *See* C.L. HAMBLIN, FALLACIES 196 (1970); CHRISTOPHER W. TINDALE, FALLACIES AND ARGUMENT APPRAISAL 46 (2007); T. EDWARD DAMER, ATTACKING FAULTY REASONING 66–74 (2005); IRVING M. COPI & CARL COHEN, INTRODUCTION TO LOGIC 244–49 (13th ed. 2008); PATRICK J. HURLEY, A CONCISE INTRODUCTION TO LOGIC 285–89 (2015). Further, it is worth noting that when logicians have discussed rules of formal logic, they have generally described a set of rules of logic applicable to categorical syllogisms. The rules for valid hypothetical and disjunctive syllogisms have sometimes taken the form of descriptions of the valid forms of those syllogistic structures. However, those descriptions can fairly be described as rules too and have been so described by some logicians. *See, e.g.*, Hurley, *id., at* 389 (describing rule of implication applicable to hypothetical syllogisms in propositional logic). Because the focus of this book is on logical fallacies and formally fallacious arguments are arguments that do not comport with the rules of logic, I will utilize the expanded concept of "rule of logic" that extends beyond categorical syllogisms, to include hypothetical and deductive syllogisms as well. According, the discussion of "rules of logic" here will include some "rules" that and not typically described as such by logic texts. However, it seems, for lawyers, to be an apt way to describe the requirements for valid deductive syllogism generally, and provides a useful framework for understanding and organizing the rules and the fallacies that result when the rules are not followed. However, these rules of logic are not the author's; they have been articulated and revised by philosophers for centuries.

4. *See, e.g.*, Hurley, *supra* note 3, at 389.

3) The middle term in a categorical syllogism has to be distributed at least once.
4) Any term distributed in the conclusion of a categorical syllogism must be distributed in the premises.
5) There can be only one negative premise in a categorical syllogism. If there is a negative premise, the conclusion must be negative.[5]

The sixth rule only applies to disjunctive syllogisms:

6) A valid disjunctive syllogism is one where the minor premise denies one of the disjuncts of the major premise and the conclusion affirms the remaining disjunct.[6]

4.2.1 A Rule that Applies to Hypothetical Syllogisms

> **Rule One**: A hypothetical syllogism must take one of two forms. First, a hypothetical syllogism is valid where the categorical premise affirms the truth of the antecedent term of the hypothetical premise and the conclusion asserts the truth of the consequent term of the hypothetical premise. Alternatively, a hypothetical syllogism is valid where the categorical premise denies truth of the consequent term of the hypothetical premise, and the conclusion denies the truth of the antecedent term of the hypothetical premise.[7]

Many legal arguments contain or take the form of a hypothetical syllogism. The rule of logic that governs such arguments focuses on the logical relationship between just two terms in a hypothetical syllogism. However, the rule of logic is important, because it frames our consideration of formal logical relationships and dictates some of formal logic's limits in evaluating sound legal argument. A syllogism is a basic building block of argument. Occasionally, the core of a legal argument can be reduced to a single syllogism, with one syllogism reaching a conclusion that finds a place as a premise in another syllogism. More frequently, legal argument is more complex and takes the form of syllogism within a syllogism. Philosophical logic calls these nested combinations *polysyllogisms*.[8]

Within such nesting, however, the rules of logic ensure the truth of an argument's conclusion one logical relationship at a time. Even in highly complex legal

5. *See* Christopher W. Tindale, Fallacies and Argument Appraisal 46 (2007).
6. *See, e.g.,* William T. Perry & Edward A. Hacker, Aristotelian Logic 387 (1991).
7. *See, e.g.,* Copi & Cohen, *supra* note 3, at 299–300.
8. "Polysyllogism is a systematic series of syllogisms leading to a single conclusion. The polysyllogism is also known as a chain of argument." Alfred Sidgwick, Elementary Logic 90 (1914). The preliminary syllogisms in a polysyllogism are referred to as prosyllogisms. *Id.* at 90–91. The final syllogism in a series of syllogisms in called an episyllogism. *Id.* at 91.

argument that might take the form of several polysyllogisms within a multiple issue legal argument, rules of logic are at work, ensuring the integrity of a single inference from two propositions.

Hypothetical syllogisms must take one of two forms to be valid. They typically start with a hypothetical premise, followed by a categorical premise.[9] When the categorical premise affirms the truth of the antecedent of the hypothetical premise and asserts the truth of the consequent term of that same hypothetical premise as its conclusion, the form is valid.[10] Alternatively, when the categorical premise asserts the falsity of the consequent of the hypothetical premise and asserts the falsity of the antecedent term of that same hypothetical premise as its conclusion, that form is also valid.[11] This logical rule focuses on managing the limits of inferences that may be drawn from a hypothetical proposition. Arguments that overstate those inferences commit either the fallacy of denying the antecedent, the subject of Chapter Five, or the fallacy of affirming the consequent, the subject of Chapter Six.

4.2.2 Rules that Apply to Categorical Syllogisms

> **Rule Two**: A categorical syllogism can only have three terms and three propositions.[12]

Like hypothetical syllogism, categorical syllogism focuses on the logical relationship between concepts at the micro level. Traditionally, categorical syllogisms have

---

9. Hypothetical syllogisms frequently take this form, which logicians call a *mixed hypothetical syllogism*, in legal argument. However, this classification of syllogism is not so limited. Argument can potentially take the form of a *pure hypothetical syllogism*. For example:

> If you are an officer of a corporation, then you are an agent of the corporation. If you are an agent of a corporation, then your authorized actions are binding on the corporation.Therefore, if you are an officer of a corporation, then your authorized actions are binding on the corporation.

Because examples of argument from pure hypothetical syllogisms are less common in case law, this book focuses instead on more commonly encountered mixed hypothetical syllogism. Throughout this book, references to hypothetical syllogisms will be to mixed hypothetical syllogisms. However, this approach should not be construed to suggest that pure hypothetical syllogisms are not recognized in logic or that they do not occur in legal argument. They are recognized in both logic and in legal argument. Moreover, like mixed hypothetical syllogism, logic recognizes that they must take a valid form. *See, e.g.*, Perry & Hacker, *supra* note 6, at 387.

10. The form of this valid hypothetical syllogism has a name: *modus ponens*. *See, e.g.*, Hurley, *supra* note 3, at 370.

11. The form of this valid hypothetical syllogism has a name: *modus tollens*. *Id.*

12. *See, e.g.*, Tindale, *supra* note 5, at 53.

been governed by a set of six rules.[13] Categorical syllogisms assert propositions and reach conclusions regarding the categorization of terms. The power of the categorical syllogism is in ensuring the certainty of the conclusion. To ensure the truth of the conclusion, the syllogism must first take proper syllogistic form. The first rule will be familiar to you, as it simply describes the form a valid categorical syllogism discussed in Chapter Three. The first rule of the categorical syllogism is as simple as limiting the number of terms and propositions that can be included in the syllogism: a categorical syllogism can only have three terms and three propositions.

This is such a fundamental rule that some logicians do not even consider it a rule of logic because it merely defines the structure of the syllogism.[14] However, it is important because it reminds a legal reasoner that formal logic does its work at the micro level, evaluating logical inferences one relationship at a time, even when they fit into larger, more complex, polysyllogistic arguments. Accordingly, each categorical syllogism has to be limited to include only three terms. Those terms must appear in only three propositions: a major premise, a minor premise, and a conclusion. For example:

> All allegations contained in a complaint are allegations that must be accepted as true for purposes of this motion to dismiss.
>
> The allegation that defendant intentionally interfered with plaintiff's contractual expectation is an allegation contained in the complaint.
>
> Therefore, the allegation that defendant intentionally interfered with plaintiff's contractual expectation must be accepted as true for purposes of this motion to dismiss.

Figure 12. *An example of a legal argument taking the form of a categorical syllogism.*

---

13. Richard Whately, a nineteenth century logician and theologian, listed six rules for the validity of syllogisms in his work *Elements of Logic. See, e.g.*, Hamblin, *supra* note 3, at 196 (1970) ("Rules of validity for syllogism stated in terms of Distribution have been a regular feature of Logic textbooks since the seventeenth century."). Whately's six rules were deduced from an original twelve rules written in Latin by Henry Aldrich, a seventeenth-century logician, who had expanded on a set of six rules originated by Aristotle's. *See id.* Logician C.L. Hamblin suggested eliminating the first two rules of Whately's list of rules, since they merely define what a syllogism is, independent of the validity of a syllogism. *Id.* at 199. He also suggested combining rules five and six of Whately's rules, because they do not operate independently from each other. *Id.* Therefore, Hamblin uses only three rules to provide a satisfactory theory of the validity for categorical syllogisms. *Id.*; *see also* Hurley, *supra* note 3, at 256. Hurley explains the distinction between five and six rules by stating "[s]ome texts include a rule stating that the three terms of a categorical syllogism must be used in the same sense throughout the argument." *Id.* at 285. Hurley and others incorporate this rule into the definition of "categorical syllogism." *Id.*

14. *Id.*

The argument in Figure 12 has three terms: allegations contained in a complaint, allegations that must be accepted as true for purposes of this motion to dismiss, and allegations that the defendant intentionally interfered with the plaintiff's contractual expectation. Furthermore, the argument in Figure 12 has three propositions. A major premise followed by a minor premise followed by a conclusion. Accordingly, the argument in Figure 12 complies with the first logical rule; it meets the definition of a syllogism.

The rules of deductive logic require that we take a complex legal argument and focus on logical relationship at the micro level—the discrete components of syllogistic argument that hold the broader argumentative structure together. The argument in Figure 12 would likely be just one argument contained in a brief that makes dozens of legal arguments, made up of hundreds of logical connections, using many of the logical tools lawyers use to fashion argument. However, formal logic problems manifest in legal argument at the micro level. Further, those problems are solved at the micro level, not the macro level. The rules of logic require that we examine legal arguments one logical relationship at a time. It is a little like examining a recently constructed steel girder bridge. The bridge is made up of steel girders and welded joints. If I wanted to inspect the structural integrity of the bridge, I might inspect the welded steel joints, and I can only inspect the joints one at a time. Each joint requires that I inspect the first steel girder, the second steel girder, and the welded joint. While a steel bridge might have thousands of welded joints, I do not necessarily have to inspect all of them to make use of my knowledge of what a bad steel and weldment joint looks like. (However, I might be taking a risk if I leave any joint uninspected.) I might want to focus in on the joints I think are most important to the structure of the bridge or that are most likely to be susceptible to failure. Of course, if a bridge has just one bad joint, then I may make some conclusions about the integrity of the entire bridge. Logic narrows the focus of its criticism of an entire legal argument to one logical connection at a time. It is focused on the relationship of three terms, and where a third term is a reliable inference from two others. The first rule of logic essentially ensures that we only look at one relationship at a time, limiting our logical analysis to three argumentative terms and maintaining our focus on the micro level.

Limiting a syllogism to three terms does require that attention be paid to the meaning of the terms logically analyzed. If one of the three terms has two meanings, then the syllogism contains four logical terms and violates the first rule of logic. This is sometimes called the fallacy of four terms or the fallacy of equivocation.[15]

15. *See, e.g.*, Douglas Walton, Fallacies Arising from Ambiguity 15–16 (2013); Jerome E. Bickenbach & Jacqueline M. Davies, Good Reasons for Better Arguments: An Introduction to the Skills and Values of Critical Thinking 251 (1996).

Rule Three: The middle term in a categorical syllogism has to be distributed at least once.[16]

The next rule of categorical syllogisms focuses on the middle term of a syllogism: the term appearing in both the major premise and the minor premise. The rule is particularly focused on whether the middle term is *distributed*. In logic, when a term is used in a way that "refers to all of the members of the class" referenced by that term, that term is said to be distributed.[17] Conversely, if a term only refers to a portion of the members of the class, it is "undistributed."[18] In the simplest case, a term modified with the word "all," or some variant of the word "all," would typically be distributed. "All cars," "every lawyer," or "no judges" are all instances of the terms "cars," "lawyers," and "judges" being distributed. Conversely, where the word "some," or a variant of the word, like "many," modifies a term, that term is undistributed. "Some cars," "many lawyers," or "most judges" are instances of undistributed terms "cars," "lawyers," and "judges" respectively. More precisely, the subjects of universal propositions are always distributed terms. The predicates of negative terms are always distributed. However, any other term in a syllogism is undistributed.[19] The propositions in categorical syllogisms always take one of four forms. Each proposition is either *universal* or *particular*[20] and either *affirmative* or *negative*.[21] Accordingly, their form can be described by one of the four combinations of universal or particular and affirmative or negative. For example, the proposition "every lawyer who signs pleadings [is a lawyer who] certifies that the pleadings are well founded in facts and law"[22] is a universal affirmative proposition. It refers to "ever lawyer," a reference to the entirely class of lawyers, rather than,

16. *See, e.g.,* Tindale, *supra* note 5, at 46.

17. Copi & Cohen, *supra* note 3, at 189–90. *See also* NICHOLAS BUNNIN & JIYUAN YU, THE BLACKWELL DICTIONARY OF WESTERN PHILOSOPHY 188 (2004) ("A term is distributed if it refers to all members of the class to which it is referring and is explicitly or implicitly prefixed by a universal quantifier."); Tindale, *supra* note 5, at 45 ("A term is said to be 'distributed' in a proposition when it is meant to refer to all members of the class of things that proposition denotes."); RICHARD WHATELY, ELEMENTS OF LOGIC 28 (1913) ("[a] term is said to be 'distributed' when it is taken universally, so as to stand for every thing it is capable of being applied to; and consequently 'undistributed,' when it stands for a portion only of the things signified by it . . . ."); JAMES A. WINANS & WILLIAM E. UTTERBACK, ARGUMENTATION 69 (1930) ("A term is said to be distributed if it refers to a class of things in its entirety.").

18. Whately, *supra* note 17 ("[a] term is said to be . . . 'undistributed,' when it stands for a portion only of the things signified by it . . . .").

19. Terence Parson, *The Doctrine of Distribution*, 27 HISTORY AND PHILOSOPHY OF LOGIC 59, 60 (2006).

20. The distinction between universal and particular is sometimes referred to as a proposition's *quantity*.

21. This distinction between affirmative and negative is sometimes referred to as a proposition's *quality*.

22. For example, in federal courts a lawyer's signature on a pleading or motion constitutes a certification that to the best of the lawyer's "knowledge, information and belief, formed after an inquiry reasonable under the circumstances," the document is not presented for an improper purpose, the claims or defenses contained in the document are warranted by existing law or a nonfrivolous argument for its extension, modification, or reversal, and that any denials of fact are warranted or based on a belief or lack of information. FED. R. CIV. P. 11(b).

for example, "some lawyers." Furthermore, it is stated in the affirmative, referring to the inclusion of lawyers who sign pleadings into the class of lawyers who certify their pleadings are well founded. Conversely, if the proposition instead excluded a class of people from the category of lawyers who certify their pleadings are well founded,[23] then it would be a negative proposition. Based on the available combinations of universal and particular and affirmative and negative, categorical propositions can take one of four forms, using the letters A through H to symbolize various terms: Every *A* is B, No *C* is *D*, Some E is F, and Some G is not *H*. In these four forms the italicized terms A, C, D and H are distributed.[24] In this list of combinations, the propositions listed take the following forms:

Every A is B	Universal Affirmative
No C is D	Universal Negative
Some E is F	Particular Affirmative
Some G is not H	Particular Negative[25]

The subject term in any universal proposition is distributed. For example, in the preceding list of propositions, A and C are subject terms of universal propositions. Predicates of negatives are always distributed. Therefore, in the preceding list of propositions, D and H are also distributed. It is straightforward to pick out universal propositions and understand why they are distributed. If the proposition refers to "every A," then it is patently clear that it is referring to the entire class of things A. The words "every," "all," and "no" are examples of words indicating a universal term. Similarly, "no C" tells us something about the entire class of things represented by C. Some examples of universal propositions are: "Every witness," "all allegations," and "both parties" (when a class of parties is limited to two).

Less obvious is why the predicate term of a negative is always distributed. For example, in the proposition "Some G is not *H*," H is distributed because it is the predicate of a negative, but why does "not H" indicate distribution? The language of the proposition does not provide a word modifying H, like "all" or "every" that suggests distribution to us. However, the rest of the proposition makes clear that "Some G is not" tells us something important about H. All of the particular members of the class G referred to are excluded from the entirely of members of the class H. Accordingly, H is distributed here. We know that whatever "some G" is referring to here, there is no chance that any member of "some G" is also a member of H.

---

23. For example, "no lawyer who signs pleadings certifies that the pleadings are well founded in facts and law."

24. Parson, *supra* note 19.

25. Each of the four forms of propositions can be combined with two other forms of propositions. Each of the potential combinations of forms is sometimes referred to as the *mood* of the syllogism. *See, e.g.*, Copi & Cohen, *supra* note 3, at 226. Logicians have historically described the mood as a combination of the letters A, E, I, or O, which represent each of the four forms of propositions. *Id.*

One of the themes of this book is that lawyers should not have to be full-time logicians in order to leverage formal logic in legal argumentation. Much of the philosophical heavy lifting has been done for lawyers who want to leverage knowledge of logic for use in legal argument. Further, much of that leverage is the consequence of spotting the logical patterns in argument. The concept of distribution is one opportunity to use these patterns to simplify what can be a difficult task evaluating deductive argument. Centuries ago, logicians solved this problem by simplifying and describing categorical propositions into their four necessary combinations of quantity and quality: universal and particular, affirmative and negative, and recognizing the distribution that follows this way:

All A is B	The subject (A) is distributed and the predicate (B) is undistributed.
No A is B	The subject (A) is distributed and the predicate (B) is distributed.
Some A is B	The subject (A) is undistributed and predicate (B) is undistributed.
Some A is not B	The subject (A) is undistributed and predicate (B) is distributed.[26]

Figure 13. *Four categorical propositions and the distribution of terms contained in each proposition.*

By arranging any argument into a syllogistic form and matching each proposition up with one of the four standard-form propositions in Figure 13, the distribution of the terms can be readily determined.[27] Once the distribution of terms is identified, the rule of logic can be applied. The middle term, which is the only term that appears in both the major and minor premises, must be distributed at least once. If it fails to be distributed at least once, the argument commits the fallacy of the undistributed middle term, which is the subject of the cases and argument techniques discussed in Chapter Seven.

26. Copi & Cohen, *supra* note 3, at 186. Tindale, *supra* note 5, at 45. Each of these four standard-form categorical propositions has a name: "All S is P" is called a *universal affirmative proposition.* "No S is P" is called a *universal negative proposition.* "Some S is P" is called a *particular affirmative proposition.* "Some S is not P" is called a *particular negative proposition.* While this terminology is not necessary to identify and describe distribution of terms, a comfort level with the terms will help ensure you understand something about the power of syllogistic form to identify the quantity and quality of the terms described in argument. In a sense, being disciplined about logical quantity and quality is much of what the rules of logic are about.

Historically, logicians have given these four forms abbreviated names. The universal affirmative form is referred to as "A," the particular affirmative form is referred to as "I," the universal negative form is referred to as "E," and the particular negative form is referred to as "O."

27. Copi & Cohen, *supra* note 3, at 182–86.

The next rule of categorical syllogisms, like the preceding rule, is a rule about distribution. However, the focus shifts a bit from the second rule. Instead of focusing on the distribution of the middle term, the focus is now on the distribution of the two terms found in the conclusion: the major and minor terms. A conclusion does not always include a distributed term—but when it does, it has to be distributed in the premises. Accordingly, the application of this rule bears some similarity the previous rule, in that it will give you a new purpose for applying what you have learned about distribution. However, the place in an argument that you will apply the rules of distribution shifts in this rule from the middle term to the terms in the conclusion.

> **Rule Four**: Any term distributed in the conclusion of a categorical syllogism must be distributed in the premises.[28]

This rule ensures that the syllogism does not reach a conclusion about all of a category when that conclusion is premised on the truth about only a portion of another category. A syllogism commits the fallacy of the illicit process, the focus of Chapter Eight, when it violates this rule.

> **Rule Five**: There can be only one negative premise. If there is a negative premise, the conclusion must be negative.[29]

The last rule of categorical syllogisms focuses on whether the premises are positive or negative. The rule provides that where both premises are negative, the syllogism cannot support any conclusion. A syllogism that violates that portion of the rule commits the fallacy of exclusive premises. Further, the rule provides that if only one of the two premises is negative, then the conclusion must be negative. A syllogism that violates that part of the rule commits the fallacy of the negative premise.[30] The fallacy of the negative premise is the focus of Chapter Nine.

4.2.3 A Rule that Applies to Disjunctive Syllogisms

The last rule applies to disjunctive syllogisms. In a disjunctive syllogism, the disjunctive premise is a disjunction (an "or" proposition) and the categorical premise asserts the truth or falsity of one of the disjuncts in the disjunctive premise. The rule provides that the valid form of this argument is one where the categorical premise denies one disjunct and the conclusion affirms the other. When this rule is not observed, the argument, typically, commits the fallacy of affirming a disjunct. The

28. *See, e.g.*, Tindale, *supra* note 5, at 46.
29. *Id.* This rule is sometimes separated into two distinct rules, one prohibiting two negative premises and a second requiring that if one premise is negative and one affirmative, the conclusion must be negative. *See, e.g.*, Copi & Cohen, *supra* note 3, at 247–48.
30. This fallacy is sometimes referred to as the fallacy of negativity. *See, e.g.*, Tindale, *supra* note 5, at 48 (citation omitted).

fallacy of affirming a disjunct and the problem of ambiguous disjunction in legal argument are the subjects of Chapter Ten.

> **Rule Six**: A valid disjunctive syllogism is one where the categorical premise denies one of the disjuncts of the disjunctive premise and the conclusion affirms the remaining disjunct.[31]

4.3 Chapter Four in Review

- Deductive arguments are governed by rules. If an argument violates just one of the rules, it is not valid, commits a logical fallacy, and does not ensure the truth of the conclusion.
- A categorical syllogism can only have three terms and three propositions.
- The middle term in a categorical syllogism has to be distributed at least once. If an argument violates this rule, it commits the fallacy of the undistributed middle term.
- Any term distributed in the conclusion of a categorical syllogism must be distributed in one of the premises. If an argument violates this rule, it commits the fallacy of the illicit process.
- There can be only one negative premise in a categorical syllogism. If there is a negative premise, the conclusion must be negative. If an argument violates this rule, it commits the fallacy of the negative premise.
- A hypothetical syllogism must take one of two forms. First, a hypothetical syllogism is valid where the categorical premise affirms the truth of the antecedent term of the hypothetical premise and the conclusion asserts the truth of the consequent term of the hypothetical premise. Alternatively, a hypothetical syllogism is valid where the categorical premise denies truth of the consequent term of the hypothetical premise, and the conclusion denies the truth of the antecedent term of the hypothetical premise. If an argument violates this rule, it commits either the fallacy of affirming the consequent or the fallacy of denying the antecedent.
- A valid disjunctive syllogism is one where the categorical premise denies one of the disjuncts of the disjunctive premise and the conclusion affirms the remaining disjunct. If an argument violates this rule, it typically commits the fallacy of affirming a disjunct.

31. *See, e.g.,* Perry & Hacker, *supra note* 6, at 337.

Chapter Five

The Fallacy of Denying the Antecedent

Our study of formal logical fallacies and legal argument begins with a fallacy that appears in hypothetical syllogisms. This chapter explains what the fallacy of denying the antecedent is, how to identify the fallacy, and how to explain what is wrong with it. It also explores how the fallacy of denying the antecedent occurs in legal argument and how courts have confronted it. As you read, focus on answers to the following questions:

- One description of a logical fallacy is an argument that appears to be logically persuasive, but is not. As you start to focus on the role logical fallacies in legal argument, consider why these arguments have the false appearance of logically valid argument. What challenge does this false appearance pose in identifying and responding to logical fallacies in legal arguments?
- The fallacy of denying the antecedent, like all fallacies, has a powerful, descriptive name. Why is this fallacy called "denying the antecedent"? What is an "antecedent" in an argument and what does it mean to "deny" it?
- Does the fallacy of denying the antecedent appear in all arguments? Or is it limited to a specific category of arguments?
- If the fallacy of denying the antecedent is an unpersuasive argument, how can it be fixed to make a better argument?
- What rule of logic is violated when an argument commits the fallacy of denying the antecedent?
- What have courts done when they encounter arguments that commit the fallacy of denying the antecedent?
- What simple pattern can you look for to remember why this is an unpersuasive argument?
- Effectively using formal logic in legal argument requires efficiently using formal logic in legal argument. Toward that end, as you read the description of this

fallacy and the cases in which courts address it, think about the patterns of logic you see in arguments that commit the fallacy of denying the consequent and how spotting those patterns of logic can help you to efficiently move from encountering an illogical legal argument to explaining its illogical architecture, rather than trying to evaluate the logical structure of an entire legal argument and testing each and every component.

5.1 Hypothetical Syllogisms, Order, and Inference

In a simple, powerful way, formal logic disciplines legal thinking and organizes legal argument. A mind is a complex, powerful, creative machine. It is like a train locomotive, in a sense. A locomotive can fire its engine, blow its whistle, move forward, come to a stop, and move backward. Importantly, it can move forward and backward with extraordinary power. We take for granted that the train will leave the station at one particular time and arrive at its destination at another. When I take the train to the District of Columbia, I can rest assured that the train will leave the place of departure and arrive at its destination. I can also be certain that the train will make a few stops along the way, and I can predict with some precision just when and where each stop will take place. All of this is possible in part because the train functions properly and is ably operated. However, the true hero of the story of a train's powerful and predictable performance is not the train locomotive or the conductor, but the train track. It is the track that focuses the power and potential of the train along a linear path, with maximum efficiency, and ensures the arrival at its final destination. Lawyers use many intellectual tools in legal argument including creativity, experience, knowledge, rhetorical techniques, and communication skill. Rules of logic discipline these tools, to ensure that they are focused along a deliberate path and that they are used to arrive at a reliable result.

Lawyers many different intellectual tools in legal argument; rules of logic discipline these tools, to ensure that they are focused along a deliberate path and that they are used to arrive at a reliable result.

For example, when I drive home this evening, I will drive my car into my garage and if my Golden Retriever, Cooper, is home, I will hear barking. Cooper is a pretty reliable guard dog, and next to going for a ride in the car, greeting family members when they arrive home is his favorite thing to do. Accordingly, when I drive my car into the garage, he will start to bark and he will not stop barking until I enter the house and greet him. I have tried to train him not to bark, but he is incorrigible; Cooper is designed to bark when someone arrives, and my long-suffering efforts to teach him another response have failed. The fact of the matter is, if I drive my car into my garage, Cooper will bark until I greet him.

Logic is a powerful tool for me as I drive into my neighborhood. I have to prepare myself to be barked at. I am not surprised to be barked at. I am not afraid when I hear the barking. I know it is coming. Logic tells me that if I am drive my car into my garage, Cooper's barking will follow. I might be tempted to make some assumptions about this fact. First, I might assume that if, instead of pulling into the garage, I park my car on the street and sneak into my house through the front door, I will not cause Cooper to bark. While I might be able to pull that off, I will ordinarily be disappointed to learn that Cooper still barks at me. The fact of the matter is that while it is true that if I pull into the garage Cooper will bark, it is not accurate to conclude that if I do not pull into the garage, Cooper will not bark. Lots of things cause Cooper to bark: he barks at his bowl when he his hungry, he barks at the bathroom door when he is thirsty, he barks at the garbage truck when it drives past my house, or the neighbor kid at the door, or another dog walking down the street; the list goes on. While pulling into the garage will ensure barking, not pulling into the garage will not ensure silence from Cooper, and it would be an error of logic—a logical fallacy—to conclude otherwise. Hunch, suspicion, or experience might lead me to guess that by inverting the propositions of the rule I can predict an opposite conclusion, but that is undisciplined thinking. In the same way the train rails prevent the train from taking a side trip before reaching its destination, rules of logic require that if we reach some conclusion not afforded by the logical structure of an argument, we need to design a different argument to get there.

Similarly, I know once a lawyer has filed an appearance with the court on behalf of a defendant in a civil case, she is responsible for accepting service of any future pleadings filed in the case.[1] I know the rule. It is one of the consequences of appearing on behalf of a party in a lawsuit. Logic makes that clear to me, and I know that is the consequence in every appearance I file. Logic requires that acceptance of service of pleadings is a logical inference of the rule. However, I have to be careful not to take that inference further than logic allows. For example, knowing it is true that if I file an appearance I accept service of future pleadings, is it also true that if I do not file an appearance, I cannot accept service of a pleading? Both logic and the law answer that question "no." The truth of the first thing might require the truth of a second, but this does not necessarily mean that the absence of the first thing requires the absent of the second. There are other ways to accept service on behalf of a client. While not appearing is one way to ensure I have not committed to accept service, it is not enough of a premise to substantiate the conclusion that there are no other

1. A lawyer formalizes her representative of a client in litigation by making an "appearance" either in the courtroom or in writing. Appearances are recorded by the clerk of the court. *See, e.g.*, FED. R. CIV. P. 79(a)(2). Once a lawyer represents a party by making her appearance on behalf of that party, any future service of court filings is made on the lawyer rather than directly on the party. *See, e.g.*, FED. R. CIV. P. 5(b)(1) ("If a party is represented by an attorney, service under this rule must be made on the attorney unless the court orders service on the party."). *See also* 28 U.S.C. § 1654 ("In all courts of the United States the parties may plead and conduct their own cases personally or by counsel as, by the rules of such courts, respectively, are permitted to manage and conduct causes therein.").

paths to my accepting service. Rules of logic discipline our thinking about order and inference, and the fallacy of denying the antecedent is a powerful tool for analyzing failed order and improper inference.

5.2 Identifying Hypothetical Arguments

The fallacy of denying the antecedent applies to hypothetical syllogisms: "if . . . then" arguments, which lawyers make regularly. For example:

> If the police obtain a confession of a defendant involuntarily, the confession must be suppressed from evidence.
>
> The police obtained the defendant's confession involuntarily.
>
> Therefore, the confession should be suppressed from evidence.
>
> —
>
> If the plaintiff proves the elements of negligence, then the defendant is liable for plaintiff's injuries.
>
> The plaintiff proved the elements of negligence.
>
> Therefore, the defendant is liable for the plaintiff's injuries.

Figure 14. *Two examples of legal arguments taking the form of a hypothetical syllogism.*

Lawyers encounter hypothetical syllogisms frequently in legal argument, because that is the nature of laws. Laws define a particular type of conduct and a consequence that follows from that conduct. For example, causation arguments are common in legal disputes, and arguments about cause and effect frequently fit into a hypothetical syllogism. If a causative event occurs, then there is a consequence. Logically speaking, lawyers spend a lot of time and resources arguing about whether the antecedent was present and what the consequence is, in a lot of different contexts, both criminal and civil, procedural and substantive. This chapter discusses several examples of these kinds of arguments. In fact, these arguments are so common that lawyers do not always think critically about the logical relationship between the cause and effect. In legal argument, this is what typically precipitates the fallacy of denying the antecedent.

Like all formal logical fallacies, the argument's defect results from failing to follow a simple logical rule. Of course, the simplicity of the rule is also what makes the fallacy so dangerous. Arguments that commit the fallacy of denying the antecedent sound or appear a lot like a valid argument that follows the rule. As a result, the fallacious pattern of argument can be easy to mistake for a valid one if you do not know the rule of logic that manages it. Fallacies of hypothetical syllogisms are the most commonly encountered formal fallacies in legal argument.[2] However, using the fallacy of denying the antecedent as a tool in litigation is as simple as understanding what kinds of legal arguments it might apply to, what rule of logic it violates, and thinking tactically about why lawyers might intentionally or unintentionally violate this rule in practice.

A hypothetical syllogism includes at least one hypothetical proposition: an "if . . . then" premise.

Logical fallacies in hypothetical syllogisms display certain patterns of argument that reveal a faulty logical structure. This pattern of faulty logical structure makes the fallacy apparent to someone evaluating the argument. The fallacious pattern also makes the logical fallacy an efficient tool for lawyers. The fallacy of denying the antecedent only applies to arguments that take the form of a hypothetical syllogism.[3] The hypothetical syllogism contains at least one compound hypothetical proposition, stating that if one of its terms is true, then the other of its terms is true.[4] That is, a hypothetical syllogism includes at least one hypothetical proposition: an "if . . . then" premise. The syllogism also has a second proposition that is either another "if . . . then" premise or a categorical premise. Legal arguments frequently employ hypothetical syllogisms.[5] For example:

> If the subject of a contract is the sale of an interest in land, then the contract is within the statute of frauds.[6]
>
> The subject of the contract is the sale of an interest in land.
>
> Therefore, the contract is within the statute of frauds.

Figure 15. *An example of a legal argument taking the form of a hypothetical syllogism.*

The first proposition includes a hypothetical component ("if the subject of a contract is the sale of an interest in land . . . ."). The second proposition is a categorical proposition.

---

2. Legence Bank v. United Mine Workers of Am., 15-cv-0144-MJR-DGW, 2015 U.S. Dist. LEXIS 123518, at *1 (S.D. Ill. Sept. 16, 2015) ("The common logical fallacy called 'denying the antecedent' is an argument of the following form: 'If p, then q. Not p. Therefore, not q.'").
3. The examples of hypothetical syllogisms found in this chapter (and the next chapter) are all "mixed hypothetical syllogisms," a subset of hypothetical syllogisms. *See* note 32 in Chapter Five.
4. *Id.*
5. *See, e.g.*, Iams v. DiamlerChrysler Corp., 883 N.E.2d 466, 492 (Ohio Ct. App. 2007); Edwards v. Riverdale Sch. Dist., 188 P.3d 317 (Or. Ct. App. 2008); Crouse-Hinds Co. v. Internorth, Inc., 634 F.2d 690, 703 (2d Cir. 1980); Zinpro Corp. v. Ridenour, No. 07-96-0008-CV, 1996 Tex. App. LEXIS 3380 (Tex. App. Aug. 1, 1996).
6. *See, e.g.,* Restatement (Second) of Contracts § 125(1) (Am. Law Inst. 1981) ("A promise to transfer to any person any interest in land is within the Statute of Frauds.").

5.3 Finding Antecedent Terms and Consequent Terms, Denied Terms and Affirmed Terms

The first step in evaluating a hypothetical syllogism is to identify the component terms of the hypothetical premise. The hypothetical premise in Figure 15 contains two terms: an *antecedent* term ("sale of interest in land") and the *consequent* term ("within the Statute of Frauds"). The second step is to determine whether the categorical premise affirms or denies a term and which term is affirmed or denied. If the categorical premise asserts that a term is true, then it is said to *affirm* the term. Conversely, if the categorical premise asserts that a term is false, then it is said to *deny* the term. In Figure 15, the categorical proposition (the subject of the contract is the sale of interest in land) affirms the antecedent term. That is, the categorical proposition declares that the first term in the hypothetical proposition is true. We could change that categorical proposition to do three other things. Instead of affirming the antecedent term, it could deny it (the contract is not a contract for the sale of interest in land). Alternatively, instead of affirming the antecedent term, it could affirm the consequent term ("the contract is within the Statute of Frauds"). Last, instead of affirming the consequent, it could deny the consequent ("the contract is not within the Statute of Frauds"). The fallacy of denying the antecedent is a pattern of argument seeking to reach a conclusion where the categorical proposition denies the antecedent term in the hypothetical proposition.

Evaluating a hypothetical syllogism begins with identifying the hypothetical premise and its antecedent and consequent terms.

Before addressing the fallacy of denying the antecedent and why it is a defective argument, it is useful to consider hypothetical syllogisms and why they are frequent and persuasive arguments. An example of a fallacious hypothetical syllogism looks like this:

> If the subject of a contract is a transfer of an interest in land, then the contract is within the Statute of Frauds.[7]
>
> The subject of the contract is not one for a transfer of interest in land.
>
> Therefore, the contract is not within the Statute of Frauds.

Figure 16. *An example of a legal argument taking the form of the fallacy of denying the antecedent.*

Understanding the nature of this logically fallacious argument requires an understanding of the rule of formal logic that applies to hypothetical syllogisms. Hypothetical syllogisms must comply with the applicable logical rule in order to be valid. If the form

7. *See, e.g.*, Restatement (Second) of Contracts § 125(1) (Am. Law Inst. 1981).

of the syllogism is invalid, the syllogism cannot be relied upon to ensure the truth of the conclusion[8] and is fallacious.[9] While a hypothetical syllogism must contain a hypothetical premise, a categorical premise, and a conclusion,[10] the conditional premise must also take one of two forms. The first form of a valid hypothetical syllogism requires that the categorical premise must affirm the truth of the antecedent of the conditional premise and the consequent of the hypothetical premise must be asserted in the conclusion. This means that we must consider the two terms of the categorical premise. If the categorical premise is "If A, then B," "A" is the antecedent term and "B" is the consequent term.

The syllogism is valid if the categorical premise affirms the truth of the antecedent term of the hypothetical and the conclusion affirms the truth of the consequent of the hypothetical. If the hypothetical syllogism takes this form, logicians sometimes give the argument the name *modus ponens.*[11]

Graphically, the valid form of argument can be illustrated this way, where the triangle represents the antecedent term in the hypothetical proposition and the diamond represents the consequent term in the hypothetical proposition:

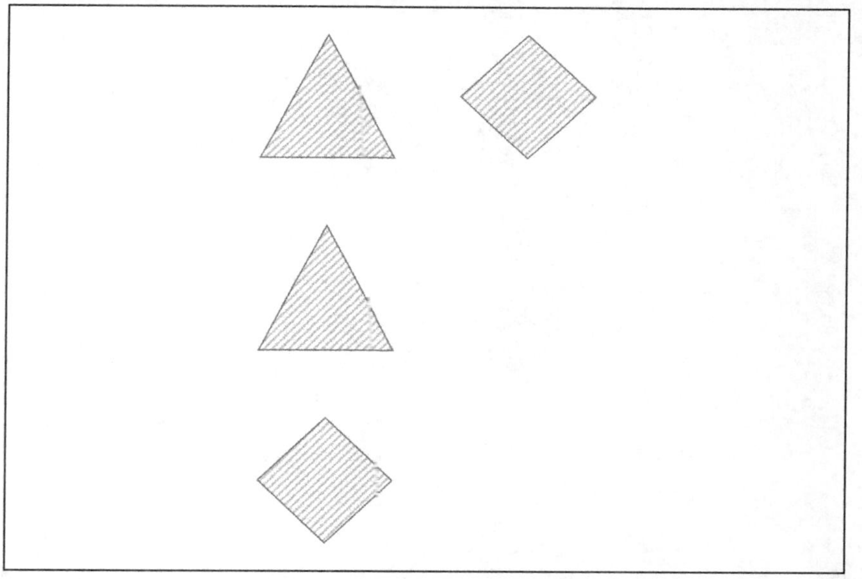

Figure 17*. The valid form of hypothetical syllogism called modus ponens.*

8. *See* DOUGLAS WALTON, INFORMAL LOGIC 22–23 (2d ed. 2008), AT 1110 ("[I]n a deductively valid argument, it is logically impossible for all the premises to be true and the conclusion false").
9. *See* C.L. HAMBLIN, FALLACIES 196 (1970); CHRISTOPHER W. TINDALE, FALLACIES AND ARGUMENT APPRAISAL 35–37 (2007).
10. *See* PATRICK J. HURLEY, A CONCISE INTRODUCTION TO LOGIC 370 (2015).
11. *See* Hamblin, *supra* note 9, at 35–37. *See also* DOUGLAS WALTON, FUNDAMENTALS OF CRITICAL ARGUMENTATION 62 (2006). *Modus ponens* is the name given to a valid hypothetical syllogism that takes this form. It is not the name of a fallacy.

In Figure 17, the top row of shapes represents a hypothetical premise. For example, we might assume the top row represents "if the judge enters the courtroom, then those in attendance will stand." The triangle represents the antecedent term "the judge enters the courtroom," and the diamond represents the consequent term "those in attendance will stand." In the second row, the triangle represents an assertion of the antecedent term. In the third row, the diamond represents the assertion of the consequent term.

There is an alternative form of the hypothetical syllogism that is also valid. If the categorical premise denies the consequent of the hypothetical premise and the conclusion denies the antecedent of that hypothetical premise, then that syllogism is also well formed and is given the name *modus tollens*.[12]

Graphically, that valid form of argument can be illustrated this way, where the triangle represents the antecedent term and the diamond represents the consequent term. Where either of the shapes appears filled with a "no" symbol, it signifies a denied term:

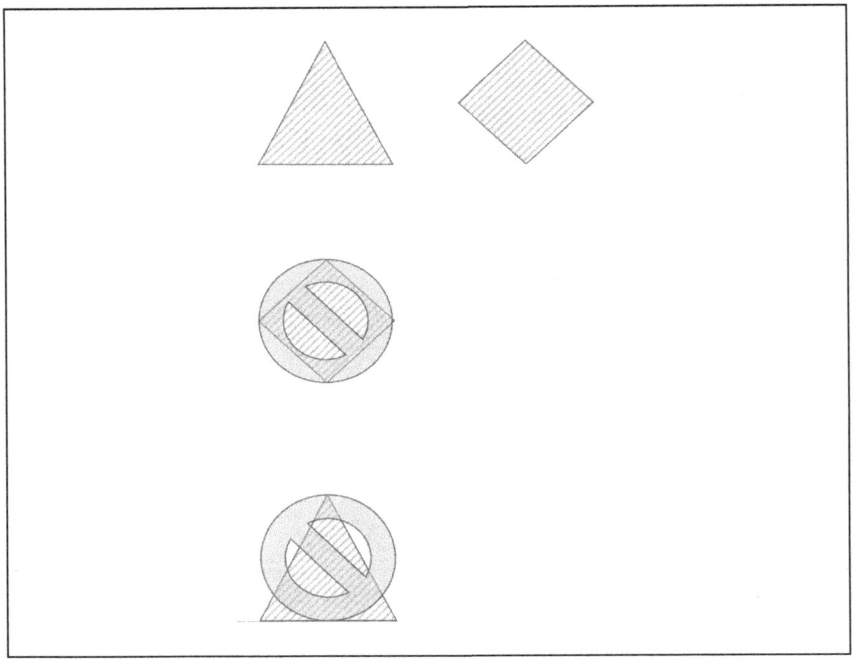

Figure 18. *The valid form of hypothetical syllogism called modus tollens.*

The rule, applicable to hypothetical syllogisms, can be described as requiring that the categorical premise denies the consequent term of the hypothetical premise and the conclusion deny the antecedent term of the hypothetical prem-

12. *See* Walton, *supra* note 11, at 62.

ise.[13] In Figure 18, the top row of shapes represents a hypothetical premise. For example, we might assume the top row represents "If the debtor files a petition for bankruptcy protection, then all collection activity is automatically stayed." The triangle represents the antecedent term "The debtor files a petition for bankruptcy protection," and the diamond represents the consequent term "All collection activity is automatically stayed." In the second row, the diamond with the "no" symbol on top of it represents a denial of the consequent term ("no collection activity is automatically stayed"). In the third row, the triangle with the "no" symbol represents the negation of the antecedent term ("the debtor has not filed a petition for bankruptcy protection").[14]

The components and rules of a well-formed hypothetical syllogism shed some light on the nature of the fallacy of denying the antecedent. The name of the fallacy is descriptive of what is wrong with the logical structure of the argument: why it fails to follow the rules. Simply put, where the previously discussed rules of logic are observed, the argument takes one of two valid forms, either *modus ponens* or *modus tollens.* Where the argument observes these rules of logic and takes one of these two forms, logic ensures that if its premises are true the argument's conclusion is true.[15]

5.4 Why Denying the Antecedent Term is Unpersuasive Argument

Conversely, when the rules of logic are not observed, the argument takes the form of a fallacy. The fallacy of denying the antecedent is one of two fallacies that result from failure to observe logical rules.[16] The other fallacy, the fallacy of affirming the consequent, is the subject of Chapter Six. Accordingly, when the antecedent term is denied, the argument commits the fallacy of denying the antecedent and is logically invalid. An example of the fallacy is:

13. Hamblin, *supra* note 9, at 35–36.

14. In bankruptcy law, a party seeking protection under the Bankruptcy Act is called "the debtor." The debtor ordinarily begins the bankruptcy process by filing a petition with the bankruptcy court. Creditors who are owed money by the debtor may have already initiated collection activity, hoping to collect their obligations from the debtor, or may have plans to initiate collection activity in the future. However, once the debtor files a petition in bankruptcy, all collection activity is automatically "stayed" or prohibited. Thereafter, creditors who wish to collect from the debtor outside of the bankruptcy process must ordinarily file a motion seeking leave from the automatic stay. Creditors who continue to collect debts without obtaining leave from the court are in violation of the court's automatic stay. 11. U.S.C. § 362.

15. *See* Walton, *supra* note 8, at 62.

16. *See, e.g.*, Hamblin, *supra* note 9, at 36–37.

> If the subject of a contract is the sale of an interest in land, then the contract is within the Statute of Frauds.[17]
>
> The subject of the contract is not the sale of an interest in land.
>
> Therefore, the contract is not within the Statute of Frauds.

Figure 19. *A legal argument taking the form of the fallacy of denying the antecedent.*

In this example, the hypothetical premise's antecedent term is "the subject of a contract is a sale of an interest in land." The argument's categorical premise denies that term by stating that "the subject of the contract is not the sale of an interest in land." That fallacious form of argument can be illustrated graphically, where the triangle represents the antecedent term and the diamond represents the consequent term. Where the shapes appear with a "no" symbol over them, they symbolize a denied term:

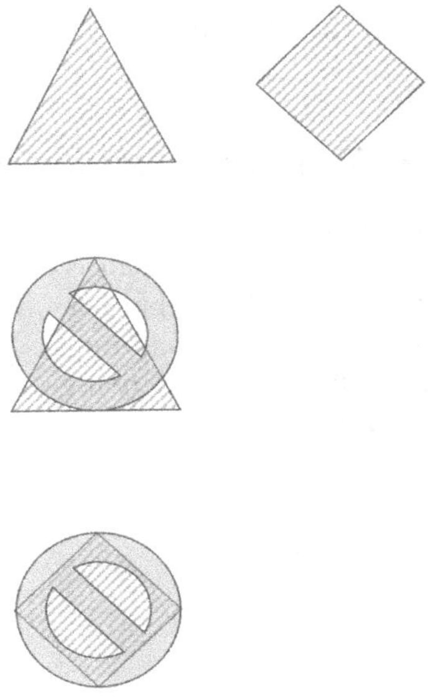

Figure 20*. The fallacious form of hypothetical syllogism called the fallacy of denying the antecedent.*

17. *See* Restatement (Second) Contracts § 12 (Am. Law Inst. 1981). Contracts that are included in one of the categories of the Statute of Frauds generally must be in writing in order to be enforced. A contract that fits within one of these categories is said to be "within" the Statute of Frauds. Those contracts that do not fall within one of the Statute of Frauds categories are said to be "without" or "outside" the Statute of Frauds.

After considering this logically invalid form of argument, it is apparent why it is invalid. The fact that the consequent term can be inferred from the truth of the antecedent terms does not provide any basis to conclude that anything can be logically inferred from the absence of the antecedent term. This is why the fallacy of denying the antecedent is sometimes referred to as the "fallacy of the inverse."[18] The argument above illustrates why assuming an inverse state of affairs is a temping but illogical conclusion. We know that, as a matter of law, a contract for the sale of land is within the Statute of Frauds. The Statute of Frauds makes that clear.[19] However, we also know that, if a contract does not involve a transfer of an interest in land, it does not necessarily require an inference that the contract is outside the Statute of Frauds. There are categories of contracts, other than contracts for the transfer of an interest in land, which are within the Statute of Frauds.[20] When we know that if one thing happens another thing always follows, we can only conclude so much from that. Logic does not require the inverse. That is, logic does not require that the absence of one thing requires the absence of another. When we assume that, we make a reasoning error and commit the fallacy of denying the antecedent. Importantly, this fallacy is not necessarily the result of either premise being false. Even when we agree with the truth of both of premises, we might still take issue with the conclusion logic allows us to draw from them.

---

18. *See, e.g.*, N.L.R.B. v. Noel Canning, 134 S. Ct. 2550 (2014) (Scalia, J., concurring) ("To assume otherwise, as the majority does, is to commit the fallacy of the inverse (otherwise known as denying the antecedent): the incorrect assumption that if P implies Q, then not-P implies not-Q."); VMG Salsoul, LLC v. Ciccone, 824 F.3d 871 (9th Cir. 2016) ("A statement that rights do not extend to a particular circumstance does not automatically mean that the rights extend to all other circumstances. In logical terms, it is a fallacy to infer the inverse of a conditional from the conditional.").

19. Restatement (Second) Contracts §125 (Am. Law Inst. 1981).

20. For example, the Restatement (Second) Contracts describes several categories of contracts that are within the Statute of Frauds:

> (1) The following classes of contracts are subject to a statute, commonly called the Statute of Frauds, forbidding enforcement unless there is a written memorandum or an applicable exception:
>
> (a) a contract of an executor or administrator to answer for a duty of his decedent (the executor-administrator provision);
>
> (b) a contract to answer for the duty of another (the suretyship provision);
>
> (c) a contract made upon consideration of marriage (the marriage provision);
>
> (d) a contract for the sale of an interest in land (the land contract provision);
>
> (e) a contract that is not to be performed within one year from the making thereof (the one-year provision).
>
> (2) The following classes of contracts, which were traditionally subject to the Statute of Frauds, are now governed by Statute of Frauds provisions of the Uniform Commercial Code . . . .

Restatement (Second) Contracts §110 (Am. Law Inst. 1981).

Furthermore, comparing the fallacious pattern of reasoning in Figure 20 to the valid patterns of reasoning in Figures 17 and 18 reveals how subtle the difference is in the argumentative patterns. This subtlety is part of the problem with formal logical fallacies: they easily go unnoticed. This is especially true when we find the truth of both premises unobjectionable. Even worse, they can also sound persuasive to a casual listener, despite the fact that they are entirely illogical and unreliable as arguments.

5.5 How Courts Have Used the Fallacy of Denying the Antecedent

Judges have applied the fallacy of denying the antecedent in evaluating litigants' arguments.[21] Reviewing a few of these cases and seeing examples of how judges use

21. *See, e.g.,* N.L.R.B. v. Noel Canning, 134 S. Ct. 2550, 2603 (2014); VMG Salsoul, LLC v. Ciccone, 824 F.3d 871 (9th Cir. 2016); United States v. Davenport, 775 F.3d 605, 610 (3d Cir. 2015); Wilson v. Clark, 372 F. App'x 745, 747 (9th Cir. 2010); Arar v. Ashcroft, 585 F.3d 559, 601 (2d Cir. 2009); Carver v. Lehman, 528 F.3d 659, 671 (9th Cir. 2008), *withdrawn*, 540 F.3d 1011 (9th Cir. 2008); AGRI Processor Co. v. NLRB, 514 F.3d 1, 6 (D.C. Cir. 2008); E. Armata, Inc. v. Korea Commercial Bank of N.Y., 367 F.3d 123, 131 (2d Cir. 2004); Tobey v. United States, 794 F. Supp. 2d 594, 601 (D. Md. 2011) (citing TorPharm, Inc. v. Ranbaxy Pharms., Inc., 336 F.3d 1322, 1329 (Fed. Cir. 2003)); EEOC v. Jetstream Ground Servs., No. 13-cv-02340-CMA-KMT, 2016 U.S. Dist. LEXIS 29500 (D. Colo. 2016); Young v. DISH Network, LLC, No. 13-CV-114-JED-PJC, 2015 U.S. Dist. LEXIS 171122 (N.D. Okla. 2015); Legence Bank v. United Mine Workers of Am., No. 15-cv-0144-MJR-DGW, 2015 U.S. Dist. LEXIS 123518 (S.D. Ill. Sept. 16, 2015); Zortman v. J.C. Christensen & Assocs., Inc., 819 F. Supp. 2d 874, 877 (D. Minn. 2011); Optigen, LLC v. Int'l Genetics, Inc., 777 F. Supp. 2d 390, 402 n. 10 (N.D.N.Y. 2011); Adelphia Recovery Trust v. Bank of Am., No. 05 Civ. 9050 (LMM), 2010 U.S. Dist. LEXIS 90836 at *45 n. 8 (S.D.N.Y. Sept. 1, 2010); Garcia v. United States, No. 08 CIV 4733 (HB), 2010 U.S. Dist. LEXIS 39287 at *15 (S.D.N.Y. Apr. 21, 2010); Cusamano v. Sobek, 604 F. Supp. 2d 416, 474 n.122 (N.D.N.Y. 2009); IMS Health Inc. v. Sorrell, 631 F. Supp. 2d 434, 447 (D. Vt. 2009), *rev'd*, 630 F.3d 263 (2d Cir. 2010), *aff'd*, 131 S. Ct. 2653 (2011); Odyssey Marine Exploration, Inc. v. Unidentified, Shipwrecked Vessel, 675 F. Supp. 2d 1126, 1132 n.5 (M.D. Fla. 2009); N.W. Steel Erection Co. v. Zurich Am. Ins. Co., No. 4:07CV3184, 2008 U.S. Dist. LEXIS 4082, at *4 (D. Neb. Jan. 18, 2008); Bell Atlantic Corp. v. MFS Commc'ns Co., 901 F. Supp. 835, 849 (D. Del. 1995); Hellweg v. Comm'r of Internal Revenue, 101 T.C.M. (CCH) 1261 (T.C. 2011); Villines v. Harris, 11 S.W.3d 516, 520 n. 2 (Ark. 2000); Thomson v. Beuchel, No. B194775, 2007 Cal. App. Unpub. LEXIS 6242, at *18 n. 6 (Cal. Ct. App. July 31, 2007); Thompson v. Clarkson Power Flow, Inc., 254 S.E.2d 401 (Ga. Ct. App. 1979); French v. State, 362 N.E.2d 834, 843 n. 1 (Ind. 1977) (DeBruler, J., concurring in part and dissenting in part); Mark v. Comm'r of Pub. Safety, No. A04-1905, 2005 Minn. App. LEXIS 500 at *5 n. 3 (Minn. Ct. App. May 10, 2005); Health Pers. v. Peterson, 629 N.W.2d 132, 134 n. 3 (Minn. Ct. App. 2001); State v. Clifford, 121 P.3d 489, 501 (Mont. 2005) (Nelson, J., concurring); State v. Wetzel, 114 P.3d 269, 275–76 (Mont. 2005) (Leaphart, J., dissenting); Dep't 56, Inc. v. Bloom, 720 N.Y.S.2d 920, 923 (N.Y. Sup. Ct. 2001); Iams v. DaimlerChrysler Corp., 883 N.E.2d 466, 478-79 (Ohio Ct. App. 2007); Edwards v. Riverdale Sch. Dist., 188 P.3d 317, 321 (Or. Ct. App. 2008); Hale v. Water Res. Dep't, 55 P.3d 497, 502 (Or. Ct. App. 2002); Thompson v. State, 108 S.W.3d 269, 278 (Tex. Crim. App. 2003) (Keasler, J., concurring in part and dissenting in part); *In re* Luna, 175 S.W.3d 315, 320 n. 4 (Tex. App. 2004), *withdrawn, In re* Luna, 275 S.W.3d 537 (Tex. App. 2008); Manchester Oaks Homeowners Ass'n v. Batt, 732 S.E.2d 690, 699 (Va. 2012); State v. Brush, 353 P.3d 213, 223, n. 8 (Wash. 2015); State v. Wiedmeyer, 881 N.W.2d 805 (Wisc. App. 2016).

this logical fallacy to evaluate legal arguments help identify the fallacy in legal argument. A sampling of such cases follows.

First, a simple application of the fallacy of denying the antecedent can be seen in *Posen Construction, Inc. v. Lee County.*[22] *Posen Construction* was a construction dispute that included several claims. One of the issues in the case was the viability of the plaintiff's claims against two defendants. The plaintiff argued that the defendants, engineers allegedly involved in the construction project, were liable to the plaintiff for breaching a duty owed to the plaintiff. The court described the plaintiff's argument this way: "engineers involved during the project owe a duty to the contractors but engineers that become involved after the completion of the project do not."[23] The court described the basis for the plaintiff's argument as being "ostensibly derived" from two cases "in which consultants hired to perform ex post facto inspections of completed work [and] were found to lack the 'requisite nexus' to establish a duty of care."[24] The court described the plaintiff's argument as committing the fallacy of denying the antecedent:

> [Plaintiff's] argument creates an artificial distinction derived from a common propositional fallacy often referred to as "denying the antecedent." The problem with denying the antecedent is that there is a logical disconnect between the antecedent and the consequent such that the predictive behavior of the consequent is not accurately linked to the nonoccurrence of the antecedent. In *Recreational Design*, the court held that if an engineer is hired after the job is completed then there will not exist the requisite close nexus to establish a duty of care. *Recreational Design*, 820 F.Supp.2d at 1301. It, however, does not logically follow (as Posen suggests) that if an engineer is hired before the completion of the job then there necessarily exists the close nexus to establish a duty of care.[25]

22. 921 F. Supp. 2d 1350 (M.D. Florida 2013).
23. *Id.* at 1363.
24. *Id.* at 1363–64.
25. *Id.* The court went on to exemplify arguments taking the form of denying the antecedent this way: "The following propositional fallacy is a common illustration: if I go to the drug store then I will buy milk. If one denies the antecedent, then one would posit that if I do not go to the drug store I will not buy milk. Of course, the logical disconnect is obvious because one could buy milk at a location other than the drug store." *Id.* n. 9. Other courts have used simple illustrations to explain fallacious reasoning. *See, e.g.,* State v. Brush, 353 P.3d 213, 223 (Wash. 2015) ("Consider the following argument, which uses "snowing" as the antecedent and "cold" as the consequent: "Premise 1: If it is snowing, then it is cold outside. Premise 2: It is not snowing. Conclusion: It is not cold outside." Plainly, the above conclusion does not follow from its premises; it can be cold without snow falling, even though snowfall requires a cold outside temperature.").

Placing the premises and conclusion in the order described by the court might look like this:

> If an engineer is hired after the job is completed, then the close nexus required to establish a duty of care does not exist.
>
> The engineer was not hired after the job was completed.
>
> Therefore, the close nexus required to establish a duty of care does exist.

The court's conclusion recognizes that the categorical premise of this argument ("The engineer was not hired after the job was completed") denies the antecedent term ("an engineer is hired after the job is completed") in an effort to justify concluding a denial of the consequent term ("the close nexus required to establish a duty of care *does* exist."). While the structure of this argument fails, at first glance, there is something about the syllogism that sounds credible. Likely, it is because we are comfortable with a *modus ponens* argument, if not by its name, then by its structure and pervasiveness in argument. Because the invalid logical structure of the fallacy of denying the antecedent is similar to the valid, familiar structure of *modus ponens*, the two forms are easily confused.[26] It is the subtle rule of a formally valid hypothetical syllogism that separates the two. Furthermore, because the antecedent term in the hypothetical premise is stated in the negative ("the close nexus required to establish a duty of care *does not* exist"), denying the antecedent term means denying a negative. Once denied, the antecedent terms is "the close nexus required to establish a duty of care does exist." Because there are no words normally associated with negation—*e.g.*, "no," "none," "not"—within the sentence, it might not readily appear as a denial of the antecedent term.

Another case that provides an example of a court using the fallacy of denying the antecedent is *Zinpro Corp. v. Ridenour*, a declaratory action for determination of the enforceability of an employer–employee confidentiality agreement.[27]

---

26. Consider how similar the logical structure of this fallacious argument is to the valid form of the argument. Taking the valid form of *modus ponens*, the argument would be:

> If an engineer is hired after the job is completed, then the close nexus required to establish a duty of care does not exist.
>
> The engineer was hired after the job was completed.
>
> Therefore, the close nexus required to establish a duty of care does not exist.

27. No. 07-96-0008-CV, 1996 Tex. App. LEXIS 3380, at *10 n. 4 (Tex. App. Aug. 1, 1996). "[A] controversy is justiciable when there are interested parties asserting adverse claims upon a state of facts which must have accrued wherein a legal decision is sought or demanded." *Id.* at 2. Conversely, in the context of an action for a declaratory judgment: "the remedy of declaratory judgment may not be used to secure an advisory opinion concerning the implications of future, contingent events, but may only be used when it will resolve an existing, justiciable controversy." *Id.* (citing Bonham State Bank v. Beadle, 907 S.W.2d 465, 467 (Tex.1995), and California Products, Inc. v. Puretex Lemon Juice, Inc., 334 S.W.2d 780, 781 (1960)).

The court reversed the trial court's judgment declaring a confidentiality agreement between the parties unenforceable and decreeing that the employee could compete against the employer.[28] The employer argued that any determination of the confidentiality agreement's validity was not a justiciable controversy.[29] The employer's argument was based on the court's prior holding that justiciability of a controversy can be shown by the imminence of litigation. The employer argued that because justiciability of a controversy could be shown by the imminence of litigation and the employee failed to establish that litigation was not imminent, the claim was not justiciable.[30]

The court rejected the employer's argument based on the fallacy of denying the antecedent, stating, "[a]lthough we have previously held that the justiciability of a controversy *can be* shown by the imminence of litigation, that holding does not compel the contrary conclusion that failure to show litigation is imminent establishes non-justiciability."[31] "If litigation is imminent, then the controversy is justiciable. A conclusion that when litigation is not imminent, a controversy is not justiciable, is described by logicians as denying the antecedent, an invalid form of reasoning."[32] While the court's description of the fallacy is limited, its application provides a clear example of how the fallacy of denying the antecedent works in legal argument. Placing the argument in syllogistic form might look like this:

> If litigation is imminent, then the controversy is justiciable.
>
> Litigation is not imminent.
>
> Therefore, the controversy is not justiciable.

The court observed that the categorical premise of this argument ("litigation is not imminent") denies the antecedent term ("litigation is imminent") in an effort to justify concluding the falsity of the consequent term ("the controversy is not justiciable").[33]

---

28. *Id.* at *34.
29. *Id.* at *10.
30. *Id.*
31. *Id.* at *10 (citation omitted).
32. *Id.* at *10 n. 4 (citing W. Edgar Moore et al., Creative and Critical Thinking (1985)).
33. Again, the logical structure of this fallacious argument is similar to the valid form of the argument. Taking the valid form of *modus ponens*, the argument would be:

> If litigation is imminent, then the controversy is justiciable.
>
> Litigation is imminent.
>
> Therefore, the controversy is justiciable.

However, this subtle difference in form makes a substantial difference in the persuasive power of the argument.

A similar result was reached in *Iams v. DaimlerChrysler.*[34] In *Iams*, the buyer of a new vehicle alleged claims under Ohio's Lemon Law and for breaches of the manufacturer's express and implied warranties under the Magnuson–Moss Warranty Act against the vehicle's manufacturer.[35] The trial court granted summary judgment in favor of the manufacturer on both the Lemon Law claim and the Magnuson–Moss Warranty Act claim.[36]

The trial court first addressed the plaintiff's Lemon Law claim and determined that it was invalid. The trial court applied the rule that if the Lemon Law claim was valid, the Magnuson–Moss Warranty Act claim is generally valid.[37] Next, the trial court concluded that because Lemon Law claim was *not* valid, the Magnuson–Moss Warranty Act claim was *not* valid.[38] The court of appeals analyzed the logic of the trial court's opinion. The court of appeals rejected the trial court's reasoning, based on the fallacy of denying the antecedent.[39] The court of appeals explained: "The court's reasoning has the following syllogistic form: If A, then B. Not A, therefore not B. This syllogistic form is the logical fallacy known as denying the antecedent, and therefore, the trial court's reasoning is erroneous."[40]

Stripped to its syllogistic essentials, the trial court's argument might be written as follows:

> If the Lemon Law claim is valid, then the Magnuson–Moss Warranty Act is valid.
>
> The Lemon Law claim is invalid.
>
> Therefore, the Magnuson–Moss Warranty Act is invalid.

34. 883 N.E.2d 466 (Ohio. App. 2007).
35. *Id.* at 469.
36. *Id.*
37. More specifically, the court observed that "To prevail under the MMWA, however, plaintiff must establish: '(i) the item at issue was subject to a warranty; (ii) the item did not conform to the warranty; (iii) the seller was given reasonable opportunity to cure any defects; and (iv) the seller failed to cure the defects within a reasonable time or a reasonable number of attempts.' Further the court observed that: 'The two causes of action are similar, but not the same. The Lemon Law requires two additional criteria not required under the MMWA: (1) the consumer must report the defect within the first year or 18,000 miles, whichever occurs first, and (2) the defect "substantially impaired the use, safety, or value of the motor vehicle to the consumer." The MMWA, on the other hand, requires only that the consumer give the manufacturer a reasonable opportunity to cure the defects. In addition, the Lemon Law provides certain reasonableness presumptions for the number of times a consumer must return the vehicle for repairs. R.C. 1345.73. The Lemon Law, thus, has in some cases more stringent and specific standards than the MMWA. Therefore, it is generally true that if a plaintiff has a valid Lemon Law claim, plaintiff also has a valid MMWA claim. However, a valid MMWA claim does not necessarily result in a valid Lemon Law claim.'" *Id.* at 479 (citations omitted).
38. *Id.* at 478-79.
39. *Id.* at 479.
40. *Id.*

The structure of the argument demonstrates the fallacy. The categorical premise, "[t]he Lemon Law claim is invalid," denies the antecedent term in the hypothetical premise. Accordingly, the argument fails to follow the rule of the hypothetical syllogism, fails to take the form of *modus ponens*, and is not logically well-formed. As a result, the premises cannot guarantee the truth of the conclusion. The court rejected the argument as committing the fallacy of denying the antecedent and therefore logically fallacious.

The opinion in *Edwards v. Riverdale School District*[41] is another example of a court using the fallacy of denying the antecedent to reject a party's legal argument. In this case, the defendant employer allegedly dismissed the respondent employee from his position as athletic director.[42] The employee appealed the decision to the Oregon Fair Dismissal Appeals Board (FDAB), arguing that the employer failed to follow procedures that apply to the dismissal of teachers.[43] The employer responded to the employee's claims, arguing that the employee was not a teacher but instead was an administrator who is not subject to the procedures that apply to the dismissal of teachers.[44] The applicable statute provided that "'administrator' includes a teacher the majority of whose work time is devoted to service as a 'supervisor, principal, vice principal or director of a department or the equivalent.'"[45] The dispute focused on the language "director of a department" in this statutory definition.[46]

The employer reasoned in favor of the *Webster's Dictionary* definition of director: "one that directs . . . the head or chief of an organized occupational group (as a bureau, foundation, institute, school)."[47] The employer further argued that "chief" refers to "the person holding the 'highest' office or ranking."[48] Therefore, the employer concluded that to qualify as an administrator, "[the] individual [must] possess[] the highest rank or degree of authority to make decisions about the department."[49]

The court rejected this reasoning: "[I]t seems clear that, while an individual who is a 'head or chief' of an occupational group may be a 'director,' merely because he or she is *not* such a head or chief does not mean that he or she is *not* a director."[50] The court went on to explain the problem with this argument in terms of formal logic: "Among other things, such reasoning relies on the logical fallacy of denying the antecedent."[51] The court explained that "[a] director, in ordinary usage, more generally refers to one

---

41. 188 P.3d 317 (Or. Ct. App. 2008).
42. *Id.* at 318.
43. *Id.*
44. *Id.* at 317–19.
45. *Id.* at 318 (citing Or. Rev. Stat. § 342.815(1) (2009)).
46. *Id.*
47. *Id.* at 320.
48. *Id.*
49. *Id.* at 321.
50. *Id.*
51. *Id.*

who 'regulate[s] the activities or course of,' one who 'administer[s],' and one who 'assist[s] by giving advice, instruction, and supervision.'"[52]

The court's opinion in *Edwards* illustrates the same syllogistic pattern of argument used in *Posen Construction*, *Zinpro*, and *Iams*:

> If the employee is a "Head," or "Chief" then he is a "Director."
>
> The employee is not a "Head" or "Chief."
>
> Therefore, the employee is not a "Director."

Because the categorical premise ("The employee is not a 'Head or Chief'") denies the antecedent term ("The employee is a 'Head' or 'Chief'"), the argument commits the fallacy of denying the antecedent.

Crouse–Hinds Co. v. InterNorth, Inc. involved a tender offer's compliance with securities laws.[53] The trial court concluded that the plaintiff, InterNorth, carried its burden of demonstrating self-interest or bad faith on the part of the directors.[54] The United States Second Circuit Court of Appeals reversed this finding, observing that the trial court had based its decision on the fallacy of denying the antecedent.[55] The court observed:

> As his starting point, the district judge gave extended consideration to [the court's prior finding] that because the [corporate] directors . . . were not to remain in office after the merger, perpetuation of their control could hardly have been their motivation for actions in furtherance of the merger . . . . Unfortunately, the district judge inferred from this that a quite different proposition must also be true—*i.e.*, that if the directors *are* to remain on the board after the merger, perpetuation of their control *must be presumed* to be their motivation. This inference has no basis in either law or logic.[56]

Considered in the form of the syllogism, the argument considered was:

> If a corporate director is not to remain in office after a merger, perpetuation of director control cannot be the motivation for their actions in furtherance of the merger.
>
> The corporate directors were to remain in office after the merger.
>
> Therefore, perpetuation of control must have been the motivation for their actions in furtherance of the merger.

52. *Id.*
53. 634 F.2d 690, 703 (2d Cir. 1980).
54. *Id.* at 698–99.
55. *Id.* at 702.
56. *Id.* (emphasis added).

The absence of "basis in either law or logic" referred to by the court is the result of a logically fallacious argument structure.[57] The court summarized the essence of the fallacy of denying the antecedent this way: "The proposition that 'A implies B' is not the equivalent of 'non-A implies non-B,' and neither proposition follows logically from the other. The process of inferring one from the other is known as 'the fallacy of denying the antecedent.'"[58]

The argument in *Crouse–Hinds* aptly demonstrates how, in entirely practical factual circumstances, this fallacious pattern of argument can be made and easily avoid detection. Here, after a casual reading of the argument, one might think the argument a sound one. The fallacious nature of the argument is further camouflaged in the syntax of the premises. The hypothetical premise is stated in the negative: "because the . . . directors . . . were not to remain in office after the merger, perpetuation of their control could hardly have been their motivation for actions in furtherance of the merger."[59] While we can simplify this premise to state "if a corporate director is not to remain in office after a merger, perpetuation of director control cannot be the motivation for their actions in furtherance of the merger," we need to include the negative terms to accurately represent the original argument. Accordingly, denying the antecedent term means denying a negative. The antecedent term "a corporate director is not to remain in office after a merger" once denied is "a corporate director is to remain in office after a merger." Because there are no words normally associated with negation—*e.g.*, "no," "none," "not"—within the sentence, it might not readily appear as a denial of the antecedent term.[60]

Second, the structural similarity between the valid form of a hypothetical syllogism and the invalid form that commits the fallacy of denying the antecedent is what makes the fallacy problematic. It is rarely obvious to a casual observer. It "looks" correct unless scrutinized at a formal level. In fact, something about the structure of the argument suggests that it is credible, as it is typically only a word or two away from taking the form of *modus ponens*, a time-tested, frequently employed, comfortable argumentative structure.

5.6 Keys to Using the Fallacy of Denying the Antecedent to Evaluate and Improve Legal Argument

The process of identifying and explaining the fallacy of denying the antecedent begins and ends with a single rule of logic. Once you have some understanding of the rules of the hypothetical syllogism, the real utility of using logical fallacies to

57. *Id.*
58. *Id.* at 703 n. 20 (citing J. Cooley, A Primer of Formal Logic 7 (1942)).
59. *Id.* at 702.
60. This was also the case in *Posen Construction*, discussed *supra*, where the antecedent term in the hypothetical premise was stated in the negative.

evaluate legal arguments is that it provides a pattern of faulty reasoning that you can use to identify and explain what is wrong with a fallacious argument. More importantly, you can recognize this pattern without spending substantial amounts of time deconstructing the form of an argument or learning the philosophical bases of logic—or even understanding all of the rules of formal logic.

Instead, understanding one simple logical fallacy provides you with an identifiable pattern of argument that is necessarily invalid. All you need to do is know the pattern, give it a name, and explain that it violates a rule of logic. This pattern empowers you to conclusively negate the argument and label it as "illogical" and "fallacious." Few judges will be comfortable accepting such an argument as persuasive.

This fallacious pattern is more obvious upon comparing the arguments described in just two of the cases discussed above. Compare the arguments described in *Zinpro* and *Iams* respectively:

> If litigation is imminent, then the controversy is justiciable.
>
> Litigation is not imminent.
>
> Therefore, the controversy is not justiciable.[61]

—

> If the Lemon Law claim is valid, then the Magnuson–Moss Warranty Act is valid.
>
> The Lemon Law claim is invalid.
>
> Therefore, the Magnuson–Moss Warranty Act is invalid.[62]

Both of the arguments take the same syllogistic form:

> If A, then B.
>
> Not A.
>
> Therefore, not B.

61. Zinpro Corp. v. Ridenour, No. 07-96-0008-CV, 1996 Tex. App. LEXIS 3380, at *10 n. 4 (Tex. App. Aug. 1, 1996).
62. Iams v. DaimlerChrysler, 883 N.E.2d 466, 497 (Ohio. Ct. App. 2008).

Similarly, they each take a pattern of argument illustrated graphically this way:

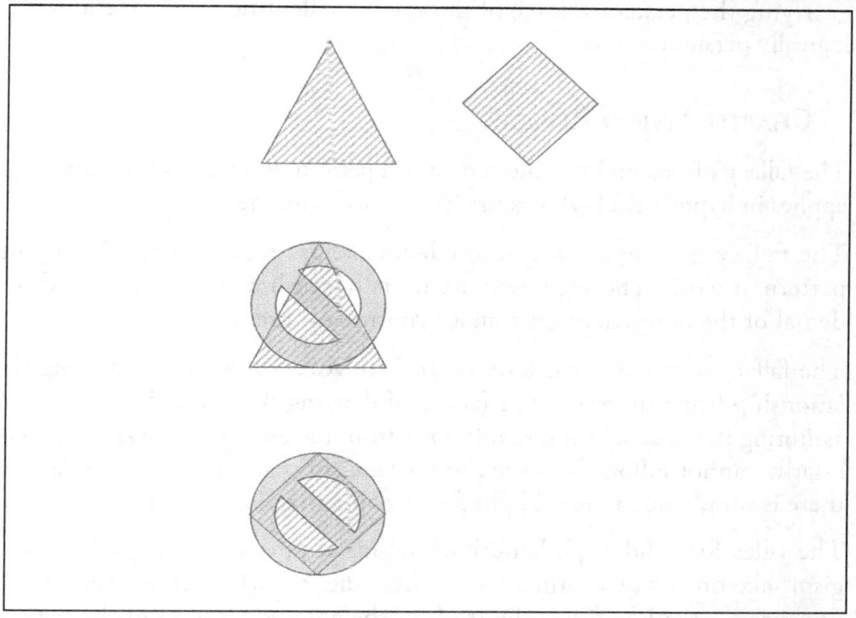

Figure 21. *The fallacious form of hypothetical syllogism called the fallacy of denying the antecedent.*

Once this pattern in legal argument is identified, the explanation for why it is logically fallacious is simple. The rule of logic in play provides that the syllogism is valid if the categorical premise affirms the truth of the antecedent term of the hypothetical and the conclusion affirms the truth of the consequent of the hypothetical. Where the argument violates this rule by denying, instead of affirming, the antecedent term of the hypothetical premise, it commits the fallacy of denying the antecedent.

Some judicial opinions have described the fallacy of denying the antecedent as the "fallacy of the inverse,"[63] which is an apt description of the fallacy and its use in legal argument. The fact the truth of one thing requires the truth of a second does not necessarily require the inverse. The rules of hypothetical syllogisms are about order and inference. Hypothetical syllogisms are powerful argumentative structures, but their power lies in maintaining an orderly relationship between the terms in the premises and the terms in the conclusion. Inverting the place of the terms will

63. *See, e.g.*, N.L.R.B. v. Noel Canning, 134 S. Ct. 2550, 2603 (2014) (Justice Scalia, concurring); United States v. Davenport, 775 F.3d 605, 610 (3d Cir. 2015); Willis-Knighton Med. Ctr. v. Caddo-Shreveport Sales & Use Tax Comm'n, 903 So.2d 1071, 1104 (La. 2005) (superseded by statute as stated in Hitachi Med. Sys. Am., Inc. v. Bridges, No. 2015 CA 0658, 2015 La. App. Unpub. LEXIS 496 (La. App. 2015)).

frequently sound like the familiar meter of *modus ponens* or *modus tollens*, but rather than carrying the persuasive force of those valid syllogistic forms, the argument is not logically persuasive at all.[64]

5.7 Chapter Five in Review

- The fallacy of denying the antecedent is a pattern of invalid argument that only applies in hypothetical syllogisms: "if . . . then" arguments.
- The fallacy of denying the antecedent's name reveals the invalid argument pattern at work. The argument attempts to reach a conclusion based on the denial of the antecedent term in a hypothetical premise.
- The fallacy of denying the antecedent involves a failure in recognizing the relationship between terms. The fallacy of denying the antecedent is an error of assuming that a conclusion that follows from the existence of a state affairs necessarily cannot follow from the nonexistence of that same state of affairs when there is simply not a logical basis for reaching that conclusion.
- The rules for valid hypothetical syllogisms require that a hypothetical syllogism take one of two forms. First, a hypothetical syllogism is valid where the categorical premise affirms the truth of the antecedent term of the hypothetical premise and the conclusion asserts the truth of the consequent term of the hypothetical premise. Alternatively, a hypothetical syllogism is valid where the categorical premise denies truth of the consequent term of the hypothetical premise, and the conclusion denies the truth of the antecedent term of the hypothetical premise. The fallacy of denying the antecedent breaks the rule by denying the truth of the antecedent term in the categorical premise in order to justify a conclusion.
- The simple logic that underlies the fallacy is this: Logic allows us to infer certain things from hypothetical premises. If one thing happens, another thing always follows. However, logic does not require the inverse. That is, logic does not require that the absence of one thing requires the absence of another. When we assume that the inverse is a necessarily conclusion, we make a reasoning error and commit the fallacy of denying the antecedent.
- This chapter is the first time you have seen how courts take the rules of logic and apply them in their evaluation of legal argument. As you continue to learn about different logical fallacies, notice how courts use the fallacies in their eval-

64. Some of the ideas developed in this chapter were first explored in Stephen M. Rice, *Conventional Logic: Using the Logical Fallacy of Denying the Antecedent as a Litigation Tool*, 43 Akron L. Rev. 79 (2010).

uation of legal arguments and consider the strengths and weaknesses of the various approaches you encounter.

- A short sample complaint in a civil case follows. Review it and see if you can spot the fallacy of denying the antecedent in the pleading. Once you find it, ask yourself why you were able to identify it, whether you would have identified it before reading this chapter, and consider how you might respond to this pleading in practice. A brief discussion of the logical fallacy in the complaint appears in the Appendix at the end of this book.

5.8 Exercise

State of Michigan
Nelson County Circuit Court

Breslin Real Estate Group, LLC
d/b/a Breslin Real Estate Solutions,
Plaintiff,

Case No: A15-000804
Judge: ________________

v.

Elderberry Software and Media, Inc.,
Defendant.

COMPLAINT

Breslin Real Estate Group, LLC d/b/a Breslin Real Estate Solutions, for its Complaint and Jury Demand, states:

1) Plaintiff, Breslin Real Estate Group, LLC d/b/a Breslin Real Estate Solutions ("BRES") is a Michigan limited liability company having its principal place of business in Nelson County, Michigan.

2) BRES has been actively engaged in the real estate brokerage business throughout Nelson County since 1985. It currently employs sixteen real estate agents who provide real estate brokerage and management services for customers.

3) Defendant Elderberry Software and Media, Inc. ("ESMI") is a software development company, having its principle place of business in Rapids, Michigan, and regularly conducting business throughout the Midwest, including in Nelson County, Michigan.

4) BRES and ESMI entered into a Software Development Agreement on May 3, 2015 (the "Software Development Agreement").

5) Pursuant to the Software Development Agreement, ESMI agreed to develop software for use by BRES and its agents to manage many of the day to day activities of its real estate agents.

6) In exchange for the software development services, BRES agreed to pay $52,500 in equal installments at the conclusion of each of three phases of development.

7) After BRES fulfilled all of its obligations to pay ESMI at the conclusion of the first two phases of the Software Development Agreement, ESMI breached the Software Development Agreement and refused to fulfil its contractual obligations.

Count I: Breach of Contract

8) Plaintiff BRES hereby incorporates each of the allegations in paragraphs 1 through 7.

9) The Software Development Agreement set out the scope of work to be performed by ESMI, the schedule of work, and the specific requirements for the software to be developed by ESMI.

10) Among the provisions on the Software Development Agreement is the following provision included in Paragraph 27 referring to BRES and ESMI as "CUSTOMER" and "DEVELOPER" respectively:

> 27. In the event CUSTOMER fails to make full and complete payment of the Phase 2 progress payment, DEVELOPER shall have no further obligations to perform any part of this Software Development Agreement, including, without limitation, completion of Phase 3 or any Post-Development Support Obligations described in paragraph 42.

11) BRES made full and complete payment of the Phase 2 progress payment and accordingly, pursuant to the contract, ESMI was required to complete Phase 3.

12) On June 4, 2015, BRES contacted ESMI and requested assurances that the development of Phase 3 was moving forward and would be completed on time.

13) During a telephone conversation between BRES's office manager and ESMI's project manager ESMI conceded that Phase 3 was no longer in progress and that ESMI refused to complete development of the software or otherwise fulfil its contractual obligations under the Software Development Agreement.

14) As a result of ESMI's refusal to complete the software, support the software or otherwise honor its obligations under the Software Development Agreement, ESMI has breached the Software Development Agreement.

15) As a result of ESMI's breach of the Software Development Agreement, BRES has been injured and continues to incur damages.

WHEREFORE, Plaintiff requests this Court enter a judgment in favor of Plaintiff in the amount of damages to which Plaintiff is entitled and award any further relief available under law.

Dated: August 31, 2016

RESPECTFULLY SUBMITTED

GOZO AND VALETTA

Attorneys for Plaintiff

____

Renee L. Valetta

Chapter Six

The Fallacy of Affirming the Consequent

This chapter will explain what the fallacy of affirming the consequent is, how to identify the fallacy, and how to explain what is wrong with it. As you read the chapter, consider focusing on answers to the following questions:

- Why is this fallacy called "affirming the consequent?" What is a "consequent" in an argument and what does it mean to "affirm" it?
- Can the fallacy of affirming the consequent appear in any argument? Is it limited to a specific category of arguments?
- How is the fallacy of affirming the consequent similar to and different from the fallacy of denying the antecedent?
- If affirming the consequent is a bad argument, how can it be fixed to make a better argument?
- What rule of logic is violated when an argument commits the fallacy of affirming the consequent?
- How do courts respond when they encounter arguments that commit the fallacy of affirming the consequent? How do they identify the fallacy, and how do they explain its application?
- What simple pattern can you look for to remember why the fallacy of affirming the consequent is a bad argument?
- What similarities and differences do you recognize between the fallacies of denying the antecedent and affirming the consequent?

6.1 More on Hypothetical Syllogisms, Order, and Inference

While I am not much of a mechanic, I am fascinated by mechanical things. I keep an old motorcycle in my garage. It was manufactured in 1968, a time when combustion engines were relatively simple devices and even inexperienced amateur mechanics could service such engines themselves. It has a very simple electronics system. The engine starts by "kicking" a kick-start pedal. In part because of the machine's simplicity, it is easy to predict whether it will run or not. To cause the motorcycle to start, I know a few things need to be in place first. The battery mounted beneath the motorcycle seat has to be connected to the engine. The fuel tank has to contain enough gas to supply the carburetors, which mix oxygen and fuel together. The spark plugs must be properly seated and attached to their wires. Last, I have to place my weight on the kick-start pedal, and lower my weight on the pedal quickly to "kick" it with enough force to start the engine. Based on what I know of motorcycles, I can assert some true premises. One premise is this: *If the motorcycle's engine starts, then there is gas in the gas tank.* That premise is undoubtedly true. Further, it is readily identifiable as a hypothetical premise. If I went out to my garage right now, I could twist open the small cap on the top of the fuel tank and look inside to see if there was any gas in it. If I can see gas in the fuel tank, I am in a position to assert a second premise: *There is gas in the gas tank.* This premise, like the first, is undoubtedly true. I might go a step further and reach a conclusion from these premises:

> If the motorcycle's engine starts, then there is gas in the gas tank.
>
> There is gas in the gas tank.
>
> Therefore, the motorcycle's engine starts.

It might be tempting to accept this argument. It, like many fallacious arguments, sounds "reasonable." Of course, I know from experience that, for example, if the battery is not connected, my motorcycle will not start, even if the tank is entirely full of gas. Further, if I do not "kick" the kick-start pedal, the motorcycle will not start. The truth of the consequent term simply will not allow me to make any logical inference about whether the engine will start.

The same rule of logic at work in the hypothetical syllogism regarding my motorcycle is at work in hypothetical syllogisms underlying legal arguments. A jury having reasonable doubt regarding the guilt or innocence of a criminal defendant will hesitate to reach a verdict when deliberating. However, a jury's hesitation to act during deliberations does not necessarily require a conclusion that it had reasonable doubt about the guilt or innocence of a criminal defendant.[1]

The fallacy of denying the antecedent, and the fallacy of affirming the consequent have some important similarities.

The fallacy addressed in Chapter Five, the fallacy of denying the antecedent, and the fallacy of affirming the consequent, have some important similarities. Understanding how they are similar will help you identify them. Seeing how they are different will help you to understand the logical rules they violate and either expose them or repair them. What they have in common is that they both apply to the same

1. *See, e.g.*, Adkins v. State, 418 S.W.3d 856, 867 (Tx. App. 2013).

kind of argumentative structure. They both apply to hypothetical syllogisms—" if . . . then" arguments. Lawyers make hypothetical arguments regularly. Accordingly, the process of finding arguments that commit the fallacy of affirming the consequent starts with identifying a legal argument with hypothetical pattern. That pattern is identified and described in the same fashion that it was in Chapter Five. The argument will be summarized into a hypothetical premise, with an antecedent term and a consequent term, followed by a categorical premise that either affirms or denies the antecedent term or the consequent term.

Once we identify a hypothetical syllogism, it has to comply with the rule of logic that describes the two valid patterns of hypothetical syllogisms. A hypothetical syllogism must take one of two forms. First, a hypothetical syllogism is valid where the categorical premise affirms the truth of the antecedent term of the hypothetical premise and the conclusion asserts the truth of the consequent term of the hypothetical premise.[2] Alternatively, a hypothetical syllogism is valid where the categorical premise denies truth of the consequent term of the hypothetical premise, and the conclusion denies the truth of the antecedent term of the hypothetical premise.[3] The argument has to take one of the two following patterns:

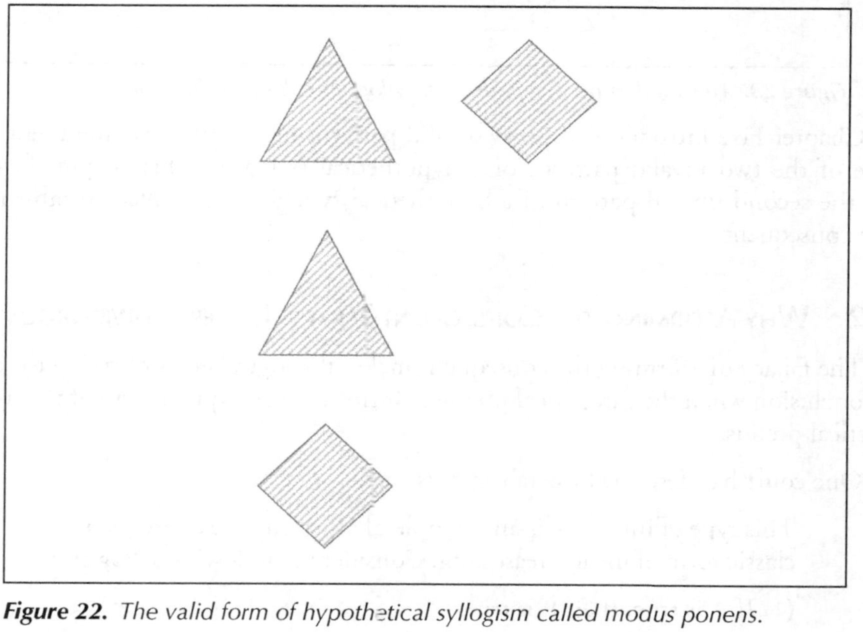

Figure 22. *The valid form of hypothetical syllogism called modus ponens.*

2. *See, e.g.*, Irving M. Copi & Carl Cohen, Introduction to Logic 244–49 (13th ed. 2008), at 299–300.
3. *Id.*

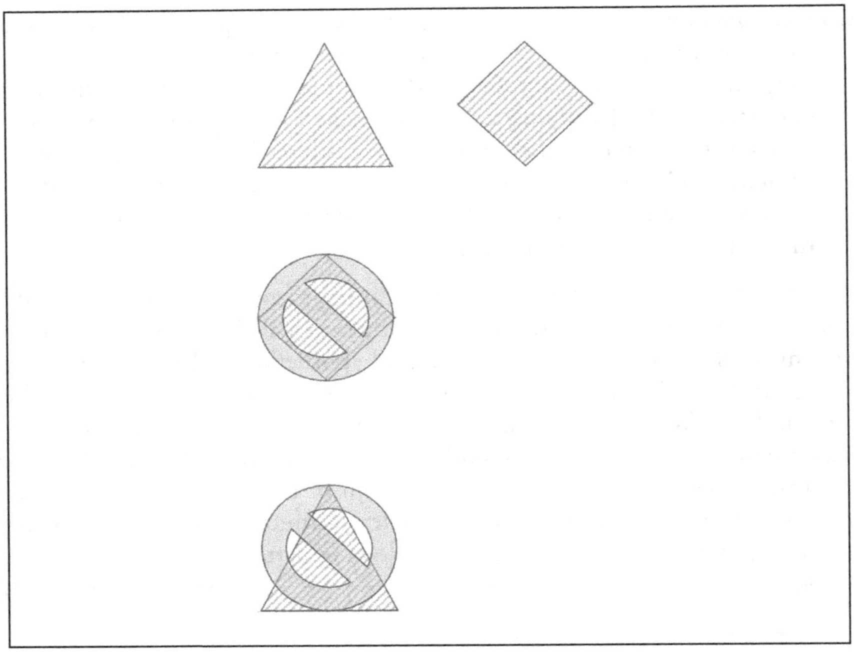

Figure 23. *The valid form of hypothetical syllogism called modus tollens.*

Chapter Five introduced these two valid patterns of hypothetical argument and one of the two invalid patterns of a hypothetical syllogism; this chapter focuses on the second invalid pattern of a hypothetical syllogism: the fallacy of affirming the consequent.

6.2 Why Affirming the Consequent Term is Unpersuasive Argument

The fallacy of affirming the consequent makes the logical error of trying to reach a conclusion when the categorical premise affirms the consequent term of the hypothetical premise.

One court has described the fallacy this way:

> This type of inference is an example of affirming the consequent, a classic form of invalid reasoning. Consider the following syllogism:
>
> (1) If A is true, then B is true.
>
> (2) B is true.
>
> (3) Therefore, A is also true.

> The conclusion that A is true does not logically follow from the premises.[4]

The logic of hypothetical syllogisms is about order and inference. The rule of logic that controls these arguments is focused on ensuring the right order of terms to justify a logical inference. Where a categorical premise affirms the consequent term of the hypothetical premise, the syllogism commits the fallacy of affirming the consequent and its conclusion cannot be relied upon. Graphically displayed, the fallacious pattern of argument takes this form:

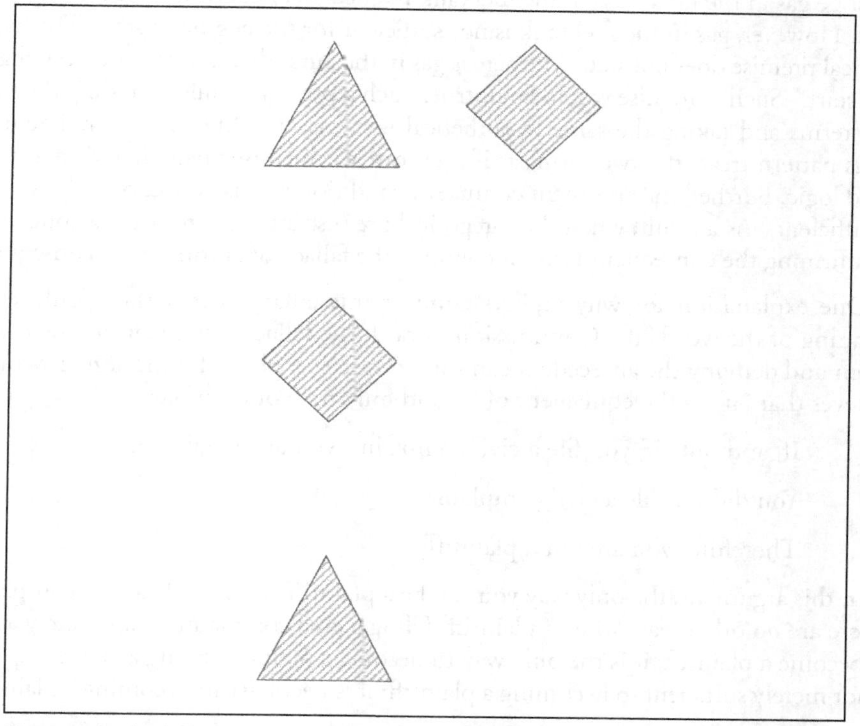

Figure 24. *The fallacious form of hypothetical syllogism called the fallacy of affirming the consequent.*

4. In re Stewart Foods, Inc., 64 F.3d 141, 145 (4th Cir. 1995). The court in *In re Steward Foods* applied the fallacy to the argument involved in that case this way:

> The district court's reasoning roughly reduces to the following syllogism:
>
> (1) If a debtor rejects a contract, then a general unsecured claim exists.
>
> (2) A general unsecured claim exists.
>
> (3) Therefore, the debtor must have rejected a contract.
>
> The district court's conclusion does not follow from its premises.

Id.

This pattern of argument is fallacious because it is not disciplined about the order of the terms in the hypothetical premise. Returning to the motorcycle argument:

> If the motorcycle's engine starts, then there is gas in the gas tank.
>
> There is gas in the gas tank.
>
> Therefore, the motorcycle's engine starts.

The hypothetical premise is true. I can be certain that if the engine starts, there must be gas in the tank. Gas in the fuel tank is a necessary condition for the engine to start. However, gas in the fuel tank is not sufficient for the engine to start. The hypothetical premise does not state: "If there is gas in the tank, then the motorcycle's engine will start." Such a premise would be untrue. Such a premise, while including the same two terms and taking the same hypothetical form, is in a different order. The fallacious pattern treats the two terms as if their order is inconsequential, and that is not good logic. Further, the argument confuses a condition that is necessary with one that is sufficient.[5] As a result, when the categorical premise attempts to reach a conclusion by affirming the consequent term, it commits the fallacy of affirming the consequent.

One explanation for why arguers commit this fallacy is that they confuse the meaning of the word "if." Commission of both the fallacies of affirming the consequent and denying the antecedent can sometimes be explained if the arguer wrongly believes that "if" is the equivalent of "if and only if." For example:

> If, and only if, you file a civil complaint, you are a plaintiff.
>
> You did not file a civil complaint.
>
> Therefore, you are not a plaintiff.

In this argument, the only way you can be a plaintiff is if you file a civil complaint. There are no other ways to be a plaintiff. Filing a civil complaint is not merely a way to become a plaintiff; it is the only way to become a plaintiff. Filing a civil complaint is not merely sufficient to becoming a plaintiff; it is necessary to becoming a plaintiff.[6]

---

5. *See* David A. Hunter, A Practical Guide to Critical Thinking: Deciding What to Do and Believe 169–71 (describing both the fallacies of affirming the consequent and denying the aAntecedent as "invalid forms of reasoning about necessary and sufficient conditions").

6. *See, e.g.*, Nigel Warburton, Thinking from A to Z, 47 (2nd ed. 1998) ("In some cases, the context and the subject matter of the argument make it clear that 'if' is to be understood as meaning 'if and only if.' These are not cases of denying the antecedent."); *see also* People v. Garcia, 237 Cal. App. 4th 666, 188 Cal. Rptr. 3d 253, 263, *review granted and opinion superseded*, 356 P.3d 279 (Cal. 2015) ("To illustrate this fallacy, start with a statement of the form, 'If P, then Q'—for example, 'If Socrates is a man, then Socrates is mortal.' In that case, the statement 'Q, therefore P,' or, 'Socrates is mortal, therefore Socrates is a man,' is a fallacy. This is because there are other ways to be mortal; perhaps Socrates is a woman, a dog, or a bristlecone pine. However, if we start with a statement of the form, 'If and only if P, then Q,' then the fallacy disappears; in that case, 'Q, therefore P' does logically follow. For example, from 'If and only if Socrates is mortal, then he can die,' we can conclude, 'Socrates can die, therefore he is mortal.').

6.3 How Courts Have Used the Fallacy of Affirming the Consequent

Like other formal logical fallacies, courts have used the fallacy of affirming the consequent as a tool to evaluate legal argument.[7] Like other courts, those evaluating the fallacy of affirming the consequent have typically identified the fallacious pattern of logical form in a legal argument, called it by its logical name, and provided some level of logical explanation for why the legal argument is not persuasive.

For example, in *Indemnity Insurance Company of North America v. W & T Offshore, Inc.*,[8] an insurer filed a declaratory action to determine whether it was required to provide coverage under its umbrella insurance policies with its insured. The umbrella polices only covered claims made by third parties against the insured, and did not provide coverage for the insured's own property damage or the insureds own "operators' extra expenses."[9] Further, coverage under umbrella policies did not require any coverage until the "Retained Limit" had been incurred by the insured under its other insurance policies. The dispute focused on whether the Retained Limit was limited to third-party claims, or whether the Retained Limit could be met based on property damage and operator's extra expense claims.[10]

One argument made in the case was that the holding in another case, *Westchester Fire Insurance Company v. Stewart & Stevenson Services, Inc.*,[11] controlled the outcome. The court observed that the insurance policy in *Westchester Fire Insurance*

---

7. *See, e.g.*, Indem. Ins. Co. of N. Am. v. W & T Offshore, Inc., 756 F.3d 347, 355 n. 5 (5th Cir. 2014); Funderburk v. Yost, No. 3:10-cv-200-KRG-KAP, 2012 U.S. Dist. LEXIS 30628 at *16 (W.D. Pa. Jan. 18, 2012) *report and recommendation adopted*, No. 3:10-cv-200-KRG-KAP, 2012 U.S. Dist. LEXIS 30081 (W.D. Pa. Mar. 7, 2012); United States v. Carlson, 67 M.J. 693, 699 (NM. Ct. Crim. App. 2009); Gilliam v. Nev. Power Co., 488 F.3d 1189, 1196 n. 7 (9th Cir. 2007); *In re* Stewart Foods, Inc. v. Broecker, 64 F.3d 141, 145 n. 3 (4th Cir. 1995); United Tel. Co. of Carolinas, Inc. v. FCC, 559 F.2d 720, 725–26 (D.C. Cir. 1977); Topliff v. Wal-Mart Stores E. LP, No. 6:04-CV-0297 (GHL), 2007 U.S. Dist. LEXIS 20533, at *183 (N.D.N.Y Mar. 22, 2007); Adams v. La.-Pac. Corp., 284 F. Supp. 2d 331, 338 (W.D.N.C. 2003), *rev'd in part, vacated in part, and remanded*, 177 F. App'x 335 (4th Cir. 2006); BMG Rights Mgmt. (US) LLC v. Cox Commc'ns, Inc., No. 1:14-cv-1611, 2015 U.S. Dist. LEXIS 161091 at *82 (E.D. Va. Dec. 1, 2015); Briggs v. Univ. of Detroit-Mercy, 22 F. Supp. 3d 798, 802 (E.D. Mich. 2014) *aff'd*, 611 F. App'x 865 (6th Cir. 2015); Morgan v. Imperial Irrigation Dist., 223 Cal. App. 4th 892, 930, 167 Cal. Rptr. 3d 687, 718 (2014), *reh'g denied* (Feb. 4, 2014), *review denied* (May 14, 2014); People v. Zavala, 2013 Cal. App. Unpub. LEXIS 7542 at *224 (Cal. Ct. App. Oct. 22, 2013), *as modified on denial of reh'g* (Nov. 21, 2013); In re Jeffery, No.H031673, 2008 Cal. App. LEXIS 7976, at *25 (Cal. Ct. App. 2008); State v. Lackey, 286 P.3d 859, 865 (Kan. 2012); City of Green Ridge v. Kreisel, 25 S.W.3d 559, 563 & n. 2 (Mo. Ct. App. 2000); United States v. Balcarczyk, 52 M.J. 809, 812 n. 4 (NM. Ct. Crim. App. 2000); Daniels v. Empty Eye, Inc., 368 S.W.3d 743, 752 (Tex. App. 2012); Adkins v. State, 418 S.W.3d 856, 867 (Tex. App. 2013); Paulson v. State, 28 S.W.3d 570, 572 (Tex. Crim. App. 2000); Culton v. State, 95 S.W.3d 401, 405 (Tex. App. 2002).
8. Indem. Ins. Co. of N. Am. v. W & T Offshore, Inc., 756 F.3d 347 (5th Cir. 2014).
9. *Id.* at 350.
10. *Id.* at 350–51.
11. *Id.* at 355 (discussing Westchester Fire Ins. Co. v. Stewart & Stevenson Servs., Inc., 31 S.W.3d 654, 656 (Tex. App. 2000)).

Company specifically provided that if the underlying policies were exhausted by losses not covered by the umbrella policy, then the umbrella coverage would not be triggered.[12] The insured argued that the court's interpretation of the policy language in the *Westchester Fire Insurance Company* required the same outcome as the dispute in the instant case. The court observed:

> [The insurer] contend[s] that [a provision in the umbrella policy at issue in the case] "mean[s] the same" thing as the provision in *Westchester* because "[o]ne provision is the converse of the other." This is a logical fallacy. Whereas the Westchester provision lays out a limitation on coverage—if not reduced or exhausted by covered claims, then no coverage—the Umbrella Policies explain two potential scenarios—if reduced or exhausted by covered claims, then either (1) pay in excess of reduced limit or (2) act as primary insurer. The two policies are not identical, and *Westchester*, rather than helping Underwriters' argument, provides an excellent example of the type of provision that would be included if the policy meant what Underwriters claim it means.[13]

The court went on to use the fallacy of affirming the consequent to police the parties' arguments and distinguish the applicability of *Westchester Fire Insurance Company* to the case before the court, stating:

> If A = "underlying policies exhausted by covered claims" and B = "coverage," the provisions work as follows:
>
> Westchester Policy:
>
> Not A → Not B (alternatively, B → A).
>
> Underwriters' Policy:
>
> A → B (alternatively, Not B → Not A).
>
> Underwriters are arguing that B A is the same as A B. This is the "affirming the consequent" fallacy, and is simply incorrect.[14]

The fallacy of affirming the consequent worked as a mechanism to explain what was logically unpersuasive about the insurer's argument. Frequently, legal arguments become convoluted. Parties might naturally use inconsistent terms and structure in drafting their arguments. Parties might be forced to derive legal rules from cases that involve different issues, facts, contractual, or statutory language. Formal logic provides a consistent framework for organizing legal argument in consistent terms and a consistent syllogistic structure. This structure allows legal thinkers to comparatively

12. *Id.*
13. *Id.* at 355 (footnote omitted).
14. *Id.* at n. 5. The arrow symbol used by the court is intended to connote a hypothetical relationship. Accordingly, where the court states "A → B," it symbolizes an "If A then B" logical relationship.

analyze legal argument, by comparing and contrasting it to necessarily valid or invalid logical structures, and reaching conclusive logical decisions about the validity or invalidity of the form of the argument. The court used the fallacy of affirming the consequent for just such a purpose in *Indemnity Insurance Company of North America.*

Similarly, in *City of Green Ridge v. Kreisel,*[15] the court evaluated a legal argument that fit into the pattern of a hypothetical syllogism. The court used the fallacy of affirming the consequent to analyze the plaintiff's argument. The defendant operated a junkyard. The City sought to regulate the junkyard by establishing an ordinance.[16] The defendant argued that the ordinance constituted a zoning ordinance and that the ordinance was invalid because it failed to meet the procedural requirements for a zoning ordinance.[17] The City responded by arguing that the ordinance was not a zoning ordinance. Because the ordinance was not a zoning ordinance, it did not have to be promulgated pursuant to the requirements for zoning ordinances.[18]

In an effort to justify its proffered conclusion that the ordinance was a zoning ordinance, the defendant designed an argument that relied on the fact that the zoning ordinance statute provided that zoning ordinances could be used to promote public health and safety.[19] The court summarized defendant's argument this way: "[The defendant] argues, therefore, that since zoning ordinances regulate health and safety through regulating the use of buildings, and since this ordinance addresses health and safety in his operation of his junkyard, therefore this ordinance is a zoning ordinance."[20]

Unlike the court in *Indemnity Insurance Company of North America*, the court in *City of Green Ridge v. Kreisel* did not break down the argument into its syllogistic components.[21] However, breaking the argument down into syllogistic form illustrates something important about both *In re Stewart Foods* and *City of Green Ridge v. Kreisel*: while both cases involved significantly different legal and factual subject matters, they were both decided on identical logical rules.

The court's description of the defendant's argument, examined syllogistically, might appear this way:

15. 25 S.W. 3d 559, 563–64 (Mo. Ct. App. 2000).

16. *Id.*

17. *Id.* at 561 (quoting Mo. Ann. Stat. § 89.09 (West 2009): "The legislative body of such municipality shall provide for the manner in which such [zoning] regulations and restrictions and the boundaries of such districts shall be determined, established, and enforced, and from time to time amended, supplemented, or changed. *However, no such regulation, restriction, or boundary shall become effective until after a public hearing in relation thereto, at which parties in interest and citizens shall have an opportunity to be heard. At least fifteen days' notice* of the time and place of such hearing shall be published in an official paper or a paper of general circulation in such municipality.") (emphasis in original).

18. *Id.* at 563.

19. *Id.*

20. *Id.*

21. However, the court did describe the pattern of fallacious reasoning this way: "The fallacy is often expressed as "If p, then q; q; therefore p." The statement is not true because there may be things other than p that also occur with q." *Id.* at 563, n. 2.

If this ordinance is a zoning ordinance, then it regulates health and safety through regulating the use of buildings.

This ordinance regulates health and safety through regulating the use of buildings.

Therefore this ordinance is a zoning ordinance.

Accordingly, the court in *City of Green Ridge v. Kreisel* was able to use the fallacy of affirming the consequent to police the parties' arguments and analyze and explain why it found Kreisel's argument unpersuasive:

> [Defendant's] argument commits the logical fallacy of "affirming the consequent." He fails to recognize that, while zoning ordinances may address health and safety issues, other types of ordinances may also address health and safety issues without becoming zoning ordinances. In other words, the mere fact that a purpose of zoning ordinances is to regulate public safety does not mean that all ordinances which regulate health and safety are zoning ordinances. To the contrary, there are many other kinds of ordinances which also regulate public health and safety.[22]

Like *City of Green Ridge v. Kreisel*, which used the fallacy of affirming the consequent to police the parties' arguments and solve a problem with a statutory definition, the court in *Paulson v. State*[23] also used the fallacy of affirming the consequent to solve a different definitional problem. In *Paulson*, the court considered the propriety of a jury instruction mandated by a previous court decision. The jury instruction dealt with the definition of "reasonable doubt." The court reviewed the previous definition of "reasonable doubt," which had provided:

> It is the kind of doubt that would make a reasonable person hesitate to act in the most important of his own affairs.
>
> Proof beyond a reasonable doubt therefore must be proof of such a convincing character that you would be willing to rely and act upon it without hesitation in the most important of your own affairs.[24]

---

22. *Id.* at 563–64.

23. 28 S.W. 3d 570, 572 (Tex. Crim. App. 2000).

24. The court was reviewing the approved instruction defining "reasonable doubt" in *Geesa v. State*, 820 S.W.2d 154 (Tex. Crim. App. 1991). The court in *Paulson* was actually addressing a three-part definition provided by the *Geesa* court. However, for purposes of logical fallacy analysis, the *Paulson* court focused on two of the *Geesa* court's three definitions. The three definitions, as described by the *Paulson* court were: "A reasonable doubt is a doubt based on reason and common sense after a careful and impartial consideration of all the evidence in the case;" "It is the kind of doubt that would make a reasonable person hesitate to act in the most important of his own affairs;" and "Proof beyond a reasonable doubt therefore must be proof of such a convincing character that you would be willing to rely and act upon it without hesitation in the most important of your own affairs." *Id.*

The court focused on the definition "proof beyond a reasonable doubt therefore must be proof of such a convincing character that you would be willing to rely and act upon it without hesitation in the most important of your own affairs."[25] The court rejected this definition because it violated a rule of logic. The court described it as a logically fallacious application of the previous definition "the kind of doubt that would make a reasonable person hesitate to act in the most important of his own affairs." The court explained its conclusion this way: "The court says that reasonable doubt makes you hesitate to act; therefore, if you hesitate to act, you have a reasonable doubt. That is like saying, 'Pneumonia makes you cough; therefore, if you cough, you have pneumonia.' This is the logical fallacy called 'affirming the consequent.'"[26]

This explanation illustrates how effective a common example of a logical fallacy can be to make a logical point without engaging in a discussion about the details of formal logic. The court makes its point without discussing categorical or hypothetical syllogisms, or even explaining the difference between antecedent and consequent terms. Instead, the court simply identifies the pattern of argument, describes the fallacy by name, and juxtaposes the description with common, non-legal examples, like coughing and pneumonia, to demonstrate why the argumentative pattern is not logically persuasive.

Similarly, in *Gilliam v. Nev. Power*[27] the court used the fallacy of affirming the consequent to police the parties' arguments and solve a legal problem. The court in *Gilliam* was faced with the issue of determining whether certain payment allegedly received by the plaintiff constituted "earnings" under her retirement plan (the "Plan").[28] The Plan defined "earnings" as "total wages and salary as reported by the Company for federal income tax purposes for the calendar year." Accordingly, the litigants focused their arguments on whether the severance payment constituted "wages and salary."

The plaintiff argued that because her employer reported the severance payment in Box 1 of her federal W-2 form, the place designated for an employer to report "wages and salary," her severance payment must be "wages and salary" under the Plan. The court used the fallacy of affirming the consequent to evaluate the plaintiff's argument:

> This argument rests on the logical fallacy of affirming the consequent. While Nevada Power Company must report "wages and salary" on Box 1 of the federal Form W-2, not all amounts reported in Box 1 of the federal Form W-2 must be "wages and salary."

25. *Id.*
26. *Id.*
27. 488 F.3d 1189, 1197 (9th Cir. 2007).
28. *Id.* at 1196.

> For example, the 1999 Instructions for Forms W-2 and W-3 explain that Box 1 includes many employee income items other than "wages and salary."[29]

Accordingly, the court in *Gilliam* appears to have interpreted the plaintiff's argument this way:

> If the employer pays "wages and salary" then the payments must be reported in Box 1.
>
> The employer reported the payments in Box 1.
>
> Therefore, the employer pays "wages and salary."

The fact that wages and salary must be reported in Box 1 does not require the inference that everything reported in Box 1 is wages and salary. Of course, this is the essence of what is "wrong" with an argument that fits the pattern of the fallacy of affirming the consequent. The logical rules of hypothetical syllogisms manage order and inference. The fallacious pattern is in the wrong order and cannot be relied upon to ensure the proffered inference.

Another case, *United Telephone Company of the Carolinas v. Federal Communications Commission*,[30] considered a logically similar argument regarding the petitioner's challenge to a formula for the division of revenues.[31] The lower court affirmed the FCC's decision to dismiss the petitioners' petitions without hearing based on the fact that neither petitioner had sufficiently challenged the reasonableness of the settlement formula for dividing revenues, which was the heart of the dispute.[32] Instead, the petitioners relied "on the implication that a settlement formula which does not provide a higher rate of return to a company whose overall operations make it a riskier economic enterprise than its co-participant is *ipso facto* unjust and unreasonable."[33] The court suggested that petitioners had provided no evidence that the result of the settlement formula was unjust. Instead, they argued that the result must be unjust since the formula was unjust.[34]

The court framed the problem with this argument in terms of the fallacy of affirming the consequent:

> The Commission properly characterized [the petitioners'] arguments as an attempt to attack the formula for dividing charges

29. *Id.* at 1197 n. 7.
30. 559 F.2d 720 (D.C. Cir. 1977); *see also* Cent. Ill. Pub. Serv. Co. v. United States, 435 U.S. 21, 25, (1978) ("Wages usually are income, but many items qualify as income and yet clearly are not wages.")
31. *Id.* at 725–26 (citing Irving Copi, Introduction to Logic 202 (3d ed. 1968) and describing the principle utilized as "fallacy of affirming the consequent").
32. *Id.* at 724–25.
33. *Id.* at 725
34. *Id.*

> without alleging that the result of that formula is in fact unjust and unreasonable. [The petitioners'] insist that if the method of dividing charges is unjust and unreasonable, its result must also be unjust and unreasonable. This exercise in sophistry miscasts the issue by reversing the logic of the inquiry. A method of determining rates, or divisions thereof, is unjust and unreasonable if the result reached does not afford a compensatory return. One cannot, as [the petitioners'] try to do, reverse the order of this proposition and preserve its logical validity.[35]

Considered syllogistically, the petitioners' argument might be arranged this way:

> If the application of the settlement formula yields an unjust result, then the settlement formula is unjust.
>
> The settlement formula is unjust.
>
> Therefore, the application of the settlement formula yields an unjust result.

Lawyers can use the force of formal logic in the same ways the courts used it in these cases by being disciplined about order and inference in hypothetical arguments. This requires understanding the simple logical patterns that underlie legal arguments that take hypothetical forms, spotting fallacious patterns, and understanding enough of the rules of logic to justify labeling the argument as fallacious.

6.4 Keys to Using the Fallacy of Affirming the Consequent to Evaluate and Improve Legal Argument

Like all of the formal logical fallacies, using the fallacy of affirming the consequent begins with understanding a simple rule of formal logic. The rule that manages hypotheticals is about order and inference. A hypothetical syllogism must take one of two forms. First, a hypothetical syllogism is valid where the categorical premise affirms the truth of the antecedent term of the hypothetical premise and the conclusion asserts the truth of the consequent term of the hypothetical premise.[36] Alternatively, a hypothetical syllogism is valid where the categorical premise denies truth of the consequent term of the hypothetical premise and the conclusion denies the truth of the antecedent term of the hypothetical premise.[37]

Conversely, in each of the cases discussed in this chapter, the court described a pattern of fallacious argument that departed from both of the two valid forms, committed

---

35. *Id.* at 725–26 (citing Irving Copi, Introduction to Logic 202 (3d ed. 1968)) (citation to record omitted).
36. *See, e.g.*, Copi & Cohen, *supra* note 2, at 299–300.
37. *Id.*

the fallacy of affirming the consequent, realized its logical unreliability, and rejected the argument on grounds of logic. For example:

> If an ordinance is a zoning ordinance, then it regulates health and safety through regulating the use of buildings.
>
> This ordinance regulates health and safety through regulating the use of buildings.
>
> Therefore this ordinance is a zoning ordinance.[38]

—

> If the employer pays "wages and salary" then the payments must be reported in Box 1.
>
> The employer reported the payments in Box 1.
>
> Therefore, the employer pays "wages and salary."[39]

—

> If the application of the settlement formula yields an unjust result, then the settlement formula is unjust.
>
> The settlement formula is unjust.
>
> Therefore, the application of the settlement formula yields an unjust result.[40]

---

38. City of Green Ridge v. Kreisel, *supra* note 15. In order to use the hypothetical premise to reach a valid conclusion, a different logical form would be necessary. For example:

> If an ordinance is a zoning ordinance, then it regulates health and safety through regulating the use of buildings.
>
> This ordinance is a zoning ordinance.
>
> Therefore, this ordinance regulates health and safety through regulating the use of buildings.

39. Gilliam, *supra* note 15. This same hypothetical premise could be used to form a valid syllogism, but it would have to take one of the two valid patterns of hypothetical syllogisms. For example".

> If the employer pays "wages and salary," then the payments must be reported in Box 1.
> The employer was not required to report the payments in Box 1.
> Therefore, the employer did not pay "wages and salary."

40. United Tel. Co. v. Federal Communications Com., *supra* note 30. Again, to use the hypothetical premise to reach a logically persuasive conclusion, the syllogism must take a valid form. For, example:

> If the application of the settlement formula yields an unjust result, then the settlement formula is unjust.
>
> The application of the settlement formula yields an unjust result.
>
> Therefore, the settlement formula is unjust.

Just as there are patterns of valid hypothetical syllogisms, there are patterns of fallacious hypothetical syllogisms. In each case, the faulty logical form manifests a pattern of argument that commits the fallacy of affirming the consequent, a pattern that looks like this:

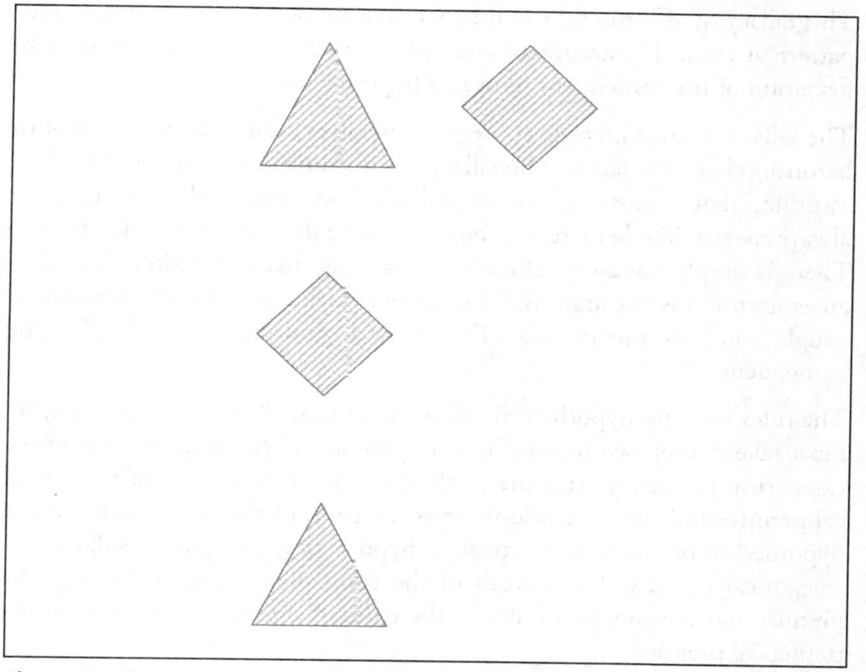

Figure 25. *The fallacious form of hypothetical syllogism called the fallacy of affirming the consequent.*

Like all of the other fallacies, once the pattern of invalid argument is identified and labeled, some explanation is generally required. More than one technique can be effective to provide a persuasive explanation for the fallacious arguments lack of persuasive value. These techniques are seen in the approaches taken by courts. Some courts, like the court in *Westchester Fire Insurance Company,* break the argument down into syllogistic components. Others, like *City of Green Ridge v. Kreisel,* do not and simply use the power of labeling an argument as committing the fallacy of affirming the consequent as a justification. Last, other courts, like *Paulson v. State,* use common examples, with terms like coughing and pneumonia, to demonstrate the logical failings of arguments.[41]

41. Some of the ideas developed in this chapter were first explored in Stephen M. Rice, *Conspicuous Logic: Using the Logical Fallacy of Affirming the Consequent as a Litigation Tool,* 14 BARRY L. REV. 1 (2010).

6.5 Chapter Six in Review

- The fallacy of affirming the consequent is a pattern of invalid argument that only applies in hypothetical syllogisms: "if . . . then" arguments.
- This fallacy of affirming the consequent's name describes the invalid argument pattern at work. The argument attempts to reach a conclusion based on the affirmation of the consequent term in a hypothetical premise.
- The fallacy of affirming the consequent involves a misunderstanding of the relationship between terms. The fallacy of affirming the consequent results from assuming that because one matter follows from another, the two matters must always coexist. While there may be cases where that is true, it is not always true. There is simply not a logical basis for reaching that conclusion. To make such an assumption is like arguing, "'Pneumonia makes you cough; therefore, if you cough, you have pneumonia.' This is the logical fallacy called 'affirming the consequent.'"[42]
- The rules for valid hypothetical syllogisms require that a hypothetical syllogism must take one of two forms. First, a hypothetical syllogism is valid where the categorical premise affirms the truth of the antecedent term of the hypothetical premise and the conclusion asserts the truth of the consequent term of the hypothetical premise. Alternatively, a hypothetical syllogism is valid where the categorical premise denies truth of the consequent term of the hypothetical premise and the conclusion denies the truth of the antecedent term of the hypothetical premise.
- The fallacy of affirming the consequent breaks the rule for valid hypothetical syllogisms by asserting the truth of the consequent term in the categorical premise to justify a conclusion asserting the truth of the antecedent term.
- A Brief in Support of a Motion for New Trial follows. Read the brief and see if you can identify the fallacy of affirming the consequent. If you find it, consider how you might use your knowledge of the rule of logic and its applicability to this argument in responding to this motion. You can review a discussion of the logic problem in this brief in the Appendix at the end of this book.

42. Paulson v. State, 28 S.W.3d 570, 572 (Tex. Crim. App. 2000); Culton v. State, 95 S.W.3d 401, 405 (Tex. App. 2002) (quoting *Paulson*)); Daniels v. Empty Eye, Inc., 368 S.W.3d 743, 752 (Tex. App. 2012) (quoting *Paulson*).

6.6 Exercise

State of Arizona
Eighteenth Judicial Circuit Court

Annalise Forester

Plaintiff,

Case No: 16-00R3927

Judge J.T. Mason

v.

Graham C. Hayes

Defendant.

Brief in Support of Defendant's Motion for a New Trial

Introduction

This is an action for injuries plaintiff alleges she sustained as a result of a car-bicycle collision that plaintiff asserts occurred when her bicycle collided with an automobile driven by defendant. At trial, defendant defended against plaintiff's allegations by introducing substantial evidence that the accident was caused when plaintiff rode her bicycle into defendant's automobile and as a result defendant was neither negligent nor the proximate cause of the accident. Furthermore, defendant argued that plaintiff's damage claim was exaggerated.

In her closing argument, Plaintiff requested damages in the amount of $100,000. The jury returned a verdict in the amount of $150,000. Since the verdict is clearly the result of passion and prejudice, defendant is entitled to a new trial. Accordingly, defendant requests this court enter an order setting aside the jury verdict and ordering a new trial on all issues.

Argument Standard of Review

Under Ariz. R. Civ. P. 59(a)(5), the court may order a new trial or a remittitur where damages are excessive. The court must decide whether the verdict is so manifestly unfair, unreasonable, and outrageous as to shock the conscience of the court. *Haralson v. Fisher Surveying, Inc.*, 201 Ariz. 1, 6 (2001). If the Court finds that the verdict was the result of passion or prejudice, it may *only* order a new trial; a reduction of the award is not permitted. *Waqui v. Tanner Bros. Contracting Co.*, 121 Ariz. 323, 326–27 (App. 1979); *Fleiger v. Reeb*, 120 Ariz. 31, 33 (App. 1978). Accordingly, where a court determines that a verdict shocks the conscience, it has discretion to either order a new trial or a remittitur. However, where a court finds the verdict was the result of passion or prejudice, it has no such discretion and must order a new trial. *Id.*

The Jury's Verdict Was the Result of Passion and/or Prejudice

The facts in this case require a new trial. There can be no doubt that the jury verdict here is the result of passion or prejudice. During the course of the trial, there were several instances during cross examination where plaintiff's counsel became argumentative with defendant and a witness called by defendant, defendant's daughter. See Exhibit A, Trial Transcript, pp. 45, 48, 52, 53, 54, 88, 89, and 90. Over Defendant's counsel's objection, plaintiff's counsel engaged both witnesses in lines of cross examination regarding the topic of plaintiff's damage claim. Both witnesses testified candidly regarding their perceptions that plaintiff's damage claims were contrived and exaggerated. The cross examination became heated and argumentative and defendant's counsel objected numerous times during both lines of cross examination. Each objection was overruled by the trial court.

Plaintiff's counsel made the topic of these heated exchanges a focus of closing argument, spending as much time discussing (and demeaning) Defendant's reasonable and honest perception of the lack of merit in plaintiff's injury claim as any aspect of plaintiff's proofs. It goes without saying that when a plaintiff in a personal injury claim seeks a specific damage award in a jury trial, they suggest the largest amount they can reasonably expect the jury to award. Plaintiff determined the largest reasonable amount of recovery to be $100,000 and during closing arguments, Plaintiff's counsel made a specific request that the jury award that amount to Plaintiff. Plaintiff's argument was that she was entitled to $50,000 in lost wages together with past and continuing pain and suffering, primarily from past and future lower back pain, in the amount of $50,000. Among the instructions provided to the jury was an instruction that it could only award compensatory damages and that it was impermissible to award punitive or exemplary damages. Nonetheless the jury returned a verdict of $150,000, exceeding the amount requested by Plaintiff by $50,000.

An award in such an amount is not only unreasonable, but shocks the conscience. The court must decide whether the verdict is so manifestly unfair, unreasonable, and outrageous as to shock the conscience of the court. *Haralson v. Fisher Surveying, Inc.*, 201 Ariz. 1, 6 (2001). Where a Court finds that the verdict was the result of passion or prejudice, it must order a new trial; a reduction of the award is not a permissible remedy under such circumstances. *Waqui v. Tanner Bros. Contracting Co.*, 121 Ariz. 323, 326–27 (App. 1979); *Fleiger v. Reeb*, 120 Ariz. 31, 33 (App. 1978).

Where a jury verdict is the result of passion or prejudice, such a verdict must shock the conscience of the court. Undoubtedly, the verdict in this case shocks the conscience. A verdict that exceeds the plaintiff's own demand by $50,000 can only be described a "shocking." Particularly when the jury is instructed that it cannot award damages to penalize the defendant. Plaintiff's counsel plainly endeavored to provoke the passions of the jury by arguing that defendant's disbelief of the severity of plaintiff's injuries was callus. No other explanation exists for the jury's decision to award substantially more than the plaintiff's demand but an effort to attempt to penalize defendant? Accordingly, the verdict here must have resulted from passion or prejudice and requires a new trial.

Conclusion

Where a jury verdict is the result of passion or prejudice, such a verdict must shock the conscience of the court. A verdict that exceeds plaintiff's own demand by $50,000 shocks the conscience. Such a verdict requires a new trial. *Waqui v. Tanner Bros. Contracting Co.*, 121 Ariz. 323, 326–27 (App. 1979). Accordingly, defendant requests this court enter an order for a new trial.

Date: August 31, 2016

Stambaugh, L'Anse & Feltch, P.C.
Counsel for Defendant

____

Daryl Feltch

Chapter Seven

The Fallacy of the Undistributed Middle Term

Fallacies of formal logic also appear in another kind of syllogistic form that appears in legal argument: categorical syllogisms. While categorical syllogisms are just one of the three kinds of deductive arguments studied in this book, they represent a substantial proportion of legal arguments because much of legal argument is about placing people, things, and conduct in legal categories. The first of three fallacies of categorical syllogisms addressed in this book, the fallacy of the undistributed middle term, was described by one court as "linguistic sleight-of-hand . . . a perennial vexation in appellate litigation."[1] When an argument draws conclusions based on placing people, things, or conduct in categories, the argument has to follow each of the rules of logic applicable to categorical syllogisms before it can be persuasive. Chapter Seven focuses on just one of those rules. This rule focuses on the concept of distribution of terms and the importance of distribution in legal argument. As you read this chapter, consider the following points.

- Like the fallacies of hypothetical syllogisms, fallacies of categorical syllogisms are frequently mistaken as logical, persuasive arguments. Mistakes about distribution of terms can be easy to make and easy to miss. As you read about the fallacy of the undistributed middle term, ask yourself why a lawyer designing an argument might exercise this "linguistic sleight-of-hand" and why a respondent might miss this fallacy and accept it as logical.
- Categorical syllogisms are common in legal argument. Why is that? How does the law use labels or categories to impose legal consequences for people, things, or conduct that fall within or without those categories?
- The fallacy of the undistributed middle term follows from improper distribution of terms. Distribution relates to whether a term is referred to universally or particularly. As you read the description of this fallacy and the cases in which courts encounter and address it, think about how some of the language of universal and particular terms can help you identify reasoning errors dealing with distribution.

1. Cooper v. Singleton, 94 A.3d 250, 258 (Md. App. 2014).

- Last, when you encounter the fallacy of the undistributed middle term in practice, you may need to explain to opposing counsel or the court what the fallacy is, why it is important, and the role logic plays in defeating fallacious argument. Consider whether you have the learned the logical and legal tools and tactics necessary to effectively do that.

7.1 Middle Terms, Distribution, and Bad Argument

Rules are an important part of lawyering and lots of other things. Musicians play by rules. Referees in football games enforce rules. A teenager learning to drive acclimates to operating a vehicle according to a set of rules. Sometimes rules allow us access to basic systems. For example, I know the rule is that I cannot watch the newest movie premier unless I purchase a ticket. All of the people who go into the theater on opening night are people who have purchased a ticket. The relationship between those people who will miss seeing the movie and those people who will gain access to the movie is whether they fit into a class of people who have a ticket. Rules allow us to do much more complex things as well. Rules of the physics of light tell us how to adjust the shutter speed and aperture of a camera to take a photograph having the desired outcome. Rules of physics allow experts to predict how fast a vehicle was traveling before it engaged its breaks in an attempt to avoid an accident.

Rules of logic are similar to other rules we encounter in music, football, driving, a trip to the theater, and photography. They can help a theater manager reach conclusions about whether a theater will be empty, full, or otherwise, just as they can help an amateur photographer predict whether a photograph they take at their child's Friday night football game will be in sharp focus or blurry. In fact, each rule of logic plays an important part in ensuring certainty about everything from the logical force of a complex legal argument to something as simple as what to serve guests for dinner.

While building a comprehensively, logically valid argument from the ground up can be difficult, knocking over a logical house of cards requires removing but a single component; identifying the fallacy of the undistributed middle term is a simple way to counter a deductive argument.

I have always loved the smell and taste of anchovies. When I was a child, I remember my grandmother making what, in my family, we regarded as a delicacy. She would painstakingly mix anchovies with chopped parsley and fresh garlic into a paste that she would then squeeze into the center of the largest green olives she could find at the grocery store. I always thought these stuffed olives were the most amazing combination of flavors. However, I remember when I was young I described this family tradition to my friends, they frequently told me that they disliked anchovies and the declared that the stuffed olives I claimed to enjoy so much sounded awful. I still love anchovies, and whether they are crammed into olives, distributed on my pepperoni pizza, or top my Caesar salad, they always provide a terrific flavor. In my opinion, many foods that contain anchovies are delicious foods. Of course, if I was feeling creative, I might assemble the ingredients for an apple pie, put some anchovies inside the apple pie, and bake the pie in my oven. While waiting for the aroma of baking pie to fill my kitchen, I might attempt to predict whether the pie would be delicious. I might even employ rules of logic to help me:

> Some food with anchovies is delicious food.
>
> Apple pie with anchovies is food with anchovies.
>
> Therefore, apple pie with anchovies is delicious food.

Of course, we do not need to know the rules of logic to predict that the conclusion is fatally flawed. I have never tried apple pie with anchovies, but I am certain that it must taste very bad. However, logic makes it entirely clear that this conclusion cannot be supported by the premises in my syllogism. The relationship between apple pie with anchovies and delicious food is insufficient to justify any conclusion about the two. That is because my syllogism only tells me something about some food with anchovies. Some kinds of food with anchovies, I am sure, are delicious; other kinds, like apple pie with anchovies, are not. However, unless I know about the quality of all foods with anchovies, this syllogism violates an important rule of formal logic and commits a fallacy.

Similarly, if I know that some enforceable contracts are contracts that are in writing and I know that some contracts to commit crimes are contracts that are in writing, I cannot draw any conclusions about the enforceability of contracts to commit crimes:

> Some enforceable contracts are contracts that are in writing.
>
> Some contracts to commit crimes are contracts that are in writing.
>
> Therefore, some enforceable contracts are contracts to commit crimes.

Just as the category "some food with anchovies" was not helpful to draw a logical relationship between, for example, anchovy pizza and apple pie with anchovies, the category "some contracts that are in writing" is not helpful to draw a logical relationship between enforceable contracts and contracts to commit crimes. A single rule of logic ensures that these arguments about food and the enforceability of contracts are not logically viable.

Chapter Four introduced the components of a categorical syllogism. Three propositions—a major premise, a minor premise, and conclusion—make up a categorical syllogism. Each proposition is comprised of two of the three terms in a syllogism:

a major term, a minor term and a middle term. Furthermore, each of these three terms can be either distributed or undistributed. That is, each term can ether refer to the class universally (referring to all members of the class) or particularly (referring to something fewer than all of the members of the class). However, the wrong combination of terms and distribution causes a problem. That combination is the essence of the first of the logical fallacies applicable to categorical syllogisms that this book will address: the fallacy of the undistributed middle term. Categorical syllogisms are the subject of Chapters Seven, Eight and Nine.

While assembling the components of a categorical syllogism and confirming that the components comply with the requirements of each of the rules of formal logic can be burdensome, finding fault with just one component or discovering a violation of just one logical rule is all that is required to extinguish the logical force of a deductive argument. That is the power of understanding logical fallacies. Simply identifying a fallacious pattern of unreliable argument conclusively defuses the logical force of the argument and leaves its proponent to return to the hard work of finding one alternative argument to support their conclusion.

Accordingly, while building a logically valid deductive argument from the ground up can be difficult, knocking over a logical house of cards requires removing but a single component. It is a little like finding one failed welded joint in a steel bridge. It is just one failure, but one that impairs the reliability of the entire structure. Identifying the fallacy of the undistributed middle term is a simple way to counter a deductive argument. It is simple because it only requires that you focus on one component, the middle term of a syllogism, and one quality, whether that middle term is distributed. The rule of logic at work here is: "The middle term in a categorical syllogism has to be distributed at least once." The process of finding arguments that commit this fallacy begins with finding the middle term in an argument.

7.2 Finding the Middle Term

The first[2] step in identifying arguments that commit the fallacy of the undistributed middle term is to locate the middle term in the argument structure. That requires putting the argument into the form of a syllogism, ensuring that the syllogism is in accurate and standard form: three propositions and three terms.

This does not require assembling the entire argument in a complaint, motion, or brief into its polysyllogistic form; that would be unnecessarily burdensome. Instead, the syllogistic focus can center on a particular element of a broader legal argument. Remember, formal logic focuses on the micro level, not the macro level.

2. This chapter and those that follow presume that the first rule of logic is complied with, that is, syllogistic relationship meets the basic requirements of a syllogism, with only three terms: two premises and a conclusion.

Accordingly, the process begins by focusing on a particular relationship among basic syllogistic components in an argument and evaluating them in the standard syllogistic form described in Chapter Four. One place to begin this process is by looking for the conclusion. A syllogistic conclusion contains only two terms. The subject is the minor term. The predicate is the major term. The conclusion can be arranged into one of the four standard categorical propositions:

All A are B.	Universal Affirmative
No A are B.	Universal Negative
Some A are B.	Particular Affirmative
Some A are not B.	Particular Negative

Occasionally, you will encounter an argument in which there might be more than one way of expressing the same logical relationship represented by a categorical proposition. For example, if you encounter an argument that claims some of the plaintiff's assertions are hearsay, would it be correct to interpret that as meaning some hearsay includes the plaintiff's assertions? Sometimes, rearranging a proposition results in an equivalent, valid proposition. Other times, it does not. Logic provides specific guidance for when the components of a standard categorical propositions can be exchanged. That guidance falls into three categories: *conversion*, *obversion*, and *contraposition*.

Conversion is the concept of exchanging subjects and predicates. Logicians have demonstrated that for some forms of categorical propositions this works, and for others it does not. Returning to the examples above, the following chart indicates when conversion is valid and when it is invalid.

All A are B.	All B are A.	Universal Affirmative	Invalid
No A are B.	No B are A.	Universal Negative	Valid
Some A are B.	Some B are A.	Particular Affirmative	Valid
Some A are not B.	Some B are not A.	Particular Negative	Invalid

That is, conversion is only valid for universal negative propositions and particular affirmative propositions. Attempts to convert universal negative propositions or particular affirmative propositions in this way are invalid.[3]

The next potential for reorganizing a categorical proposition is called obversion. This does not involve exchanging predicates for subjects. Instead, there are times when the quality of a proposition can be changed (from affirmative to negative, or vice versa) and the predicate term can be replaced with a complementary version

3. Irving M. Copi & Carl Cohen, Introduction to Logic 198–99 (13th ed. 2008); Patrick J. Hurley, A Concise Introduction to Logic 221–23 (2015).

of that term. For example, the complement of the term "hearsay" is "nonhearsay." Obversion is valid for all four of the standard categorical propositions.[4]

All A are B.	No A are non B.	Universal Affirmative	Valid
No A are B.	All A are non B.	Universal Negative	Valid
Some A are B.	Some A are non B.	Particular Affirmative	Valid
Some A are not B.	Some A are non B.	Particular Negative	Valid

The last form of equivalency is call contraposition. It includes elements seen in both conversion and obversion. Contraposition entails exchanging the subject and predicate terms and replacing both terms with their respective complements.[5]

All A are B.	All non B are non A.	Universal Affirmative	Valid
No A are B.	No non B are non A.	Universal Negative	Invalid
Some A are B.	Some non B are non A.	Particular Affirmative	Invalid
Some A are not B.	Some non B are not non A.	Particular Negative	Valid

Hopefully, in legal argument, it will be unusual to encounter an argument that, for example, fits into the patterns seen in obversion. However, problems of conversion are more commonly encountered. Regardless of whether the equivalency takes the form of conversion, obversion, or contraposition, one should ensure that equivalent propositions are used and that the equivalent proposition used is a valid one.

Once in standard form, the middle term is readily apparent. The middle term of a categorical syllogism is the term that appears in both the major premise and the minor premise; it does not appear in the conclusion. The middle term is the only term that appears once in both premises, if the syllogism is in correct form. The

4. Copi & Cohen, *supra* note 3, at 201; Hurley, *supra* note 3, at 223–25.
5. Copi & Cohen, *supra* note 3, at 202–04; Hurley, *supra* note 3, at 226–28.

middle term can be the subject or the predicate in the premise in which it appears.[6] For example, in the following simple arguments,[7] the middle term is highlighted.

> Every **seller of a residential property in South Dakota** is a person required to comply with the residential property disclosure requirements under South Dakota statute.
>
> The defendant was not a **seller of residential property in South Dakota**.
>
> Therefore, the defendant is not a person required to comply with the residential property disclosure requirements.

Figure 26. *An example of a legal argument taking the form of a categorical syllogism.*

> The court does not have jurisdiction over **defendants who are residents of another state**.
>
> Some of the defendants named in the complaint are **defendants who are residents of another state**.
>
> Therefore the court does not have jurisdiction over some of the defendants named in the complaint.

Figure 27. *An example of a legal argument taking the form of a categorical syllogism.*

> No **evidence regarding damages** is admissible during the liability phase of the bifurcated trial.
>
> The plaintiff's testimony regarding his extended hospitalization is **evidence regarding damages.**
>
> Therefore, the plaintiff's testimony regarding his extended hospitalization is not admissible during the liability phase of the bifurcated trial.

Figure 28. *An example of a legal argument taking the form of a categorical syllogism.*

6. *See, e.g.*, Copi & Cohen, *supra* note 3, at 227. Most of the examples in this book intentionally place the middle term as the predicate of both premises in order provide a consistent presentation of syllogistic form. However, that is not required. Logicians use the location of the middle term to more precisely describe the *figure* of the syllogism. *Id.* at 227–28.

7. Note the simple arguments that follow in Figures 14, 15, and 16 do not always appear in strict syllogistic form. This is not always required to apply the rule of logic here. The only part of the structure that needs to be revealed is the middle term and its level of distribution. Organizing ordinary English arguments into strict syllogistic form can require a lot of additional effort. Approaches to systematically translating English arguments into proper categorical forms can be found in most introductory logic texts. For one approach, see ARNOLD VANDER NAT, SIMPLE FORMAL LOGIC: WITH COMMON-SENSE SYMBOLIC TECHNIQUES 150–69 (2010).

Because making tactical use of logical fallacies begins with spotting logical fallacies in legal argument, the first order of business in logical analysis of legal argument is developing a sense of what these logical fallacies of categorical syllogisms look like in their natural habitat. Figures 26, 27, and 28 are a little bit like going to the zoo and having a friend point out the bear lounging in the back of the zoo's relatively small, artificially designed, bear habitat. They are easy to see because they are presented in an artificial context designed to ensure we notice them. Noticing a bear and cubs in the woods is a more valuable skill, but one that requires we start diligently looking for bears when we are hiking along a mountain trail, where a bear might be camouflaged by trees and shrubs. This is a more difficult task than finding bears while walking through the zoo.

Similarly, logical fallacies are not always apparent to us, in part because their argumentative context is not designed to give them away. In fact, logical fallacies can, upon casual inspection, look like legitimate, logical, persuasive arguments. However, lawyers can improve their ability to spot logical fallacies by being intentional about looking for logical patterns in legal argument. Further, the more familiar we are with the patterns of fallacious legal argument, the more efficient and consistent we become at spotting them.

Consider an argument you might encounter in a brief in support of a motion for recusal of a judge[8] and see if you can develop a methodology for spotting the middle term in the argument.

> On December 7, plaintiff's counsel conducted the deposition of Emily Rainey, a member of defendant's board of directors and the chairperson of defendant's board of directors' finance committee. During the course of the deposition, Ms. Rainey disclosed that defendant had "partnered" with the County Economic Development Commission each of the past four years at biannual workshops (the "CEDC Workshops"). Ms. Rainey indicated that she and various other members of defendant's board had worked closely with various business, education, and government leaders during the CEDC Workshops. Among those community leaders Ms. Rainey worked with was, Judge Analise Davidson, the judge presently assigned to hear this case. Ms. Rainey indicated that she had several discussions with Judge Davidson and specifically recalled a conversation she and Judge Davidson had regarding defendant and its longtime support for the efforts of the CEDC.

8. If a litigant has a concern that a judge may not be qualified to hear a case, because, for example, the judge has an interest in the outcome of the case, the judge may recuse themselves and the case can be assigned to another judge. Alternatively, where the judge does not initiate the recusal, a party may ask the court to recuse itself. For example, 28 U.S.C. § 455(b)(1) requires recusal where the presiding federal judge has "a personal bias or prejudice concerning a party, or personal knowledge of disputed evidentiary facts concerning the proceeding."

> In *In re Brody*, the court held that a judge's special relationship with persons involved who were significant participants in a case was a sufficient basis for recusal, despite a lack of evidence showing actual bias. In the present case, Judge Davidson, in her involvement with the CEDC, has a special relationship with a significant representative of defendant. Accordingly Judge Davidson clearly must be recused from hearing the instant dispute.

While one methodology for identifying the logic problem in this argument might be to comprehensively deconstruct the argument into its syllogistic components, that extensive an effort might not be required here. However, focusing on the right component is essential to expediting a logical analysis of the argument. A reading of the argument should leave us wondering if the defendant should be as confident about concluding that "Judge Davidson clearly must be recused" as it suggests. The problem with the defendant's argument lies in its middle term. Here the middle term is the term that bridges the inferential gap between the terms in the premises. The argument includes three terms: 1) judges who have special knowledge of a litigant, 2) [judges who are] Judge Davidson, 3) judges who must recuse themselves. The term "judges who have special knowledge of a litigant" is the term that the defendant wants to leverage to justify its conclusion. The argument is essentially that Judge Davidson and judges who have to be recused have something in common—they are all judges who have special knowledge of a litigant. This common category is the middle term. Seeing this example, it becomes apparent how frequently the logic of legal arguments' is found in placing people, things, and conduct into categories, and the persuasive work done by the middle term in these arguments. The middle term is the logical component that relates the case facts to the result advocated. It is the term that appears in both the major premise and the minor premise. It is the term that connects the minor term and the major term in the conclusion. We will see shortly, it is the term that effectuates the persuasive force of logic to justify the truth of the argument's conclusion in a categorical syllogism, if the form of the argument is valid.

Reducing the argument into its syllogistic structure brings the role of the middle term into sharper focus:

> Some judges who have a special relationship with a litigant are [judges who are] required to recuse themselves.
>
> Judge Davidson is a judge who has a special relationship with a litigant.
>
> Therefore, Judge Davidson is a judge who is required to recuse herself.

Figure 29. *An example of a legal argument taking the form of a categorical syllogism.*

The example helps reveal the middle term, something that might initially seem like a very technical concept of formal logic, as a practical tool for evaluating argument.

Arguments that rely on categorization, at the micro level, work by associating membership in categories with the relationship between two categories. A categorical syllogism has to have just three terms; that is a requirement of the second rule of logic discussed in Chapter Four. Accordingly, in a categorical syllogism, one term—the middle term—ensures that the connection between the other two is justified. Accordingly, the middle term plays an important role in argument. Spotting that middle term is as simple as asking, what do the terms in the conclusion have in common?

In Figure 26, "defendant" and "persons required to comply with the residential property disclosure requirements" have something in common: they are "sellers of residential property in South Dakota." In Figure 27, "some defendants named in the complaint" and "defendants the court has no jurisdiction over" have something in common: they are "defendants who are residents of another state." In Figure 28, "evidence admissible during the liability phase of a bifurcated trial" and "testimony regarding extended hospitalization" have something in common: they are "evidence regarding damages." In Figure 29, the defendant claims that Judge Davidson and judges who are required to recuse themselves have something in common: they are "judges with a special relationship with a litigant."

The argument relating to Judge Davidson in Figure 29 can be placed into a syllogistic form and has a middle term. However, it is not enough to have a middle term. The middle term has to comply with the rules of logic. From a logic perspective, there is something unpersuasive about the defendant's argument for recusal. Applying a single rule of logic is the key to understanding what essential role this middle term plays in this syllogism: "The middle term in a categorical syllogism has to be distributed at least once."

7.3 Spotting Distribution, or Lack Thereof, in the Middle Term

After identifying the middle term, the second step in using the fallacy of the undistributed middle term is applying the important logical rule that "the middle term in a categorical syllogism has to be distributed at least once."

The middle term in a categorical syllogism has to be distributed at least once.

Understanding that rule and its relationship to the fallacy of the undistributed middle term is a function of assessing the middle term's distribution. We know the middle term appears in both the major premise and the minor premise; that is one of the characteristics of the middle term. Accordingly, compliance with this rule of logic, or commission of the fallacy of the undistributed middle term, is determined by whether that middle term is distributed once, twice, or not at all. This requires understanding the logical concept of distribution and applying it to assess the middle term.

Chapter Four introduced the concept of distribution. In logic, when a term is used in a way that "refers to all of the members of the class" referenced by that term, that term is said to be distributed.[9] Conversely, if a term only refers to a portion of the members of the class, it is "undistributed."[10] Returning to the argument regarding Judge Davidson's recusal, we should be able to scrutinize the middle term, now highlighted, and assess whether it has been distributed at least once.

> Some **judges who have a special relationship with a litigant** are [judges who are] required to recuse themselves.
>
> Judge Davidson is a **judge who has a special relationship with a litigant**.
>
> Therefore, Judge Davidson is a judge who is required to recuse herself.

Figure 30. *An example of a legal argument taking the form of a categorical syllogism.*

The middle term is undistributed in the major premise: "Some judges who have a special relationship with a litigant . . . ." The word "some" makes it clear that the major premise is not referring to all judges with a special relationships with a litigant. Instead, it only refers to a part of that class of judges. Formal logic is not concerned with the exact number of judges referred to here. Even if we substituted the word "most" or "nearly all" for the word "some," the logical result would still be the same: the term is undistributed. A term is distributed or undistributed in formal logic. Accordingly, the middle term is undistributed in the major premise because the distribution of this term is express in the premise.

There is additional evidence of the middle term's undistributed quality in the major premise. The major premise fits the pattern of a particular affirmative proposition described in Chapter Four. In a particular affirmative proposition, the subject term is always undistributed. Because "some judges who have a special relationship with a litigant" is the subject term of a particular affirmative proposition, it must be undistributed.[11] However, the logical analysis should not end there; the rule says that the middle term only has to be distributed in one of the premises, not both of them. Accordingly, failure to distribute the middle term in the major premise is not fatal to the logical force of the argument unless the middle term is also undistributed in the minor premise.

However, analyzing the middle term's appearance in the minor premise confirms that the middle term is not distributed there either. The minor premise, "Judge Davidson is a judge who has a special relationship with a litigant," takes the form

9. Copi & Cohen, *supra* note 3, at 189–90; RICHARD WHATELY, ELEMENTS OF LOGIC 28 (1913); JAMES A. WINANS & WILLIAM E. UTTERBACK, ARGUMENTATION 69 (1930); NICHOLAS BUNNIN & JIYUAN YU, THE BLACKWELL DICTIONARY OF WESTERN PHILOSOPHY 188 (2004).

10. Whately, *supra* note 9 ("[a] term is said to be . . . 'undistributed,' when it stands for a portion only of the things signified by it . . . .").

11. In a particular affirmative proposition, both the subject and the predicate are undistributed.

of a universal affirmative. As we learned in Chapter Four, a universal affirmative proposition includes a distributed subject and an undistributed predicate term. Here, the middle term is the predicate term. When the subject is distributed, we usually get language cues—words like "some" or "most"—that make that clear to us. This makes it easy to spot undistributed middle terms when they are subject terms. Conversely, undistributed predicates are not always so obvious. However, if we classify the form of the proposition, that classification provides just as reliable a method for assessing distribution as seeing the word "some" would. Of course, we also can see from the language of the proposition that there is only one Judge Davidson. That reveals the subject term, Judge Davidson, is distributed. But surely the proposition is not suggesting reference to the entirely of the class of judges who have special relationships with litigants. Judge Davidson is only one judge, and there are other judges who are not Judge Davidson. The predicate refers to something less than the entire class of judges who have special relationships with litigants, and is therefore undistributed in the major premise and the minor premise. This analysis confirms that the middle term is undistributed in both premises and yields an important conclusion. The argument violates the rule of logic and commits the fallacy of the undistributed middle term.

7.4 Why an Undistributed Middle Term Makes an Argument Unpersuasive

The first time you read the argument for recusal of Judge Davidson, you might not have been persuaded that it should succeed. It is not a persuasive argument, but it does, at the very least, have the appearance of an argument and it sounds like it might be true. That is, it takes the common argumentative form of a syllogism and there is not anything in the premises that appears to be false. When a judge has a special relationship with a litigant, the judge's objectivity and disinterest is potentially in question, so we would not be surprised to learn that, in some cases, judges who know or even have a special relationship with a litigant have to recuse themselves from hearing cases which involve the litigant. Additionally, Judge Davidson knows one of the parties. There might be some question in our mind regarding just what constitutes a "special relationship" and whether Judge Davidson's limited interactions with the defendant's directors is special enough to qualify. Beyond that, there are not too many concerns with the truth of the premises.

One of the problems with fallacious arguments is not just that they are illogical, but that they frequently have the false appearance of logical appeal.[12] This similarity

12. Others have described and debated the meaning of the term fallaciousness as a philosophical definition. For a thorough discussion of the meaning of fallacy throughout the history of the philosophy of logic, see H. V. Hansen, *The Straw Thing of Fallacy Theory: The Standard Definition of 'Fallacy'*, 16 Argumentation 133 (2002). Hanson considers a variety of definitions of fallacy: "A fallacious argument, as almost every account from Aristotle onwards tells you, is one that *seems to be valid* but *is*

to persuasive, logically sound, deductive arguments is one of the risks that should motivate lawyers to be aware of the potential to be misled by fallacious arguments. However, part of the power of labeling an argument as fallacious is the persuasive force of that label. Nothing degrades the quality of an argument like labeling it as "illogical," and labeling an argument as illogical requires some justification in logic. The rules of logic provide an authoritative justification for labeling legal argument as fallacious.

There is a reason why violation of the rule makes the argument justifiably unpersuasive. Deduction makes a powerful claim. If the premises are true, then the conclusion must be true, so long as the form of the argument is valid. The rules ensure the validity of the form of the argument. The rule that the middle term be distributed in at least one premises is necessary[13] to ensure the validity of the argument's form and thereby the truth of the argument's conclusion.

Distribution of the middle term ensures that there is a certain relationship between the minor term and the major term.

Distribution of the middle term ensures that there is a certain relationship between the minor term and the major term. It ensures that we do not use a truth about a part of a category (like "some judges") in the same way we can use a truth about all of a category (like "all judges"). Judge Davidson may or may not need to recuse herself in this case. However, we can never reach a certain conclusion regarding her recusal based on what we know about "some judges." If some judges have to recuse themselves because of their special relationship with litigants, it is also true that other judges with special relationships with litigants do not have to be recused. A reasoner cannot conclude anything about Judge Davidson until we resolve that uncertainty regarding which category of judges Judge Davidson is a part of. The fallacy of the undistributed middle term ensures we are not reaching a conclusion regarding categorization without certainty regarding what category Judge Davidson falls within. Without a distributed middle term, we cannot achieve requisite certainty and the defendant will have to formulate and justify some other argument in support of its conclusion.

---

not so." Id. at 133 C.L. Hamblin, Fallacies 12 (1970)); "A *fallacious* argument in logic is an incorrect argument. It is also customary to restrict the word 'fallacious' to incorrect arguments which in certain contexts *seem* to some to be correct." *Id.* at 141 (quoting James D. Carney and Richard K. Scheer, Fundamentals of Logic 11 (2d ed. 1974)).

13. Note that complying with the rule is necessary, but not sufficient, to the logical integrity of an argument. An argument has to comply with all of the rules of categorical syllogisms before it can be entirely valid.

7.5 How Courts Have Used the Fallacy of the Undistributed Middle to Evaluate Legal Argument

The problem of legal argument taking form of the fallacy of the undistributed middle term has been described by one court as a "linguistic sleight-of-hand . . . a perennial vexation in appellate litigation."[14]

The fallacy of the undistributed middle term has been described by one court as a "linguistic sleight-of-hand . . . a perennial vexation in appellate litigation."

Accordingly, studying how courts have used the rules of logic and the fallacy of the undistributed middle term to evaluate legal argument is useful not only for seeing how the fallacy works in practical application, but how rules of logic have a place among the procedural and substantive rules more commonly associated with legal argument.[15]

One example can be found in the court's opinion in *Rushing v. Commonwealth of Virginia.*[16] *Rushing* involved a claim that an appellant in a criminal prosecution was

14. Cooper v. Singleton, 94 A.3d 250, 258 (Md. App. 2014).

15. *See, e.g.,* Spencer v. Texas, 385 U.S. 554, 578 (1967) (Warren, C.J., concurring in part and dissenting in part); Funk Bros. Seed Co. v. Kalo Inoculant Co., 333 U.S. 127, 134 (1948) (Frankfurter, J., concurring); Allied Erecting & Dismantling, Co. v. USX Corp., 249 F.3d 191, 202 & n. 1 (3d Cir. 2001); Aylett v. Sec'y of Hous. & Urban Dev., 54 F.3d 1560, 1569 (10th Cir. 1995); Hernandez v. Denton, 861 F.2d 1421, 1439 (9th Cir.1988) (Aldisert, J., concurring in part and dissenting in part), *vacated and remanded,* 493 U.S. 801 (1989); In re LF Centennial Ltd., No. 2015-1931, 2016 U.S. App. LEXIS 11854 (Fed. Cir. June 29, 2016); Infonow Corp. v. Zyme Solutions, Inc., No. 12-cv-03255-MSK-MEH, 2013 U.S. Dist. LEXIS 113324 at *10 (Aug. 6, 2013 D. Colo. 2013); McHugh v. Hillerich & Bradsby Co., No. C 07-03677 JSW, 2010 U.S. Dist. LEXIS 16164 at *9 (N.D. Cal. Feb. 24, 2010), *aff'd,* 413 F. App'x 240 (Fed. Cir. 2011); Regalado v. City of Chicago, No. 96 C 3634, 1999 U.S. Dist. LEXIS 14902, at *4 (N.D. Ill. Aug. 31, 1999); British Steel PLC v. United States, 929 F. Supp. 426, 436 n. 11 (Ct. Int'l Trade 1996); Lucas Aerospace, Ltd. v. Unison Indus., L.P., 899 F. Supp. 1268, 1287 (D. Del. 1995); Foster v. McGrail, 844 F. Supp. 16, 21 (D. Mass. 1994); Pearson v. Bowen, 648 F. Supp. 782, 792 n. 26 (N.D. Ill. 1986); United States v. Gambale, 610 F. Supp. 1515, 1525 (D. Mass. 1985); Amusement Equip., Inc. v. Mordelt, 595 F. Supp. 125, 130 n. 4 (E.D. La. 1984), *aff'd in part, rev'd in part,* 779 F.2d 264 (5th Cir. 1985); Menora v. Ill. High Sch. Ass'n, 527 F. Supp. 632, 636 (N.D. Ill. 1981); Lakeland Constr. Co. v. Operative Plasterers & Cement Masons Local No. 362, No. 79 C 3101, 1981 U.S. Dist. LEXIS 11584, at *4 (N.D. Ill. Mar. 24, 1981); PPL Corp. v. Comm'r of Internal Revenue, 135 T.C. 176, 186, 191 n. 11 (T.C. 2010); Desilu Prods., Inc. v. Comm'r of Internal Revenue, 24 T.C.M. (CCH) 1695 (T.C. 1965); Batty v. Ariz. State Dental Bd., 112 P.2d 870, 873 (Ariz. 1941); Nickolas F. v. Super. Ct., 50 Cal. Rptr. 3d 208, 222 n. 17 (Cal. Ct. App. 2006); People v. Martinez, 74 P.3d 316, 321 (Colo. 2003); Royer v. State, 389 So.2d 1007, 1016 (Fla. Dist. Ct. App. 1979); Barham v. Richard, 692 So. 2d 1357, 1359 (La. Ct. App. 1997); State v. Star Enter., 691 So.2d 1221, 1229 n. 8 (La. Ct. App. 1996); Cooper v. Singleton, 94 A.3d 250, 256–58 (Md. App. 2013); Wein v. Carey, 362 N.E.2d 587, 590–91 (N.Y. 1977); Hicks v. State, 241 S.W.3d 543, 546 (Tex. Crim. App. 2007); Rushing v. Commonwealth, 726 S.E.2d 333, 338 n.2 (Va. 2012); State v. Zespy, 723 P.2d 564, 570 n. 1 (Wyo. 1986) (Urbigkit, J., concurring in part and dissenting in part).

16. *Rushing v. Com.,* 726 S.E.2d 333 (2012), *abrogated by* Va. Code Ann. § 19.2-324.1.

a member of a "street gang" as defined by Virginia statute.[17] The appellant argued that the Commonwealth had produced insufficient evidence to prove the appellant was involved with an identifiable street gang.[18] Specifically, the appellant challenged the value of the Commonwealth's argument that because members of an alleged street gang were known to wear particular colored beads and because another person named Clark had allegedly been observed wearing the same colored beads, Clark was a member of a street gang.[19] The Virginia Supreme Court rejected any persuasive force of this argument, applying the rules of formal logic and the fallacy of the undistributed middle term as authority:

> The Commonwealth's reasoning illustrates the celebrated fallacy of the undistributed middle term in Aristotelian Logic. In the syllogism: "All gang members wear beads; Clark wears beads; therefore Clark is a gang member," the conclusion is fallacious because it does not account for those who wear beads who are not gang members. Some may wear them because they wish to become or be perceived as members, or for protection from members, or because they are enemies or even law enforcement officers seeking to infiltrate the gang, or because they simply like beads.[20]

The court's use of the fallacy of the undisturbed middle term illustrates how utilizing formal logic can be effective in legal argument. The court's explanation is efficient, authoritative, and provides a sound justification for why the Commonwealth's legal argument was not persuasive. Legal argument sometimes focuses on issues other than the application of legal rules to facts. *Rushing* illustrates an instance of that kind of legal reasoning and the usefulness of formal logic for disciplining the process of argument in such circumstances. If wearing beads is sufficient evidence to prove membership in a street gang, evaluating the relationship between a person, the beads they wear, and indicia of street gang membership is not a process that requires

---

17. *Id.* at 277–78. The description of facts comes from the court's opinion which begins by stating that they were described "in the light most favorable to the Commonwealth." The court framed the issues on appeal by first describing the Commonwealth's burden to establish four elements:

> The Commonwealth, therefore, had the burden of proving, beyond a reasonable doubt, that (1) [appellant] had committed a "predicate criminal act," (2) that [an alleged street gang] existed as an identifiable street gang, (3) that [an alleged street gang] was a criminal street gang because its *members* had committed two or more "predicate criminal acts," at least one of which was a crime of violence, and (4) that [appellant] committed his "predicate criminal act" as a member of or active participant with the gang.

Id.

18. *Id.* at 278.

19. *Id.*

20. *Id.* at 278, n. 2 (citing *Spencer v. Texas*, 385 U.S. 554, 578–79 (1967) (Warren, C.J., dissenting), and *Allied Erecting & Dismantling Co. v. USX Corp.*, 249 F.3d 191, 202 n. 1 (3d Cir. 2001).

the application of a legal rule to case facts.[21] While legal argument frequently features a legal rule as the major premise, sometimes, the major premise is some other general principal. Here, the proffered major premise might be described as "some persons who wear particular beads are members of a street gang."

Formal logic can provide a useful framework for making and responding to fact-centered arguments that do not fit within the traditional IRAC framework for legal argument.

In addition to serving as an example of the fallacy of the undistributed middle term as a tool for legal argument, the case illustrates how formal logic can provide a useful framework for making and responding to arguments that do not fit within the traditional IRAC framework.[22] Here, the focus of the argument is at the micro level, on an issue that is not the typical application of law to fact that lawyers are so comfortable with. The focus of the argument is, instead, on a purely factual proof matter, where the traditional tools for argument and persuasion are less structured and well-defined as IRAC. Additionally, it presents an example of a case where the court rested its decision, not on the application of a specific rule of law, but instead on the application of a specific rule of logic.

The court in *Infonow Corp. v. Zyme Solutions, Inc.*[23] also used the fallacy of the undistributed middle term as a tool for policing legal argument and explaining

---

21. The conclusion arrived at in a purely fact-based argument generally has a place in another syllogism, where a legal rule supplies the major premise.

22. A similar pattern of reasoning toward a factual conclusion is found in *Evans v. State*, 26 So.3d 85 (Fla. Dist. Ct. App. 2010). In *Evans* the court also used the Fallacy of the Undistributed Middle to evaluate the prosecution's evidentiary argument:

> However, the State's reliance on the gloves is an example of the logical fallacy of the undistributed middle. Presented in the form of a syllogism, the State's argument was as follows: 1. Drug distributors wear latex gloves. 2. Mr. Evans was wearing latex gloves. 3. Therefore, Mr. Evans was a drug distributor. Even if all drug distributors wear latex gloves to protect themselves and their merchandise, most people who wear latex gloves are not drug distributors. Many people wear latex gloves for legitimate purposes, e.g., food preparation, cleaning, and rendering medical and dental services. Law enforcement officers and other persons engaged in forensic work frequently wear latex gloves to avoid contaminating a crime scene. Clearly, the jury's verdict finding Mr. Evans guilty of trafficking in cocaine could not have been reached without resort to a pyramiding of inferences.

Id. at 95–96. *See also* Royer v. State, 389 So.2d 1007, 1016 (Fla. Dist. Ct. App. 1979) *aff'd*, 460 U.S. 491 (1983) ("It may be fairly said as to all of the officers' bases of 'suspicion' that, although they may indeed be characteristic of those who carry narcotics, they are at least equally, and usually far more frequently, consistent with complete innocence. The fallacy of the undistributed middle directly applies: all narcotics couriers act like parts of the profile, but most people who act like parts of the profile are not narcotics couriers.").

23. Infonow Corp. v. Zyme Solutions, Inc., 2013 U.S. Dist. LEXIS 113324 (D. Colo. Aug. 6, 2013).

logical form in its opinion. This time, the fallacy had a place in the application of a jurisdictional issue. The issue in *Infonow Corp.* was whether the court had jurisdiction over the defendant, who moved to dismiss the complaint, arguing that it lacked sufficient contacts with the State of Colorado to fall within the jurisdiction of the United States District Court there.[24] One argument advanced in the case was that the defendant's alleged business transactions with Best Buy, a company which has locations in Colorado, created sufficient contacts with the state to create jurisdiction over defendant there. The court rejected the plaintiff's argument as insufficient to support a conclusion that the defendant had sufficient contacts with Colorado to create jurisdiction stating: "Thus, the mere fact that [defendant] may have contacts with a company like Best Buy, and that Best Buy has locations in Colorado, does not mean that [defendant] necessarily has contacts with the State of Colorado."[25] The court justified this conclusion, using the fallacy of the undistributed middle term:

> Practitioners of logic will recognize this as the fallacy of the undistributed middle term. To be a valid statement, one would have to include the premise that "contacts with Best Buy constitute contacts with all of Best Buy's locations." Needless to say, nothing in the law or the record supports such a proposition.[26]

The argument as described by the court in *Infonow Corp.* might be placed into the following syllogistic form:

> The defendant is a person with contacts with Best Buy locations.
>
> Some people with contacts with Best Buy locations are people with contacts with the State of Colorado.
>
> Therefore, the defendant is a person with contacts with locations in the State of Colorado.

The middle term, persons with contacts with Best Buy locations, is the term appearing in both the major premise and the minor premise. It is the term that links the minor and major terms in the conclusion. The essence of the plaintiff's argument is that the defendant's relationship to Best Buy is what justifies the defendant's relationship to Colorado. The rule of logic in play here requires that the middle term be distributed at least once. The major premise is a universal affirmative. A universal affirmative proposition distributes the subject but not the predicate. The middle term is the predicate of the major premise. Accordingly, the middle term in the major premise is undistributed. The minor premise is a particular affirmative. A particular affirmative proposition distributes neither

24. *Id.* at *1.
25. *Id.* at *3.
26. *Id.* n. 3.

the subject nor the predicate. Accordingly, the middle term is undistributed in the minor premise as well. Accordingly, the court concluded that the argument committed the fallacy of the undistributed middle term.[27]

Another example of a court using the logical fallacy of the undistributed middle term to decide a legal issue is seen in *Grand Victoria Casino & Resort, L.P. v. Indiana Department of State*,[28] involving a state tax dispute. Grand Victoria Casino & Resort claimed it was exempt from state use tax on the purchase of a riverboat used as a riverboat casino.[29] One of the issues in *Grand Victoria Casino & Resort* was whether the riverboat fit the definition of "motorboat" under the Indiana Code.[30]

Indiana Code Section 9-31-3-1, states: "[E]very motorboat principally used on the waters of Indiana must be registered [with the Bureau of Motor Vehicles] and numbered."[31] The Indiana Department of State argued that because riverboats are watercraft and motorboats are watercraft, then riverboat were motorboats required to register with the Bureau of Motor Vehicles.[32] The court rejected this argument as "fall[ing] prey to the fallacy of the undistributed middle." The court summarized the Department's argument in its syllogistic form: "the Department argues that

27. Notably, courts, like the court in *Infonow Corp.*, do not always reveal all of the details of their specific logical basis for their conclusion when deciding a case on a basis of formal logic. *See, e.g.*, PPL *Corp. v. C.I.R.*, 135 T.C. 176, 186 (2010) ("The middle term is the one (the sale of an electric service) that appears in both the major (first) and minor (second) premises. It is undistributed because neither premise describes *every* sale of an electric service; rather, the premises describe subsets of those sales that do not necessarily coincide. Therefore, the middle term fails to connect the sale of street and area lighting to the sale of electricity; both kinds of sales could separately constitute sales of electric services.") (emphasis in original); McHugh v. Hillerich & Bradsby Co., 2010 U.S. Dist. LEXIS 16164 at *9 (N.D. Cal. Feb. 24, 2010), *aff'd*, 413 F. App'x 240 (Fed. Cir. 2011) ("McHugh concludes that, because both the Bionic finger pads and the proximal digital crease of the user's hand are located in the proximal phalanx A2 pulley region, the pads must be located in the proximal digital crease of the user's hand. Accordingly, McHugh argues that, under the Court's claim construction, the pads are located 'in a gap between a palm of the user's hand and the base of the user's fingers.' Such logic is unsound because it parallels the classic fallacy of the undistributed middle."); Wein v. Carey, 41 N.Y.2d 498, 503, 362 N.E.2d 587, 590-91 (1977) ("His syllogism is simple but mistaken. It is, in effect, that a planned deficit is unconstitutional (which it is); that two successive annual deficits occurred (which is true); and, therefore, that there must have been a planned deficit (which results in a classic example of the fallacy of the undistributed middle term). On the basis of this disjointed syllogism, he argues, therefore, that the anticipation notes of 1976–1977 were invalid, and, to make matters worse, by implication and necessary consequence from the relief he seeks, that the plan to issue more anticipation notes in 1977–1978 would be an ill-disguised 'rollover' or unconstitutional refinancing of a planned deficit.").

28. 789 N.E.2d 1041 (Ind. Tax. 2003).

29. *Id.*

30. *Id.* at 1047.

31. *Id.* at 1048 (quoting Ind. Code § 9-31-3-1 (1998)).

32. *Id.*

(1) riverboats are watercraft, (2) motorboats are watercraft, therefore, (3) riverboats are motorboats and, thus, the registration requirements apply."[33]

The fallacy becomes clear when we more specifically identify the components of this syllogism. In the major premise "riverboats are watercraft," the term "watercraft" is not distributed. "Watercraft" as used in this premise is not universal. It is not referring to all watercraft. Some riverboats are watercraft, but not all watercraft are riverboats. To the contrary, a riverboat is just one example, one particular subset of all of the watercraft.

Similarly, in the minor premise "motorboats are watercraft," the term "watercraft" is not distributed. Here, the term "watercraft," as in the major premise, does not describe all watercraft. Instead, it merely refers to another subset of the universe of all watercraft. The court recognized this, stating: "the Department's argument falls prey to the fallacy of the undistributed middle. 'The nature of this fallacy becomes more obvious in the following example: Cats are mammals. Dogs are mammals. Therefore, cats are dogs.'"[34]

Like *Grand Victoria Casino & Resort, Hoatson v. New York Archdiocese*[35] is another decision that employed the fallacy of the undistributed middle to evaluate the parties' arguments. The plaintiff, in *Hoatson*, argued for recusal of the trial court judge. One basis for recusal argued by the plaintiff was the trial court judge's alleged relationship with the mayor of New York City. The plaintiff claimed that the trial judge had known the mayor during the mayor's first term in office. Additionally, plaintiff claimed that the mayor knew an employee of the defendant archdiocese, the monsignor.[36] Because

---

33. *Id.* Another way to present this argument is to say:

> All riverboats are watercraft.
>
> All motorboats are watercraft.
>
> Therefore, all riverboats are motorboats.

Both premises are universal affirmatives, so regardless of whether the *subject* term is distributed, the *predicate* term must be undistributed. Since the predicate term, "watercraft" is the middle term, the form of the syllogism is one where the middle term is undistributed in both premises, and therefore violates the rule of logic that requires that term be distributed at least once.

34. *Id.* at 1048, n. 10 (quoting State v. Star Enter., 691 So.2d 1221, 1229 n. 8 (La. App. 4 Cir. 1996)). Note that while the this example syllogism described by the court is patently illogical, explaining why, in terms of syllogistic logic this is so requires some understanding of the nature of distribution. Both premises refer to the subject terms universally, but not the predicate terms. Universal affirmative propositions distribute the subject, but not the predicate term. *See also* Amusement Equip., Inc. v. Mordelt, 595 F. Supp. 125, 131, n. 4 (E.D. La. 1984), *aff'd in part, rev'd in part,* 779 F.2d 264 (5th Cir. 1985) ("It is easy to see why this syllogism is invalid. Both dogs and cats are members of the larger class of mammals. This does not mean, however, that the class of dogs is identical to, or even overlaps with, the class of cats.").

35. 2006 U.S. Dist. LEXIS 87877 (S.D.N.Y. Dec. 1, 2006).

36. The court observed that the plaintiff was publicly critical of the Monsignor prior to this suit against the New York Archdiocese. *Id.* at *28.

both the mayor and the monsignor were alleged to have had a common acquaintance in the trial court judge, the plaintiff argued that the trial court judge should recuse himself.

The court held that the plaintiff's argument suffered from the fallacy of the undistributed middle term. While the argument, as described in the court's opinion, does not seem to fit neatly into a syllogism, a little analysis of the basic components of the plaintiff's argument reveals the argument's syllogistic form. In essence, the plaintiff's argument is this:

> The judge is a friend of the mayor.
>
> The monsignor is a friend of the mayor.
>
> Therefore, the monsignor is a friend of the judge.[37]

The middle term appears in both the major and minor premises: "[persons who are] friend[s] of the mayor." Indeed, it is undistributed in both the major premise and the minor premise. Neither the trial court judge nor the monsignor encompassed the totality of the mayor's set of friends. If the mayor truly counted either of these men as a friend, either would be but a single representative of a larger set. Of course, from this we cannot draw any conclusions about the relationship between the judge and the monsignor. Accordingly, the court recognized the existence of fallacy in the logical structure of the argument.[38]

While the argument is fallacious, this infirmity only demonstrates that the form of the argument is logically invalid. The fallacious nature of the argument does not require the negation of its proffered conclusion, i.e., that the monsignor was no friend of the trial judge.[39] However, if the plaintiff were to prove his intended conclusion, he would have to develop some other logically valid argument to do it.

Similarly, *Graceland College Center for Professional Development and Life-Long Learning, Inc. v. Kansas Department of Labor*[40] involved a labor dispute between an employer and its former employee. The opinion reports that the employee in that case worked for her employer for two years. At the time she left her employment, she had accrued hourly wages, vacation time, and sick pay. She had also

---

37. *Id.*

38. *Id.* at p. 7.

39. Ruggero J. Aldisert, Logic for Lawyers, A Guide to Clear Thinking 68–69 (3d ed. 1997) ("The validity of a syllogism and the validity of the argument's structure deal only with the relations between the premises. Validity deals only with form. It has absolutely nothing to do with content. Arguments, therefore, may be logically valid, yet nonsensical. Assuming valid form, the essence of argument must always be a search for the truth or falsity of the premises . . . . Once this determination is made in constructing the premise in a deductive syllogism, however, we do not say that the conclusion probably will follow; the conclusion must follow.").

40. Graceland College Center for Professional Development and Life-Long Learning, Inc. v. Kansas Department of Labor, 131 P.3d 1281 (Table), 2006 Kan. App. Unpub. LEXIS 1030 (Kan. Ct. App. Apr. 14, 2006).

accrued prepaid commissions that the employer claimed she had not earned.[41] The employer offset the employee's accrued hourly wages[42] against the employee's prepaid commissions.[43]

One issue in the case was whether these accrued hourly wages, vacation time, and sick pay constituted "wages" or "commissions." The employer's policy provided that "[p]rograms that are not paid in full at the time of separation will be debited from [the employee's] final commissions."[44] The employer argued that the definition of the word "commissions" in this policy must be read in light of a Kansas statute that defines "wages" as "compensation for labor or services rendered by an employee, whether the amount is determined on a time, task, piece, commission or other basis."[45] The court here concluded that the employer's argument suffered from an undistributed middle.[46]

The court described the fallacy in the claimant's argument this way:

> Apparently, the logic is that, because the term "wages" includes hourly wages and commissions, then the term "commissions" must include hourly wages. If the argument were to be structured as a categorical syllogism, it would be stated as: hourly wages are wages; commissions are wages; therefore commissions are hourly wages. The conclusion is deductively invalid for violating the fallacy of the undistributed middle, i.e., hourly wages and commissions are subsets of the general wages category but the subsets do not necessarily overlap. By analogy, a contract to purchase all of a neighbor's cows does not entitle the buyer to purchase the neighbor's horses, even though the statutory definition of "domestic animals" in K.S.A. 60-4001(b) includes, inter alia, both cows and horses.[47]

The court considered the syllogism and identified the fallacy of the undistributed middle term in claimant's argument:

> All hourly wages are wages.
>
> All commissions are wages.
>
> Therefore, all commissions are hourly wages.

---

41. *Id.*
42. While the court referred to "hourly wages," the offset was made as to hourly wages, vacation time, and sick pay. *Id.* at *1.
43. *Id.* at *1.
44. *Id.*
45. *Id.* at *12.
46. *Id.* at *12–13.
47. *Id.*

Once again, the middle term, "wages," is undistributed in both premises.[48] Because the middle term is not distributed in at least one premise, it committed the fallacy of the undistributed middle term, and the court rejected the argument as a result.

Another case, *Aylett v. Secretary of Housing and Urban Development*,[49] involved the Secretary of Housing and Urban Development's decision overturning the findings of an administrative law judge's (the "ALJ") decision. The court's opinion in *Aylett* explains that the defendant Secretary of Housing and Urban Development's designee (the "HUD Designee") decided to find the claimant's testimony more credible than the testimony of the respondent. Here, Judge Ruggaro J. Aldisert,[50] writing for the court, held that the HUD Designee committed an "egregious" error of logic.[51]

According to the court, the HUD Designee "credited the testimony of [the intervenor], who had a profound personal financial stake in the outcome of this case, quantified at the final hearing to the tune of $100,000." However, the court observed that the HUD Designee also "corrected the ALJ for crediting [the respondent's] testimony" because the respondent had "a personal stake in the outcome of this litigation." The court recognized that "the reviewing officer cannot have it both ways. When it comes to finding credibility, he cannot fault [the respondent] for having a personal stake because of his relationship to his parents and ignore the personal stake of [the intervenor]."[52]

The court held that by "having it both ways," the HUD designee had "committed the formal fallacy of the undistributed middle." The court went on to explain that the applicable rule of logic

> provides that the middle term (the subject of the major premise and usually the predicate of the minor premise) must be distributed in at least one premise, that is to say, the term must be broad or general: If narrow or particular, it is called "undistributed." It is

48. Like the argument in *Grand Victoria Casino & Resort, L.P., Hoatson v. New York Archdiocese*, the argument here consists of two universal affirmative propositions. Since universal affirmatives do not distribute the predicate term, neither occurrence of the predicate middle term, "wages," is distributed.
49. *Aylett v. Secretary of Housing and Urban Development*, 54 F.3d 1560 C.A.10, 1995.
50. Ruggero J. Aldisert, Senior Judge for the United States Court of Appeals for the Third Circuit, sitting by designation. Judge Aldisert wrote several opinions discussing faulty logic in legal argument. He authored two other works specifically addressing formal logic in legal reasoning: Ruggero J. Aldisert, Logic for Lawyers, A Guide to Clear Thinking 68 (3d ed. 1997), and *Logic for Law Students: How to Think Like a Lawyer*, 69 U. Pitt. L. Rev. 1 (2007), in addition to several other books focusing on the judicial process.
51. Aylett v. Secretary of Housing and Urban Development, 54 F.3d 1560, 1596 (10th Cir. 1995) (citing Irving Copi, Introduction To Logic 219 (7th ed. 1986)).
52. *Id.*

> distributed only when the major and minor terms can be connected through or by means of the middle term, and for the two terms that become part of the conclusion to be reached (minor and major) to be connected through a third, at least one of the two must be related to the whole of the class designated by the third or middle term.[53]

The court went on to put the argument in syllogistic form, starting with the major premise and focusing on the middle term:

> "*Some* persons who have a personal stake are not credible." When an undistributed middle term is present, the conclusion cannot be justified: this is the fallacy of the undistributed middle. With respect to this stated reason for rejecting the credibility of [the respondent], the reviewing officer's reasons lack formal, valid or cogent logical support.[54]

The opinion suggests the following syllogism representing the HUD designee's reasoning:

> Some persons who have a personal stake in litigation are persons who are not credible.
>
> The respondent is a person who has a personal stake in this litigation.
>
> Therefore, the respondent is a person who is not credible.

The middle term is "persons who have a personal stake in litigation." The term is distributed in neither the major nor the minor premise.[55] The court explained that, changing the word "some" to "all" in the major premise would have a dramatic impact on the validity of the form of the argument. "All persons who have a personal stake in litigation are not credible" would distribute the middle term "persons who have a personal stake in litigation."[56] However, because "some" indicates an undistributed middle term, the argument was logically fallacious.[57]

In *Atlantic Aluminum & Metal Distributors v. United States*,[58] the plaintiff was an importer of extruded aluminum tubes. The issue in the case was whether the tubes fell within the definition of the words "rods" or "bars" as used in paragraph 397 of the 1930 Tariff Act.[59] The United States claimed that the extruded aluminum tubes

53. *Id.*
54. *Id.* (emphasis in original).
55. *Id.*
56. While the logical form of the syllogism would no longer suffer from an undistributed middle, the major premise would be false. While a witness with a personal stake in litigation may have their credibility scrutinized, their personal stake does not necessarily require that their testimony be incredible.
57. Aylett v. Secretary of Housing and Urban Development, 54 F.3d 1560, 1569 (10th Cir. 1995).
58. 47 C.C.P.A. 88, 89 (Cust. & Pat. App. 1960).
59. 19 U.S.C.A. § 1001, par. 397, as modified by T.D. 51802.

at issue were neither bars nor rods, and therefore fell outside of the definition in this section. Accordingly, the issue in the case was whether the hollow aluminum tubes constituted "bars" or "rods" or neither. In analyzing this issue, the plaintiff argued that the aluminum tubes were "hollow bars" and "hollow rods" and that therefore the tubes fell within the common meaning of "bars" and "rods."[60] In an attempt to bolster this argument, the plaintiff relied upon various dictionary definitions of the words "bars" and "rods." Examples of the respective definitions included:

> The present record contains definitions from various lexicons introduced to show the common meaning of the terms "bars" and "rods."
>
> bar 1. A piece of wood, metal or other material, long in proportion to its breadth and thickness, and having, in general, considerable rigidity, such as one used for a lever, support, hindrance, obstruction, fastening, etc. * * *3. A piece of some substance, of indefinite size, shaped so as to be long in proportion to its breadth and thickness; * * *
>
> rod 1. A straight or slender stick; a wand; hence, any slender bar, as of wood or metal.[61]

The court held that the definitions established

> that a bar or a rod is "long in proportion to its breadth and thickness" and that the evidence established that the tubes at issue were "long in proportion to [their] breadth[s] and thickness[es]." From these premises the importer argued for the court to conclude that "tubes are bars and rods." The court rejected the argument finding that the argument "constitutes an invalid syllogism.[62]

The court appears to have construed plaintiff's argument to take the following syllogistic form:

> Aluminum tubes are objects that are long in proportion to their breadth and thickness.
>
> Bars and rods are objects that are long in proportion to their breadth and thickness.
>
> Therefore, aluminum tubes are bars and rods.[63]

60. 47 C.C.P.A. 88, 90 (1960).
61. *Id.*
62. *Id.*
63. *Id.*

The court found that this argument's middle term was undistributed:

> The undistributed middle term prevents reliance upon the premises to support the importer's conclusion. If we were to agree with this argument, we would then be required logically to hold that every item having length would be a rod or bar, since every item having length is, by definition, long in proportion to its breadth and thickness.[64]

7.6 Keys to Using the Fallacy of the Undistributed Middle to Evaluate and Improve Legal Argument

These cases illustrate the two methodologies suggested in Chapter Four for assessing argument for commission of the fallacy of the undistributed middle term. First, one can focus on the logic inference in question, reduce it to syllogistic form, and test it against a logical rule to see if it applies. For example, in *Grand Victoria Casino & Resort, L.P. v. Indiana Department of State*,[65] a case discussed above in section 7.5, the court considered the following syllogism:

> All riverboats are watercraft.
>
> All motorboats are watercraft.
>
> Therefore, all riverboats are motorboats.

The court determined that the middle term was undistributed in both premises. Each of the premises takes to form of a universal affirmative, which means the subject is distributed and the predicate is not. Since the middle term is the predicate of each premise, it is not distributed in either premise and commits the fallacy of the undistributed middle term.

Another way to think about this logical error is by looking for fallacious patterns that can be described as committing the fallacy of the undistributed middle term.

64. *Id.* at 2. Another example of legal arguments revolving around the construction of language, this time contractual rather than statutory, can be found in *Ruede v. City of Florence*, 220 P.3d 113 (2009).
65. 789 N.E.2d 1041 (Ind. Tax. 2003).

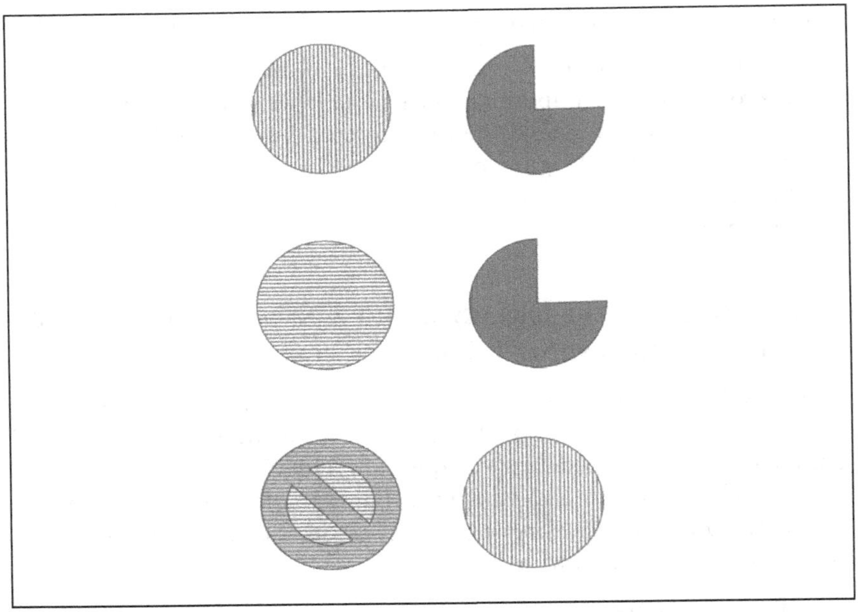

Figure 31. *An example of one fallacious pattern of categorical syllogism called the fallacy of the undistributed middle term.*

There are three shapes in Figure 31; each shape occurs twice. The shape with the vertical lines represents the major term. The shape with the horizontal lines represents the minor term. We will expect to see those shapes in the conclusion. The shapes with no lines are represent the middle term. It is not a term that will be found in the conclusion. For purposes of identifying the fallacy of the undistributed middle term, our focus and be on the two shapes in the premise representing this middle term. It is, however, the term that allows us to reach a logical inference regarding the major and minor term. When the term is represented by a complete circle, it is representing a distributed term. When the term is represented by a partial circle, it is representing an undistributed term. When a shape has a "no" symbol on it, it indicates a negative premise, where one term is excluded from the other.[66] Accordingly, the top line Figure 31 is a graphical depiction of a major premise with a distributed major term and an undistributed middle term. The second line depicts a distributed minor term and an undistributed middle term. The third line depicts a negative conclusion including a distributed minor term and a distributed major term. Graphically, this depiction illustrates the terms and distributions in the

66. For example, "no parol evidence is evidence admissible to contradict the terms of a completely integrated contract" and "some out of court statements are not hearsay" are two examples of negative premises where one term is excluded from another. The first example is a universal negative. The second example is a particular negative. In the first, parol evidence is excluded from the term "evidence admissible to contradict the terms of a completely integrated agreement." In the second example, some out of course statements are excluded from the term "[statements that are] hearsay."

riverboats and motorboats argument described in *Grand Victoria Casino & Resort, L.P. v. Indiana Department of State.*[67] The middle term was undistributed in both premises and commits the fallacy of the undistributed middle term.

If we are searching for argumentative patterns that are hallmarks of this fallacy and we can identify the middle term, we do not even need to look for such complex patterns of shapes and lines. Instead, we can simply focus on the shapes representing the middle terms.

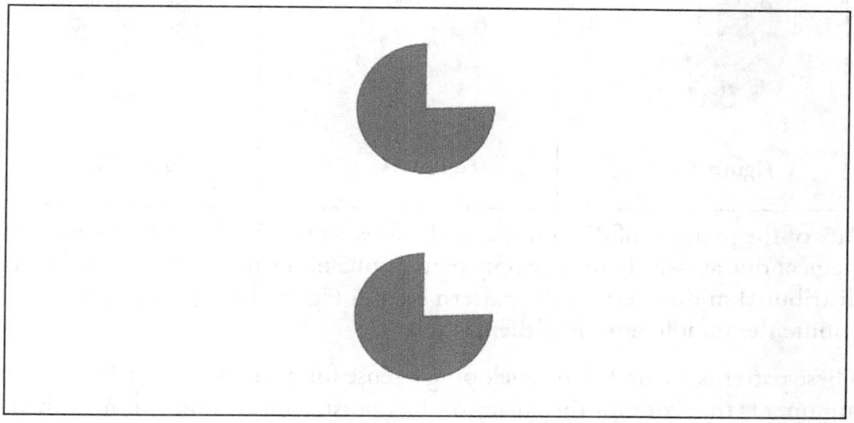

Figure 32. *The example of the pattern of two undistributed middle terms, as seen in the major and minor premises of Figure 31.*

Figure 32 depicts the distribution of the middle term in the riverboats and motorboats argument from *Grand Victoria Casino & Resort*. Once we become adept at determining the middle term, the term that supports and inference between the major and minor terms, we can simply focus on the nature of that relationship and whether it is distributed in a way that ensures that the proffered inference is true. Importantly, any combination that does not include at least one complete circle will fail the test of the rule of logic and commit the fallacy of the undistributed middle term.

67. The pattern seen in Figure 19 is consistent with the pattern seen in *Rushing, Grand Victoria Casino & Resort, L.P., Graceland College Center for Professional Development and Life-Long Learning, Inc.*, and *Atlantic Aluminum & Metal Distributors*. While *Infonow Corp., Aylett* take a slightly different syllogistic pattern from those cases, the difference is in the distribution of minor and major terms, not the middle terms, and they still commit the fallacy of the undistributed middle term.

Figure 33.

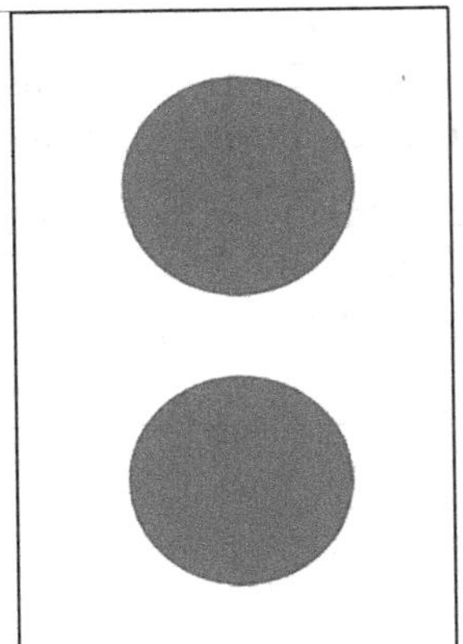

Figure 34.

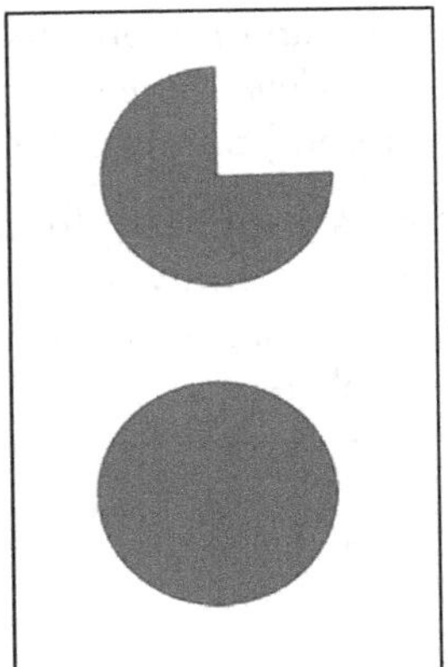

Figure 35.

Any of the patterns of distribution in Figures 33 to 35 will be sufficient to satisfy the logical rule at issue here. The only pattern one needs to identify the fallacy of the undistributed middle term is the pattern seen in Figure 32, representing a failure to distribute the middle term in either premise.

These patterns are useful in developing a sense for what logical weaknesses underlie arguments that commit the fallacy of the undistributed middle term at the micro level. However, other patterns in these arguments can serve as red flags for this fallacy, and that should make us look more specifically for this logical weakness at the more abstract macro level of argument. We see from the cases discussed above that at least two general types of argument that are commonly made in briefs and courtroom arguments commit this fallacy—first, cases in which the arguer treats a particular middle term as though it was a universal. For example:

> Eyewitnesses who are not paying complete attention to the scene of the crime make errors in recalling the details of the crime. The prosecution's witness, Mr. Hudson, admitted that when he saw the perpetrator at the gas station drive away, Mr. Hudson was in the process of retrieving his wallet from his own vehicle. Mr. Hudson wasn't focused on the scene of the crime; he was focused on his wallet. The witness was not paying complete attention to the scene of the crime. Therefore, he cannot be relied upon to identify the person who committed this crime. He simply, by his own admission, wasn't paying attention.

The logical essence of this argument is an effort to relate two categories of people: Mr. Hudson and people who make errors in reporting their eyewitness accounts. The arguer attempts to do this with a middle term: "eyewitnesses who are not paying complete attention to the scene of the crime." Of course, this may be a true premise as it applies to particular eyewitnesses. While the word "some" is not included in the statement, it can fairly be implied. The defense attorney here is arguing that the conclusion's categorization of Mr. Hudson as an unreliable witness is justified by his inclusion in the term "some eyewitnesses who are not paying complete attention to the scene of the crime." The problem is the middle term is particular, not universal. It is unclear how many people fit into that category. Surely some inattentive eyewitnesses are not accurate or reliable reporters of what they have seen. However, others report observed crimes very accurately, even when they are fumbling for their wallets. Because the term is undistributed throughout the argument, it cannot lead us to a certain conclusion. Accordingly, at a macro level, one pattern of argument to look for in spotting the fallacy of the undistributed middle term, is the pattern of argument that uses undistributed categories (references to some, or a few, or even most) to justify a conclusion about two other terms. Arguments like this cannot justify a deductive conclusion because they do not comply with the rules of logic.

Just as argument about the facts can commit the fallacy of the undistributed middle term, treating a rule of law like a universal when it has some exceptions (as they frequently do) is another pattern to look for. Of course, advocates who base their arguments on a general rule of law focus on the general rule because it supports their conclusion. Further, these advocates deflect attention away from the exceptions to the rule that might apply. For example:

> Contracts for the sale of goods of $500 or more must be in writing or they are unenforceable. The alleged contract between the parties for the defendant to pay $34,000 for the aluminum flashing sold by the plaintiff is a contract for the sale of goods in an amount of $500 or more. Because the contract is not in writing, it is certainly unenforceable.

The argument suggests that the instant contract is one that is an unenforceable oral agreement. It argues for this logical inference based on a middle term: "contracts for the sale of goods for $500 or more." However, not all contracts for the sale of goods for $500 or more require a writing. The advocate has accurately stated the general rule, but ignored the some exceptions to the rule.[68] For example, if a party admits in a pleading that the contract was made, the contract is still enforceable, even when not memorialized in writing.[69] One might respond to this argument by saying that the major premise is simply untrue because it is incomplete and omits mention of an applicable exception. Further, if the major premise is revised to accurately reflect the general rule and its exceptions, it makes the advocate's proffered conclusion anything but certain. The argument's logical form is undoubtedly fallacious and necessarily illogical. The term "contracts for the sale of goods for $500 or more" is the middle term, and the law makes clear that the rule applies to some, not all, such contracts. Because the terms describe only a particular subset of contracts for the sale of goods for $500 or more, it is an undistributed middle term.[70] Logic provides a persuasive label, and even a well-defined method for justifying the label—important tools in making convincing argument. We do not always have good ways to explain why an advocate's overstatement of the scope of a promise is illogical (possibly even wrongful), without some structure and methodology to do that. Logic provides such a structure.[71]

7.7 Chapter Seven in Review

- The middle term in an argument is an important logical component. It is the concept that justifies a relationship between the two terms in the conclusion.

---

68. Section 2-201 of the Uniform Commercial Code, which governs contracts for the sale of goods, provides:

> Except as otherwise provided in this section a contract for the sale of goods for the price of $500 or more is not enforceable by way of action or defense unless there is some writing sufficient to indicate that a contract for sale has been made between the parties and signed by the party against whom enforcement is sought or by his authorized agent or broker. A writing is not insufficient because it omits or incorrectly states a term agreed upon but the contract is not enforceable under this paragraph beyond the quantity of goods shown in such writing.

However, there are exceptions to this rule found in the balance of the section. First, between merchants, a party can provide a sufficient written confirmation of the contract. U.C.C. 2-201(2). If the written confirmation and the circumstances surrounding the provision of the written confirmation meet the requirements of 2-201(2), the writing requirement is satisfied, unless the recipient of the writing timely objects. *Id.* Second, an exception exists for "specially manufactured" goods. U.C.C. 2-201(3)(a). Third, an exception exists where the party makes an admission that the contract was made in a "pleading." U.C.C. 2-201(3)(b). Fourth, an exception exits for "goods for which payment has been made and accepted or which have been received and accepted." U.C.C. 2-201(3)(c).

69. *Id.*

70. The advocate could fix this logic problem by revising the middle term to be a distributed one. For example, changing the middle term to: "all contracts for the sale of goods of $500 or more that do not fit into one of the exceptions found in U.C.C. 2-201" would be a distributed middle term, and the form of the syllogism would be valid. Then the argument would focus on the minor term, and whether the contract at issue fit into that newly, narrowly defined, universal term.

71. Some of the ideas developed in this chapter were first explored in Stephen M. Rice, *Indispensable Logic: Using the Logical Fallacy of the Undistributed Middle as a Litigation Tool*, 79 Miss. L. J. 699 (2010).

- The middle term's role is important and has to play by a specific rule to justify the conclusion. That rule requires that the middle term be distributed at least once in either of the two premises, or in both of them.
- Sometimes determining distribution is easy—for example, when the proposition refers to "all" or "some" of a term. The distribution of those terms is apparent from the words used to describe them. Other times, distribution is not so obvious and we may need to think about the argument in syllogistic form to determine distribution. However, whenever a term is not referred to universally, it is undistributed.
- If the middle term is not distributed in either or both premises, the argument commits the fallacy of the undistributed middle term.
- Courts have encountered arguments that commit the fallacy of the undistributed middle term and dealt with those arguments using formal logic.
- One way to spot the fallacy of the undistributed middle term is to look for patterns of argument featuring exclusively undistributed middle terms.
- At the macro level, one of the hallmarks of legal argument that commits the fallacy of the undistributed middle term basing a conclusion on a truth about a part of a category. Express or implied reference to "some witnesses," "some contracts," or "some hearsay" are references to undistributed terms. Because undistributed terms do not refer to all of the category, they cannot justify a conclusion unless they are distributed elsewhere in the argument. The middle term has to be distributed in at least one premise.
- A short sample Brief in Support of a Motion for Partial Summary Judgment in a civil case follows. Review it and see if you can spot the fallacy of the undistributed middle term in the motion. Once you find it, ask yourself why you were able to identify it, whether you would have identified it before reading this chapter, and consider how you might respond to this argument in practice.
- After you work though the sample brief, you will find commentary in the Appendix at the end of this book explaining how the fallacy of the undistributed middle term comes into play in the sample brief.

7.8 Exercise

State of Ohio
Finch County Circuit Court

Mack Bryce,
Plaintiff,

Case No: A15-CF7-04242
Judge: Barton L. Scheetz

v.

Eastern Ohio College,
Defendant.

Plaintiff's Brief in Support of Motion for Partial Summary Judgment on the Issue of Agency

Introduction

Plaintiff, Mack Bryce ("Mr. Bryce") filed this action to recover damages for injuries he incurred on the premises of defendant Eastern Ohio College ("EOC") when an employee of EOC struck Mr. Bryce with a golf cart that was being utilized as a utility vehicle during tailgating and other pregame activities prior to EOC's 2015 Homecoming football game. For the reasons that follow, Bryce is entitled to partial summary judgment on EOC's defense that the driver of the golf cart was not an agent of EOC. Because there is no genuine dispute as to a material fact on the issue of agency, Plaintiff requests this court enter an order holding that the driver of the golf cart was an agent of EOC for purposes of trial.

Standard of Review

A motion for summary judgment must be granted where no genuine dispute as to a material fact exists for trial, and the moving party is entitled to judgment as a matter of law. Ohio R. Civ. P. 56(C). The moving party must show that no genuine dispute as to a material fact exists for trial. *Dresher v. Burt* (1996), 75 Ohio St.3d 280, 293, 662 N.E.2d 264. The motion must be granted where the issue is "so one-sided that one party must prevail as a matter of law." *Turner v. Turner* (1993), 67 Ohio St.3d 337, 340, 617 N.E.2d 1123. When the moving party satisfies its burden, the non-moving party must produce specific facts showing that there is a genuine issue for trial. If the nonmoving party does not, summary judgment in favor of the moving party is required. *Dresher*, 75 Ohio St.3d at 293.

Statement of Facts

The facts of this case are simple. On October 24, 2015, Plaintiff, Mr. Bryce, was on the EOC campus for EOC's annual homecoming football game and festivities. EOC facilitated opportunities and forums for ticketholders for the football game to appear on campus before the game and engage in pre-game festivities, including an EOC sponsored "spirit rally," a "homecoming parade" featuring participants from the university, and "tailgating" throughout the campus parking lots and green spaces. In fact, several parking lots were specifically designated as tailgating areas and participants seeking to use them for tailgating were required to purchase a tailgating pass in order to park their vehicles in the lots. Mr. Bryce purchased a pass to tailgate in the "Grant Hall Parking Lot" located adjacent to the EOC football stadium. The lot was policed by an EOC parking official wearing a florescent yellow vest with the word "parking" on the front and back of the vest.

At approximately 2:15 p.m., Mr. Bryce was walking from the Grant Hall restrooms to his vehicle in the Grant Hall Parking Lot. As he stepped into the parking lot, he was struck by a golf cart. The driver was described as a "college-aged male" driving a green golf cart, wearing a green EOC baseball cap and wearing a green tee shirt with a yellow EOC logo on the back (the "Driver"). The cart struck Mr. Bryce along the left side of Mr. Bryce's body, causing him to stumble. As a result of the collision, Mr. Bryce suffered a tear to his medial collateral ligament in his left knee, requiring surgery followed by physical therapy, further medical treatment, and resulting in permanent limitations to Mr. Bryce's ability to use his left knee and permanent pain and suffering.

The Driver of the golf cart made no effort to assist Mr. Bryce after the collision. Instead, the driver drove away from the scene of the accident without ever stopping.

Discussion

Since the Driver of the golf cart left the scene of the accident he has not been specifically identified or named as a defendant in this lawsuit. Further, EOC has refused to identify the Driver, claiming that it is unaware of the Driver's identity. In fact, EOC has taken the position that the Driver was not an employee or agent of EOC and seeks to take advantage of the "hit and run" nature of the Driver's actions to avoid taking responsibility for them. However, because there can be no genuine issue of fact regarding the Driver's agency, this argument must fail and the issue of agency must be resolved in favor of Mr. Bryce as a matter of law.

The relationship of principal and agent exists when one party exercises the right of control over the actions of another, and those actions are directed toward the attainment of an objective which the former seeks. *Hanson v. Kynast*, 24 Ohio St. 3d 171, 173, 494 N.E.2d 1091, 1094 (1986) (citing *Baird v. Sickler* (1982), 69 Ohio St.2d 652, 654, 433 N.E.2d 593.) Further, "[i]f one's actions or omissions indicate an apparent authority on the part of another, the fact that the latter had no actual authority does not preclude a third party from holding the former liable if his acts or negligence are such as to lead a reasonable and prudent person to believe the authority existed." *Able Equip., Inc. v. Tom S.A., Inc.*, No. 84-006, 1984 Ohio App. LEXIS 9874, at *6 (Ohio Ct. App. June 1, 1984) (citing 3 OHIO JURISPRUDENCE 3d 36–37, Agency by Estoppel, Section 20)).

Here the Driver was, literally, clothed in authority by EOC. Both Mr. Bryce and another witness, Mr. Miller, testified in their depositions that the Driver was driving a green golf cart. The school colors of EOC are green and gold. See Exhibits A and B, Excerpts of Depositions of Mr. Bryce and Mr. Miller. Further, Mr. Miller, who was the first to come to the assistance of Mr. Bryce, testified that he had a clear view of the Driver, and that the Driver was wearing a green baseball cap with the gold letters "EOC" on the front. Moreover, as the Driver passed him, he turned and noticed that the back of the driver's green tee shirt appeared to be adorned with an EOC logo. Importantly, the parking lot attendant who granted Mr. Bryce access to the Grant Hall Lot, was similarly clothed, also wearing a green baseball cap and green shirt under their yellow parking vest. EOC does not deny that the parking lot attendant was an agent of EOC.

In response to Mr. Bryce's allegation that EOC's agent caused his injuries, Defendant's response can be best summarized as "I don't know." Defendant claims it did not have any employees or agents driving golf carts in the Grant Hall Parking Lot between 2:00 and 3:30 on the date of the accident. It claims it does not know the identity of the Driver of the golf cart. It concedes that it employs hundreds of people to work in various capacities on campus during various homecoming activities. See Exhibit 3, Answer, paragraph 32. Further, it concedes that many of the EOC employees wear green or yellow EOC apparel while working. See Exhibit 3, Defendant's Answer, paragraph 33. Last, EOC has admitted that some EOC employees use golf carts for transportation on campus during game days. Importantly, EOC produces no evidence whatsoever suggesting the Driver was someone other than an agent of EOC. EOC's absence of evidence is insufficient to defeat a motion for summary judgment. It must come forward with some evidence that the Driver was not its agent.

Conclusion

Here the record is clear. Hundreds of EOC agents were on campus at the time of the accident. Virtually all of them were wearing EOC apparel and some of them were driving golf carts. There can be no room for dispute that the Driver was an EOC agent or employee at the time of the accident. Further, EOC's failure to rebut this argument with evidence identifying the Driver as someone not an agent or employee of EOC is fatal to its defense. Accordingly, Mr. Bryce is entitled to summary judgment on the issue of agency as a matter of law.

Watts & Jackson, LLP

Attorneys for Plaintiff

____

David D. Duff

Chapter Eight

The Fallacy of the Illicit Process

Like the fallacy of the undistributed middle term, the second of the formal logical fallacies confronted in this book applies to categorical syllogisms. In Chapter Seven, you saw how courts frequently deal with arguments about categorization of the subjects of litigation. Persons who are credible, persons who are friends of the judge, boats that are motorboats, parties who have contacts within a state, and people who are members of a street gang were all subjects of categorical syllogisms in Chapter Seven. That theme continues in Chapter Eight, which also deals with a fallacy of categorical syllogisms: the fallacy of the illicit process. This chapter focuses on another rule of distribution that ensures the integrity of legal argument when it takes the form of a categorical syllogism.

As you read this chapter, consider the following points.

- This chapter, in the overview above, has already suggested an important similarity between the fallacy of the undistributed middle term and the fallacy of the illicit process. As you read this chapter, consider the role of distribution, common errors of distribution, and why distribution is so important in argument.
- As you become more familiar with the logical concept of distribution, consider the role distribution plays in legal argument. Does the theory of legal argument have good language tools to describe errors in distribution? If not, how can logic supply such terms?
- One goal of this book is to challenge you to find ways to make efficient use of logic in legal argument, helping you learn how to use logic as a tool in the craft of legal argument, without requiring that you become an expert logician. Can you identify common patterns of argument that help you spot the fallacy of the illicit process in legal argument? Are there efficient ways to explain this logical failure to judges or opposing counsel when you discover the failure in the arguments you confront?

8.1 Two Kinds of Illicit Processes and Bad Argument

I hate getting sick. I am particular displeased to get the flu; who isn't? I am not a doctor, but I have been sick with the flu enough over the years to be able to identify some of the symptoms: fatigue, headache, muscle pain. When I get a combination of these symptoms, I can generally diagnose myself with the flu, without the need to visit my doctor. If I was really feeling poorly, I might take my temperature with a thermometer and discover that I had a fever. Of course, having a fever is a symptom of illness, but it is distinct from fatigue, headache, and muscle pain. Confronted with new information about a new symptom, I might, for purposes of self-diagnosis, arrange my knowledge of the flu and symptoms into a syllogism:

> All symptoms of fatigue, headache, and muscle pain[1] are symptoms indicative of the flu.
>
> No fever symptoms are symptoms of fatigue, headache, and muscle pain.
>
> Therefore, no fever symptoms are symptoms indicative of the flu.

Figure 36. *An example of a fallacious categorical syllogism taking the form of the fallacy of the illicit process.*

Of course, my conclusion is incorrect. The rigors of medical school are not necessary to confirm that fever can be a flu symptom. However, both of the premises in my syllogism are true. It is true that fatigue, headache, and muscle pain are symptoms of the flu. Further, it is true that fever is a symptom distinct from fatigue, headache, and muscle pain. If the premises are true but the conclusion is not, the syllogism must suffer from some malaise of logical form. The problem is in the place of the major term: "symptoms indicative of the flu." While fatigue, headache, and muscle pain are undoubtedly some of the symptoms of the flu, they are not all of the symptoms of the flu. "Symptoms indicative of the flu" is undistributed in the major premise. While I know that premises are true and the conclusion is false, forcing myself to justify what is logically amiss in this syllogism helps me understand an important logical rule.

Law, like medicine, frequently involves labeling conduct based on elements. Just as my doctor will ask me about my symptoms before diagnosing a health concern and prescribing a course of treatment, lawyers assess whether, for example, the elements of a crime are present before assessing consequences of being subject to prosecution for that crime. Entering into a store with the intent to commit larceny would meet the requirements for the elements of the crime of burglary. Entering into a barn is not entering into a store, of course. However, it would be wrong to reach a conclusion from them that entering into a barn is not an element of burglary. That conclusion would suffer from the same infirmity that the conclusion about the flu did. The major premise asserts something about some of the elements of burglary but not all of them. In fact, entering a barn with the intent to commit larceny is just

1. Here, "symptoms of fatigue, headache, and muscle pain" is used as a single term, rather than three independent terms.

as much burglary as entering a store with the intent to commit larceny.[2] To assert otherwise, based on the premises here, is logically fallacious.

The next logical fallacy, the fallacy of the illicit process, like the fallacy of the undistributed middle term, involves a rule that regulates the distribution of terms in a categorical syllogism. The rule of logic at work in the fallacy of the undistributed middle term requires that the middle term be distributed in either or both of the appearances of the middle term in the premises. The rule of logic at work in this chapter, and the fallacy that follows from violating this rule, moves its focus away from the middle term and toward the two terms that appear in the conclusion: the minor term and the major term.

The rule of logic at issue in the fallacy of the illicit process provides: "Any term distributed in the conclusion of a categorical syllogism must be distributed in the premises."[3] Because the conclusion of a syllogism includes only two terms, the minor term and the major term, this rule only applies where one or both of those terms are distributed. If a term is distributed in the conclusion, then it must also be distributed in the premise in which it appears. Since this rule could be violated by either the major term or the minor term, logic supplies two different names for the two potential species of the fallacy of the illicit process. Those fallacies—the "fallacy of the illicit minor term" and the "fallacy of the illicit major term"—are intended to capture the essence of why these patterns of argument are inherently unreliable. Where a conclusion includes a distributed major term but does not distribute the major term in the major premise, the argument commits the fallacy of the illicit major term. Where a conclusion includes a distributed minor term but does not distribute the minor term in the minor premise, the argument commits the fallacy of the illicit minor term. In the same way that the first step toward detecting the

---

2. For example, in California the elements of burglary as provided by statute as:

> Every person who enters any house, room, apartment, tenement, *shop*, warehouse, store, mill, *barn*, stable, outhouse or other building, tent, vessel, as defined in Section 21 of the Harbors and Navigation Code, floating home, as defined in subdivision (d) of Section 18075.55 of the Health and Safety Code, railroad car, locked or sealed cargo container, whether or not mounted on a vehicle, trailer coach, as defined in Section 635 of the Vehicle Code, any house car, as defined in Section 362 of the Vehicle Code, inhabited camper, as defined in Section 243 of the Vehicle Code, vehicle as defined by the Vehicle Code, when the doors are locked, aircraft as defined by Section 21012 of the Public Utilities Code, or mine or any underground portion thereof, *with intent to commit grand or petit larceny* or any felony is guilty of burglary. As used in this chapter, "inhabited" means currently being used for dwelling purposes, whether occupied or not. A house, trailer, vessel designed for habitation, or portion of a building is currently being used for dwelling purposes if, at the time of the burglary, it was not occupied solely because a natural or other disaster caused the occupants to leave the premises.

Cal. Penal Code § 459 (emphasis added).

3. Christopher W. Tindale, Fallacies and Argument Appraisal 45 (2007).

fallacy of the undistributed middle term is identifying the middle term in an argument, the first step toward detecting the fallacy of the illicit process is identifying the major and minor terms.

Returning to my case of the flu in Figure 36, the major premise takes the form of a universal affirmative proposition, and the major term is undistributed there. The major term takes the place of the predicate in the major premise here. The predicate term of a universal affirmative proposition is undistributed. Conversely, the conclusion uses this major term differently. Rather than using the major term in the undistributed form found in the major premise, the conclusion purports to use it in the distributed form. The conclusion takes the form of a universal negative proposition, one that distributes the subject and predicate terms in the conclusion. Like the rule that manages how argument uses the middle term, another rule of logic manages the major and minor terms, and how that can be used in the conclusion.

8.2 Finding the Major or Minor Terms

The first step toward identifying arguments that commit the fallacy of the illicit process is to locate the major and minor terms in argument structures. Locating them typically requires putting the argument into the form of a syllogism and ensuring it is in accurate and standard form: three propositions and three terms in proper syllogistic form. It is not necessary to deconstruct the entire legal argument into a series of syllogisms. Instead, it is enough to focus on one important or suspect logical relationship. The syllogistic focus can center on a particular element of a broader legal argument, because formal logic focuses on the micro, rather than macro, level.

The process of identifying major and minor terms begins by focusing on a particular relationship among the basic logical elements in an argument and arranging them in standard syllogistic form. Arranging an argument into a syllogism generally begins with identifying the conclusion and the two terms in that conclusion. The first term, the subject term, in the syllogistic conclusion is called the *minor term.* The second term, the predicate term, is called the *major term.* Unlike the middle term, which appears in both premises and not at all in the conclusion, the major and minor terms appear together in the conclusion and in one premise respectively. The premise containing the major term is the *major premise.* The premise containing the minor term is the *minor premise.* In the following syllogisms, the minor term is underlined and the major term is italicized.[4]

4. The term that is neither in bold type nor italicized is the middle term.

> Every [person who is a] seller of a residential property in South Dakota is *[a person who is] required to comply with the residential property disclosure requirements* under South Dakota statute.
>
> The defendant was not a [person who is a] seller of residential property in South Dakota.
>
> Therefore, the defendant was not *[a person who is] required to comply with the residential property disclosure requirements.*

Figure 37. *An example of a legal argument taking the form of a categorical syllogism.*[5]

> The *defendants that the court does not have jurisdiction over* are defendants who are residents of another state.
>
> Some of the defendants named in the complaint are defendants who are residents of another state.
>
> Therefore, the defendants named in the complaint are the *defendants that the court does not have jurisdiction over.*

Figure 38. *An example of a legal argument taking the form of a categorical syllogism.*

> No evidence regarding damages is *[evidence which is] admissible during the liability phase of the bifurcated trial.*
>
> The plaintiff's testimony regarding his extended hospitalization is evidence regarding damages.
>
> Therefore, the plaintiff's testimony regarding his extended hospitalization is not *[evidence which is] admissible during the liability phase of the bifurcated trial.*

Figure 39. *An example of a legal argument taking the form of a categorical syllogism.*

It was helpful in spotting middle terms in Chapter Seven to know that the middle term connected the minor and major terms but did not appear in the conclusion. Similarly, in spotting major and minor terms, it is helpful to know

5. You may note that the example in Figures 37–39 are based on the simple arguments that appear in Chapter Four. Some modifications and parenthetical additions to the syllogisms from the way they appear in Chapter Four have been made to clarify the separate major and minor terms. However, these arguments have not been arranged in strict syllogistic form the way a logician might. For example, in Figure 37, the conclusion might be more precisely stated as "no Defendant is a person who is required to comply with the residential property disclosure requirements." As you read the case descriptions later in this chapter, you will see that courts are, similarly, not always strict regarding how they articulate the syllogistic structure of arguments. However, it is important to accurately identify the major, minor, and middle terms and their distribution in order to determine if the form is valid.

that they have specific places in the conclusion and that they each appear in only one premise. The minor term can be spotted in the conclusion because it is always the subject in the conclusion. The major term can be spotted in the conclusion because it is always the predicate in the conclusion. Since frequently in legal argument the major term is a general proposition of law, we can expect to see it as the predicate of the conclusion. We see this pattern of legal conclusion in legal argument regularly, for example: (1) "Defendant's proffered testimony must be excluded from evidence as hearsay;" (2) "Plaintiff's documentary evidence fails to create a genuine dispute as to a material fact;" (3) "Defendant's explanation of the contract's meaning is inadmissible under the parol evidence rule;" (4) "Defendant's failure to make the property reasonably safe for invited members of the public constitutes a breach of the standard of care;" (5) "Defendant's use of misleading labels constitutes a violation of the Consumer Protection Act." Each of these argumentative conclusions includes two terms. The subject term is a reference to the facts of a case; it is the minor term. The predicate term is a reference to a proposition of law; it is the major term. Identifying the major and minor terms is as straightforward as identifying the subject and predicate terms in the argument's conclusion.

8.3 Spotting Distribution, or Lack Thereof, in the Major or Minor Terms

Chapter Seven explained how to test distribution in assessing the distribution of the middle term. The lessons of distribution learned there can be leveraged to assess the distribution of major and minor terms in the conclusion. Since the rule of logic at work in the fallacy of the illicit process requires that if a term is distributed in the conclusion it must be distributed in the premise, we simply have to test whether one or both terms in the conclusion are distributed, and then confirm distribution in the respective premise or premises. Further, in the same way we evaluated the structure of the major and minor premises to test the distribution of the middle term in Chapter Seven, we can evaluate the structure of the conclusion to test the distribution of the minor and major terms.

In a universal affirmative proposition (All S is P), the subject term is distributed and the predicate term is undistributed. In a universal negative proposition (No S is P), both the subject and predicate terms are distributed. Conversely, in a particular affirmative proposition (Some S is P), both the subject and predicate terms are undistributed. Last, in a particular negative proposition (Some S is not P), the subject term is undistributed and the predicate term is distributed. Accordingly, by labeling the conclusion, the distribution of the terms becomes straightforward.

If neither term is distributed in the conclusion,[6] then there is no chance the fallacy of the illicit process can exist, since this fallacy only manages distributed terms in the conclusion. However, if a term is distributed in the conclusion, then it must be distributed in its premise. Additionally, if both terms are distributed in the conclusion, then both terms must be distributed in their respective premises. The same process used to assess distribution in the conclusion can be used to assess distribution in the applicable premise. If the syllogism fails to comply with this logical rule, then it commits the fallacy of the illicit process.

8.4 Why an Illicit Process Makes an Argument Unpersuasive

This discussion regarding how to identify the major and minor terms and how to assess their level of distribution is helpful in understanding why illicit major or minor terms are problematic. It is not logical to make a claim about all of a class when that claim is supported by a statement relating to a subset of that same class. For example, a lawyer should not argue that all out-of-court statements are inadmissible hearsay statements when only some out of court statements are hearsay. Because many legal rules have exceptions, lawyers should be disciplined in how they describe them, and when they are not so disciplined about their descriptions, this rule of logic affords an explanation of why their argument is unreliable: "Any term distributed in the conclusion of a categorical syllogism must be distributed in the premises." For example, consider this argument:

> Plaintiff submits the deposition of Defendant's general manager, Mr. Greenbriar, in support of its claim that defendant's deposition testimony raises a genuine dispute as to a material fact. However, Mr. Greenbriar, during his deposition, repeatedly denied writing the statements that plaintiff asserts were libelous in this action. In fact, Mr. Greenbriar, on pages 23, 34, 37 and 112 of his deposition transcript expressly denied that he authored the letters that are the subject of plaintiff's complaint. Evidence *denying* the allegations of plaintiff's claim cannot create a genuine dispute of material. Mr. Greenbriar's deposition includes four separate denials of plaintiff's allegation. Therefore, plaintiff's evidence cannot create a genuine dispute as to a material fact in this case

Figure 40. *An example of an excerpt of a legal argument in support of a motion for summary judgment.*

Figure 40 is a typical pattern of argument that a defendant might make in support of a motion for summary judgment seeking to dismiss a claim of libel asserted

6. This would only happen if the conclusion took the form of a particular affirmative ("Some S is P"). As will be discussed below, this form is unusual in legal argument.

by the plaintiff.[7] The defendant is arguing that no evidence supports the plaintiff's claim. However, what if, in making this argument, the defendant is directing the court's attention to some, but not all, of Mr. Greenbriar's deposition testimony. Assume that Mr. Greenbriar also made other statements that call into question whether he made the libelous statements, but that these statements were not raised in the defendant's argument for summary judgment. An objective description of the defendant's argument might look something like this:

> No evidence denying the plaintiff's allegations of libel is evidence that creates a genuine dispute as to any material fact.
>
> Some of the plaintiff's evidence is evidence denying the plaintiff's allegations of libel.
>
> Therefore, none of the plaintiff's evidence is evidence that creates a genuine dispute as to any material fact.

Figure 41. *An example of a legal argument taking the form of a categorical syllogism.*

The conclusion of the argument takes the form of a universal negative proposition. The conclusion distributes the minor term, "plaintiff's evidence" and the major term "evidence that creates a genuine dispute as to a material fact." However, the minor term is not distributed in the minor premise: "Some of the plaintiff's evidence is evidence denying the plaintiff's allegations of libel." Of course, the defendant is trying to pull a bit of a "fast one" here. The defendant's argument focuses on the particular parts of the plaintiff's proffered evidence that support the defendant's position. However, the defendant's argument ignores the rest of the deposition testimony. As lawyers, we are trained to focus on the favorable facts in our case and deemphasize the facts that are unfavorable. Further, we, in many contexts, are forced to make arguments that reach universal conclusions with distributed terms. A movant's lawyer arguing a motion for summary judgment would never conclude by stating that "much of the evidence attached to plaintiff's brief in opposition to this motion fails to create a genuine dispute as to a material fact." That would likely ensure that the movant's lawyer loses his motion. Instead, we frequently make the kinds of claims in legal argument that only deduction can provide. They sound

7. A motion for summary judgment is generally raised by a defendant in a civil case at the close of the discovery phase of litigation. If the defendant can establish that there are no genuine disputes as to material facts, the court must dismiss those undisputed claims. FED. R. CIV. P. 56(a) ("A party may move for summary judgment, identifying each claim or defense—or the part of each claim or defense—on which summary judgment is sought. The court shall grant summary judgment if the movant shows that there is no genuine dispute as to any material fact and the movant is entitled to judgment as a matter of law. The court should state on the record the reasons for granting or denying the motion.").

something like, "plaintiff has had six months of discovery[8] to develop some evidence to create a fact issue for trial, and has produced, depositions, affidavits and documents with their brief in opposition, but *none* of this evidence creates a genuine dispute as to a material fact." Further, in oral argument, counsel will likely emphasize the word "none." Speaking logically, that word, "none," a universal term, will ensure that their argument commits the fallacy of the illicit minor term unless it is based on a premise that includes a distributed minor term.

Understanding this logical consequence provides another tool to understand, analyze, and explain why the defendant's motion should be denied. Yes, plaintiffs will typically parse out the material in the deposition that suggests a fact issue remains for trial and tell the court that the evidence in the balance of the deposition is sufficient to create a genuine dispute as to a material fact. However, that point can be made more completely by explaining that not only is the defendant's conclusion factually inaccurate, it is logically unsound. The laws of logic prohibit a litigant from drawing any universal conclusion about the entirety of the plaintiff's evidence from a few examples of the plaintiff's evidence. When they do that, they commit a logical fallacy—here, the fallacy of the illicit minor term.

This illustration demonstrates what is so unpersuasive about arguments that commit the fallacy of the illicit process. Categorical syllogisms reach conclusions by putting concepts in categories.[9] That is why logicians call this form of argument a categorical syllogism. It is the relationship between the categories that justifies drawing a valid logical inference from the premises in the conclusion. In cases of the fallacy of the undistributed middle term and the fallacy of illicit process, when a syllogism treats undistributed terms as if they were distributed terms, the reliability of the inference breaks down. Once that happens, you can no longer rely on the argument's conclusion. That is why logic calls the argument "fallacious."

Just as this rule applies, in our example, to a minor term in the conclusion that is distributed in the conclusion but not distributed in one of the premises resulting in the fallacy of the illicit minor term, it may also apply to a major term. Where the conclusion distributes the major term without it being distributed in at least one premise, it is referred to as the fallacy of the illicit major term. Both fallacies result from violations of the same logical rule: if a term is distributed in the conclusion, then it must be distributed in at least one premise.

8. In a civil case, parties are generally provided a period of time to conduct discovery before they are expected to demonstrate that a genuine dispute as to material fact exists for trial. *See, e.g.*, THI-Hawaii, Inc. v. First Commerce Fin. Corp., 627 F.2d 991, 994 (9th Cir. 1980) ("Where the opposing party has not had sufficient time to complete discovery or otherwise marshal facts to oppose the motion, application may be made under Rule 56(f) [now codified in Rule 56(d)] for a continuance of the proceedings pending completion of discovery.').

9. W. Edgar Moore, Creative and Critical Thinking 194 (1967) ("[A] *categorical* proposition names or describes two classes and states a relationship between them.").

We encounter arguments that take this form in litigation and elsewhere, and their logical structure is not always readily apparent. Two reasons explain how easily camouflaged formal logical fallacies can be. First, logically fallacious arguments are generally made with seemingly true premises. The fact that the arguer claims a conclusion results from two truthful premises suggests that there is something sound about the conclusion. While logic tells us this is not the case, there seems to be a psychological tendency in some cases to find a conclusion "truthful by association."[10] Where a conclusion keeps the company of two seemingly truthful premises, we tend to give the conclusion the benefit of the doubt unless and until we scrutinize it.

Second, the syllogism, like good poetry, has an inviting, familiar, meter, or rhythm, to it. Audiences are comfortable with the meter of syllogistic argument (even if they have not learned the terminology or components of the syllogism). Syllogistic argument tends to have, by its argumentative structure alone, some credibility with its audience. Accordingly, when an argument takes a syllogistic form, audiences are comfortable with accepting that form. However, a lawyer understanding those laws of logic that allow us to test the logical form of a syllogism will know the difference between an argument that merely sounds good and one that is logically reliable.

8.5 How Courts Have Used the Fallacy of the Illicit Process to Evaluate Legal Argument

The logical fallacy of the illicit process is a practical tool with persuasive force in legal argument. Lawyers and judges searching for theoretical justification and language tools for describing what is wrong with a legal argument have used the fallacy of the illicit process to analyze legal arguments and articulate what is logically right or wrong with them.[11] A few examples of judicial opinions that have employed the

10. Some psychological research has revealed that humans are psychologically predisposed to sometimes accept certain conclusions just because they take a particular syllogistic form. Psychologists have studied the application of one theory known as the "atmosphere effect." Some researchers have considered the moods of the premises created by an "atmosphere" regarding the types of conclusions humans are prone to accept as valid. Deborah J. Bennett, Logic Made Easy 88 (2004). "The atmosphere of the premises has been shown to be a contributing factor to difficulties in syllogistic deduction." *Id.* at 88. Psychologists have argued that "if two premises are of the same logical form, then 'atmosphere' makes it likely that a conclusion of that form will be thought to follow." N.E. Wetherick & K.J. Gilhooly, *'Atmosphere', Matching, and Logic in Syllogistic Reasoning*, 14 Current Psychology 169, 2 (1995).

11. *See, e.g.*, In re Scoggins, 517 B.R. 206, 218–19 (Bankr. E.D. Cal. 2014); Baker v. Amoco Oil Co., 761 F. Supp. 1386, 1392 (E.D. Wis. 1991); State v. Zespy, 723 P.2d 564, 570 n.1 (Wyo. 1986); Hernandez v. Denton, 861 F.2d 1421, 1439 (9th Cir. 1988), *vacated and remanded*, 493 U.S. 801 (1989); Caterpillar, Inc. v. United States, 941 F. Supp. 1241, 1245 (Ct. Int'l Trade 1996); Idaho Press Club, Inc. v. State Legislature, 123 P.3d 397, 407 (Idaho 2006); Shirley v. Kansas Dep't of Revenue, 243 P.3d 708, 712 (Kan. Ct. App. 2010); State v. Deal, 206 P.3d 529, 544 (Kan. Ct. App. 2009), *aff'd*, 269 P.3d 1282 (Kan. 2012); Cent. Dauphin Sch. Dist. v. Pa. Mfrs. Ass'n Ins. Co., 1992 Pa. D. & C.4th 289, 296 (1992); State v. Euman, 558 S.E.2d 319, 324 (W. Va. 2001).

fallacies of the illicit major and illicit minor terms provide some authority for and examples of the usefulness of the fallacy of the illicit process in legal argument.

One example is seen in *Shirley v. Kansas Dept. of Revenue*,[12] where the court explicitly cited the fallacy of the illicit process of the major term as a basis for its decision. The court focused its analysis, as categorical syllogisms in legal argument frequently do, on the definition of terms and whether conduct falls within defined categories for which there are legal consequences. The definition at issue in *Shirley* was whether an alleged operator of a "minitruck"[13] was an operator of a "vehicle" such that the operator was subject to penalties under the Kansas implied consent law.[14] The court considered the plaintiff's argument and arranged it into a syllogism:

> Major Premise: All operators of vehicles that can be legally operated on a public highway must comply with the Kansas implied consent law.
>
> Minor Premise: Operators of vehicles that cannot be legally operated on a public highway are not operators of vehicles that can be legally operated on a public highway.
>
> Conclusion: Therefore, operators of vehicles that cannot be legally operated on a public highway are not required to comply with the Kansas implied consent law.[15]

The court went on to describe the argument as committing the fallacy of the illicit major term[16]—that is, the conclusion was a function of the logical relationship between two terms: the minor term ("operators of vehicles that cannot be legally operated on a public highway") and the major term ("operators who must comply with the Kansas implied consent law"). The major term ("[operators who must comply with the] Kansas implied consent law") was distributed in the conclusion, but not distributed in the major premise. That term was undistributed in the major premise because the major premise took the form of a universal affirmative proposition, where the predicate is always undistributed.[17]

12. 243 P.3d 708 (Kan. Ct. App. 2010).
13. Evidence was submitted to the hearing officer, describing "the minitruck [as] as weighing 1,400 pounds and having a 3- or 4-cylinder, 650 cc. 45-horsepower motor. According to the sales brochure, the minitruck is 52 inches wide, has a 4-speed transmission, and will run about 60 miles per hour."
14. *Id.* at 46.
15. *Id.* at 48. Note that "operators of vehicles that can be legally operated on a public highway" and "operators of vehicles that cannot be legally operated on a public highway" are two separate terms in this syllogism.
16. *Id.* at 48.
17. *Id.*

In *State of Kansas v. Deal,*[18] the defendant in a criminal case argued for a Sixth Amendment right to a trial transcript for purposes of arguing a motion for a new trial.[19] The defendant argued that the Sixth Amendment ensures the right of an indigent defendant to a trial transcript on appeal as a component of the right to counsel, since a transcript is necessary to perfect an appeal.[20] Because a trial transcript was just as essential to arguing a motion for a new trial as it would be for perfecting an appeal, the defendant argued that the Sixth Amendment also entitled him to a trial transcript for the purpose of arguing a motion for a new trial.[21] The court characterized the argument this way:

> All appellate attorneys in perfecting appeals from indigent defendants are constitutionally entitled to trial transcripts [Major Premise];
>
> Some trial attorneys (that are appointed after trial to handle post-trial motions for indigent defendants) are like appellate attorneys [Minor Premise];
>
> [The Defendant's] two-part deduction leaves out an essential statement:
>
> Therefore, all trial attorneys who are appointed after the trial to handle posttrial motions for indigent defendants should be entitled to trial transcripts [Conclusion].[22]

The court's syllogistic description of the defendant's argument suggests what it would next conclude as well as the essence of why the fallacy of the illicit process makes legal argument unpersuasive:

> [The defendant] moves from considering part of the category of attorneys (appellate attorneys) that are constitutionally entitled to trial transcripts to broadening his claim to include all the attorneys mentioned in the conclusion. [The defendant's] argument commits the fallacy of the illicit minor term. This results "[w]hen the minor term is undistributed in the minor premise but distributed in the conclusion." Here, the minor term [some trial attorneys who are

18. 206 P.3d 529 (Kan. Ct. App. 2009).

19. *Id.* at 544.

20. *Id.* The defendant cited *State v. Andrews*, 614 P.2d 447 (Kan. Ct. App. 1980). In *Andrews*, the Kansas Supreme Court stated that "an indigent defendant has a right to appointed counsel in perfecting his appeal, including the right to a trial transcript and the right to file an appeal without a filing fee."

21. *Id.*

22. *Id.* (bracketed syllogistic labels in the original). While the form of the argument is not described in the precise language of the categorical syllogism, especially the use of "are like" in the minor premise, the court acknowledged that the defendant's argument was described as analogical rather than deductive: "Although [the defendant] characterizes his argument as an analogy, it reads like a partial syllogism or enthymeme." *Id.* (emphasis in original). An enthymeme is an argument that can be expressed as a syllogism, but excludes a premise or conclusion. Patrick J. Hurley, A Concise Introduction to Logic 301 (2015).

> appointed after trial to handle posttrial motions for indigent defendants] is not distributed in the minor premise, where it appears as the subject term in a particular affirmative categorical proposition.[23]

The court's description nicely encapsulates the essence of the fallacy of the illicit process. The conclusion asserted by the argument applies to all trial attorneys, when the premise relating to that term only applied to some trial attorneys. Spotting the pattern of fallacious argument is as simple as seeing a distributed term in the conclusion, justified by only an undistributed premise.

In an administrative appeal before the United States Department of Health and Human Services Departmental Appeal Board, *Patel v. CMS*,[24] an administrative law judge set out the argument of the respondent in clear syllogistic terms. One issue in that hearing was the effective date of the petitioner's Medicare billing privileges. Specifically at issue was the right of the petitioner to appeal the determination of that effective date. The administrative law judge described CMS's argument in syllogistic terms:

> All § 489.13(a)(1) effective date determinations are reviewable[.]
>
> Supplier enrollment effective date determinations are not § 489.13(a)(1) effective date determinations[.]
>
> [T]herefore, supplier enrollment effective date determinations are not reviewable.[25]

---

23. *Id.* at 544–45 (citing Ruggero J. Aldisert, Logic for Lawyers 55–58, 153 (1997)). The court went on to aptly explain this logical conclusion:

> [The defendant's] conclusion goes beyond what the premises warrant. His conclusion makes an assertion about all trial attorneys appointed after trial. Nevertheless, the premises make no such contention. They say nothing about all trial attorneys appointed after the trial. Moreover, we acknowledge that for [the defendant] to drive home his point, he would have to broaden his claim to all trial attorneys appointed after trial. Otherwise, [the defendant's] argument is drastically weakened if he is contending that only some trial attorneys appointed after trial should be entitled to trial transcripts. Based on the latter assertion that only some trial attorneys appointed after trial should be entitled to trial transcripts, Deal's argument is enormously less appealing. For example, [the defendant] would have to argue that his appointed trial counsel was a member of the class of some attorneys appointed after trial. Also, he would have to argue that his appointed trial counsel was a member of the class of those trial attorneys that should be entitled to trial transcripts. This second argument is very difficult. Under a particular affirmative proposition, there may be only one member of both classes. Moreover, [the defendant's] appointed trial counsel may not have been that one member of both classes.

Id. at 545.

24. Patel v. CMS, No. C-10-181, 2010 WL 9938105, n. 3.

25. *Id.*

The court demonstrated the lack of persuasiveness of arguments that commit the fallacy of the illicit process by exemplifying this fallacious argument structure:

> In logic, CMS's argument would be considered a syllogistic fallacy of the illicit major term: all A=B; no C=A; therefore, no C=B. More concrete examples illustrate the flaws in the reasoning: all dogs are mammals; no cats are dogs; therefore no cats are mammals; or, as here: all § 489.13(a)(1) effective date determinations are reviewable; supplier enrollment effective date determinations are not § 489.13(a)(1) effective date determinations; therefore, supplier enrollment effective date determinations are not reviewable.[26]

This discussion in *Patel* demonstrates an effective way of explaining the fallacious nature of a legal argument. Rather than describe the rule of logic or the syllogistic components at work in the logical analysis, the court provides a common example of the fallacy to illustrate the lack of persuasive value in the argument's logical pattern. When the reader sees the same pattern of fallacious reasoning in the relationship among mammals, cats, and dogs, the pattern makes its point effectively: the invalid pattern of argument is just as unpersuasive in the relationship between cats and dogs as it would be in any other kinds of relationship, including the more technical categorical relationships at issue in *Patel.*

In *State of Wyoming v. Zespy,*[27] a justice used the logical fallacy of the illicit process to evaluate an evidentiary issue. *Zespy* involved the admissibility of expert testimony.[28] In his separate opinion, concurring in part and dissenting in part, Justice Urbigkit described the State's argument regarding the admissibility of expert testimony this way:

> It is not logical to contend, as did the witness (Coleman), and now the State of Wyoming in this bill of exceptions, that if the witness challenges the validity of specific processes he can also logically deny the validity of all processes without first demonstrating knowledge and expertise about every possible process or combination of processes that may or may not have been utilized by the examining expert witness on the subject of constitutionality and statutorily required absence of mental illness or deficiency.[29]

Justice Urbigkit, described the State's syllogism this way:

> Some evaluative processes are invalid.
>
> Other experts may use those processes.
>
> The conclusions of those experts are invalid.

---

26. *Id.*
27. 723 P.2d 564 (Wyo. 1986).
28. *Id.* at 570 (Urbigkit, J., concurring in part and dissenting in part).
29. *Id.*

> This appears to be the fallacy of an undistributed middle term and illicit process of a major or minor term.[30]

This description breaks the argument down into three terms. The major term is "processes that area invalid." The minor term is "some experts' conclusions." The middle term is "some evaluative processes."[31]

Justice Urbigkit also provided an alternative description of the argument as:

> I am an expert about some evaluative processes.
>
> Those processes are invalid.
>
> All evaluative processes are invalid.[32]

This second logical interpretation of the argument makes finding the pattern of fallacious argument easier; however, the respective terms of the syllogism are still not as clear as are found in some other opinions. Nevertheless, it demonstrates how courts sometimes simply look for the hallmarks of a fallacy to identify logical weaknesses in an argument rather than provide an exhaustive, detailed syllogistic analysis of the components of the argument. In the second description of the logical form of the argument, the major, minor, and middle terms are not entirely clear. What is apparent is the major term: "evaluative processes." Furthermore, what is just as clear is the distribution of that major term in the conclusion: "all evaluative processes." Last, it is equally clear that that same term is not distributed in the major premise: "some evaluative processes." This pattern of argument represents the essence of the fallacy of the illicit major term, an argument reaching a conclusion about all evaluative processes based on a truth about some evaluative processes.

8.6 Keys to Using the Fallacy of the Illicit Process to Evaluate and Improve Legal Argument

Just as the previous chapter featured two ways courts used the fallacy of the undistributed middle term to police the logical form of legal argument, this chapter has also reported examples of two similar uses of the fallacy of the illicit process by courts. First, sometimes courts focus on the logical inference in question, reduce it to syllogistic form, and test it against a logical rule to see if it applies. Other times, the court does not take the time to articulate the syllogism entirely, but simply

30. *Id.* at 570 n.1 (citing Stuart Chase, Guides to Straight Thinking, With 13 Common Fallacies 205 (1956)). Justice Urbigkit recognized that formal fallacies are not mutually exclusive and an argument can suffer from more than one logical infirmity. Here, he recognized that the argument, as described, committed the fallacy of the illicit process, but also committed the fallacy of the undistributed middle term, discussed in Chapter Five.

31. This is not entirely clear; there seems to be some ambiguity about what "those" is referring to in the conclusion. Regardless of the precise wording of the middle term, the conclusion attempts to reach a universal conclusion based on a particular premise.

32. *Id.*

recognizes the hallmark of the fallacious argument and describes the fallacy committed. For example, in *Shirley v. Kansas Department of Revenue*,[33] the court utilized the first method, breaking the legal argument down into syllogistic form:

> All operators of vehicles that can be legally operated on a public highway must comply with the Kansas implied consent law.
>
> Operators of vehicles that cannot be legally operated on a public highway are not operators of vehicles that can be legally operated on a public highway.
>
> Therefore, operators of vehicles that cannot be legally operated on a public highway are not required to comply with the Kansas implied consent law.[34]

The *Shirley* court noted that the major term ("[operators who must comply with the] Kansas implied consent law") was distributed in the conclusion, but not distributed in the major premise. The court demonstrated this by providing a complete syllogism that, in its opinion, explained why the major term was distributed in the conclusion, and why the major term was undistributed in the major premise.

Another way to think about this logical problem is by looking for fallacious patterns that can be described as committing the fallacy of the illicit process.

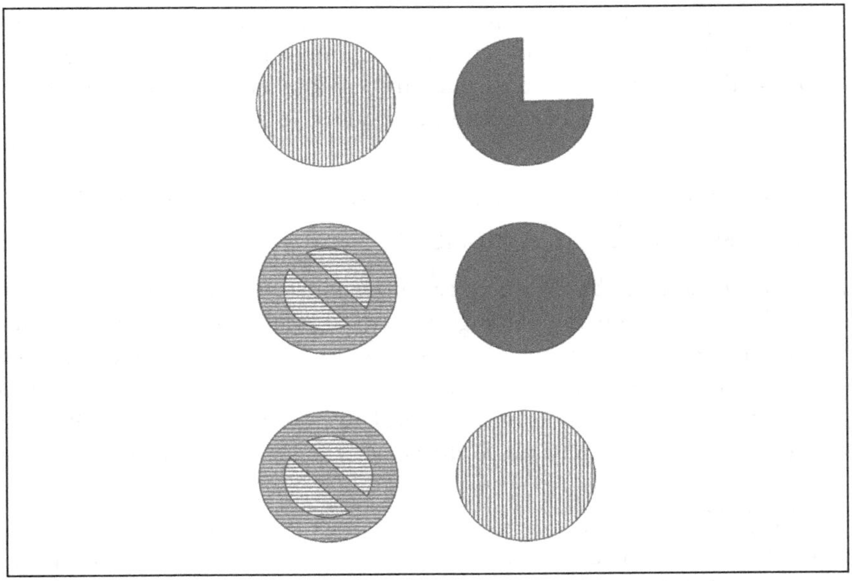

Figure 42. *An example of a pattern of valid distribution of terms in a categorical syllogism.*

33. 243 P.3d 708, 712 (Kan. Ct. App. 2010) (syllogistic premise labels omitted).
34. *Id.*

In Figure 42, there are three shapes, each occurring twice. The shape with the vertical lines represents the major term. The shape with the horizontal lines represents the minor term. We will expect to see those shapes in the conclusion. The shapes with no lines are representative of the middle term. It is not a term that will be found in the conclusion. When any term is represented by a complete circle, it is representing a distributed term. When the term is represented by a partial circle, it is representing an undistributed term. If any of the shapes appear filled with a "no" symbol, it signifies a negative term. Accordingly, the top line Figure 42 is a graphical depiction of a major premise with a distributed major term and an undistributed middle term. The second line depicts a negative distributed minor term and a distributed middle term. The third line depicts a negative conclusion including a distributed minor term and a distributed major term.

Analyzing the fallacy of the illicit process begins with the conclusion and determining whether the terms in the conclusion are distributed. If the conclusion distributes neither term, then there is no chance that the argument commits the fallacy of the illicit process. Accordingly, any of the following combinations of distributed or undistributed terms in the conclusion of an argument has the potential commit this fallacy.

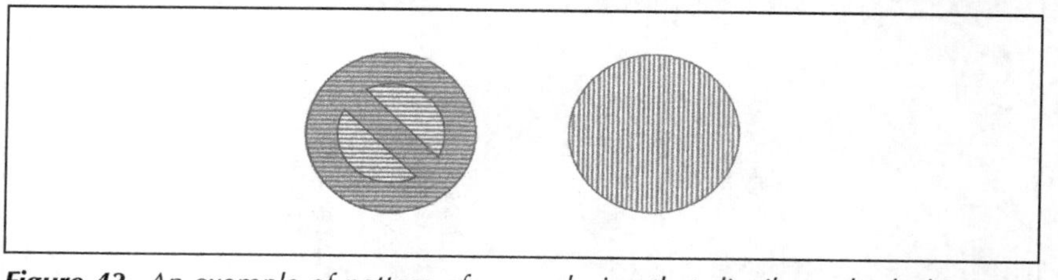

Figure 43. *An example of pattern of a conclusion that distributes both the minor and major terms.*

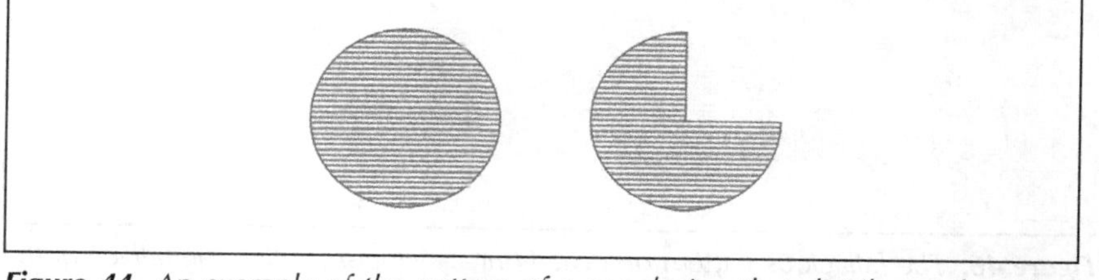

Figure 44. *An example of the pattern of a conclusion that distributes the minor term but not the major term.*

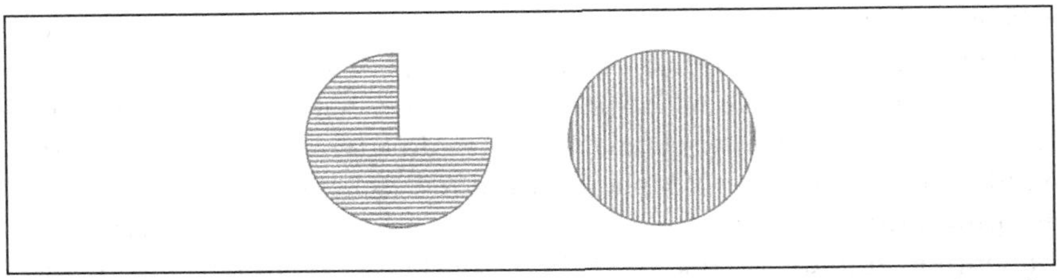

Figure 45. *An example of the pattern of a conclusion that does not distribute the minor term but distributes the major term.*

Figures 43 through 45 each represent conclusions with at least one distributed term. Accordingly, in order to avoid the fallacy of the illicit process, that same distributed term must also be distributed in the premise in which it occurs.

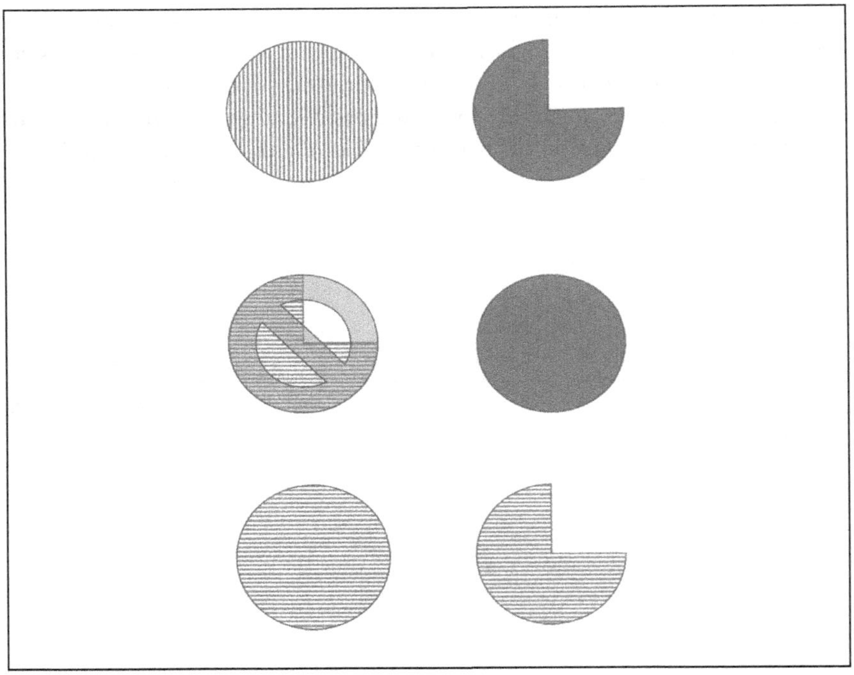

Figure 46. *The fallacious pattern of a categorical syllogism called the fallacy of the illicit minor term.*

Figure 46 represents an argument where the minor term is distributed in the conclusion. However, it is undistributed in the minor premise and commits the fallacy of the illicit process. This graphical illustration demonstrates that the focus here is on the pattern of a distributed term in the conclusion without a distributed term in the premise in which it appears.

These patterns are useful in developing a sense for what logical weaknesses underlie arguments, at the micro level, that commit the fallacy of the illicit process. However, other patterns in these arguments, at the more abstract macro level of argument, can serve as red flags for this fallacy and suggest that lawyers look more specifically for this logical weakness. At a macro level, the fallacy of the illicit process follows from reaching a universal conclusion based on particular premises. This might look like reaching a conclusion about *all* of the evidence or *none* of the evidence based on a characteristic of *most* of the evidence or *some* of the evidence. For example, it might result from considering a few examples of how courts have construed a statute to suggest a conclusion regarding how all courts must construe a statute.

Take, for example, the following argument made in the closing paragraph of a plaintiff's brief in support of its argument that the trial court should have granted its motion for judgment notwithstanding a jury verdict in the defendant's favor.[35]

> The jury verdict in this case must be set aside and a judgment in [the] plaintiff's favor entered as a matter of law. The only evidence in support of [the] defendant's claim that it met the standard of care for performing [the] plaintiff's medical procedure was the testimony of [the] defendant's expert witness, Dr. Hodges. Dr. Hodges testimony lacked credibility, particularly since he conceded that he had known [the] defendant since medical school and had failed to review all of the medical records in this. No other evidence whatsoever was offered by [the] defendant on the issue of negligence in this case, and the jury verdict cannot be said to be supported by substantial evidence.

One might begin considering the logic of this argument by describing the plaintiff's conclusion which might be summarized as, "No evidence introduced by the defendant is sufficient to avoid entry of a judgment notwithstanding the verdict." This conclusion contains two terms: "evidence introduced by the defendant" and "evidence sufficient to avoid entry of a judgment notwithstanding the verdict." The conclusion takes the form of a universal negative: "no evidence introduced by the defendant is evidence sufficient to avoid entry of a judgment notwithstanding the verdict." Universal negative propositions distribute both the subject and predicate terms. That means both terms have to be distributed in the premises in order to comply with the rule of logic and avoid the fallacy of the illicit process.

35. At the close of proofs, "If a party has been fully heard on an issue during a jury trial and the court finds that a reasonable jury would not have a legally sufficient evidentiary basis to find for the party on that issue, the court may: (A) resolve the issue against the party; and (B) grant a motion for judgment as a matter of law against the party on a claim or defense that, under the controlling law, can be maintained or defeated only with a favorable finding on that issue." Fed. R. Civ. P. 50(a)(1). The motion may be renewed after trail. Fed. R. Civ. P. (b). When made after a jury verdict, this motion is sometimes referred to as a judgment notwithstanding the verdict or "JNOV."

The problem with the plaintiff's argument is that it attempts to reach an unjustified universal conclusion about the defendant's evidence. The plaintiff argues that none of the defendant's evidence supported the verdict, when, in fact, according to the plaintiff's own argument, some does. In fact, logically speaking, the plaintiff concedes as much by focusing on the how limited the evidence proffered by the defendant was (one expert witness) and how incredible the evidence proffered by the defendant was (a potentially biased expert who had not reviewed all of the medical records). Logically speaking, however, the plaintiff's premise amounts to a concession that some of the evidence introduced by the defendant supports the verdict. "Some evidence introduced by the defendant" connotes an undistributed term. Therein lay the logic problem with the plaintiff's argument: it attempts to reach a conclusion about all of the defendant's evidence when it only has a premise informing the court about some of the defendant's evidence. The rule of logic forbids such an inferential leap and ensures that the plaintiff's conclusion must fail unless the plaintiff can design a different argument to support it.

This example also demonstrates a bit of a short cut in fallacy-based reasoning. The logic problem in this argument could be described without breaking the entire argument down into syllogistic form. It could be simplified by recognizing the conclusion attempts to assert something about all of a class based on evidence of only some of the class. This can be a persuasive explanation for the failure of an argument. Take, for example, the following opinion, in which a court used the fallacy of the illicit process to evaluate an argument:

> The trustees' compensation argument depends on context but they exploit the fallacy of the illicit major by arguing out of context with a narrow focus on only a segment of compensation.
>
> . . . .
>
> But the main flaw in the trustees' argument is that it proves too much. It is one thing to say that *the basic* § 330(a)(7) "commission" is designed to subsidize the no-asset cases without offending the § 330(a)(1) requirement that the fee be "reasonable." It is quite another thing to say, as the trustees and the U.S. trustee contend, that *every* § 330(a)(7) commission, even (for example) on artificially inflated estates, is reasonable compensation.[36]

The italicized words focus on the essential logic problem recognized by the court. One party was trying to reach a conclusion about "every . . . commission" based on a characteristic of "the basic . . . commissions." The court recognized this hallmark of the fallacy of the illicit process—here, the illicit major term—and used it to explain the problem with the argument it confronted.

36. *In re Scoggins*, 517 B.R. 206, 218–19 (Bankr. E.D. Cal. 2014) (emphasis added).

This method of spotting a logical fallacies by focusing on the pattern of a distributed minor term in the conclusion following an undistributed appearance of the term in a premise stands in contrast to the approach used in *Shirley, Deal,* and *Zespy*, where the court reduced the argument to distinct logical terms, arranged the terms in a syllogism, and then explained the logical failure of the arguments. The court in *Patel* reaches the same logical conclusion that the courts in the other cases reached, but does so without providing the detailed justification that the other cases provide. Nonetheless, it seems the court opinion in *Patel* is just as effective. That might be a function of the authority logic has in argument. Few are willing to advance an argument that is "illogical" and when the court is able to label the argument at issue in *Patel* as "fallacious" the label is a powerful and efficient advocacy tool for evaluating argument.[37]

8.7 Chapter Eight in Review

- The minor term and major term in an argument are important logical components. They are the only two terms that appear in the conclusion, and the entire syllogistic argument is an effort to justify an inference about the relationship between those two terms.
- These terms in the conclusion have to play by a rule of logic if the conclusion is to be reliable. If the minor or major terms are distributed in the conclusion, then the distributed terms must also be distributed in the premise in which they appear.
- Sometimes determining distribution is easy. For example, when the proposition refers to "all" or "some" of a term, the term's distribution is apparent. Other times, distribution is not so obvious and we may need to think about the argument in syllogistic form to determine distribution.
- If the minor term is distributed in the conclusion but not the minor premise, the argument commits the fallacy of the illicit minor term.
- If the major term is distributed in the conclusion but not the major premise, the argument commits the fallacy of the illicit major term.
- The fallacies of the illicit major term and illicit minor term are sometimes referred to generically as the fallacy of the illicit process.
- Courts have encountered arguments that commit the fallacy of the illicit process and dealt with those arguments in terms of formal logic.
- One way to spot the fallacy of the illicit process is to look for patterns of argument featuring distributed terms in the conclusion that are not distributed in the premises.

---

37. Some of the ideas developed in this chapter were first explored in Stephen M. Rice, *Indiscernible Logic: Using the Logical Fallacy of the Illicit Process as a Litigation Tool*, 47 Willamette L. Rev. 101 (2010).

- At the macro level, one of the common hallmarks of legal argument that commits the fallacy of the illicit process is reaching a conclusion about all of a category when the premise only establishes a truth about some of the category.
- A short sample Reply Brief in Support of a Motion for Sanctions in a civil case follows. Review it and see if you can spot the fallacy of the illicit process in the motion. Once you find it, ask yourself why you were able to identify it, whether you would have identified it before reading this chapter, and consider how you might respond to this argument in practice. As you read the sample brief, assume that you represent the respondent. The sample brief cites some cases standing for the proposition that a court can sanction a party represented by a deponent in a 30(b)(6) deposition if the deponent is not sufficiently knowledgeable about the subjects of the deposition, if the deponent's limited knowledge is unjustified. Assume that not cited by the movant are other cases that suggest that not every deponent who is unable to answer questions during a 30(b)(6) deposition subjects the entity represented in the deposition to sanctions.
- After you work though the problem, you will find commentary in the appendix at the end of this book explaining how the fallacy of the illicit process comes into play in the sample brief.

8.8 Exercise

State of Georgia
Line County Superior Court

SquareBarrel Solutions, LLC

Plaintiff, Case No: A15-00061

Judge: Hon. James St. Andre

v.

Interior Diameter, Inc.

Defendant.

Plaintiff SquareBarrel Solutions, LLC's Brief in Support of Motion for Sanctions Against Defendant Interior Diameter, Inc.

This action was filed by plaintiff against Defendant Interior Diameter, Inc. as a result of Defendant's negligence in designing and manufacturing a set of hydraulic elevator guide tubes. Plaintiff builds specialty elevators for various industrial applications. Plaintiff contracted with Defendant for essential components for an elevator project being executed by Plaintiff. The essential components were a set of custom designed steel guide tube assemblies designed and manufactured by Defendant. One of the primary issues in this litigation is Defendant's defective design process and failure to properly manufacture the guide tubes.

On April 4, Plaintiff served Defendant with a Notice of Deposition Pursuant to Fed. R. Civ. Pro. 30(b)(6). The notice required Defendant to produce a corporate representative for a deposition and, as required by Fed. R. Civ. Pro. 30(b)(6), particularly identified subject areas that the representative would be questioned regarding. Defendant produced a witness, but the witness was unprepared to answer questions in the subject areas specified in the notice. As a result Plaintiff incurred substantial expenses in retaining counsel to prepare for and conduct the deposition. As a result of the failure, this Court entered an order on June 28, requiring Defendant to produce a witness for a continued 30(b)(6) deposition. However, that order did not address the issue of sanctions. Accordingly, Plaintiff moves that Defendant be sanctioned in the amount of attorney fees incurred by Plaintiff in preparing for and conducting the deposition on May 5, 2016.

Where a party's refusal to allow discovery is not substantially justified, the court must award sanctions in the amount of costs and attorney fees incurred in obtaining the order to compel.

> If the Motion Is Granted (or Disclosure or Discovery Is Provided After Filing). If the motion is granted—or if the disclosure or requested discovery is provided after the motion was filed—***the court must***, after giving an opportunity to be heard, ***require the party or deponent whose conduct necessitated the motion***, the party or attorney advising that conduct, or both to pay the movant's reasonable expenses incurred in making the motion, including attorney's fees. But the court must not order this payment if:
>
> . . .
>
> (ii) the opposing party's nondisclosure, response, or objection ***was substantially justified***; . . . .

Fed. R. Civ. Pro. 37(5)(A) (emphasis added). Defendant was required to produce witness for a deposition pursuant to Fed. R. Civ. Pro. 30(b)(6). Fed. R. Civ. Pro. 30(b)(6) requires that upon receipt of a notice of deposition describing the matters for examination, an organizational defendant must "designate one or more officers, directors, or managing agents, or designate other persons who consent to testify on its behalf; and it may set out the matters on which each person designated will testify." *Id.* In response to Plaintiff's 30(b)(6) deposition notice, defendant produced Defendant's general manager, Wallace Drone. The notice specifically described "the process utilized by Defendant to design the Guide Tubes at issue in this litigation and the identities of all persons engaged in that that process." See Exhibit A, Notice of Deposition Pursuant to Fed. R. Civ. Pro. 30(b)(6). Despite receipt of particular notice that this would be a topic of the deposition, Mr. Drone appeared for the deposition without knowledge of this topic. See Exhibit B, Transcript, Deposition of Wallace Drone, pp. 68, 70, 71, 72, 73, 75, 88, 89, 90, and 92. When asked to respond to questions regarding Defendant's design process for the Guide Tubes at issue in this litigation, Mr. Drone responded twelve different times by indicating "I don't know" or "I don't have that information." *Id.*

Failure to produce an appropriate 30(b)(6) witness has been grounds for sanctions in other cases. Several courts have held that where parties have produced a witness in response to a 30(b)(6) deposition, and the witness was unknowledgeable about the topics specified in the notice, that the failure to produce a knowledgeable witness was not substantially justified and sanctions were required. *Starlight Int'l Inc. v. Herlihy*, 186 F.R.D. 626, 649 (D. Kan. 1999); *United States v. Taylor*, 166 F.R.D. 356, 363 (M.D.N.C.) *aff'd*, 166 F.R.D. 367 (M.D.N.C. 1996) ("Producing an unprepared witness is tantamount to a failure to appear."); *State Farm Mut. Auto. Ins. Co. v. New Horizont, Inc.*, 250 F.R.D. 203, 219 (E.D. Pa. 2008); *Black Horse Lane Assoc., L.P. v. Dow Chem. Corp.*, 228 F.3d 275, 305 (3d Cir. 2000).

Accordingly, parties who fail to produce knowledgeable witnesses for 30(b)(6) depositions are without substantial justification for their failure to comply with discovery rules. Defendant's failure to comply with the discovery rules here is a failure to produce a knowledgeable witness for a 30(b)(6) deposition. Defendant's failure to produce a knowledgeable witness for a 30(b)(6) deposition is not substantially justified and requires an award of sanctions pursuant to Fed. R. Civ. Pro. 37(5)(a). *Starlight Int'l Inc. v. Herlihy*, 186 F.R.D. 626, 649 (D. Kan. 1999); *United States v. Taylor*, 166 F.R.D. 356, 363 (M.D.N.C.) *aff'd*, 166 F.R.D. 367 (M.D.N.C. 1996) ("Producing an unprepared witness is tantamount to a failure to appear."); *State Farm Mut. Auto. Ins. Co. v. New Horizont, Inc.*, 250 F.R.D. 203, 219 (E.D. Pa. 2008); *Black Horse Lane Assoc., L.P. v. Dow Chem. Corp.*, 228 F.3d 275, 305 (3d Cir. 2000).

For these reasons, Plaintiff requests this Court enter an order requiring Defendant to pay Plaintiff's attorney fees incurred in preparing for taking the deposition of Mr. Drone on May 5, 2016. An affidavit detailing the fees incurred is attached as Exhibit D.

Calamari and Associates
Attorneys for Plaintiff

____

Leonard Calamari

Chapter Nine

The Fallacy of the Negative Premise

The third of the formal logical fallacies confronted in this book, like the fallacy of the undistributed middle term and the fallacy of the illicit process applies to categorical syllogisms. Chapters Seven and Eight explored how courts frequently deal with arguments about categorization of the subjects of litigation. That theme continues in this chapter, which also explores a fallacy of categorical syllogisms: the fallacy of the negative premise. In this chapter, we will see how courts use another rule to ensure the integrity of legal reasoning when it takes the form of a categorical syllogism.

As you read this chapter consider the following points:

- The fallacy of the undistributed middle term and the fallacy of the illicit process share an important common characteristic with the fallacy of the negative premise in that they all relate to categorical syllogisms. As your challenge evolves from understanding individual fallacies to managing the application of several potential fallacies, consider how grouping the fallacies by syllogistic form might help you to manage this task.
- The fallacy of the negative premise deals with whether the premises and conclusion of an argument are affirmative or negative. As you read this chapter, consider how the role of distribution, seen in the fallacy of the undistributed middle term and the fallacy of the illicit process, is different from the role of the affirmative or negative state of the premises and conclusion, seen in the fallacy of the negative premise.
- As you encounter this third formal fallacy, consider why these three necessarily illogical arguments are sometimes accepted by lawyers and judges as persuasive ones.
- Once understood, the fallacy of the negative premise is fairly simple to identify and explain in legal argument. As you read this chapter, consider what kinds of arguments are susceptible to the fallacy of the negative premise and how you might respond to these kinds of fallacies in the legal arguments you face.

9.1 Negative Premises and Positive Conclusions

I love to visit Chicago. There are many ways drive to Chicago. You can look at a map and whether you are traveling from Detroit, Indianapolis, St. Louis, or Milwaukee, there is an interstate that will take you into the heart of Chicago to visit all it has to offer. One westbound route is to take Interstate 94 into the city. For example, if you are traveling from Detroit, I-94 will take you into Chicago. However, if you are traveling from Indianapolis, I-94 is not an efficient route to the Windy City. Accordingly, if my friends from Indianapolis wanted to know what interstate to take to Chicago, I might tell them that I-94 is not the best route. Certainly, that is useful information to my friends, but it is not what they really need to know. My friends need to know how to get to Chicago from Indianapolis, and my bit of navigation advice really does not help them get there. They want to know what routes *will* take them to Chicago. They do not want to know what routes *will not*.

My friends need to reach an affirmative conclusion if they are going to do something useful with my bit of travel advice. They need an affirmative statement about the roads that lead to Chicago from Indianapolis if they are going to reach an affirmative conclusion. They could reach a negative conclusion from negative statements—a list of interstates that will not get them to Chicago—but that really is not what they want to conclude. Further, if they did attempt to reach an affirmative conclusion from a negative premise, they would be taking a chance rather than reaching a certain conclusion. There are several interstates leading to Chicago, including I-94, I-90, I-65, I-55, and others. If my friend from Indianapolis used my limited advice that "I-94 is not a viable route to Chicago from Indianapolis," he might conclude that "I-90 is a viable route to Chicago." If he reached this conclusion, he would make a significant navigational error: I-90 does not run through Indianapolis. In fact, even if I provided a second bit of navigational advice to him, adding a second premise to his argument for directions to Chicago from Indianapolis such as, "I-90 is not a viable route to Chicago," he would not be in a position to reach an affirmative conclusion. Armed with two negative premises, he would not be in a position to reach any conclusion about the best route to Chicago from Indianapolis.

A negative premise describing how one term is excluded from another cannot support an affirmative conclusion.

Logic ensures this result in the context of arguments about navigation, as well as arguments about legal conclusions. A negative premise describing how one categorical term is excluded from another cannot support an affirmative conclusion about any categorical term. For example, in a criminal assault prosecution, one of the elements of the crime of assault is proof that the defendant intended to create a reasonable apprehension of harm in the victim.[1] Accordingly, if the prosecution bases its case on the defendant's state of mind by establishing that the defendant's intention was not to come to the aid of the victim, that evidence is not particularly helpful to establishing that the defendant intended to create apprehension of harm. It might remove from consideration one kind of intent, among the vast universe of potential intentions harbored by a criminal defendant, but that is not any more conclusive about a defendant's intent than knowing I-94 is not a viable route from Indianapolis to Chicago. Rules of logic ensure that if an argument reaches an affirmative conclusion, it must do so based on two affirmative premises; an argument that asserts an affirmative conclusion, based on a premise that merely states a negative proposition, commits a logical fallacy.

The fallacy of the negative premise, like the fallacy of the undistributed middle term and the fallacy of the illicit process, involves a rule that regulates categorical syllogisms. The rules of logic at work in the first two fallacies focused on the distribution of terms. The preceding discussion of those two fallacies centered on rules that managed the distribution of the middle term and the terms in the conclusion respectively. The rule of logic at issue in this chapter, and the fallacy that follows from violation of this rule, moves its focus away from distribution. Instead, the fallacy of the negative premise focuses on whether the conclusion is affirmative and, when it is, whether it is supported by an affirmative premise.

The rule of logic at work in the fallacy of the negative premise has been stated this way: "There can be only one negative premise. If there is a negative premise, the conclusion must be negative."[2] Distribution is sometimes easy to identify, but other times the organization of an argument makes distribution difficult to uncover. While distribution is an unfamiliar concept to most people who have not studied logic, the concept of affirmative and negative statements is more intuitive. While it is easy to explain the difference between "some" and "all" to most people, the explanation of why the predicate term of a universal negative premise is always distributed requires some effort. Conversely, positive and negative statements are straightforward, both to identify and explain. Accordingly, the fallacy of the negative premise is easier to police, identify, and explain than the other two fallacies of categorical syllogisms.

9.2 The Force of an Affirmative Conclusion

Policing negative premises begins with understanding the scope of the rule of logic at work: "There can be only one negative premise. If there is a negative premise the conclusion must be negative."[3] This statement of the rule of logic at work is really asserting two related logical principles. In fact, some logicians describe this as

1. *See, e.g.*, Wash. v. Wilson, 883 P.2d 320 (Wash. 1994).
2. Christopher W. Tindale, Fallacies and Argument Appraisal 46 (2007).
3. *Id.*

two separate rules, and seeing them stated separately is valuable.[4] First, a syllogism based exclusively on negative premises is always invalid. This first variety of the fallacy is called the fallacy of exclusive premises. A valid syllogism requires at least one affirmative premise in order to justify any conclusion. Telling my friends from Indianapolis that I-94 is not a viable route and telling my friend that I-90 is not a viable route does not allow them to reach any logical inference from those propositions. They can believe what I have told them. Both of my statements to them are entirely true. However, my friend cannot learn anything new from my premises. They cannot reach a logical inference, which is the purpose and power of formal logic.

Second, a syllogism that has one negative premise and one affirmative premise can still yield a conclusion. However, such a syllogism can only reach a negative conclusion.[5] If there is a negative premise, it must be paired with another, affirmative, premise, and those two premises must support a negative conclusion. Where a syllogism has a different combination of affirmative and negative premises and conclusions, the syllogism commits the fallacy of the negative premise.

9.3 Finding Positive Conclusions and Supporting Them with Positive Premises

Identifying the right combination of premises and conclusions to fit the pattern of the fallacy of the negative premise involves assessing whether the respective premises and conclusion are affirmative or negative. First, if a categorical argument reaches an affirmative conclusion, it cannot be based on a negative premise. Spotting this form of fallacy is as simple as seeing the pattern of an affirmative conclusion and a negative premise. An affirmative conclusion can take either of two syllogistic forms:

> All A are B.
>
> or
>
> Some A are B.

Examples of affirmative conclusions in legal arguments include:

> All the plaintiff's witnesses lack credibility.
>
> All the defendant's affirmative defenses were timely asserted.
>
> All of the elements of negligence are included in the plaintiff's Complaint.
>
> Some of the expert's opinions are supported by an appropriate evidentiary foundation.

4. *See, e.g.*, Patrick J. Hurley, A Concise Introduction to Logic 230–31 (2015).
5. *See, e.g.*, Irving M. Copi & Carl Cohen, Introduction to Logic 247–48 (13th ed. 2008).

> Some of the documents within defendant's possession and control are included in its response to the plaintiff's Request for Production of Documents.

Logic prevents an argument from reaching an affirmative conclusion, like those listed above, from a negative premise. Cases dealing with arguments that commit the fallacy of the negative premise generally fit into this pattern. Negative premises take one of the following syllogistic patterns:

> No A are B.
>
> or
>
> Some A are not B.

Examples of negative premises in legal argument follow.

> Some of the plaintiff's witnesses are not credible witness.
>
> None of the defendant's affirmative defenses were timely asserted.
>
> None of the elements of negligence are included in the plaintiff's Complaint.
>
> Some of the expert's opinions are not supported by an appropriate evidentiary foundation.
>
> Some of the documents within defendant's possession and control are not included in its response to the plaintiff's Request for Production of Documents.

Accordingly, the process of identifying the fallacy of the negative premise is spotting a combination of an affirmative conclusion and a negative premise. Determining the distribution of a proposition, sometimes referred to as its *quantity*,[6] can be challenging. Conversely, determining whether a proposition is affirmative or negative, sometimes referred to as its *quality*,[7] is generally apparent from the language of the proposition and is rarely difficult to identify. Language that excludes one categorical term from another, like "no," "none," or "is not," is indicative of a negative proposition. For example, language excluding categorical terms in the following proposition is highlighted:

> ***None*** of the witness's statements are protected by the attorney–client privilege.
>
> Some of the witness's statements are ***not*** protected by the attorney–client privilege.

6. *See, e.g.*, Hurley, *supra* note 4, at 204.
7. *Id.*

I-94 ***is not*** an interstate that goes from Indianapolis to Chicago.

Some of the witness's testimony ***is not*** hearsay.

Some of the witnesses called by defendant's counsel ***are not*** on the defendant's witness list.

An argument can still reach a conclusion based on one negative premise, but the conclusion cannot be affirmative. This leads to the second form of this fallacy. If an argument is based on two negative premises, it can reach no conclusion whatsoever. Two assertions that exclude their respective terms from another cannot result in any inference:

No A is B

No C is B

Therefore, some A is C.

This form of the fallacy, sometimes referred to as the fallacy of exclusive premises because both premises exclude one term from another term, cannot provide any logical inference regarding the relationship between the two terms and is fallacious.

9.4 How Courts Have Used the Fallacy of the Negative Premise to Evaluate Legal Argument

Courts have employed the rules of logic related to negative premises just as they have used rules that regulate distribution in legal argument.[8] An example is found in *Wiehe v. Kissick Construction Company*,[9] in which the Kansas Court of Appeals reviewed a decision by the Kansas Worker's Compensation Board. The court was reviewing a decision by the Board finding that the claimant was entitled to worker's compensation benefits.[10] The claimant was injured while operating heavy construction equipment at work, but his employer argued the injuries occurred while he was

8. *See, e.g.*, Cook v. Moffat, 46 U.S. (5 How.) 295, 299 (1847); Walmsley v. City of Philadelphia, 872 F.2d 546, 554 (3d Cir. 1989) (Aldisert, J., dissenting); Kolakowski v. Sec'y of Health & Human Servs., No. 99-0625V, 2010 U.S. Claims LEXIS 1035 at *422 (Fed. Cl. Nov. 23, 2010); Posey v. State, No. CACR04-610, 2005 Ark. App. LEXIS 397 (Ark. Ct. App. May 18, 2005); State v. Lackey, 208 P.3d 793, 797 (Kan. Ct. App. 2009), *rev'd*, 286 P.3d 859 (Kan. 2012); Jones v. State, 203 P.3d 739 (Kan. Ct. App. 2009); Ochsner v. Idealife Ins. Co., 945 So. 2d 128, 135 (La. Ct. App. 2006) (Kirby, J., dissenting); Bailey v. State, 294 A.2d 123, 129 n. 4 (Md. Ct. Spec. App. 1972); Council of Orgs. & Others for Educ. about Parochiaid v. Governor of Mich., 548 N.W.2d 909, 920 n. 7 (Mich. Ct. App. 1996) (O'Connell, J., dissenting); Dunn v. City of Milwaukie, 328 P.3d 1261, 1273 n. 17 (Ore. 2014); State v. Weber, 247 P.3d 782, 786 (Wash. App. 2011).

9. 232 P.3d 866, 869–70 (Kan. App. 2010).

10. Most workers compensation statutes proscribe a system under which employers pay for insurance for their employees. The insurance policy generally covers certain losses incurred by employees who are injured at work, even when the injury was the fault of the employee.

under the influence of marijuana.[11] The worker's compensation statute at issue provided that employers were not responsible for payment of worker's compensation benefits for injured workers when consumption of alcohol or drugs contributed to the injury.[12] Further, the statute provided for a conclusive presumption that alcohol or drugs contributed to the injury "if certain quantitative alcohol or drug levels are shown from an employee's chemical test."[13]

The Board determined that despite the evidence that "drug test results revealed. . . a level of marijuana. . . more than four times the level to establish a conclusive presumption of impairment [under the statute],"[14] the impairment exception did not relieve the employer of an obligation to pay worker's compensation benefits because there was not sufficient evidence that any impairment contributed to the accident.[15]

> But based on the evidence contained within this record, there is little if any credible evidence that claimant's presumptive impairment contributed to his accident. He drove to work, apparently without incident. He began his work day at approximately 7:15 a.m. He worked continuously for four hours until the time of the accident. He was told to keep his machine moving which he did. One coworker points to his unusual approach to the spreading of this dirt pile, but the pictures reveal a significant pile of dirt with one large clod of dirt. It is not surprising that the machine claimant was operating, which both parties agree is unstable, would tip over as he was trying [to] smooth the area out.
>
> As was noted early on in this claim, claimant may have exhibited poor judgment in his method of operating the machine. But if claimant was so impaired as Dr. Brown suggests, one would expect at least one of his coworkers to say or do something to prevent him from continuing on with his job on that day long before he tipped the equipment over and was injured. Instead, all we are left with is an allegation that one coworker made eye contact with him at the moment of the accident and gestured in a manner telling him 'no' and another coworker who alleges, after driving by him, that claimant was acting squirrely [*sic*]. And the last of respondent's witnesses was found to be less than straightforward with his testimony. Thus, none of these were persuasive on the issue of claimant's impairment or his ability—or inability—to perform his job duties on the day of his accident.[16]

11. 232 P.3d 866, 868–69.
12. *Id.* at 873–74.
13. *Id.* at 874.
14. *Id.* at 869–70.
15. *Id.* at 739.
16. *Id.* at 875 (bracketed material in the original).

The court evaluated this argument using formal logic, beginning by summarizing the Board's decision as being founded on a list of negative premises:

> The Board's decision revolves around its determination that there was no credible evidence that [the claimaint] was acting erratically or unusually on the morning of the accident. From this negative evidence, the Board drew a conclusion that [the claimaint's] presumptive impairment did not cause or contribute to the accident. The logic of that conclusion is based upon a syllogism, which is essentially as follows:
>
> No employee's presumptive impairment will contribute to the employee's accident when no evidence exists that the employee was "acting erratically or unusually" before the accident occurred.
>
> Although employee A was presumptively impaired when the accident occurred, no evidence exists that employee A was "acting erratically or unusually" before the accident happened.
>
> Therefore, employee A's presumptive impairment did not contribute to the accident.[17]

The court went on to evaluate the Board's reasoning as suffering from the fallacy of exclusive premises, and provided an explanation for the fallacious nature of this pattern of legal argument along the way:

> The Board's logic is flawed for it would compel the conclusion that whenever an employee showed no signs of erratic or unusual behavior before the accident occurred, the employee's presumptive impairment would not have caused or contributed to the employee's accident. Nevertheless, just because an employee does not display any erratic or unusual behavior does not mean that the employee's presumptive impairment would not have caused or contributed to the accident.
>
> Moreover, the Board's reasoning is an example of what logicians describe as the "Fallacy of Exclusive Premises."[18] From two negative premises no conclusion can be drawn. The reason is that we cannot argue about the relation between two classes from the mere fact that they are both excluded, wholly or in part, from a third class. In our case, the third class is the following: No evidence exists that the employee was "acting erratically or unusually" before the accident

17. *Id.* at 875–76.

18. As mentioned above, logicians, like the court here, sometimes refer to the fallacy of the negative premise, when it takes the form of reaching a conclusion from two negative premises, as the "fallacy of exclusive premises." *See, e.g.*, Hurley, *supra* note 4, at 287.

> occurred. When each premise contains an exclusion, the argument is not a syllogism; that is, its premises do not jointly imply the conclusion, as is in this case.
>
> For example, "No native-born Sooners are persons born in Kansas" and "No native-born Hoosiers are persons born in Kansas" furnishes no basis for inferring any connection whatsoever between the native-born Sooners and the native-born Hoosiers. To attempt to draw an inference from such a connection is to commit the fallacy of exclusive premises.[19]

Another example of a court using the fallacy of the negative premise can be found in *Dunn v. City of Milwaukie*.[20] In *Dunn*, the Oregon Supreme Court considered the sufficiency of evidence of intent necessary to establish a case of inverse condemnation. The plaintiff sued the City of Milwaukie, Oregon, claiming that her sewer system backed up, causing water damage in her house. The plaintiff alleged that the backup occurred after the city used a high-pressure water technique ("hydrocleaning") to clean the city sewer lines. The plaintiff sued the city on theories of negligence and inverse condemnation. The negligence claim was dismissed prior to trial.[21]

The plaintiff endeavored to establish that the sewage backup was intentionally caused. The court held that plaintiff was required to show that the sewage backup was the necessary result of the city's intentional actions[22] and that the standard for such proof was that the backup was the "necessary, certain, predicable, or inevitable result of the city's intentional manner of hydrocleaning the sewer."[23]

> Of course, on this record, there is no evidence or jury determination that the city was "not negligent." There instead is simply a void left by the dismissal of plaintiff's negligence claim. Even if, however, this record established that the city was "not negligent," as plaintiff argues, the argument fails, as we have explained. Classic logic provides a further explanation for why it fails. Plaintiff's argument suffers from the "fallacy of negative premises."[24]

The court considered the impact of evidence that the plaintiff's damages were not caused by the defendant's negligence. The court recognized that such a negative finding could not support an affirmative conclusion that the damages were inflicted intentionally. As the court explained, "the person could have acted with intent, but a

19. *Id.* at 876 (citing Copi & Cohen, Introduction to Logic 239 (12th ed. 2005)).
20. 328 P.3d 1261 (Ore. 2014).
21. *Id.* at 1263.
22. *Id.* at 1274.
23. *Id.*
24. *Id.* at 1274, n. 17 (citing Judge Ruggero J. Aldisert, Logic for Lawyers: A Guide to Clear Legal Thinking 156 (3d ed. 1997)).

range of other possibilities exists as well, including the possibility that what happened was purely accidental or inadvertent, and not due either to negligence or intent."[25]

Another example of a court using formal logic and the fallacy of the negative premise is found in *State v. Weber*.[26] There, the appellate court scrutinized the trial court's reasoning, using the fallacy of the negative premise to evaluate a motion to suppress evidence in a criminal case. In *Weber*, the defendant moved to suppress evidence obtained by the state after a Washington state trooper stopped the defendant while defendant was driving his vehicle.[27] The trooper reported observing the defendant failing to stop before pulling his vehicle into the street and speeding at 2:53 a.m.[28] The trooper indicated that he pulled over the defendant and administered a sobriety test, which the defendant allegedly failed.[29] Breath tests allegedly suggested the defendant was driving under the influence of alcohol.[30] The trooper testified that while he is "always looking for DUI's [*sic*]," he stopped the defendant for failing to stop and for exceeding the posted speed limit.[31] The defendant moved to suppress the evidence obtained after the stop, claiming the claimed justification for the stop was a pretext.[32] The trial court granted the defendant's motion.[33] The decision was subsequently reversed by the superior court.[34]

The Washington Court of Appeals reviewed the findings of fact and scrutinized the basis for the trial court's conclusion that the stop was a pretext[35] to investigate whether the defendant was operating his vehicle under the influence of alcohol. The court began by assessing what facts the court concluded that "[t]he trial court did not make any express statement about the trooper's credibility, nor did it squarely find what motivated him to make the traffic stop."[36]

Having noted that the trial court did not squarely determine what *did* motivate the trooper, the court of appeals reviewed the evidence of pretext.

> While we have an obligation to reasonably infer facts from the trial court's judgment, it is difficult to determine what should be inferred here. Perhaps it could be inferred that the officer was motivated by something other than enforcing the speeding law,

25. *Id.* at 1273–74.
26. *State v. Weber*, 247 P.3d 782 (Wash. Ct. App. 2011).
27. *Id.* at 782.
28. *Id.*
29. *Id.* at 782–83.
30. *Id.* at 783.
31. *Id.* at 783–84 (emphasis omitted).
32. *Id.* at 783.
33. *Id.* at 785.
34. *Id.*
35. "A pretextual stop occurs when an officer stops a vehicle in order to conduct a speculative criminal investigation unrelated to the driving, and not for the purpose of enforcing the traffic code." *Id.* at 787 (citing State v. Nichols, 162 P.3d 1122 (2007)).
36. *Id.* at 786–87.

> although there is not much in the record to support such an inference. To go any further and infer a specific motivation, however, fails on two accounts. First, nothing in the record would support such an inference, and a reviewing court must only infer facts that have substantial evidentiary support in the record. Second, it is a long-recognized logical fallacy to draw an affirmative conclusion from a negative premise. Thus, even if a reviewing court infers that the trial court factually found the trooper was not motivated to enforce the traffic law, it is not in a position to infer what the motive actually was.[37]

The court went on to affirm the superior court's reversal of the trial court's order to suppress the evidence as being obtained from a pretextual stop.[38]

The fallacy of the negative premise was raised in another case, in an argument about construction of statutory language. In *City of Wichita v. Stevenson*,[39] the court faced the application of a simple city ordinance. The ordinance[40] provided, in the applicable part, that "No person shall permit overcrowding or admittance of any person beyond the approved capacity of a building or a portion thereof."[41] The appellant was convicted of violating the ordinance on three occasions in 2009.[42] She was allegedly present at a tavern on each of those three occasions.[43] However, she argued that she was neither the owner nor a manager on duty on any of the three occasions for which she was charged, but merely a patron drinking and socializing in a tavern.[44] The appellant's legal argument on appeal was that the ordinance was unconstitutionally vague, since the term "no person" did not define who *was* responsible for ensuring compliance with the statute.[45]

---

37. *Id.* at 786–87 (citations omitted).
38. *Id.* at 788. The court utilized the fallacy of the negative premise to explain why the superior court's opinion reversing the trial court could not be based on a fallacious argument. It did so, in the quoted portion of the opinion, by confirming the logic of the superior court's limited substantiation of its decision to reverse the trial court. The court of appeals went on to affirm the superior court's reversal of the trial court's decision that the stop was pretextual, concluding: "In light of the nonexistence of an improper motive, there is no basis for finding that this traffic stop was a pretext." *Id.* at 791.
39. *City of Wichita v. Stevenson*, 265 P.3d 593, 2011 Kan. App. Unpub. LEXIS 1058 (Kan. Ct. App. 2011, an unpublished decision of the Kansas Court of Appeals).
40. *Id.* at *1.
41. *Id.*
42. *Id.* at *1–2.
43. *Id.* at *2.
44. *Id.* ("Stevenson argued the ordinance unconstitutionally failed to place limits on who police officers could cite for permitting overcrowding as evidenced by the fact that (1) she was not the owner of [the tavern], (2) she was not the manager on duty on February 7, April 11, or April 18, 2009, and (3) although she was in the [tavern] on all three occasions, it was only because she was socializing with friends.").
45. *Id.* at *2.

The court disagreed with this argument, ultimately holding that "[n]o person shall permit overcrowding"

> makes it clear that the individual who is culpable under the ordinance is the individual who actually permits the building to be over capacity. It is the responsibility of the police and fire departments to determine who permits, gives consent, authorizes, makes possible, or gives opportunity for the building to be occupied over capacity. The common and well-understood meaning of the word "permit" provides a clear standard for those who enforce the ordinance.[46]

However, the dissenting judge, Henry W. Green, Jr., would have construed this language otherwise, and he justified his conclusion in terms of formal logic.

> Subsection 15.01.480 of the Wichita City Ordinance states: "No person shall permit overcrowding or admittance of any person beyond the approved capacity of a building or a portion thereof." Stevenson alleges that this subsection of the ordinance is unconstitutionally vague because the word "person" could mean "any human being." And "person" is a term that can be applied without limitation. Stevenson is correct. For example, "[n]o person shall permit overcrowding" is a universal negative proposition: all persons are excluded from the class of things that allow overcrowding; and all members of the class of things that allow overcrowding are excluded from the class of persons. Thus, "[n]o person shall permit overcrowding" asserts that if anyone is a person, then he or she will not allow overcrowding. This negative premise can be reconstructed into the following syllogism:
>
> > Major Premise: No person shall permit overcrowding.
> >
> > Minor Premise: The bartender is a person.
> >
> > Conclusion: Therefore, the bartender shall not allow overcrowding.
>
> By not explaining who is "no person," the ordinance is deficient. Persons of common intelligence would be required to guess at the phrase's meaning and differ as to how the regulations should be enforced. For example, the ordinance contains no guidelines to assist either a person who desires to know whether he or she is the person who is not to allow overcrowding or an official who is charged with the enforcement of the ordinance.[47]

46. *Id.* at *18.
47. *Id.* at *20-21 (Green, J., dissenting).

Judge Green also wrote the majority opinion in *State v. Lackey*, another case where the fallacy of the negative premise makes an appearance in a court's analysis.[48] While Judge Green does not provide an explanation of the fallacy of the negative premise in *City of Wichita v. Stevenson*, his recitation of this rule of logic from *State v. Lackey* is just as applicable here: "[I]f one premise is negative, the conclusion must be negative."[49] Accordingly, logic precludes drawing a positive conclusion from a negative premise, such as "no person shall permit overcrowding." It seems that Judge Green's point in his dissenting opinion in *Stevenson* is not to assert that a fallacious argument is being made.[50] Instead, it is to demonstrate the consequence of a universal negative proposition: the only conclusion that can be drawn from a negative premise is a negative conclusion. Therefore, no person can conclude whether they are allowed to permit overcrowding from the major premise provided by the statute.[51] This was the basis for Judge Green's conclusion that the ordinance was unconstitutionally vague.

Ochsner v. Idealife Insurance Company[52] is another case involving the construction of language. In *Ochsner*, the court was construing language in an insurance policy. The dissenting judge took the position that the appellate court committed the fallacy of the negative premise when it rendered its opinion. The appellant, the surviving spouse of the insured, attempted to compel the insured's life insurance company to pay death benefits to the appellant.[53] The insurer claimed that the insured had quit paying his policy premiums nine years before his death.[54] As a result, the insurer cancelled the insured's life insurance policy without giving notice to him.[55] The court ruled that an applicable Louisiana statute provided that "**No life insurer shall within one year** after default in payment of any premium, . . . **declare forfeited** or lapsed any policy. . . [without giving the statutorily prescribed notice]."[56] The insurer argued that it provided notice of cancellation to the insured's bank, but not to the insured himself.[57] However, the court held that the notice of cancellation sent to the bank did not meet the requirements of the statute.[58]

48. State v. Lackey, 208 P.3d 793 (Kan. App 2009), *rev'd*, 286 P.3d 859 (Kan. 2012).
49. *Id.* at 797.
50. Judge Green never asserts that the fallacy of the negative premise is committed here.
51. *Stevenson*, 265 P.3d at 598 at *21 ("For example, the ordinance contains no guidelines to assist either a person who desires to know whether he or she is the person who is not to allow overcrowding or an official who is charged with the enforcement of the ordinance.").
52. 945 So. 2d 128 (La. Ct. App. 2006).
53. *Id.* at 129–30.
54. *Id.* at 130.
55. *Id.* The policy had been pledged to the insured's bank, which later assigned its interest in the policy. *Id.* The insurer also assigned and delegated its rights and obligations under the policy to another entity. *Id.*
56. *Id.* at 135 (Kirby, J., dissenting) (emphasis in the original).
57. *Id.* at 131.
58. *Id.*

The insurer focused on the "within one year" provision of the statute to argue that because the nonpayment of the premium extended beyond one year, no written notice was required.[59] The insurer argued that after one year of nonpayment, "all life insurers shall declare the subject policy forfeited or lapsed" regardless of notice.[60] The court accepted this argument. However, the dissenting opinion evaluated the argument in terms of formal logic and opined that such a conclusion could not logically be drawn from the negative premise upon which the argument was based, since doing so would be a fallacy of the negative premise.[61] Apparently,[62] the dissenting judge would evaluate the argument in something like this syllogistic form:

> No life insurer less than one year after default in payment of any premium is a life insurer that may declare lapsed any policy without first providing notice.
>
> No defendant is a life insurer less than one year after default in payment.
>
> Therefore, the defendant is a life insurer that may declare lapsed any policy without first providing notice.

Seen in this syllogistic form, the argument is described in a way that commits the fallacy of the negative premise. The major premise states a principle of law. This principle of law is described as a universal negative proposition. It describes a class of life insurers who are precluded from declaring a policy lapse without notice to their insured. The minor premise is a universal negative proposition as well. It describes the entire class of the defendant and excludes the defendant from the category of life insurers that find themselves less than one year after default in payment. The conclusion is a universal affirmative proposition. Of course, one might be tempted to believe that logic compels this conclusion.[63] However, there are likely other circumstances that limit an insurer's ability to declare a life insurance policy lapsed. It would be a leap of logic to conclude that because one category

59. *Id.* at 132.
60. *Id.* at 135.
61. *Id.*
62. The dissenting opinion does not detail the argument in specific syllogistic form.
63. Just why, at first glance, this argument might be tempting is unclear. Psychologically speaking, however, there may be some explanations. *See, e.g.*, Timothy L. Hubbard, *Logic and Reasoning, in* 3 Salem Health: Psychol. & Mental Health 1121, 1123 (Nancy A. Piotrowski, ed. 2010) ("When quantifiers such as "all," "some," and "none" are used within syllogisms, additional errors in reasoning occur. People are more likely to accept positive conclusions to positive premises and negative conclusions to negative premises, *negative conclusions if premises are mixed*, a universal conclusion if premises are universal (all or none), a particular conclusion if premises are particular (some), and a particular conclusion if one premise is general and the other is particular. These observations led to the atmosphere hypothesis, which suggests that the quantifiers within the premises create an "atmosphere" predisposing subjects to accept as valid conclusions that use the same quantifiers.") (emphasis added).

of insurers cannot declare a policy lapsed without notice that another category of insurers can declare a policy lapsed without notice. It would be logically equivalent to letting friends in Indianapolis conclude that because I-94 is not a viable route to Chicago from Indianapolis, I-90 must be a viable route to Chicago from Indianapolis.[64]

9.5 Keys to Using the Fallacy of the Negative Premise to Evaluate and Improve Legal Argument

The patterns of the fallacy of the negative premise are simple to spot. In the following graphical depictions of arguments, the major term is represented by a circle with vertical lines. When the major term is negative (that is, when it is excluded from the middle term), it includes a circle with a diagonal line. For example, the following Figure 47 represents a negative premise having a distributed major term excluded from a distributed middle term, like "No defendant is a life insurer that may declare a policy lapsed."

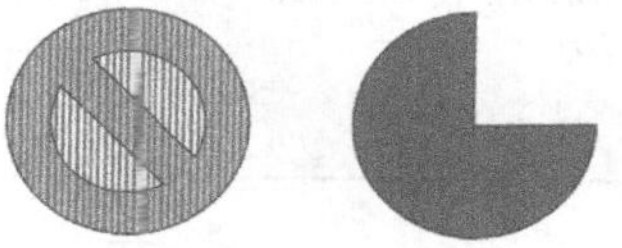

Figure 47. *An example of a pattern of a negative premise.*

For purposes of assessing quality, we can ignore whether any term is distributed or not. Instead, the focus is on whether the premise is negative. If one term is negative, then the quality of proposition is negative. Accordingly, syllogisms committing the fallacy of the negative premise will take the pattern of an affirmative conclusion and at least one negative premise. For example, the pattern is apparent in each of the following three syllogisms:

64. By now, you may be thinking that a negative premise might justify an affirmative conclusion if the premise ruled out one of only two alternatives. For example, what if there were only two routes leaving Indianapolis, and one premise excluded one of the routes from consideration as viable routes to Chicago? Would that negative premise require a conclusion that the other route is a viable route to Chicago? Another kind of syllogism, a disjunctive syllogism, does allow for this kind of an argument. However, a categorical syllogism does not. The valid, and invalid, patterns of disjunctive syllogisms are the subject of Chapter Ten.

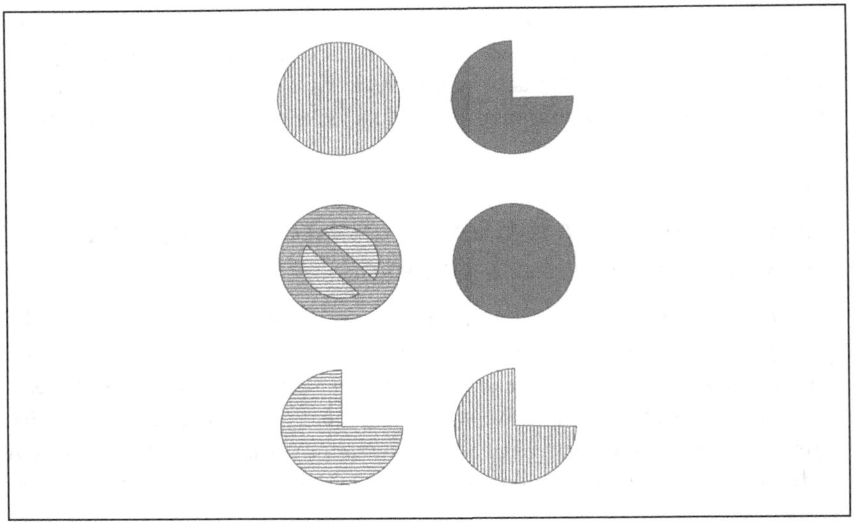

Figure 48. *An example of a fallacious categorical syllogism taking the form called the fallacy of the negative premise, including an affirmative conclusion, supported by a negative minor premise.*

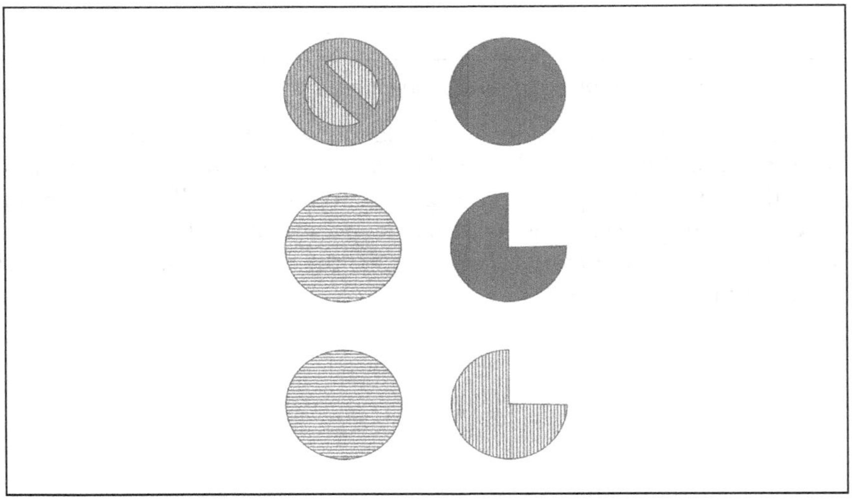

Figure 49. *An example of a fallacious categorical syllogism taking the form called the fallacy of the negative premise, including an affirmative conclusion, supported by a negative major premise.*

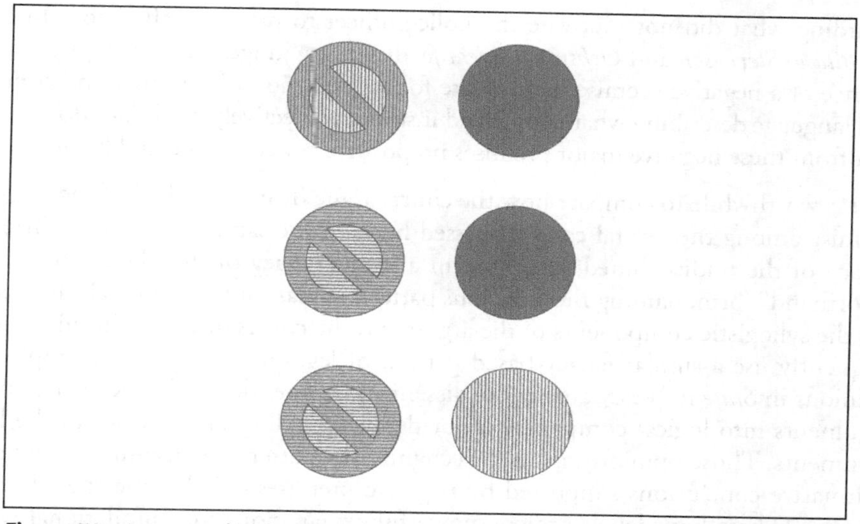

Figure 50. *An example of a categorical syllogism taking the form called the fallacy of the exclusive premises, including a negative conclusion, supported by a negative major premise and a major minor premise.*[65]

There could be more variations on these three patterns if some different combinations of quality and quantity were included in the examples, but because distribution does not affect whether a syllogism commits the fallacy of the negative premise, variations of quantity are not logically significant here.[66] Figures 48 and 49 are examples of arguments that reach a positive conclusion from a negative premise. Figure 50 is an example of an argument that reaches a conclusion from two negative premises and commits the fallacy of exclusive premises.

Comparing these patterns of argument that commit the fallacy of the negative premise with the cases discussed above demonstrates how these patterns of logical fallacy appear in legal argument. In *Wiehe v. Kissick Construction Company*, the court held that it held could not conclude anything about whether impairment caused the accident from the negative premise that the employee was not acting erratically or unusually. In *Dunne v. Milwaukie*, the court held that it could not conclude that the City's actions were intentional from the negative premise that the City's actions were not negligent. In *State v. Weber*, the court held that it could not reach a conclusion about what did motivate the police officer to make a traffic stop from a premise

65. Note that although the conclusion in Figure 50 is negative it still violates the rule of logic. No conclusion can be drawn, positive or negative, from two negative premises. This is sometimes referred to as the fallacy of exclusive premises.

66. That is not to say that distribution is not logically significant, since fallacies are not mutually exclusive. Further, whether a premise is positive or negative impacts the quantity of the terms. Arguments have to comply with all of the rules of logic, and the fact that an argument manages the *quantity* of terms properly does not ensure that it manages the *quality* of terms properly.

regarding what did not motivate the police officer to make a traffic stop. In both *Wichita v. Stevenson* and *Ochsner v. Idealife*, dissenting judges used the logical consequence of a negative premise to advocate for construction of statutory and contractual language describing what people and insurers, respectively, could not do, arguing that from these negative major premises no positive conclusions could be drawn.

It is worthwhile to compare how the courts argue from the fallacy of the negative premise among the several cases discussed here. In the same way courts utilize the fallacy of the undistributed middle term and the fallacy of the illicit process in a "shorthand" form, naming the fallacious pattern of reasoning without always detailing the syllogistic components of the argument, the courts discussed in this chapter frequently use a similar fallacy-based pattern of legal reasoning. For example, the opinions in *State v. Weber* and in the dissent in *Ochsner* do not break the down the arguments into logical components, nor detail the syllogisms at work in the legal arguments. Those opinions, instead, recognize the patterns of argument at work—affirmative conclusions supported by negative premises—and name the fallacious patterns. These logic labels provide powerful explanations for foundational weaknesses in the arguments addressed by the courts.[67]

9.6 Chapter Nine in Review

- Propositions in a categorical syllogism are either affirmative or negative.
- The propositions in a categorical syllogism have to comply with a rule of logic that requires that if either premise is negative, the conclusion must be negative.
- The propositions in a categorical syllogism also have to comply with a rule of logic that requires that at least one premise must be affirmative.
- The pattern of argument that commits the fallacy of the negative premise is one that argues what something is from a premise about what something is not.
- Courts have encountered arguments that commit the fallacy of the negative premise and dealt with those arguments in terms of formal logic.
- A short sample deposition transcript excerpt in in a civil case follows. Assume a primary issue in the case is whether the defendant landlord's breach of a plaintiff tenant's commercial lease agreement resulted in damages for lost profits to the plaintiff. Assume that in the case the plaintiff, a toy retailer, was forced to move from its location in a shopping mall to a new location. When the plaintiff could not move to defendant's space in another shopping mall ("The Shoppes Property"), it had to move to a third property, located near the local airport.

67. Some of the ideas developed in this chapter were first explored in Stephen M. Rice, *False Persuasion, Superficial Heuristics, and the Power of Logical Form to Test the Integrity of Legal Argument*, 34 Pace L. Rev. 76 (2014).

Despite operating the business under the same name, management, employees, and business model, the business incurred losses at the airport location, rather than the profits it had historically enjoyed at the mall. Review the transcript and see if you can spot the fallacy of the illicit process in the line of questioning pursued by the lawyer taking the deposition. Once you find it, ask yourself why you were able to identify it, whether you would have identified it before reading this chapter, and consider how you might respond to this line of questioning in practice. A discussion of the fallacy in this example can be found in the appendix at the end of this book.

9.7 Exercise

In the District Court of the 23rd Judicial District, Montana

Toy-Vo, Inc. d/b/a Toypocalypse
Plaintiff,

Case No. B16-3927

v.

Collin Lewis,
Defendant.

Deposition of Collin Lewis

Q: Mr. Lewis, would you please state your name for the record?

A: Collin Martin Lewis. I spell my first name C-O-L-L-I-N.

Q: Mr. Lewis, what do you understand this lawsuit is about?

A: Well, my understanding is that your client says I breached a lease for the ground floor of my property in The Shoppes Development.

Q: What's the address of that property?

A: It's 1601 Shoppes Circle.

Q: Is it okay with you if I refer to that property today as The Shoppes Property?

A: That's what I call it.

Q: So, if I refer to it as The Shoppes Property in this deposition we can agree that I'm talking about the property you own at 1601 Shoppes Circle here in town?

A: Sounds good.

Q: What do you understand the legal issue to be in this lawsuit?

MS. BOCHANE: I'll object to the question to the extent it calls for a legal conclusion.

Q: Go ahead and answer the question as best you can.

A: Well, I understand that there are two issues. For one, your client ended up leasing another property near the airport, and I just do not see why they have anything to complain about. They ended up with a less expensive lease near the airport. Next, I never thought we had an enforceable lease. I send a copy of my lease agreement to them to sign but I never got a signed copy back from them. So I don't think there was ever a lease in the first place.

Q: Let's talk about the first issue you mentioned. Your position is that my client, Toy-Vo, did not suffer any loss as a result of any breach of contract, right?

A: Yeah. They were not harmed. They do not have any losses.

Q: Okay. Let me ask you this. Do you know how much money Toy-Vo was making before it talked to you about leasing The Shoppes Property?

A: I have no idea.

Q: Well, you know Toy-Vo was operating a toy store before you talked to them about leasing The Shoppes Property?

A: Yes.

Q: And you know they'd been operating their toy store in the West Side Mall for five years before they talked to you about leasing The Shoppes Property?

A: Yes. But I don't think they were making any money there.

MS. BOCHANE: Listen to his question.

Q: Why don't you think they were making money at their West Side Mall location?

A: I guess I don't know that for sure. I just never saw much traffic in their store at West Side Mall and I assumed that had they hadn't been profitable there or they would not have been looking to move to my property.

Q: When you say "my property" you are referring to The Shoppes Property, right?

A: Yes. The Shoppes Property.

Q: Are there any other reasons why you believe that Toy-Vo was unprofitable at the West Side Mall location?

A: No.

Q: Did you know that Toy-Vo made profits of $108,000 in the year before they left the West Side Mall?

A: I didn't know that.

Q: Did you know that Toy-Vo made profits of $88,000 in the year before that?

A: Didn't know that. I guess I still don't know that. You're just telling me that.

Q: You cannot agree to those figures because you just do not know if they are accurate, right?

A: Right.

Q: And you don't know if they are wrong either, do you?

A: I guess that is true too.

Q: If Toy-Vo was profitable before it left the West Side Mall, do you know why they lost $204,000 last year, while they were in their latest location near the airport?

A: I do not.

Q: You don't know why a business that had profits exceeding $80,000 in the two years preceding deciding to move locations suddenly had six-figure losses in the year following moving locations?

A: No.

Q: Well Toy-Vo had a history managing a retail toy store, didn't they?

A: Yes.

Q: So lack of management experience could not be the cause of the loss?

A: Right.

Q: If they were selling the same assortment and quality of toys at their new location, the inventory could not be the cause of their loss of profits, could it?

MS. BOCHANE: Objection as to form.

Q: Go ahead and answer.

A: I guess not.

Q: Are you aware of whether the recent economic improvement in retail sales locally could causes Toy-Vo to lose profits?

A: I don't know.

Q: Do you know that Toy-Vo employs the same managers now that they did at the West Side Mall location?

A: I don't know that.

Q: If the management team is the same, that couldn't be the cause of their recent losses, right?

MS. BOCHANE: Objection as to form, speculation.

A: I suppose that is right.

Q: If the sales staff is the same, that couldn't be the cause of their recently losses either right?

MS. BOCHANE: Objection as to form.

A: Okay.

Q: Is that a "yes?"

A: Yes.

Q: So if I understand your testimony today, you'd agree that if Toy-Vo is losing money, and that loss is not caused by inexperience, inventory, management, sales, or local economic factors, that the cause of its lost profits is its current location near the airport, right?

A: I don't know.

Q: Well what do you think is causing the lost profits?

A: I guess I just don't know.

. . . .

Chapter Ten

The Fallacy of Affirming a Disjunct

This chapter will focus on a third kind of syllogism, a disjunctive syllogism, and a fallacy some disjunctive syllogisms commit, the fallacy of affirming a disjunct. The chapter will explain how to identify the fallacy and how to explain what is wrong with disjunctive syllogisms that commit it. Unlike the fallacies described in the preceding chapters, the pattern of the fallacy of affirming a disjunct is not always fallacious. As you read the chapter, consider focusing on answering the following questions:

- Why is this fallacy called "affirming a disjunct?" What is a "disjunct" in an argument, and what does it mean to "affirm" it?
- Can the fallacy of affirming a disjunct appear in any argument? Is it limited to a specific category of arguments?
- If affirming a disjunct is an unpersuasive argument, how can it be fixed to make a compelling argument?
- What rule of logic is violated when an argument commits the fallacy of affirming a disjunct?
- What simple pattern can you look for to identify why the fallacy of affirming a disjunct?
- What similarities and differences do you recognize among the fallacies of categorical syllogisms, hypothetical syllogisms, and disjunctive syllogisms?
- When is the pattern of argument that identifies the fallacy of affirming a disjunct fallacious, and when is it not fallacious?

10.1 Disjunctive Syllogisms and the Problem with "Or"

The last type of syllogistic argument this book addresses is the disjunctive syllogism. In Chapters Five and Six, hypothetical syllogisms generally took the "if . . . then" form. In Chapters Seven, Eight, and Nine, categorical syllogisms were frequently marked by use of the words "some," "all," or "no." Disjunctive syllogisms are typically marked by the simple, but problematic, word: "or."

When we use the word "or" in ordinary conversation, there is rarely any ambiguity in what we intend. If I ask a colleague who works down the hall from my office what he usually eats for lunch, he might tell me "a salad or a sandwich." If I ask a friend what kind of cake she likes for her birthday, she might respond by saying "German chocolate or carrot cake." I know what they mean when they answer me. I know that my colleague means that he either goes to the large cafeteria on our campus and purchases a salad at the salad bar or that he walks over to the opposite section of the cafeteria, where the sandwich shop staff will prepare a sandwich for him, and purchases a sandwich of his specifications for lunch. While it would not be extraordinary for a person to have both a salad and a sandwich for their lunch, I do not infer that from his answer. He did not tell me that he has a salad and a sandwich; he told me he has a salad or a sandwich. Similarly, while my friend likely deserves both a German chocolate cake and a carrot cake for her birthday, I do not infer that she is wishing for two cakes on her birthday. If that is what she wanted, she would have answered my question by saying she wanted a German chocolate cake and a carrot cake. Instead, she answered my question by saying she wanted a German chocolate cake or a carrot cake. In both cases, the word "or" is intended to mean one or the other, but not both.

In legal argument, the intention behind the word "or" is not always so apparent. For example, under the rules of Civil Procedure:

> B) A party must serve an answer to a counterclaim or crossclaim within 21 days after being served with the pleading that states the counterclaim or crossclaim.[1]

This provision in the Federal Rules of Civil Procedure provides guidance to a party in a lawsuit who, for example, finds themselves a defendant in a counterclaim and a defendant in a crossclaim.[2] Pursuant to the rule, they must serve an answer to both the counterclaim and crossclaim within twenty-one days. The rule does not authorize a party to choose between responding to one pleading or the other. However, while I would not expect the word "or" to include both a salad and a sandwich when my colleagues is speaking about lunch, a lawyer reading Fed. R. Civ. Pro. 12(a)(1)(B) would expect the word "or" to refer to both counterclaims and crossclaims.

The word "or" in both English and logic is referred to as a disjunction. In both English and in logic, the short word "or" is not as simple as it might appear.

The word "or" in both English and logic is referred to as a disjunction. In both English and in logic, the short word "or" is not as simple as it might appear. This chapter considers the potential ambiguity in disjunction and how disjunction

1. Fed. R. Civ. P. 12(a)(1)(B). A counterclaim is a claim filed by the defendant against the plaintiff. A crossclaim is a claim filed by one co-defendant against another co-defendant.
2. A party could be a counter-defendant and cross-defendant in a case where that party was named as a co-defendant and filed a third-party complaint, if one of their co-defendants filed a crossclaim and the third party defendant filed a counterclaim.

is used in legal argument. Further, this chapter considers a formal logical fallacy that occurs in disjunctive argument, the fallacy of affirming a disjunct, when a particular rule of logic is not followed.

10.2 Identifying Disjunctive Arguments and Disjuncts

Consider the following argument that might be made at the conclusion of a defendant's motion for summary judgment in a negligence[3] case: "In this negligence case, the plaintiff has failed to raise a genuine dispute about any material fact regarding duty or damages in this case." The meaning of that statement at first glance seems clear. However, does the sentence mean that the plaintiff failed to raise a genuine dispute of material fact regarding duty and the plaintiff failed to raise a genuine dispute of material fact regarding damages? Alternatively, does the sentence mean that the plaintiff failed to raise an issue of material fact regarding duty or failed to raise a genuine dispute regarding damages, but not both? The ambiguity is a consequence of what the word "or" means. Explaining the result is a function of learning logical nature of disjunction.

The solution to identifying and solving logic problems in disjunctive legal arguments begins with identifying disjunctive argument. Frequently, this is as simple as spotting the word "or." The word "or" in logic is a logical connective, just like the words "and" and "if . . . then" in other types of syllogistic arguments.[4] In logic, a disjunctive statement includes two terms; the two terms are called *disjuncts*.[5] The disjunction is the relationship between the two disjuncts.

The solution to identifying and solving logic problems in disjunctive legal arguments begins with identifying disjunctive argument. Frequently, this is as simple as spotting the word "or."

Logic recognizes two forms of disjunction not expressed in the English word "or." One form is said to be an inclusive disjunction.[6] "An inclusive disjunction is true if one . . . or both [of the] disjuncts are true; only if both disjuncts are false is their inclusive disjunction false."[7] Consider the following statement: "A contract is within the statute of frauds if it is a suretyship or if it is a contract requires more than one year to

3. A plaintiff has the burden of proving four elements in a negligence case: duty, breach of that duty, causation, and damages.
4. *See, e.g.*, Vladimir M. Sloutsky & Yevgeniya Goldvarg, *Mental Representation of Logical Connectives*, 57 Q.J. Experimental Psychol. Sec. A 636, 636 (2004) ("Logical connectives, such as 'AND', 'OR', 'IF . . . THEN', and 'IF AND ONLY IF' are ubiquitous in both language and cognition. Their role is particularly prominent in propositional reasoning, for which outcomes often depend on how logical connectives are construed.").
5. Irving M. Copi & Carl Cohen, Introduction to Logic 321 (13th ed. 2008).
6. *Id.* This form of disjunction is sometimes called the weak form of disjunction.
7. *Id.*; *See also* Layman E. Allen, *Symbolic Logic: A Razor-Edged Tool for Drafting and Interpreting Legal Documents*, 66 Yale L. J. 833, 842 (1957).

complete."[8] Under the inclusive form of disjunction, this statement would be true (1) if a contract was for a suretyship, but could be completed within one year; (2) if the contract required more than one year to complete, but was not for a suretyship; and (3) if the contract was for a suretyship that required more than one year to complete.

Alternatively, another form of disjunction is the exclusive disjunction; an exclusive disjunction is true only if one disjunct is true and the other is false.[9] If the word "or" is intended to be used as an exclusive disjunction, then the example above regarding the statute of frauds would be false because a contract will be within the statute of frauds even if it is both a suretyship and requires more than one year to complete.

Even this limited discussion of the logic of disjunction illuminates the potential problem of disjunction in legal argument. Consider the earlier statement: "In this negligence case, the plaintiff has failed to raise a genuine dispute about any material fact regarding duty or damages in this case." In this statement, there are two disjuncts. One disjunct is "duty." The other disjunct is "damages." We can see now that, as a matter of logic, there is likely an unintended ambiguity. Logic recognizes two specific types of disjunction. The English word "or" is not specific, resulting in some ambiguity. Accordingly, the lawyer who drafted this sentence likely had no understanding of the ambiguity inherent in the word "or," but fully intended to use it in its inclusive sense. The lawyer probably believed that she would be right not only if the plaintiff had failed to establish either disjunct, but also if the plaintiff had failed to establish both disjuncts.[10]

---

8. Restatement (Second) of Contracts § 110 cmts. a–b (Am. Law Inst. 1981).

9. *See* Copi & Cohen, *supra* note 5, at 321.

10. Logicians occasionally use a device called a *truth table* to evaluate and illustrate the importance of logical operators like disjunctions. A truth table is most effective when a logical statement is reduced to its most basic logical structure. This can be accomplished by identifying the logical operator and assigning simple names, or letters, to represent the terms in the statement. In the above example, we might use the letter A to represent the disjunct "raised a genuine dispute of material fact regarding duty" and the letter B to represent the disjunct "raised a genuine dispute of material fact regarding damages." A truth table evaluates the status of the statement after each of the disjuncts is assigned a truth value (either "true" or "false"). An inclusive disjunction's truth table looks like this:

A	B	A or B
T	T	T
T	F	T
F	T	T
F	F	F

An exclusive disjunction's truth table contains a significant difference:

A	*B*	*A* or *B*
T	T	F
T	F	T
F	T	T
F	F	F

See Colin Howson, Logic with Trees: An Introduction to Symbolic Logic 7 (2005); Joel Rudinow & Vincent E. Barry, Invitation to Critical Thinking 205 (6th ed. 2008).

10.3 Why Affirming a Disjunct Might Be Unpersuasive Argument

Disjunctions, just like the other logical operators we have considered, are used is the design and execution of arguments. When a disjunction is used in a syllogism, the syllogism is called a disjunctive syllogism. Like other syllogisms, syllogistic disjunction is a common way to argue both factual disputes, legal disputes, and disputes about the application of law to facts. The disjunctive syllogism discussed above focused on a legal question of whether the answer to a counterclaim and crossclaim would be due. Similarly, factual disjunctions can also serve as the premise of a disjunctive syllogism. For example:

The driver was watching the car in front of him or he was texting his client. The driver was not texting his client. Therefore, the driver was watching the car in front of him.

Figure 51. *An example of a disjunctive syllogism taking the valid form of denying a disjunct.*

In a disjunctive syllogism, the disjunctive statement is called the *disjunctive proposition*[11] or a *disjunctive premise.*[12] The disjunctive proposition in Figure 51 contains two terms: (1) "the driver was watching the car in front of him"; and (2) "[the driver] was texting his client." Following this disjunctive proposition is a second premise, taking a form we have seen in both categorical syllogisms and hypothetical syllogisms: a categorical premise. Here, the categorical premise is expressed in negated terms: "driver was not texting his client." The last element of the disjunctive syllogism is the conclusion.

When evaluating the form of a disjunctive syllogism, it must be tested against the applicable rule of logic: A valid disjunctive syllogism is one where the categorical premise denies one of the disjuncts of the disjunctive premise and the conclusion affirms the remaining disjunct.[13] Testing the argument in Figure 51 against this rule, the argument takes a valid form. If it is true that the driver was either watching the car in front of him or texting his client, then disproving that he was texting his client requires the conclusion that the driver was watching the car in front of him.

Conversely, some disjunctive syllogisms take an invalid form and commit the fallacy of affirming a disjunct. The rule requires that the categorical premise deny

11. *See* Copi & Cohen, *supra* note 5, at 298.
12. *See* Patrick J. Hurley, A Concise Introduction to Logic 318 (2015).
13. *See, e.g.*, William T. Perry & Edward A. Hacker, Aristotelian Logic 387 (1991).

a disjunct if the syllogism is to ensure the truth of the conclusion.[14] When a disjunctive syllogism affirms the disjunct and tries to reach a conclusion, the form of the syllogism is fallacious. For example:

> The driver was watching the car in front of him or he was texting his client.
>
> The driver was texting his client.
>
> Therefore, the driver was not watching the car in front of him.

Figure 52. *An example of a fallacious disjunctive syllogism taking the form called the fallacy of affirming a disjunct.*

Here, the categorical premise affirms one of the disjuncts. The conclusion attempts to conclude the negation of the other disjunction from this categorical premise. However, the rule of logic does not allow such a conclusion. The reason for the rule of logic, and the reason why this argument is fallacious, goes back to the two kinds of disjunction. The rule does not assume that disjunction is used in the exclusive sense. That is, a driver could be texting his client and watching the car in front of him. If that was the case, then the fact that the diver was doing one thing cannot guarantee the truth of a conclusion that he was not doing the other. Of course, if it was made clear that the disjunctive proposition was used in the exclusive sense, then the syllogism would be valid.[15]

Like the other formal logical fallacies, the proper and improper form of disjunctive syllogisms can be illustrated graphically. The following form uses a square to represent each of the two disjuncts. One disjunct is represented by a square with vertical lines. The other disjunct is represented by a square with horizontal lines. The first line represents the disjunctive premise, including two disjuncts. The second line represents the categorical premise, either affirming or denying one of the disjuncts. Where the disjunct is denied in the categorical premise, the "no" symbol appears over the square. The third line represents the conclusion, either affirming or denying another disjunct. Accordingly, the valid form of the disjunctive syllogism is illustrated this way:

14. Contrast this rule with the rule at work in the fallacy of the negative premise. In that rule, applicable only to categorical syllogisms, a negative premise cannot lead to a positive conclusion. Conversely, in a disjunctive syllogism, a negative premise can lead to an affirmative conclusion. The key to the proper application of these logical rules is to recognize the distinction between categorical syllogisms and disjunctive syllogisms.

15. *See* George W. Rainbolt & Sandra L. Dwyer, Critical Thinking: The Art Of Argument 168 (2d ed. 2015) ("If a disjunction is exclusive, then affirming a disjunct is a valid form. If a disjunction is inclusive, then affirming a disjunct is an invalid form.").

Figure 53. *An example of a valid form of a disjunctive syllogism.*[16]

Conversely, the invalid, fallacious form of a disjunctive syllogism is illustrated this way:

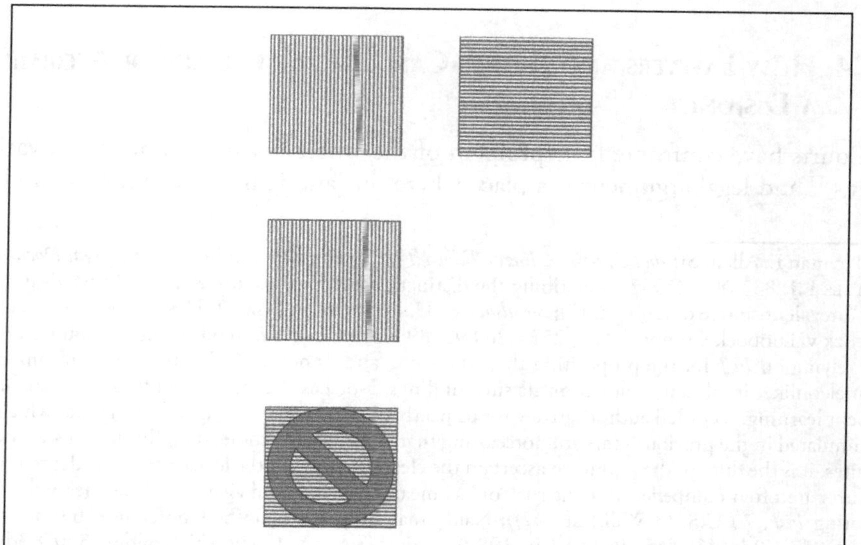

Figure 54. *One example of the fallacious form of a disjunctive syllogism called the fallacy of affirming a disjunct.*

16. This is just one of two possible examples. A valid disjunctive syllogism could deny either disjunct.

Figure 55. *Another example of a fallacious disjunctive syllogism taking the form called the fallacy of affirming a disjunct.*

10.4 How Lawyers and Judges Can Use the Fallacy of Affirming a Disjunct

Courts have confronted the problem of the ambiguity of disjunction in various forms,[17] and legal argument is a place where this ambiguity of disjunction and the

17. Layman E. Allen, *Symbolic Logic: A Razor-Edged Tool for Drafting and Interpreting Legal Documents*, 66 Yale L.J. 833, 842 (1957) (describing the distinction between exclusive and inclusive disjunction as a "prevalent source of ambiguity"); *see also, e.g.*, United States v. Fisk, 70 U.S. (3 Wall.) 445 (1865); Peacock v. Lubbock Compress Co., 252 F.2d 892, 893 (5th Cir. 1958) (construing a conjunctive term and relying on *Fisk* for the proposition that "the word 'and' is not a word with a single meaning, for chameleonlike, it takes its color from its surroundings. Nor has the law looked upon it as such. It is ancient learning, recorded authoritatively for us nearly one hundred years ago, echoing that which had accumulated in the previous years and forecasting that which was to come, that, 'In the construction of statutes, it is the duty of the [c]ourt to ascertain the clear intention of the legislature. In order to do this, [c]ourts are often compelled to construe "or" as meaning "and," and again "and" as meaning "or"'") (quoting *Fisk*, 70 U.S. (3 Wall.) at 447)); Nat'l Small Shipments Traffic Conference, Inc. v. United States, 887 F.2d 443, 445–46 (3d Cir. 1989); United States v. Gomez-Hernandez, 300 F.3d 974, 978 (8th Cir. 2002); Bruce v. First Fed. Sav. & Loan Ass'n of Conroe, Inc., 837 F.2d 712, 715 & n. 2, 719 (5th Cir. 1988); Morpho Detection, Inc. v. Transp. Sec. Admin., 717 F.3d 975, 979 (D.C. Cir. 2013); De Sylva v. Ballentine, 351 U.S. 570, 573–74 (1956); Vasudevan Software, Inc. v. MicroStrategy, Inc., No. C 11-06637, 2013 U.S. Dist. LEXIS 134310 (N.D. Cal. Sept. 19, 2013); United States v. 890 Noyac Rd., 739 F. Supp. 111, 113 (E.D.N.Y. 1990), *rev'd*, 945 F.2d 1252 (2d Cir. 1991); Weavertown Transp. Leasing, Inc. v. Moran, 834 A.2d 1169, 1173 (Pa. Super. Ct. 2003).

rule of formal logic governing disjunctive syllogisms intersect. The result is a common pattern of legal argument with the potential for misunderstanding or unjustified persuasion. An example of a court using the structure of a disjunctive syllogism to analyze an issue in a civil discovery dispute can be found in *Harmon v. Wal-Mart Stores, Inc.*[18] The legal issue in *Harmon* revolved around whether subject matter jurisdiction existed over the defendant. During discovery, the defendant requested admissions of the plaintiff regarding whether the amount in controversy exceeded the $75,000 threshold amount necessary to obtain subject matter jurisdiction based on diversity of citizenship of the parties.[19] The defendant requested admission from the plaintiff, which included a request that the plaintiff admit: "That you do not claim in excess of $75,000.00 as total damages in this case" and five similar requests relating to jurisdiction. The plaintiff denied all six of the requests for admission.[20] The court described the logic issue in the case this way:

> Defendant cannot create an end-run around the jurisdictional requirements by forcing a denial of a negative and then claim the positive is admitted and conclusively determined. It is true that in formal logic, and even in everyday language, that what is may be inferred from a statement about what is not. Or, that denial is the opposite of affirmation. Or, in a universe where only A and B are possible, but one of either A or B must be, one can construct a sound disjunctive syllogism like this one:
>
> Either A or B.
>
> Not A,
>
> Therefore B.[21]

The court went on to describe the intersection of logic and legal argument in *Harmon*:

> One could particularize this syllogism for Defendant's argument in the following way:
>
> Either > $75,000 is not in controversy (A) or > $75,000 is in controversy (B).

18. Harmon v. Wal-Mart Stores, Inc., No. 3:08-cv-309-MEF (WO), 2009 U.S. Dist. LEXIS 21040 at *1 (M.D. Ala. Mar. 16, 2009)).

19. "Article III of the Constitution empowers the Federal Courts to hear suits between citizens of different states, and 28 U.S.C. § 1332 provides the necessary statutory authorization for that jurisdiction. That familiar statute provides that 'The district courts shall have original jurisdiction of all civil actions where the matter in controversy exceeds the sum or value of $75,000, exclusive of interest and costs, and is between . . . citizens of different states.'" *Id.* at *9 (M.D. Ala. Mar. 16, 2009).

20. *Id.* at *2.

21. *Id.* at *10, n. 2 (explaining that "This and the disjunctions that follow are all exclusive, which means that only one of the disjuncts is true.").

It is not the case that > $75,000 is not in controversy (Not A),
Therefore > $75,000 is in controversy (B).[22]

The court held that: "Plaintiff's denial of the six questions propounded by Defendant serves not to establish that an amount in excess of $75,000 is in dispute, but rather that Plaintiff is not willing to concede the issue and that an amount in excess of $75,000 is in dispute is itself in dispute."[23]

Harmon is an example of a valid use of disjunctive argument to assist legal reasoning.[24] The court structured an argument that complied with the rule of logic for disjunctive syllogisms, and because the denial of one of the disjuncts preceded the conclusion of the other disjunct, the form of the syllogism was valid. The facts of the syllogism in *Harmon* are such at an exclusive disjunction has to be intended by the disjunctive proposition. The amount in controversy has to be an amount less than $75,000 or an amount $75,000 or more. Both disjuncts cannot be true. Because affirming a disjunct is a valid form of argument when the disjuncts are exclusive,[25] *Harmon* is not a good example to illustrate the fallacy of affirming a disjunct.

However, in cases where disjuncts are not exclusive, the pattern of affirming one disjunct and concluding the negation of the other disjunct is an invalid pattern of reasoning. Imagine a criminal larceny prosecution for the theft of a piece of heavy construction equipment. The equipment was locked in a gated construction yard, and the gate to the yard was secured by a padlock. The lock was found locked and undamaged on the morning the heavy equipment was discovered missing. Only two employees of the construction company had possession or access to the keys to the padlock to the construction yard. One of them was a defendant in the larceny prosecution. The following closing argument might be offered by the defendant's attorney.

> There were only two keys to that construction yard and only two people who could possibly have opened the gate and removed the equipment. One of them is Daryl Anderson, the general manager. The other, is the defendant, Landry Powell. You have heard the evidence regarding Mr. Anderson's possession of the key on

---

22. *Id.* at *10, n. 3

23. *Id.*

24. Other examples of arguments taking the valid form of reasoning exist. *See, e.g.*, Herrin v. United States, 349 F.3d 544, 547 (8th Cir. 2003) ("The prosecutor framed his closing argument in the form of a disjunctive syllogism, beginning with a statement of alternatives: '[I]t boils down to whether the defendant committed the robbery or whether [another person] committed the robbery.' The prosecutor next eliminated [the other person] as an alternative, arguing "[I]f [the other person] did not commit this robbery, there is only one logical possibility under common sense, the evidence, and the law; and that's that the defendant committed the robbery." The prosecutor then proceeded to contrast the personal characteristics of [the other person] with those of [the defendant]."); Nat'l Small Shipments Traffic Conference, Inc. v. United States, 887 F.2d 443, 445–46 (3d Cir. 1989); Griffith v. Wal-Mart Stores E., L.P., 884 F. Supp. 2d 1218, 1225 (N.D. Ala. 2012)

25. *See, e.g.*, Rainbolt & Dwyer, *supra* note 15.

> his key ring. You watched him as he testified that he was at the office the night before the equipment was discovered missing. You learned about Mr. Anderson's familiarity with the market for heavy equipment and his contacts in the business of buying and selling heavy equipment. Mr. Anderson had the ability and motivation and know-how to open the gate, move the equipment out of the yard, and move the equipment into the marketplace where it could be sold. There were only two people who could open that gate: Mr. Anderson and Mr. Powell. If you find it more likely that Mr. Anderson stole the equipment, then you must conclude that Mr. Powell did not steal the equipment.

Here, the argument advanced by defendant's lawyer commits the fallacy of affirming a disjunct. The prosecution could use the rules of disjunctive syllogism to respond to what might sound like a persuasive argument to a court or jury. The disjunctive premise is likely true. Only Mr. Anderson or Mr. Powell had access to the equipment. However, the categorical proposition affirms one disjunct in an effort to justify a conclusion that the other disjunct is not true. The pattern of argument is fallacious because the disjunctive premise is not exclusive. Both Mr. Anderson and Mr. Powell could have committed the crime. If they did, the fact that evidence exists that Mr. Anderson committed the crime does not justify a conclusion that Mr. Powell did not.

For example, the rebuttal to the logic of the defense counsel's closing argument might include the following argument:

> The defendant's lawyer, in his closing argument, has asked you to believe something that is simply illogical. He argues that either Mr. Anderson or Mr. Powell could have stolen that equipment. He argues that the evidence suggests that Mr. Anderson could have stolen the equipment. But then, he argues that if Mr. Anderson could have stolen the equipment, you cannot conclude that Mr. Powell could have stolen the equipment. Well, that's just not logical. It's like arguing that because I would love a bowl of strawberry ice cream or vanilla ice cream and choose to enjoy a bowl of strawberry ice cream, I must not like vanilla ice cream. Well, a lot of people love strawberry and vanilla ice cream. It's like saying I like to vacation in the mountains or at the beach, and when I elect to vacation in the mountains, concluding that I must hate the idea of spending the weekend at the beach. See, there is no reason we can't like both strawberry and vanilla, andthere is no reason we can't like the beach and the mountains, and there is no reason we can't conclude that both Mr. Anderson and Mr. Powell could have had motive and opportunity to take that equipment.

Understanding the logic of defense counsel's argument changes the options for rebutting defense counsel's argument, and provides a structure for organizing the rebuttal. A first reaction to defense counsel's argument might be to confront his description of the evidence about Mr. Anderson's motive and opportunity to steal the equipment. If the evidence is persuasive that Mr. Anderson had motive and opportunity to steal the equipment, that might be a losing fight. You might lose credibility with that argument. You might distract the focus of the judge or jurors with that argument. It's a case where we might agree (or have to concede that the jurors will agree) on opposing counsel's view of the facts as they relate to Mr. Anderson. If so, the better argument is about the logical consequence of defense counsel's argument. The fact that Mr. Anderson might have stolen the equipment doesn't mean Mr. Powell didn't. But, unless we understand that, we might miss the value of a logic-based argument like this one.

10.5 Keys to Using the Fallacy of Affirming a Disjunct

From these examples, the patterns of valid and fallacious reasoning should be apparent. While the concept of disjunction is more familiar that the concepts of distribution in categorical syllogisms or the various combination of forms of hypothetical syllogisms, the primary point of confusion in applying the rules of disjunctive syllogisms is the ambiguous nature of disjunction. Disjunction can be exclusive or inclusive. When the disjunction is inclusive, then affirming one disjunct does not require the denial of the other. Conversely, where the disjunction is exclusive either pattern is valid.[26]

Accordingly, once an inclusive disjunctive proposition is identified, the next step is to assess whether the argument affirms or denies one of the disjuncts. If it denies a disjunct, then the argument complies with the rule of logic that applies to disjunctive syllogisms. If it affirms a disjunct, then the argument commits the fallacy of affirming a disjunct[27] and will fit one of the two following patterns:

26. George Rainbolt and Sandra Dwyer, Critical Thinking: The Art of Argument 168 ("If a disjunction is exclusive, then affirming a disjunct is a valid form. If a disjunctive is inclusive, then affirming a disjunct is an invalid form.").

27. William Jackson Kilgore, An Introductory Logic 512 (defining "fallacy of affirming a disjunct" as "[a] faulty argument using an inclusive disjunctive statement as a premise and holding that since one disjunct is true, the other disjuncts must be false."). *See also* W. Kent Wilson, Cambridge Dictionary of Philosophy, "Formal Fallacy" 316 (describing the fallacy as an "[i]mproper disjunctive syllogism (affirming one disjunct)" and noting the proper form of the syllogism when the disjunction is used exclusively).

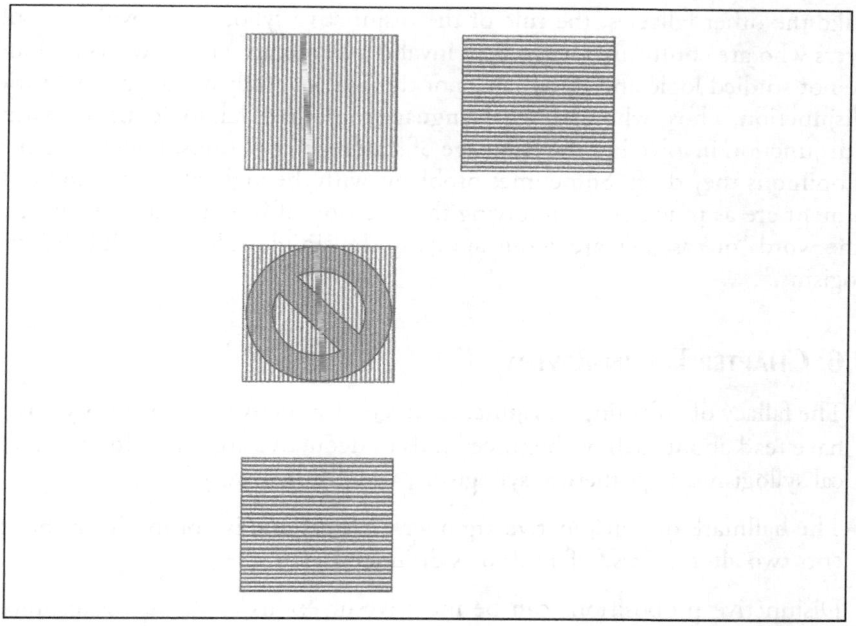

***Figure 56.** An example of a fallacious disjunctive syllogism taking the form called the fallacy of affirming a disjunct.*

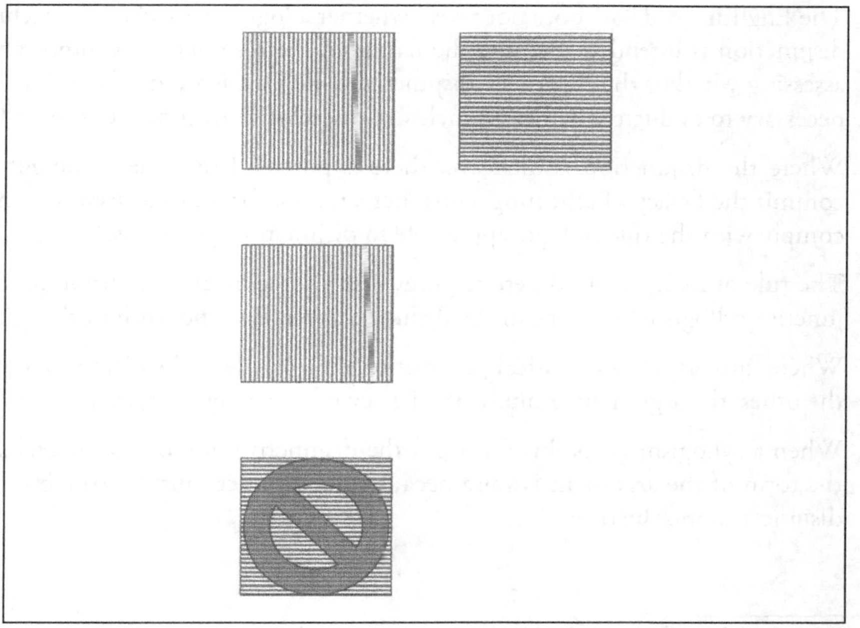

***Figure 57.** An example of a fallacious disjunctive syllogism taking the form called the fallacy of affirming a disjunct.*

Like the other fallacies, the rule of the disjunctive syllogism provides a tool for lawyers who are confronted with these invalid arguments. Most lawyers and judges have not studied logic and likely have not thought carefully about the two varieties of disjunction. Those who draft legal language sometimes fail to define the nature of the disjunction involved in the language of statutes, regulations, policies, contracts, and opinions they draft. Sometimes problems with the logic of disjunction in legal argument are as much about resolving the question of intent in ambiguous usages of the word "or" as they are about applying the simple rules for valid disjunctive syllogisms.[28]

10.6 Chapter Ten in Review

- The fallacy of affirming a disjunct occurs in disjunctive syllogisms. By now, you have read about each of the three kinds of deductive argument forms: categorical syllogisms, hypothetical syllogisms, and disjunctive syllogisms.
- The hallmark of a disjunctive argument is a disjunctive proposition that presents two alternatives, referred to as disjuncts.
- Disjunctive propositions can be inclusive or exclusive. Inclusive disjunctions require that one disjunct, the other, or both disjuncts be true. Exclusive disjunctions require that only one disjunct or the other, but not both, be true.
- The English word "or" does not reveal whether a logically inclusive or exclusive disjunction is intended. Because the nature of the disjunction is important to assessing whether the form of a disjunctive syllogism is valid, context may be necessary to evaluate whether an inclusive or exclusive disjunctive is intended.
- Where the disjunction is inclusive, there is potential that the argument will commit the fallacy of affirming a disjunct, and the form of the argument must comply with the rule of logic applicable to disjunctive syllogisms.
- The rule of logic involved here requires that a categorical proposition in a disjunctive syllogism deny one of the disjuncts and affirm the truth of the other.
- Where, instead, the categorical proposition affirms one of the disjuncts to deny the other, the argument commits the fallacy of affirming a disjunct.
- When a syllogism takes this form but the disjunctive proposition is exclusive, the form of the argument is valid because one disjunct must be true but both disjuncts cannot be true.

28. Some of the ideas developed in this chapter were first explored in Stephen M. Rice, *Leveraging Logical Form in Legal Argument: The Inherent Ambiguity in Logical Disjunction and Its Implication in Legal Argument*, 40 Okla. City U. L. Rev. 551 (2015).

- A sample Special Interrogatory follows. As you read the Special Interrogatory and the hypothetical facts that follow it, consider how the logic of disjunction might play a role in the arguments made by each side. How can the language and rules of logic help you to explain why the jury responded to the Special Interrogatory the way they did, the logical errors that might be made in the parties' arguments on appeal, and the limits of logic in solving problems like this one? What objection might the parties have raised at trial to the form of the Special Interrogatory? How might the Special Interrogatory have been drafted differently in anticipation of the problems caused by the ambiguity of disjunction? If you had not learned about the fallacy of affirming a disjunct, would you have noticed the potential for this logical error?

10.7 Exercise

STATE OF GEORGIA
TALL COUNTY CIRCUIT COURT

Marathon Logistics III, Inc.,

Plaintiff ,

Case No: A15-00061

Judge: Hon. Samantha Cornwall

v.

Brule River Capital, LP,

Defendant.

Special Interrogatory Regarding Attorney Fees

This Interrogatory shall be answered only in the event your verdict is rendered in favor of Plaintiff on any of its claims against Defendant.

Generally, parties to a lawsuit bear their own costs and expenses incurred in pursuing and defending their claims. Expenses of litigation, including attorney's fees are not generally allowed as part of damages. However, if a party has acted in bad faith or has been stubbornly litigious, the jury may allow them.

Stubbornly litigious means that a defendant has been guilty of a wanton and excessive indulgence in litigation beyond that demanded by the nature of the controversy.

Bad faith means actual or constructive fraud or a design to mislead or deceive another or a neglect or refusal to fulfill some duty or some contractual obligation.

Do you find that Defendant acted in bad faith or has been stubbornly litigious?

Answer: ________________________________

For purposes of this problem, assume that this Special Interrogatory was submitted to the jury. Further, assume that the jury responded to the Special Interrogatory, but handwrote the following on the "Answer" line: "The Defendant acted in bad faith."

Last, assume on appeal that the defendant successfully argues that the jury was errantly instructed on the definition of bad faith in the Special Interrogatory. In light of the defendant's successful argument on appeal, what consequence to you anticipate the parties will advocate for, and what role would you expect the logic of disjunction might have in those arguments?

Chapter Eleven

A Fallacy-Based Perspective on Legal Argumentation for Litigators and Judges

The preceding six chapters introduced the six most common formal logical fallacies in legal argument. While those chapters sought to explain each fallacy individually, this chapter compiles those fallacies in a formal logic "toolbox" that provides a lawyer or judge options for solving logic problems in legal argument. Outfitted with these logic tools for legal argument, a lawyer can consider legal argument from a new perspective. Using formal logical fallacies as a perspective for evaluating legal argument provides you with conceptual and language tools to help you understand and explain logical strengths and weaknesses in legal argument. As you read this chapter, consider the following:

- This book began by describing the place of logic in legal argument and describing formal deductive logic as one logical tool among others, including inductive logic and analogy. Now that you have studied the fallacies of formal logic, consider how formal logic differs from induction and analogy in legal argument.
- The formal logical fallacies featured in this book apply to three kinds of deductive arguments: categorical, hypothetical, and disjunctive arguments. Are you able to describe and identify the three kinds of deductive arguments?
- Each of the formal logical fallacies can be identified by its pattern of argument. Are you able to describe and identify the distinct patterns of the six formal logical fallacies described in this book?
- Identifying fallacious arguments is only half of the battle for lawyers who want to use formal logic in legal argument. Lawyers who identify fallacious arguments tendered by opposing counsel must describe and explain the fallacy in order to effectively rebut it. Judges who identify fallacious arguments tendered by litigants have to respond to the defective logic with an appropriate justification for its lack of persuasiveness. Lawyers who identify fallacies in their own argument have to know how to repair the argument's logical framework before the argument is delivered. As you read this chapter, think about what techniques you might use to respond to fallacious arguments.

- Think generally about how you measured the strength of legal arguments before reading this book, or whether you measured them at all with any kind of systematic methodology. Does considering a formal logic, fallacy-based perspective on legal argument make you think more intentionally about what makes a good legal argument and what makes a bad one?

11.1 Three Kinds of Legal Arguments and a Fallacy-Based Perspective on Evaluating Legal Argument

This book began by describing legal argument generally as an assembly of three different tools of logical persuasion: deductive logic, inductive logic, and analogy. This book has focused on formal deductive logic, which is only one tool of logic lawyers use to evaluate legal issues and advocate for legal outcomes. The cases described in this book demonstrate how formal logic has an important and sometimes explicit role to play in legal argument, where the lawyers and judges sometimes evaluate and discuss the argument from the perspective of and utilizing the language of formal logic. Of course, in the vast majority cases, formal logic does not play an explicit role, and the arguments and opinions do not mention the language and principles of logic. Nonetheless, even in those cases, formal logic still operates in the background of the arguments advanced by the lawyers and the decisions justified by the judges who hear the arguments.

This book has focused on formal deductive logic, which is only one tool of logic lawyers use to evaluate legal issues and advocate for legal outcomes.

Understanding formal logic's role in legal argument provides a new perspective for thinking about legal argument. Most lawyers are trained to understand, evaluate, and respond to legal argument in terms of the strength of legal rules, the volume of factual support, and the underlying policies supporting an argument. Lawyers typically encounter a legal argument in a brief or oral argument in court and respond to the argument based on the assumption that the argument they confront is logically coherent. This typical approach focuses on evaluating the premises of a legal argument, without really thinking or talking about these components as "premises" at all. The typical strategy for responding to and defeating the legal argument advanced is a matter of responding to opposing counsel's position regarding the parameters, viability, and applicability of the legal principles cited in the argument and the interpretation of the facts described in the argument. In a motion in limine to exclude evidence at trial, the response will focus on arguing about what the proper applicable legal principles are and what factual issues are relevant to those legal principles. The argument does not typically start with or focus on the logical structure or logical justification for the argument's conclusions.

Taking a logical, fallacy-based approach to designing or responding to legal argument simply requires taking one additional step in this traditional process. It does not supplant that process; it merely disposes of the presupposition that every legal argument is logical and that all of the logic tools lawyers use are equally persuasive. Instead, a fallacy-based evaluation of legal argument requires testing the argument's logical architecture for the most common patterns of illogical deductive argument and recognizing that where legal arguments take a fallacious logical form, the responding lawyer has one more important argument to make in response. A fallacy-based perspective offers one more facet to the already multifaceted process for evaluating and responding to legal argument. A fallacy-based perspective provides additional tools for identifying and describing strengths and weaknesses in the logical structure of a legal conclusion.

Lawyers generally make arguments that sound like they are reaching conclusions justifiable only by deduction. That is, they almost always describe their argument as the only right conclusion.

Among the benefits to analyzing the logical integrity of legal argument is the ability to distinguish the relative persuasiveness of the different logical tools lawyers use. Lawyers generally make arguments that sound like they are reaching conclusions justifiable only by deduction. That is, they almost always describe their argument advancing the only right conclusion. They argue that the law and facts *require* that the court grant their motion. They argue to the jurors that the *only* correct verdict is a "not guilty" verdict. They suggest to the court that the interpretations of the rule of evidence at issue in their case *dictate* that the evidence be excluded at trial. This is the language of deductive logic. Deduction is powerful; if the premises of the argument are true, then the conclusion is required, so long as the argument takes a valid form. When an argument can be shown to be invalid, either because its premises are uncertain or its form is invalid, it requires that the argument move out of the realm of deduction and into an alternative logical framework, either induction or analogy, where the conclusions are not certain but instead merely take some degree of probability. While the ability to recognize and describe the different kinds of logical frameworks of legal argument is preliminary to spotting the fallacies of formal deductive logic, this ability alone is a powerful tool for advocacy.

First, recognizing the different tools of logic in legal argument reveals that all arguments are neither logically equal nor equally persuasive. Second, different logical tools play by different rules. Third, legal arguments that present different logical patterns require different logical strategies. Where the logical tool is analogy, the strategy for confronting an analogical argument is typically centered on attacking the analogical similarities between the cases, facts, or outcomes compared. Where the logical tool is induction, the strategy for confronting the inductive argument is typically centered on the richness or reliability of the sample size, be it a sample of legal decisions or factual observations, to justify the proffered generalization. Where the logical tool is deduction, the strategy for confronting a deductive argument is typically centered on choosing the right premises, attacking the credibility of the premises, and evaluating the logical form of the deductive argument. Unlike analogy and induction, deduction's persuasiveness is ensured by adherence to a few strict rules of logic.

11.2 The Rules of Deductive Logic and Patterns of Fallacious Argument Revisited

Evaluating the logical persuasive force of legal argument requires understanding the basic rules of formal logic and the fallacies that follow when arguments do not comply with those rules. In the same way rules of law allow lawyers to communicate and evaluate legal issues, problems, and solutions, rules of logic allow them to communicate and evaluate logic issues, problems, and solutions. Each of the three kinds of deductive logical forms—hypothetical syllogisms, categorical syllogisms, and disjunctive syllogisms—have their own rule or rules of logic that ensure their logical reliability.

The first rule applies only to hypothetical syllogisms. The rule requires that a hypothetical syllogism fit into one of two patterns to be valid. First, a hypothetical syllogism is valid where the categorical premise affirms the truth of the antecedent term of the hypothetical premise and the conclusion asserts the truth of the consequent term of the hypothetical premise. Alternatively, a hypothetical syllogism is valid where the categorical premise denies the consequent term of the hypothetical premise and the conclusion asserts the falsity of the antecedent term of that hypothetical premise.[1] Where a hypothetical syllogism fails to fit into one of these two patterns, it commits either the fallacy of denying the antecedent or the fallacy of affirming the consequent.[2]

The next four rules apply to categorical syllogisms. A categorical syllogism can only have three terms and three propositions. The middle term in a categorical syllogism must be distributed at least once. Any term distributed in the conclusion of a categorical syllogism must be distributed in the premise in which it appears. This book explained the two fallacies that follow from failure to comply with the latter two rules. Where the middle term is not distributed in at least one premise, it commits the fallacy of the undistributed middle term. Where any term is distributed in the conclusion but not distributed in one of the premises, the argument commits the fallacy of the illicit process. Additionally, there can be only one negative premise;

1. *See, e.g.*, Irving M. Copi & Carl Cohen, Introduction to Logic 229–300 (13th ed. 2008).
2. *See, e.g.*, C.L. Hamblin, Fallacies 35–37 (1970).

if there is a negative premise the conclusion must be negative. Where a categorical syllogism fails this fourth rule, it commits the fallacy of the negative premise.[3]

The last rule applies only to disjunctive syllogisms. A valid disjunctive syllogism is one where the categorical premise denies one of the disjuncts in the disjunctive premise to reach a conclusion affirming the other disjunct. Where the form of a disjunctive syllogism fails to comply with this rule, it commits the fallacy of affirming a disjunct.[4]

Lawyers do not focus on the logical form of legal argument, in part, because they assume most legal arguments are logical and comply with these rules of logic—an assumption entirely correct. Generally, illogical arguments are patently unpersuasive, even silly. As a result, lawyers typically avoid such arguments altogether and they are not regularly advanced. However, "[a] fallacious argument, as almost every account from Aristotle onwards explains, is one that *seems to be valid* but *is not so.*"[5] This is the danger with the subtleties of formal logic and the logical fallacies that follow from failing to comply with the rules; unless lawyers exercise some logical vigilance, they will make or accept some fallacious arguments unknowingly. Judges and jurors can find fallacious arguments persuasive, even when the arguments should have no persuasive logical value. Accordingly, being able to identify and respond to fallacious arguments is an important consequence of knowing and understanding the rules of formal logic and how they discipline legal argument.

11.3 The Hallmarks of Six Formal Fallacies in Legal Argument

The six most common formal logical fallacies in legal argument have been described and illustrated in this book by their logical patterns. These patterns are the hallmarks of arguments that contradict a specific rule of logic. Thinking about arguments in terms of logical patterns becomes an important skill for using the rules of formal logic in making and evaluating legal argument. Breaking legal arguments down to every conceivable syllogistic relationship would be possible, but it would not be efficient enough to be useful for busy practitioners. Conversely, spotting patterns of invalid argument at the most essential intersections of legal argument is efficient and effective.

The six fallacious patterns of argument described in this book are summarized below. The first two patterns of fallacious arguments are patterns of hypothetical syllogisms. The rule of logic applicable to hypothetical syllogisms prohibits hypothetical

3. *See, e.g.*, Christopher W. Tindale, Fallacies and Argument Appraisal 48 (2007) (citation omitted).
4. As discussed in Chapter Ten, an exception to this rule exists when the disjunction is used exclusively. In the case of an exclusive disjunction, a disjunctive syllogism affirming a disjunction may properly reach a conclusion denying the other disjunct.
5. Hamblin, *supra* note 2, at 12 (emphasis in original).

arguments that fit into one of two forms: the fallacy of denying the antecedent and the fallacy of affirming the consequent. A hypothetical argument that denies the antecedent term of a hypothetical premise in an effort to justify a conclusion denying of the consequent term commits the fallacy of denying the antecedent.[6] A hypothetical argument that affirms the consequent term of a hypothetical premise in an effort to justify a conclusion affirming the antecedent term commits the fallacy of affirming the consequent. Triangles and diamond shapes are used here to represent the antecedent and consequent terms, respectively, in hypothetical syllogisms. The "no" symbol over either shape indicates the denial of that term. The pattern of the fallacy of denying the antecedent takes the following form.[7]

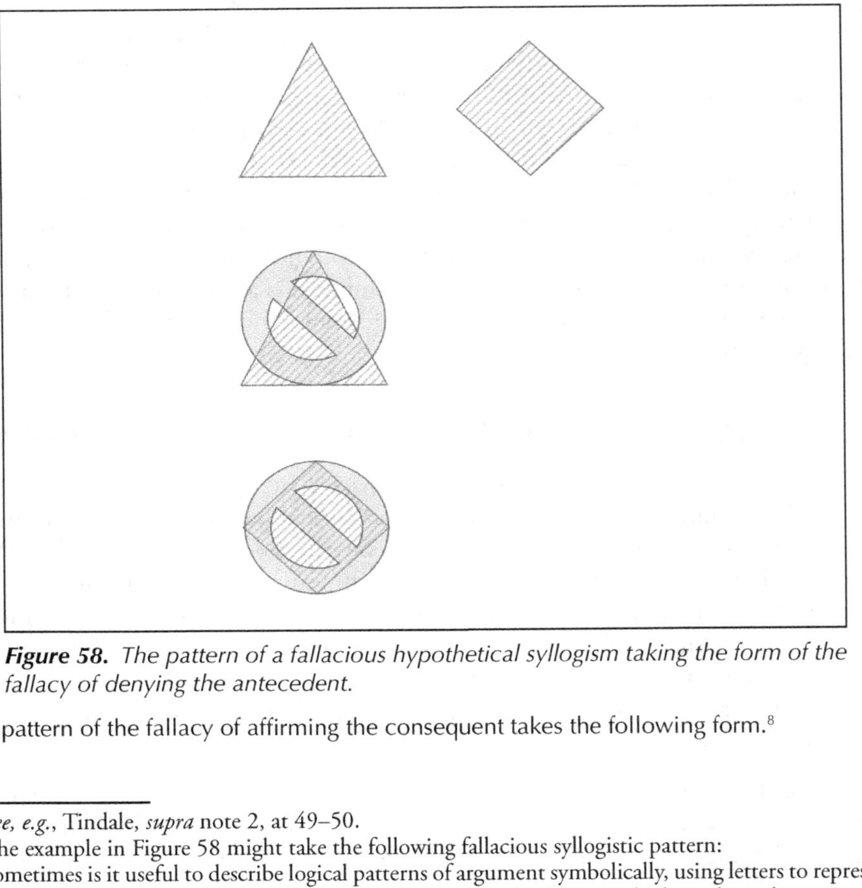

Figure 58. *The pattern of a fallacious hypothetical syllogism taking the form of the fallacy of denying the antecedent.*

The pattern of the fallacy of affirming the consequent takes the following form.[8]

6. *See, e.g.*, Tindale, *supra* note 2, at 49–50.
7. The example in Figure 58 might take the following fallacious syllogistic pattern:
8. Sometimes is it useful to describe logical patterns of argument symbolically, using letters to represent the logical terms in a syllogistic argument. In a hypothetical syllogism, the hypothetical premise will take the form "If A, then B." "A" represents the antecedent term and "B" represents the consequent term. The next line in the symbolically represented hypothetical syllogism is the categorical premise. Where the categorical premise is affirmative, it will simply contain the letter matching the antecedent term or the consequent term. Where the categorical premise is negative, it will include the word "not," followed by either the letter representing the antecedent term or the letter representing the consequent term. Last, the third line in the symbolically expressed hypothetical syllogism will be a categorical

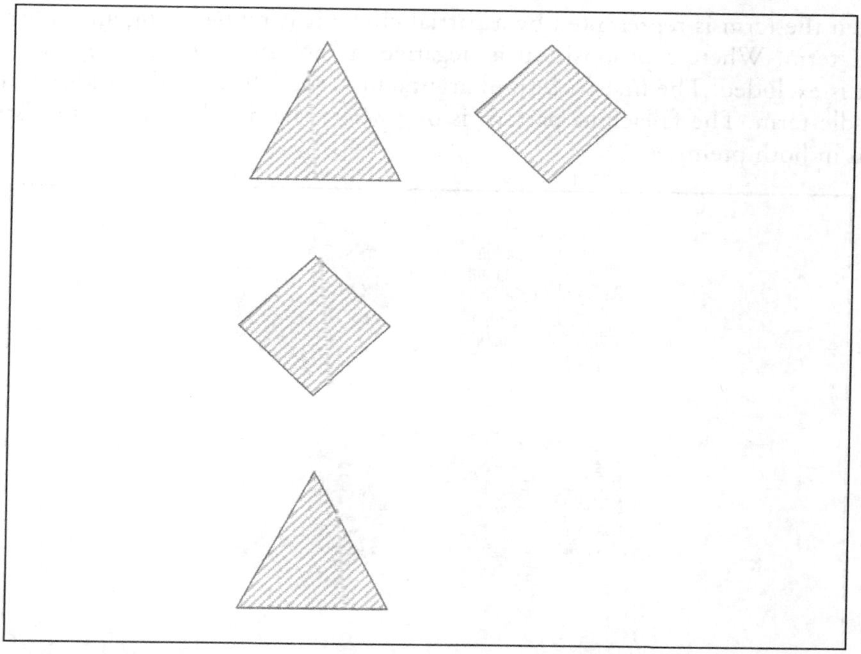

Figure 59. *The pattern of a fallacious hypothetical syllogism taking the form of the fallacy of affirming the consequent.*

The logical rule that manages hypothetical syllogisms focuses on order and inference. Undisciplined use of hypothetical argument seeks to reach a conclusion not justified by the relationship between these two terms.

The next three patterns are fallacies of categorical syllogisms. In Figures 60–62 and 64–66, below, there are three shapes, each occurring twice. The circle with the vertical lines represents the major term. The circle with the horizontal lines represents the minor term. We will expect to see those two shapes in the conclusion, since a conclusion in a standard categorical syllogism includes the minor term followed by the major term. The solid circles represent the middle term. The middle term is not found in the conclusion. It is however, the term that allows us to reach a logical inference regarding the major and minor term. When any term is represented by a complete circle, it is representing a distributed term.

---

concussion either affirming or denying the antecedent or consequent term. The example in Figure 59 might take the following fallacious syllogistic pattern:

> If A then B.
>
> B.
>
> Therefore, A.

When the term is represented by a partial circle, it is representing an undistributed term. Where a proposition is negative, a "no" symbol indicates the term that is excluded. The first pattern of argument is the fallacy of the undistributed middle term. The fallacious pattern is one where the middle term is undistributed in both premises.

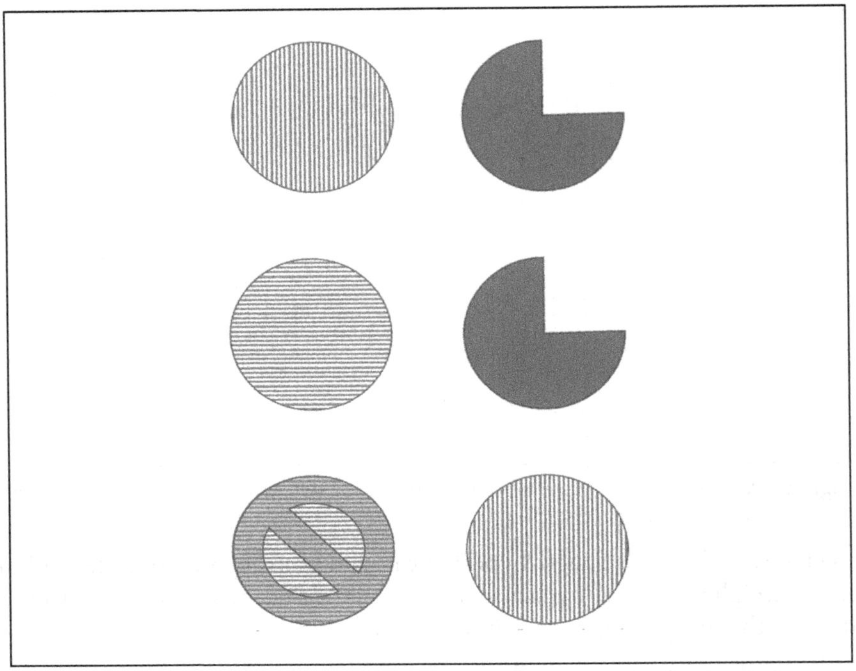

Figure 60. *An example of the pattern of the fallacy of the undistributed middle term.*

Accordingly, the top line of Figure 60 depicts a major premise with a distributed major term and an undistributed middle term. The second line depicts a distributed minor term and an undistributed middle term. The conclusion depicts a distributed minor term excluded from a distributed major term. Graphically, this depiction illustrates the fallacy of the undistributed middle term.[9]

The next pattern of fallacious categorical argument is the fallacy of the illicit process. The fallacy of the illicit process occurs when a term is distributed in the

9. Substituting letters for terms, an example of the fallacy of the undistributed middle term illustrated in Figure 60 might be:

All A is B.

All C is B.

Therefore, no C is A.

conclusion, but not in the premise in which it occurs. In Figure 61, like Figure 60, there are three shapes, each occurring twice. The shape with the vertical lines represents the major term. The shape with the horizontal lines represents the minor term. As with all categorical syllogisms, those two shapes appear together in the conclusion. The shapes with no lines are representative of the middle term. Again, any distributed term is represented by a complete circle. When the term is represented by a partial circle, it is representing an undistributed term. When a premise is negative a term includes a circle with the "no" symbol on it.

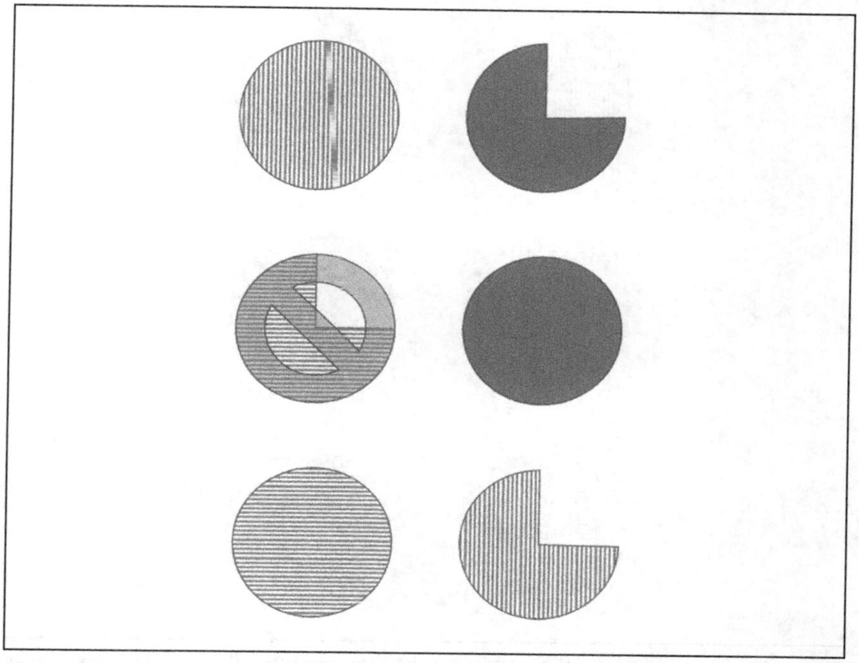

Figure 61. *An example of the pattern of the fallacy of the illicit minor term.*

Accordingly, the top line Figure 61 is a graphical depiction of a major premise with a distributed major term and an undistributed middle term. The second line depicts a negative premise with an undistributed minor term and a distributed middle term. The third line depicts a negative conclusion including a distributed minor term and an undistributed major term.[10] Because the minor

10. Substituting letters for terms, an example of the fallacy of the undistributed middle term illustrated in Figure 61, might be:

All A is B.

Some C is not B.

Therefore, all C is A.

term is distributed in the conclusion but undistributed in the minor premise, it commits the fallacy of the illicit process. There are two variations on that fallacy. Figure 61 represents one variation called the fallacy of the illicit minor term. If the pattern varied slightly, where the major term was distributed in the conclusion but not in the major premise, the variation would be called the fallacy of the illicit major term. The pattern of the fallacy of the illicit major term is illustrated below, in Figure 62.

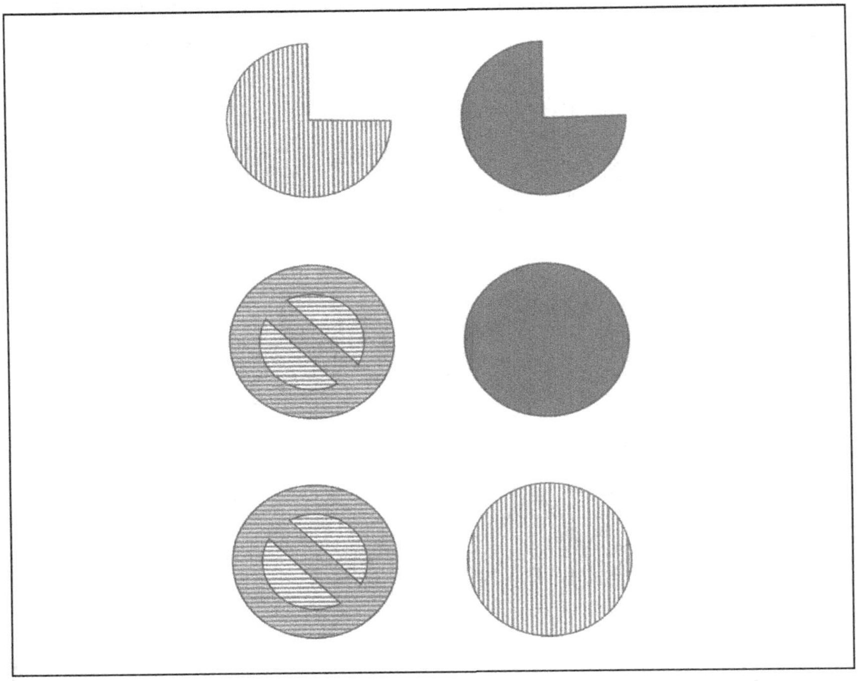

Figure 62. *An example of the pattern of the fallacy of the illicit major term.*

The next pattern, the pattern of the fallacy of the negative premise, is simple to identify.[11] Since the rule at issue in this fallacy is one that precludes reaching

11. The fallacy of the illicit major term, illustrated in Figure 62, might be:

Some A is B.

No C is B.

Therefore, no C is A.

an affirmative conclusion from a negative premise, the focus of the pattern here is on whether the term is affirmative or negative. In the following graphical depictions of arguments, like the preceding one, the negative major term is represented by a circle with vertical lines. When the term is negative it includes a circle with a diagonal line: the "no" symbol. For example, the following figure represents a negative, distributed major term and a distributed middle term:

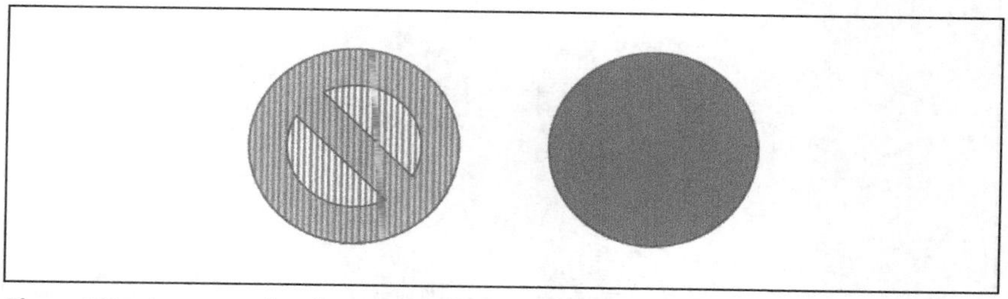

Figure 63. *An example of a negative major premise.*

Accordingly, syllogisms committing the fallacy of the negative premise will take a pattern of a negative premise and an affirmative conclusion—for example:

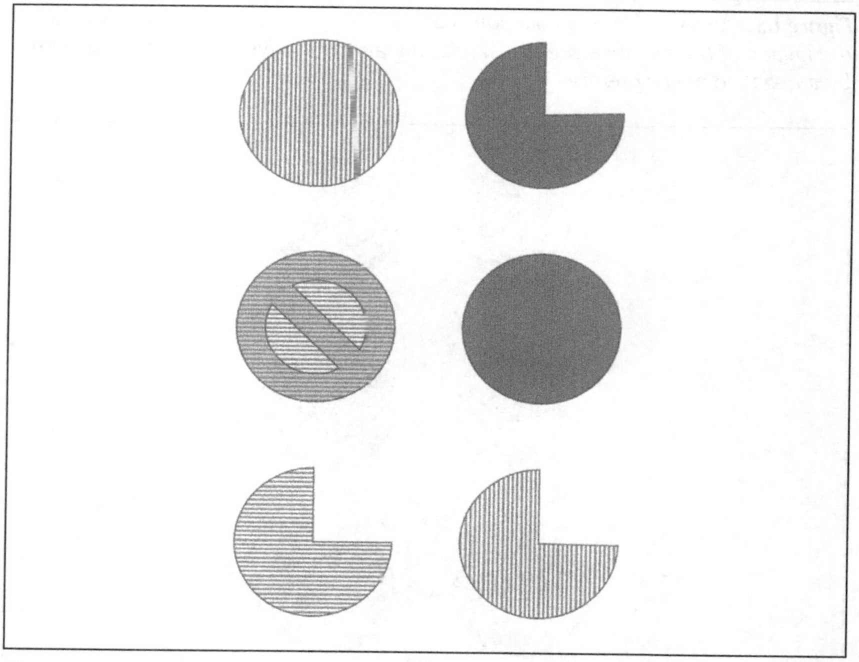

Figure 64. *An example of a fallacious categorical syllogism taking the form called the fallacy of the negative premise, including an affirmative conclusion, supported by a negative minor premise.*

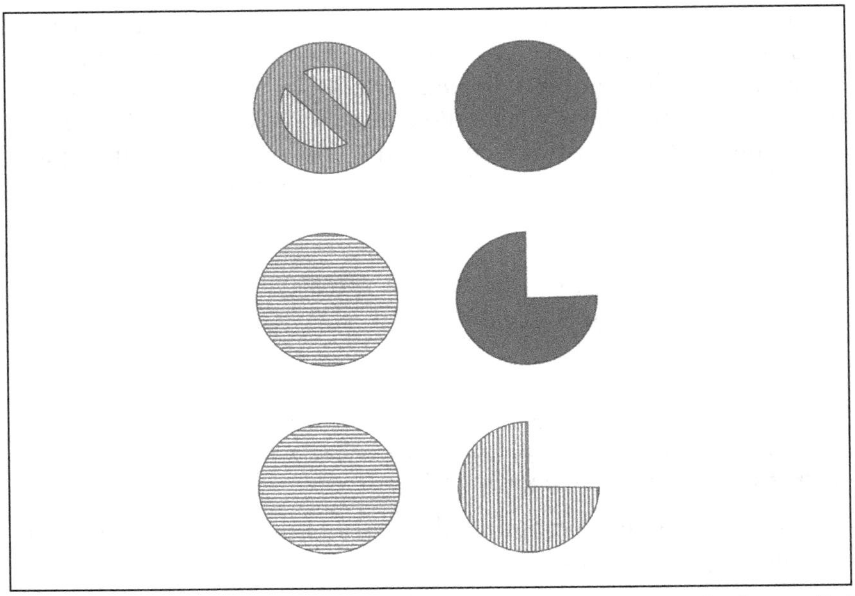

Figure 65. *An example of a fallacious categorical syllogism taking the form called the fallacy of the negative premise, including an affirmative conclusion, supported by a negative major premise.*

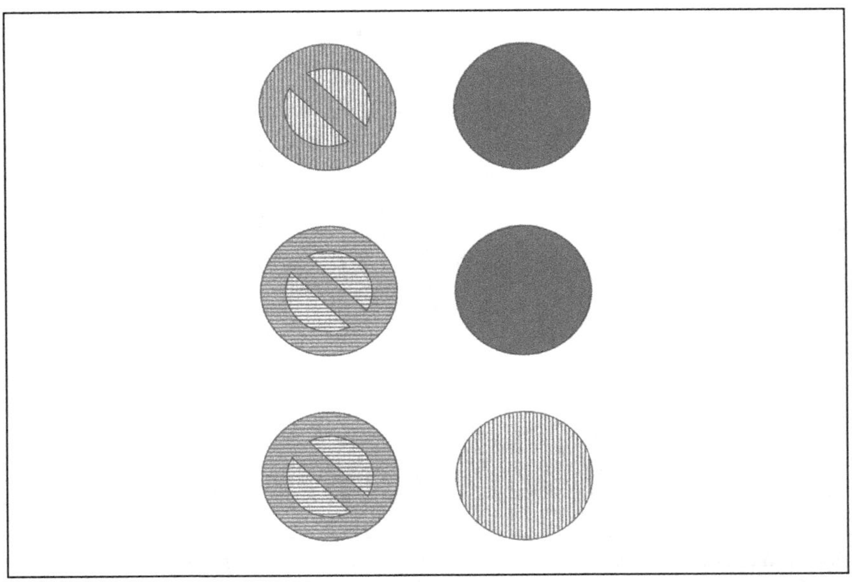

Figure 66. *An example of a fallacious categorical syllogism taking the form called the fallacy of the exclusive premises, including a negative conclusion, supported by a negative major premise and a negative major minor premise.*

There could be more variations on these three patterns if some different combinations of quality and quantity were included in the examples, but the essence of a pattern identifying the fallacy of the negative premise is an affirmative conclusion coupled with a negative premise.[12] The examples in Figures 64[13] and 65[14] provide examples of arguments that reach an affirmative conclusion from a negative premise. The third example, in Figure 66,[15] is an example of an argument that reaches a conclusion from two negative premises and commits the fallacy of exclusive premises.

The last of the three categories of deductive argument considered in this book was disjunctive argument. A disjunctive syllogism is valid only where the categorical premise denies one disjunct to affirm the other in the conclusion. The fallacious form of a disjunctive syllogism affirms one disjunct in an effort to justify the conclusion denying the other disjunct. As discussed in Chapter Ten, an exception to this rule exists when the disjunction is used exclusively. In the case of an exclusive disjunction, a disjunctive syllogism affirming a disjunction may properly reach a conclusion denying the other disjunct. Each of the disjuncts is represented below by a square, one having vertical lines and the other having horizontal lines. When a disjunct is denied, it is represented by the "no" symbol on the square. This pattern represents the fallacy of affirming a disjunct:

---

12. That is not to say that distribution is not logically significant, since fallacies are not mutually exclusive. Arguments have to comply with all of the rules of logic, and the fact that an argument manages the quantity of terms properly does not ensure that it manages the quality of terms properly.

13. The example of the fallacy of the negative premise in Figure 64 might take the following fallacious syllogistic pattern:

All A is B.

No C is B.

Therefore, Some C is A.

14. The example of the fallacy of the negative premise in Figure 65 might take the following fallacious syllogistic pattern:

No A is B.

All C is B.

All C is A.

15. The example of the fallacy of exclusive premises in Figure 66 might take the following fallacious syllogistic pattern:

No A is B.

No C is B.

Therefore, no C is A.

Figure 67. *Two patterns of fallacious disjunctive syllogisms, each taking the form called the fallacy of affirming a disjunct.*

Here, the pattern is a simple one to spot. The focus is on the categorical premise. If it denies a disjunct, then it can reach a valid result. However, if the categorical premise affirms one of the disjuncts, then it cannot reach a conclusion. Accordingly, both of the examples in Figure 67[16] are fallacious, unless the disjunction is an exclusive one.

11.4 Different Tools, Different Skills, and Different Perspectives for Thinking about Legal Argument

Learning about the different logical tools in legal argument leads us to consider the different ways we can use these tools in the daily work trial lawyers do making and evaluating legal argument.

16. The examples of the fallacy of affirming a disjunct in Figure 67 would appear in their syllogistic form the following ways. The first example is:

A or B.

A.

Therefore, not B.

The second example is:

A or B.

B.

Therefore, not A.

11.4.1 A Multifaceted Approach to Legal Argument

A logical, fallacy-based perspective on legal argument leverages ancient rules of logical thinking to achieve a new perspective for evaluating and communicating about legal arguments. It is a perspective not directly centered on the law or the facts, but on the logical structure that supports arguments about law and facts. There is a story about a closing argument in a trial that hinged on the credibility of key witness. The details of the witness's story seemed to meander between the beginning of direct examination and the end of cross-examination, and back to redirect, as witness testimony sometimes does. One of the lawyers made an argument that focused on a simple bit of common wisdom: "If a witness tells the truth, their story is always the same." I have always liked that turn of phrase. It seems true. It is easy to remember. The comma suggests a nice place for a dramatic pause. Witnesses who provide honest testimony typically testify consistently, even when asked to tell the same story more than once. Further, it is a saying virtually everyone can relate to, whether they have caught someone telling a false story, or have been caught up in such a story themselves.

A logical, fallacy-based perspective on legal argument leverages ancient rules of logical thinking to achieve a new perspective for thinking and communicating about legal arguments.

The turn of phrase is also useful, because it does something that students of argument have long recognized as powerful advocacy: it allows the audience to reach the proffered conclusion themselves, that because the story is not always the same, the witness was not telling the truth. The jurors in this case heard a lot of testimony, some of it conflicting, and are faced with the hard work of deciding which witnesses to believe, which witnesses to disbelieve, and how to reconcile the different perspectives they heard during trial. This can be a difficult job for jurors. They need some guidance, and a pithy, memorable argumentative premise like this one might be just what the jurors think back on as they deliberate on how to reconcile the witness's inconsistent testimony.

A fallacy-based perspective on this legal argument empowers lawyers to look at this argument from another perspective:

> If a witness tells the truth, then their story is always the same.
>
> The witness's story was not always the same.
>
> Therefore, the witness is not telling the truth.

As Chapter Five explains, this argument is a hypothetical syllogism and complies with the rule of logic that governs hypothetical syllogisms. It reaches a conclusion by denying the consequent term. That is a valid pattern of reasoning. Accordingly, the only way to respond to the argument is to argue that one of the premises is false. The respondent needs to confront the hypothetical premise and demonstrate that there are other explanations for inconsistent witness testimony. Alternatively, the respondent would have to convince the jury that the witness's story was "the same" and entirely consistent. Deduction helps classify and organize the argument, here narrowing the field of opposing arguments. Further, the only methods of opposition are relatively structured. If the form of the argument is valid, the respondent has to attack the truth of a premise in order to succeed.[17]

If the argument had played out a little differently, the respondent might have advanced a variation on this argument using the same hypothetical premise but a different categorical premise. For example:

> If a witness tells the truth, their story is always the same.
>
> The witness's story was always the same.
>
> Therefore, the witness is telling the truth.

This subtle change in the categorical premise, changes the logical pattern of the argument from a valid one to a fallacious one:

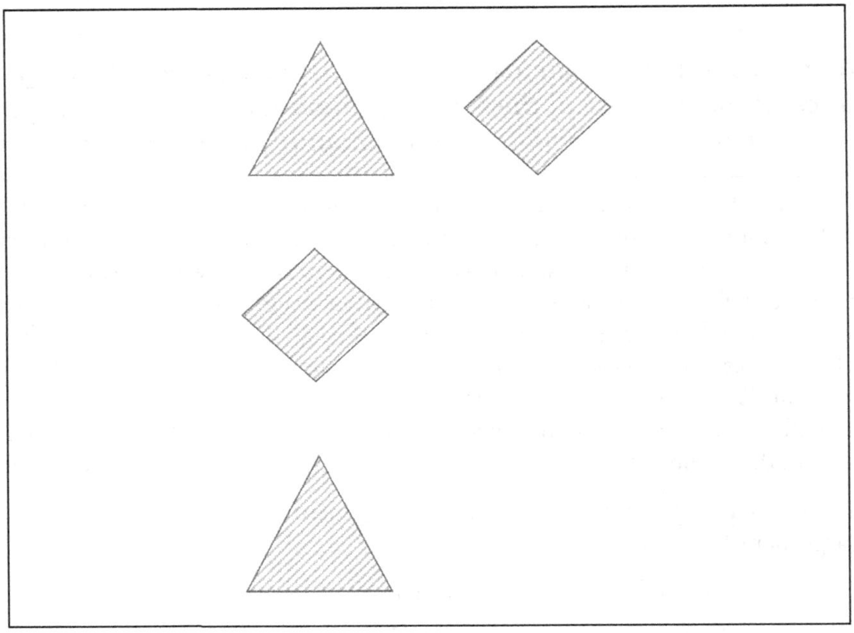

Figure 68. *A fallacious hypothetical syllogism taking the pattern of the fallacy of affirming the consequent.*

17. Comparatively, inductive and analogous arguments do not play by such strict rules, and the paths to opposing them are not well defined. If an argument takes the form of analogy, a response typically focuses on what is disanalogus about the things compared. There might be a variety of factors that distinguish one thing from the others. Furthermore, an alternative or additional response might be to suggest that some other comparison is more analogous. There are no well-defined rules that guide the respondent in designing an argument in response to analogous or inductive arguments.

Knowing the fallacious pattern of the second argument unlocks the potential to recognize something significant, and deficient, about its logical integrity. A fallacy-based perspective also provides tools to describe why the argument is unpersuasive. This knowledge and approach to evaluating legal argument has a role to play in two different areas of legal analysis: lawyers' self-assessment of their own legal arguments and lawyers' responses to the arguments they oppose.

11.4.2 Self-Assessment

Using formal logic as a practical tool of persuasion can focus on self-assessment. Once lawyers learn the rules of logic and recognize their value, these rules should inform and refine the arguments lawyers make. Lawyers should commit to making logically sound arguments. This commitment should lead them to craft and refine the logical architecture of their arguments, designing arguments that are persuasive and logically supportive of their proffered conclusions. Lawyers might even begin to think about that logical architecture before they begin to write an argument. Even recognizing that there are several logical tools and that formal deductive logic is not always the right tool should impact how lawyers craft the best legal argument using the best logical tools.

Once lawyers learn the rules of logic and recognize their value, these rules should inform and refine the arguments lawyers make.

For example, formal logic is not an effective tool when the truth of one of the premises is in doubt. Knowing the strengths and weaknesses of deduction might lead a lawyer to select another logical tool, like deduction or analogy. If deduction is an available tool, a lawyer armed with an understanding of the formal fallacies would want to avoid committing the fallacies themselves. Accordingly, assessment of the logical structure of legal arguments should be a regular part of disciplined legal reasoning and argumentation. Lawyers should identify the most persuasive logical tools available and then maximize their persuasive value by using the right logical tool well. When legal arguments fit into a deductive pattern, lawyers should ensure they comply with the rules: ensuring categorical arguments manage "some" and "all" effectively, ensuring hypothetical arguments are disciplined about order and inference, and being attentive to the potential ambiguity in disjunctive arguments. The rules of logic provide the details necessary to craft deductive legal arguments that are disciplined and persuasive.

11.4.3 Responding to Fallacious Arguments

Formal logic works not only to assist lawyers in crafting their own arguments; understanding the logical weakness in legal argument also provides a new perspective and new tools for responding to legal argument's weak logical foundations. In the same way that knowing rules of law is prerequisite to lawyers spotting legal issues, knowing rules of logic is prerequisite to lawyers spotting logical weaknesses in arguments they face.

Most lawyers wrestled with legal "issue spotting" for the first time in law school. Spotting legal issues in a set of facts can be frustrating at first. To do so, the student must first understand the rules of law. If you do not know, for example, that there is a Statute of Frauds that requires some contracts be in writing to be enforceable, then you will never understand why an oral agreement gives rise to that legal issue. Knowing that rule of law is necessary, but not sufficient, to spotting that legal issue.

Similarly, if you know that hypothetical arguments are only persuasive when they maintain discipline about the relationship between the antecedent and consequent terms, knowledge of that rule of logic enables you to spot logical issues in legal argument. If you do not know about the rules of logic and the fallacies that follow from their breach, you will likely struggle to spot those logical issues.

The rules of logic not only empower you to spot logic problems in legal arguments, they also enable you to describe the problem. The rules of logic provide language tools for describing what is wrong with fallacious arguments, and why fallacious arguments are wrong. Depending on the circumstances, it might be appropriate to point out the fallacious nature of the argument, describing the logical fallacy and why it invalidates the argument, just as many courts did in Chapters Five through Ten. Even a responsive argument that avoids some of the technical terminology of formal logic, logical distribution, or antecedent and consequent terms might be useful. Some courts wresting with logic problems in legal argument have illustrated the problem by example, rather than using the technical, and frequently unfamiliar, terms of logic. For example:

> Consider the following argument, which uses "snowing" as the antecedent and "cold" as the consequent: "Premise 1: If it is snowing, then it is cold outside. Premise 2: It is not snowing. Conclusion: It is not cold outside." Plainly, the above conclusion does not follow from its premises; it can be cold without snow falling, even though snowfall requires a cold outside temperature."[18]

18. State v. Brush, 353 P.3d 213, 223 (Wash. 2015); *see also* VMG Salsoul, LLC v. Ciccone, 824 F.3d 871 (9th Cir. 2016) ("For example, take as a given the proposition that 'if it has rained, then the grass is not dry.' It does not necessarily follow that 'if it has not rained, then the grass is dry.' Someone may have watered the lawn, for instance. We cannot infer the second if-then statement from the first."); In re LF Centennial Ltd., No. 2015-1931, 2016 U.S. App. LEXIS 11854 (Fed. Cir. June 29, 2016) ("That suggestion is fallacious: it employs a version of the fallacy of the undistributed middle, under which the two statements, "a dog is a four-legged pet" and "a cat is a four-legged pet," are asserted to give rise to the inference that a dog is a cat."); Herring v. Colvin, No. 15-CV-1021-CJW, 2016 U.S. Dist. LEXIS 78312 at *9 (N.D. Iowa June 16, 2016) ("If a fish lives in water, and a whale lives in water, therefore a whale must be a fish," is an example of a logical fallacy. Claimant engages in a similar logical fallacy."); Posen Construction, Inc. v. Lee County, 921 F.Supp. 2d 1350 (M.D. Fla. 2013) ("[I]f I go to the drug store then I will buy milk. If one denies the antecedent, then one would posit that if I do not go to the drug store I will not buy milk. Of course, the logical disconnect is obvious because one could buy milk at a location other than the drug store."); Wiehe v. Kissick Construction Co., 232 P.3d 866, 876 (Kan. App. 2010) ("For example, "No native-born Sooners are persons born in Kansas" and "No

Moreover, even without entirely defusing the persuasive force of the argument, demonstrating the logical failings of the argument at least positions the respondent on equal logical footing with their opponent. If there is no logically sound deductive argument being made, then the lawyers will likely be making arguments using the tools of inductive and analogical argument. There is nothing wrong with using those logical tools, but they do not yield conclusive answers in the way deduction does. These alternative tools might be persuasive, their conclusions might be likely—but they should not be allowed to masquerade as deduction. Reconsider this argument:

> If a witness tells the truth, their story is always the same.
>
> The witness's story was always the same.
>
> Therefore, the witness is telling the truth.

The fact that the witness's story was the same may very well be persuasive. It might suggest something about the credibility of the witness. However, that witness's consistency does not require a conclusion that the witness is truthful. Reaching that point in a responsive argument at least provides you, as the responding lawyer, with a chance to deliver your own argument, and suggest your own conclusion, using your own tools of logic.

11.4.4 Thinking, Speaking, Reading, and Listening Syllogistically

This book began by using a tool of logic—analogy—to draw a comparison between the role of rules of logic in legal argument and the role of rules of music in improvisational jazz. The suggestion in that analogy is this: principles of music that help jazz musicians craft sounds into music that is persuasive and pleasing to listen to are like principles of logic that help lawyers craft arguments that are persuasive and pleasing to the judges, jurors, and opposing counsel who read and hear them. Now that you have considered these rules of logic, it is worthwhile to return to that analogy.

The rules of logic provide an important structure to most legal reasoning and argument. If you learn the rules of logic and become comfortable, even proficient, in understanding and using them, then logic provides a new framework for designing and responding to legal argument. When you become comfortable with the logical foundation of legal argument, it encourages and empowers you to think and communicate precisely, consistently, and in ways that are logically coherent and persuasive. Consider just some summaries of the patterns of valid and fallacious argument

---

native-born Hoosiers are persons born in Kansas" furnishes no basis for inferring any connection whatsoever between the native-born Sooners and the native-born Hoosiers. To attempt to draw an inference from such a connection is to commit the fallacy of exclusive premises."); Grand Victoria Casino & Resort, L.P. v. Ind. Dep't of State Revenue, 789 N.E.2d 1041 (Ind. Tax Ct. 2003) ("the Department's argument falls prey to the fallacy of the undistributed middle. 'The nature of this fallacy becomes more obvious in the following example: Cats are mammals. Dogs are mammals. Therefore, cats are dogs.'").

discussed in this book that are easy to remember: if an argument begins with a disjunctive premise, arguing from a categorical premise that denies one of the disjuncts is good, logical, persuasive argument. Arguing from a categorical premise that affirms one disjunct is generally not good argument. Hypothetical syllogisms need to balance order and inference; when they balance order and inference, they are good, logical, persuasive arguments. When they do not, they fit into fallacious patterns that might sound persuasive, but cannot be. Categorical arguments have to be disciplined about distribution; words like "some," "all," "no" and "none" have logical importance that might require more deliberate analysis, logical scrutiny, and understanding of fallacies of distribution and negation. Negative premises support only the most limited inferences, and two negative premises support no conclusions at all.

Familiarity with the structure and language of formal logic and the alternative logical tools of induction and analogy, and deploying them in legal argument, also provides an important structure for legal argument. Logical writing and speaking is clear, organized, and persuasive. Further, logically disciplined argument provides an architecture for you to return to when arguments are challenged or go "off script." Many points in legal arguments can be associated with either a major premise or a minor premise in a syllogism. When a trial court judge asks an unexpected or even off-the-wall question during oral argument about the limits of the minor premise, that structure provides you a logical framework to answer from, and a secure architecture to return to, to complete the argument and move the argument forward toward a conclusion.

The logical architecture—the formal logic framework—can be an effective tool that allows you to elegantly move from prepared argument, to response to a question, or response to a rebuttal argument, back to the syllogism and intended conclusion. Like Miles Davis's handwritten sketches that outlined the structure of the music his sextet would execute on March 2, 1959, formal logic provides a means of organizing argument. It is a means of organization just as powerful for contemplatively designing a complaint or appellate brief as it is the improvisation that goes on when depositing a witness, responding to questions in a motion in limine, or delivering an impromptu rebuttal argument that responds to defense counsel's closing argument. Without some structure, many lawyers simply rely on their instinctive ability to articulate argument to respond to the unexpected, improvise, and move the argument forward to their conclusion. Some lawyers do that very well, but the tools for legal argumentation can be better developed than that. Lawyers make music out of their arguments; argument is our craft. Formal logic is just one of the tools for learning and developing proficiency in this craft, but one that nearly every lawyer can make better use of.

11.5 Limits of a Fallacy-Based Perspective on Legal Argument

Formal logic is a useful tool for framing, organizing, and testing legal argument. However, deduction and the fallacies that follow from ignoring the rules of formal logic only take legal argument and advocates so far. First, the fact that an argument commits a fallacy does not mean that the conclusion is necessarily false. Instead, it means that the argument does not ensure the truth of the conclusion. Another argument might be offered that supports the conclusion. For example, in the preceding argument, revealing the fallacious nature of the argument does not require a conclusion that the witness was telling the truth. Instead, it only means that the argument does not ensure the conclusion that the witness was truthful. The conclusion might be entirely supportable by some other argument. For example, the argument might be reformed into an inductive argument, where pointing out several occasions where the witness provided consistent false testimony might be strong evidence that the witness is unreliable. Alternatively, a new major premise might be offered to support the conclusion. When a witness is unreliable, their testimony should be disregarded, or discounted, and more reliable witness or documentary evidence should be preferred by the jury. Accordingly, a fallacy-based response merely defuses the persuasive power of the deductive argument offered. It does not necessarily ensure the proffered conclusion is wrong. It does necessarily preclude the possibility other arguments, deductive, inductive, or analogical, might support the conclusion.

Deduction and the fallacies that follow from ignoring the rules of formal logic only take legal argument and advocates so far.

Additionally, while formal logic has an important place as a tool for designing and assessing legal argument, it is tempting, but not always appropriate, to use in other related advocacy tasks. For example, faced with ambiguity about the meaning of contractual or statutory language, the rules of logic might be applied as canons of construction. However, contract and statute drafters do not always utilize strict formal logic when writing, and where the court's role is to consider argument regarding the intention of statutory or contractual drafters, tools of logic might not always ensure that such intent is understood. While there may be a place for using formal logic as a tool for assessing intended meaning, it should be used with some caution. Where there is no other persuasive evidence of intent or controlling cannons of construction, the presumption that language was intended to be construed in a manner consistent with formal logic might have appeal, but has not always been embraced.[19] Conversely, fallacious arguments should be consistently rejected as unpersuasive. They simply cannot logically justify the conclusions they purport

19. *See, e.g.*, EarthGrains Baking Companies, Inc. v. Sycamore Family Bakery, Inc., 573 F. App'x 676, 678 (10th Cir. 2014) (utilizing formal logic in contract interpretation); United States v. Certain Real Prop. & Premises Known as 890 Noyac Rd., Noyac, N.Y., 739 F. Supp. 111 (E.D.N.Y. 1990), *rev'd*, 945 F.2d 1252 (2d Cir. 1991) (rejecting arguments based on concepts of formal logic in statutory interpretation); Vasudevan Software, Inc. v. MicroStrategy Inc., No. C 11-06637, 2013 U.S. Dist. LEXIS 134310 (N.D. Cal. Sept. 19, 2013) (rejecting arguments based on concepts of formal logic in interpreting a patent claim).

to justify. That is not to say the conclusions are necessarily unsupportable. However, where an advocate advances a fallacious deductive argument in support of a conclusion, they should be required to develop some other argument to persuasively support it.

Further, formal logic requires strict adherence to many formal rules. In fact, there are many more rules necessary to perform comprehensive, formal logical analysis of arguments. The few rules that have been described in this book are just those rules of classical, formal logic that result in the most common logical fallacies. Further, strict formal logic is not designed to handle complex arguments efficiently.[20] In many cases, factual or legal indeterminacy are the focus of the arguments: the parties are not in disagreement about the logical relationships between the premises and the inferences the support at all; they are instead focused on whether the proffered premises are true.

These weakness in the application of formal logic return us to the strength and value of the formal logical fallacy in legal argument. Formal logical fallacies are never good arguments. For all of the potential complexity required of strict adherence to the traditional approach to syllogistic logic, a fallacy-based perspective on legal argument can largely be reduced to a handful of those rules. While building a syllogistic argument "from the ground up" might require an impracticable number of terms, syllogisms, translation of common language to formal terms, and polysyllogistic relationships, a fallacy-based perspective on legal argument is as simple as evaluating one suspect syllogistic relationship, ensuring it has the hallmark pattern of one of the formal fallacies, and calling it by name. Last, where the dispute is not one of formal logic, the perspective of fallacy-based legal argument puts, at the very least, the legal argument in a logical context and allows your knowledge about the different logical tools to place the appropriate persuasive value on an argument that is really inductive or analogical rather than one masquerading as deduction.

11.6 Chapter Eleven in Review

- Understanding the rules of logic provides lawyers and judges with an additional facet in an already multifaceted system of legal argument.
- The rules of formal logic are the keys to determining whether the logical structure of an argument is valid or not. They are also the keys to explaining why cer-

20. *See* Arnold Vander Nat, Simple Formal Logic: With Common-Sense Symbolic Techniques 149 (2010) (describing the customary approach to traditional logic as "consist[ing] of making many *technical distinctions* regarding the various ways that permissible arguments, called *categorical syllogisms*, can be composed" and prefacing an approach to formal logic that recognizes that traditional deductive logic can be understood as "a *commonsense* system of deduction, a system that is complete and formal in the *style* of the deductive system for Propositional Logic") (emphasis in original).

tain patterns of argument are potentially persuasive and others must certainly be unpersuasive.

- Each logical fallacy manifests a pattern of argument that serves as a hallmark of fallacious reasoning. Familiarity with these patterns is important to making efficient use of formal logic in designing and evaluating persuasive logical form.
- Armed with an understanding of the rules of formal logic and the patterns of fallacious argument, sharpen your own arguments by designing them upon firm logical foundations.
- Additionally, armed with an understanding of the rules of formal logic and the patterns of fallacious argument, you should police opposing arguments for fallaciousness,and use the rules and case law, rejecting fallacious argument as tools to advocate for the rejection of the opposing argument and the conclusion it purports to justify.
- Formal logical fallacies provide a new perspective from which to evaluate legal argument. Some arguments should fail because they are not supported by facts. Some arguments should fail because they are not supported by law. Some arguments should fail because they are not supported by logic.
- Formal logic is an important, foundational tool for argument, but it is not the only tool lawyers use to craft and evaluate arguments.
- Formal logic has limits in legal argument and is but a single tool and not a system of legal argument in and of itself. It supplements the process of legal argument, but does not supplant it.

Chapter Twelve

Logic's Value to Lawyers Who Solve Legal Problems with Argument

This book concludes by considering the importance of formal logic in legal reasoning generally. If legal argument is to be a discipline, it requires some objective criteria for describing and evaluating the merit of legal argument. The integrity of this discipline has been ensured by systematically applying sound principles of law to established facts, bound by consistent logical justification, toward just conclusions. Understanding and using formal logic is foundational for legal argument, necessary for a principled legal system, valuable to lawyers and judges who want to distinguish their legal argument and analytical skills, and important to legal educators and students who want to communicate and comprehend the discipline of legal argument. However, knowing the proper place, and limits, of formal logic as a tool for legal argument is just as foundational.

- The role that lawyers play in the process of legal reasoning and judicial decision-making is focused on making and evaluating argument. The arguments that lawyers advance within the judicial decision-making process are important components of the adversarial judicial system.
- Before you read this book, did you think about the framework within which legal arguments are made or evaluated? If not, do you think formal logic providing an important framework for legal argument?
- Before your read this book, what were the five or six most important words you would have used to describe and justify your description of good legal arguments and bad legal arguments? After reading this book, would you still use the same words to assess legal argument, or would you use different or additional words?
- This book has focused on formal deductive logic, and that is just one of the logical tools lawyers use. Why do you think deductive arguments are persuasive? Are there times when you might make an argument that does not take a deductive form or fit into the pattern of a syllogism? Why?
- Does considering legal argument from the perspective of formal logic provide a perspective you had not considered before? Do you find this perspective useful for solving problems of legal argument?

12.1 The Place of Formal Logic in Legal Reasoning

This book has been designed to avoid discussing "legal reasoning" and "the judicial process," two important jurisprudential topics, within which formal logic in legal argument has a proper place. In part, this effort to avoid discussing legal reasoning has been a function of the intended audience for and purpose of this book. This has been a discussion about how a tool of philosophy can be used by trial lawyers to craft and evaluate legal argument. However, the broader ongoing discussion of legal reasoning generally is an important one. Much has been and continues to be written in an effort to articulate both positive and normative accounts of legal reasoning.[1] This book does not endeavor to add to that body of work. Instead, the aim of this book is to take a decidedly narrower focus, one designed not to describe what the judicial reasoning process is or ought to be. The focus here has been on how to improve legal arguments, based on a modest, uncontroversial, but important idea: persuasive legal argument should never be logically fallacious. Logic has persuasive force. Leveraging that persuasive force is an important tool for lawyers who practice the craft of legal argument in the courtroom. Learning the rules of logic helps lawyers think more intentionally about the arguments they design and respond to. The rules of logic and the formal logical fallacies that follow from errant deduction can be seen at work in the decisions of courts using those rules and fallacies. These examples provide useful tools for lawyers engaged in crafting and evaluating legal arguments.

The focus here has been on how to make legal arguments better, based on a modest, uncontroversial, but important idea: legal argument should never be logically fallacious.

However, within the vast body of literature regarding legal reasoning generally are differing views of whether that process is a deductive one or to what extent it is

1. One approach to this topic is offered in Larry Alexander & Emily Sherwin, Demystifying Legal Reasoning (2008). The authors' account begins with a summary of historical and contemporary writings on legal reasoning. *Id.* at 1. That summary begins with Sir Edward Coke, The First Part of the Institutes of the Law of England, § 138 ¶ 97b (1628), reprinted in II The Selected Writings of Sir Edward Coke 577, 701 (1639) (Steve Sheppard, ed., Indianapolis: Liberty Fund 2003), and lists several additional important historical works. Their list also lists several contemporary works on the topic including: "Lloyd L. Weinreb, Legal Reason: The Use of Analogy in Legal Argument (Cambridge: Cambridge University Press 2005); Cass R. Sunstein, Legal Reasoning and Political Conflict (1996); Steven J. Burton, An Introduction to Law and Legal Reasoning (1995); Henry M. Hart Jr. & Albert M. Sacks, The Legal Process: Basic Problems in the Making and Application of Law (1994); Steven J. Burton, Judging in Good Faith 35–68 (1992); Oliver Wendell Holmes, The Common Law (Dover Publications 1991); Melvin Aron Eisenberg, The Nature of the Common Law (1988); Ronald Dworkin, Law's Empire (1986); Ronald Dworkin, Taking Rights Seriously 14–130 (1978); Karl N. Llewellyn, The Common Law Tradition: Deciding Appeals (1960); Roscoe Pound, Law Finding through Experience and Reason (1960); Benjamin N. Cardozo, The Nature of the Judicial Process (1949); and Edward H. Levi, An Introduction to Legal Reasoning (1948)."

deductive. Some have described deduction's limitations in the legal reasoning process as including the complexity of legal argument and lack of agreement in legal argument.[2] Surely, there are many legal arguments where even the scope and details of the legal rule that supplies the major premise are uncertain. When that is the case, deduction is the wrong logical tool.

However, one writer has described the place of formal logic in a way most would find agreeable:

> [T]he ordinary canons of logic would be implied to determine whether the conclusion reached indeed follows from the premises selected. To insist that legal justification be logical in this sense is to impose no greater and no lesser requirement here than in most other types of argumentation and justification. But the familiarity of the requirement does not excuse its neglect. Although questions related to the formal validity of an argument may be only preliminary to an examination of the material desirability of the premises assumed, they are among the most important of preliminary questions.[3]

Formal logic might not always be the right tool in legal argument or judicial decision making. However, when it is employed, it should be employed with some care, and deductively fallacious argument should never be accepted as persuasive. Just as the foundation of a house is an essential step in its construction, the design of the logical structure of argument is essential to its stability. The rules and techniques described in the preceding chapters provide uncontroversial rules for making arguments. Formal logic is a starting point for argument, but arguments that ignore their formal logical structure are susceptible to significant instability.

12.2 A Focus on Framework

Lawyers who consider the logical framework of arguments not only have insights into argumentative stability, but their understanding of logical tools empowers them to respond to arguments by organizing legal arguments logically. I recall hearing two lawyers make an argument in a courtroom. The argument focused on whether the conduct of the defendant met the definition of "outrageous" under a certain rule of law. The rule itself did not define "outrageous," but outrageousness was an

2. *See, e.g.*, Richard A. Posner, *The Jurisprudence of Skepticism*, 86 Mich. L. Rev. 827, 833 (1988) ("There are two serious general limitations on the use of syllogisms in law, and they are still imperfectly acknowledged in legal opinions and advocacy, including the advocacy scholarship that dominates the law reviews. First, numerous and contestable minor premises often are necessary to connect the major premise to the conclusion. Second, the major premise often is not an agreed-upon definition, comparable to the definition of 'man' as a mortal being . . . . Logic and inference must be distinguished. A syllogism is valid if the conclusion follows from the premises; but the conclusion is true only if, in addition, the premises are true. Often in legal reasoning the premises cannot be shown to be true.").
3. Richard A. Wasserstrom, The Judicial Decision 192 (1961).

essential element of the plaintiff's case. There were only a few cases in the jurisdiction that provided examples of conduct that met or fell short of outrageousness. One of those cases was a case where the conduct was particularly bad. I'll call it the *Cooper* case. I cannot imagine too many people disagreeing that the conduct in *Cooper* was outrageous. In that case, the court held that the defendant's conduct was outrageous.

In the argument I heard, the defendant cited the *Cooper* case in support of the argument that defendant's conduct was not outrageous. The argument could be summarized this way:

> *Defendant's Counsel*: *Cooper* provides some guidance of what courts in this jurisdiction have held to be outrageous conduct. The facts in the instant case are entirely distinguishable. My client's alleged conduct did not involve conduct nearly as unexpected or uninvited as the conduct in *Cooper*. Further, the alleged conduct here did not take place over nearly as long a period of time as in *Cooper*.
>
> Accordingly, the court must determine that the plaintiff has failed establish that my client's conduct met the standard for outrageous conduct.

Considering the three logical tools discussed in this book, the argument fit into the category of argument by analogy. The defendant's counsel argued that the facts of the case were so dissimilar from those of *Cooper* that the court must reach a dissimilar conclusion, and hold that the defendant's conduct was not outrageous.

Lawyers are comfortable with analogous argument. Analogy is an important and effective logical tool for legal argument. It is not surprising that plaintiff's counsel responded to this argument with an analogical tool of their own. The plaintiff's argument might begin this way:

> *Plaintiff's Counsel*: Your Honor, the defendant has failed to discuss any of the other cases in this jurisdiction where courts have found conduct to be outrageous. Two of those cases involve facts with important similarities to the facts of my client's case.

So often, lawyers focus on one logical tool. They spend their time discussing the facts of cases and argue about similarities and dissimilarities in those facts. Judges entertain the comparisons and ask hard questions about what facts are important and what facts are not. However, if a lawyer understands analogy to be just one tool in legal argument, they are able to utilize a different tool to change the framework of the argument. For example, instead of seeing this dispute as limited to analogical argument, plaintiff's counsel might have responded with a different tool, offering a different perspective:

> *Plaintiff's Counsel*: Your Honor, the defendant's argument is founded on a logical error. It's logically fallacious. The defendant's

> argument is that *Cooper* is an example of conduct that is outrageous. The defendant goes on to argue that the facts of this case are different from the facts of *Cooper*, and therefore the facts of this case could not be held to be outrageous. Courts have never articulated such a limited definition of outrageousness. For example, there are two other cases, factually inapposite to *Cooper*, where the court also held the conduct to be outrageous.

Plaintiff's counsel's argument uses two tools. They begin by using the tool of formal logic. The defendant tried to reach a definitive conclusion, and analogy is not an appropriate tool to justify such a conclusion. Further, plaintiff's counsel subtlety points out that the defendant's argument is fallacious. It commits the fallacy of denying the antecedent term:

> If the facts are like Cooper, then the conduct is outrageous.
>
> The facts are not like Cooper.
>
> Therefore, the conduct is not outrageous.

The addition of a second tool, a tool of formal logic, to the plaintiff's argument helps in several ways. First, plaintiff's counsel communicates something about their understanding of both arguments in their logical context, providing some argumentative bearing. Plaintiff's counsel communicates that level of respect for the defendant's argument, but has an objective framework for understanding the place of that argument in relation to the plaintiff's argument. Second, plaintiff's counsel's fallacy-based response puts the defendant's argument in its proper place. The defendant's argument, in its current form, is logically fallacious and cannot do what it purports to do: compel the proffered conclusion. Third, the plaintiff's response puts a nametag on plaintiff's argument—it is fallacious. Such a label has persuasive value and calls the defendant's argument into question. Last, putting the defendant's argument in its place empowers the plaintiff to do two things. The plaintiff can respond with a deductive argument, based on a definition of "outrageous" and describe why the facts of the case fit within that definition. Additionally, or alternatively, the plaintiff can return to an analogical argument, having firmed up a foundation that, at least, puts the plaintiff's argument on equal or better footing, compared to the defendant's.

Otherwise, it would be easy for a lawyer to get trapped in this analogical argument. Plaintiff's counsel might spend a lot of time discussing the facts of *Cooper*, parsing out the legally significant facts, and trying to explain how the facts in evidence really are a lot like *Cooper*. Plaintiff's counsel might be significantly disadvantaged by framing the logical issue in terms of analogy, especially if the facts of *Cooper* are far from the facts in evidence. Most lawyers have been here before, seemingly confined to the arena of analogical argument. A lawyer "stuck" solving the problem of *Cooper* with only the tools of analogical argument might find this problem frustrating. This is especially true when lawyers confront the argument unexpectedly. They might struggle, and even sputter a little, trying to argue that there are legally significant factual similarities to *Cooper*, and therefor advocate that this limited the similarities require the same result as the *Cooper* court. Analogy might not be the best logical tool for convincing the court that the result in the case should be the same as in Cooper. Choosing the right logical tool requires knowledge of the logical framework of the arguments you face.

A firm understanding of the logical framework that lawyers work within provides a methodology for organizing legal argument and responses to arguments. Appreciating the differences among these frameworks provides you with a way to organize your responses to argument, even when arguing extemporaneously and dealing with unexpected questions, testimony, or arguments. The logical framework provides a foundation on which to fall back, evaluate the argument, and respond, with an argument that uses the best logical and legal tools. Plaintiff's counsel would be better off putting the problem of *Cooper* in its deductive place, and responding with a deductive argument or a better analogical one.

Last, the foundational structure of deductive logic, the syllogism, provides a framework for assessing and comparing argument. If we can reduce arguments to their syllogistic components, we can understand their logical form (categorical, hypothetical, or disjunctive). From there, we can test their form for conformity with the rules of formal logic, and focus our evaluation more precisely on their weakest components, seeing the justification for the inference drawn in the conclusion from the premises. The syllogistic form provides an objective, consistent format for organizing, understanding, and testing the logical components of legal argument.

12.3 Logic as a Metalanguage for Argument

In addition to a framework for making and evaluating legal argument, formal logic also provides language tools for communicating about argument. What makes a good legal argument good has not been comprehensively and consistently defined.[4]

4. Some have described the qualities of good legal argument. *See, e.g.*, Jack M. Balkin & Sanford Levinson, *Legal Historicism and Legal Academics: The Roles of Law Professors in the Wake of* Bush v. Gore, 90 Geo. L. J. 173, 181 (2001) ("Therefore the internal norms of good legal argument are always changing; they are being changed by political, social, and historical forces in ways that the internal norms of legal reasoning do not always directly acknowledge or sufficiently recognize."); Lawrence M. Friedman, *Taking Law and Society Seriously*, 74 Chi.–Kent L. Rev. 529, 530 (1999) ("Hence, a good legal argument might be defined objectively as an argument that judges treat with respect. Such an argument may not actually change the minds of judges, but at least they have to handle it with care."); Michael Sean Quinn, *Argument and Authority in Common Law Advocacy and Adjudication: An Irreducible Pluralism of Principles*, 74 Chi.–Kent L. Rev. 655, 777 (1999) ("There are two concepts of good legal argument. (a) In one sense, a legal argument is a good one when it is rhetorically well-structured and highly polished in delivery. In legal context, rhetorically-good arguments will cite obviously-relevant cases in a sensible way. (b) In another sense, a legal argument is a good one substantively and normatively. A good legal argument is one that entails a conclusion consistent with the legal system, including its surface provisions, its patterns, and its deep structure. These arguments attend to precedent with both depth and integrity. They attend to context and change. Empirically, such arguments

Nonetheless, logic provides one set of objective criteria for evaluating the persuasive force of argument. It also provides language tools for evaluating the nature and soundness of legal argument.[5] The language of formal logic helps lawyers divide and discuss arguments into components that are useful for them and for judges. If a concern for the success of an argument lies in the truth of its premises, logic provides language tools for focusing on that. If an argument's error is in incorrectly assessing the universality of a term in the argument, logic provides language tools for that. If an argument fails to be disciplined in the relationship between terms in hypothetical syllogisms, logic provides language tools for that. If an argument ignores the ambiguity in logical disjunction, logic provides language tools for that. The ability to name the different kinds of logical argument—deduction, induction, and analogy—provides an important means of describing argument. Last, the formal logical fallacies themselves serve as argumentation tools that, when understood, communicate something powerfully and succinctly about the persuasive force of logic in an argument.

Once you have language tools to discuss the persuasive force of argument, you are empowered to evaluate and communicate your valuation judgments about argument. This enriches the argumentative process, by providing new tools and perspectives on legal argument. While formal logic does not provide all of the conceptual and language tools necessary to communicate about legal argument, it does provide important foundational tools for this process. Of course, even a logically precise argument can be delivered ineffectively and rendered entirely unpersuasive. Legal argument is multifaceted, and formal logic represents just one facet necessary to make and evaluate legal argument. Other facets have their own concepts and language tools, and legal argument is about more than just sound logical form.

12.4 Logic's Persuasive Force

Logic not only provides conceptual and language tools for making and evaluating argument, it has persuasive force. Crafting legal arguments built on sound logical foundations wins cases. Logically framed conclusions are intuitively acceptable to

---

do not always win. In a perfect legal system, they would always prevail. In sense (b), legal argument should be taken very seriously indeed. Of course, it does not always happen in the real world. No legal system is perfect."); Mark Tushnet, *Interdisciplinary Legal Scholarship: The Case of History-in-Law*, 71 Chi.–Kent L. Rev. 909, 912 (1996) ("A good legal argument has many components. The authority of the person making the argument itself has weight, for example, in a way that may not happen in philosophy. A good legal argument quite often is one that is simple enough to encapsulate in the obligatory parenthetical when it is cited, even though arguments that are rationally compelling may be quite complicated. And, finally, good legal arguments often have a certain rhetorical flair.") (citations omitted).

5. Jacquette et al., Philosophy of Logic 43 (2006) ("it's necessary to distinguish between the logician's language with its concepts, and the reasoner's language with its concepts. For convenience let's call the logician's language the metalanguage and the reasoner's language the object language.") (emphasis in original).

audiences of legal argument.[6] However, in the same way that deduction is not the only logical tool for making legal argument, logic is just one among other extralogical tools for legal argument.[7] Logical form supports the persuasive force of argument because it is orderly and familiar.[8] Illogical arguments are confusing. A confused audience will struggle to understand a message. An audience unable to understand a message will struggle to be persuaded by it. Logic helps organize, and discipline, premises and conclusions in a way that can be understood.

Second, because lawyers, judges, and others generally endeavor to think logically—at least seeking some general rule or principle to justify a proffered conclusion—a logically sound argument will likely sound plausible, if not compelling, to an audience. While some logically fallacious arguments might sound persuasive, most do not, and ensuring the logical integrity of an argument can only help the audience to understand and consider the argument. Carefully planned arguments, based on a sound logical framework, lay a foundation for persuasion.

Third, deductive arguments that take an illogical, fallacious form should be unpersuasive once their fallaciousness is identified.[9] That is not to say that their conclusions are unsupportable, but a formally fallacious argument is no argument at all and should be abandoned for another, valid argument. In fact, in some contexts,

6. *See, e.g.*, JAMES A. GARDNER, LEGAL ARGUMENT: THE STRUCTURE AND LANGUAGE OF EFFECTIVE ADVOCACY 6 (1993) ("When presented with the property framed major and minor premises of a syllogism, the human mind seems to produce the conclusion without any additional prompting. Moreover, the mind recognizes the conclusion to be of such compelling force that the conclusion simply cannot be denied."). *See also* CELIA W. CHILDRESS, PERSUASIVE DELIVERY IN THE COURTROOM (1995) ("It is my contention that winning lawyers today enter the courtroom prepared with their major ideas and premises which they will enunciate during their opening statements because they, in their mental review of their cases, know what they wish to prove. Then after seeking corroboration of their premises during direct, cross-examination, and redirects which exploit adversarial dialect, they use those premises and conclusion within their closing arguments.").

7. *See, e.g.*, DAVID J. DEMPSEY, LEGALLY SPEAKING, 40 POWERFUL PRESENTATION PRINCIPLES LAWYERS NEED TO KNOW, 195–99 (2002) (listing logical persuasion as just one method of persuasion in legal argument among psychological persuasion, personal appeal and emotional appeal.); *see also* Posner, *supra* note 2, at 838 (listing "anecdote, introspection, imagination, common sense, intuition (due apparently to how the brain structures perceptions, so that, for example, we ascribe causal significance to acts without being able to observe—we never do observe—causality), empathy, imputation of motives, speaker's authority, metaphor, analogy, precedent, custom, memory, 'induction' (the expectation of regularities, related both to intuition and to analogy), 'experience'" amount the methods of investigation and persuasion used in "practical reason."

8. Joel L. Cornwell, *Legal Writing as a Kind of Philosophy*, 48 MERCER L. REV. 1091, 1113 (1997) ("The deductive syllogism is the backbone of traditional legal rhetoric even when it is not expressly acknowledged.").

9. "An argument that is correctly reasoned may be wrong, but an argument that is incorrectly reasoned can never be right." Ruggero J. Aldisert et al., *Logic for Law Students: How to Think Like a Lawyer*, 69 U. PITT. L. REV. 1, 22 (2007).

offering illogical arguments or explanations is associated with evidence of intent to hinder, delay, and defraud.[10]

12.5 A New Way of Thinking about Logic and Legal Argument—and Jazz

My grandfather was a hard worker. He told me a story once that, as he likely intended, I will not forget. It was a story about his first day at his first job. His job was a simple one that day: he was to help build a concrete sidewalk. The concrete for the sidewalk had to be mixed by hand. There were several laborers involved in making the sidewalk, each with his own distinct job to perform. My grandfather, being the newest laborer on the jobsite, was given a simple job to do. A large load of bags of concrete mix had been unloaded at the beginning of the sidewalk. He was told to carry bags of concrete along the path of the sidewalk so that the next day, when the concrete was being mixed with water and poured, ample supplies of concrete would be within arm's reach of the laborers tasked with mixing and pouring the concrete.

Excited for his first day and first job, my grandfather picked up two of the bags of concrete from the large stack, walked five or six steps to the beginning of the sidewalk's eventual location, dropped the bags of concrete to the ground, and neatly arranged both bags next to each other. He returned to the large stack of bags, picked up two more, and walked seven or eight strides toward the sidewalk location, and dropped off the bags there. He continued this process throughout the day, picking up bags, moving them to the linear path of the planned side walk and dropping off the bags, each time a little further away from the large stack.

As the day went on, those bags of concrete got heavier in my grandfather's hands. Rather than toting two at a time, he started carrying just one. His fingers became sore and his hands started to swell. The morning shade was dismissed and overtaken by a hot June sun. The soft, cool ground became warm and unforgiving. His feet started to sweat and ache in his boots. Each bag required that he travel further and further to deposit it. The more he hauled bags of concrete, the less energized and enthusiastic he became to do his job. It was exhausted and unenthusiastic that he found himself having to carry what seemed like the heaviest bags the longest distance.

Nonetheless, he did his work and did it well. But, by the time he had finished, he realized he had made an error. In his zealousness to do a job and do it well, he had

10. *See, e.g.*, In re Evans, 538 B.R. 268, 286 (Bankr. W.D. Va. 2015) ("the debtor's logical fallacies in explaining the reasons the debtor either forgot or declined to disclose the property are relevant. *See* Kaye v. Hirsch (In re Hirsch), 14 B.R. 59, 63 (Bankr.S.D.Fla.1981) ("The incongruity and illogic of the debtors' explanations regarding their financial affairs, and particularly the . . . checking account, leads the court to conclude that their actions were taken with the intent to hinder, delay or defraud creditors and to conceal property . . . ."); In re Butler, 38 B.R. 884, 888 (Bankr. D. Kan. 1984).

begun his work without any careful design for how best to do it. Had he considered the best path to complete this work, he would have deposited the first bags at the end of the line, rather than the beginning. Then, when he was the most tired and the elements were the most hostile, he would have found himself with the shortest distance to travel. He would have done "the heavy lifting" first.

Legal argument involves some heavy lifting too. However, lawyers frequently do not begin the process of designing their arguments with the same attention to the argument's logical architecture that they do to the other important aspects of the argument. Many lawyers get a sense for the arguments they will make, and their merit, when they meet with their client for the first time. The client reports a story that includes some important facts, the story suggests that justice requires a certain result, and the lawyer builds arguments around the facts that are most compelling and credibly established at trial. Many times, their hunches, intuition, and experience provide excellent guidance for constructing theories of their cases and even formulating specific arguments. Sometimes lawyers learn, in something like the heat of the afternoon sun, that the arguments they were energized and enthusiastic to make at the outset of the case could have been more thoughtfully and elegantly designed had they taken some time to consider the argumentative structure that would provide a foundation for the presentation and use of those compelling factual and legal premises that attracted them to the client's just cause in the first place.

The first song that plays on Miles Davis's *Kind of Blue* album is titled "So What." It is my favorite song on the album. It is a modal jazz song. If you were to listen to the song right now, you will hear different instruments, different solos, different artists playing, and different improvisations. You will hear a lot of "different" in that song. However, what I think about when I listen to that song is something that is not different. I think about the same two chords played by the pianist, Bill Evans, in a consistent, then varied, rhythm. These two chords change throughout the song, introducing the song, organizing the musical structure of the song, and at the end, bringing the song to a beautiful conclusion. The piano chords provide a foundational background and organization to the music, and allow the musicians freedom to improvise solos, move from sound to sound, solo to solo, artist to artist, difference to difference, in a way that seems cohesive, organized and, to me and many others, compelling and persuasive.[11]

Understanding of the rules of music, especially modal jazz, provides some insight into why that music is so interesting to so many. Further, understanding something of the rules, order, and language of jazz music theory provides tools for understanding and communicating my perceptions, experiences with, and reaction to that music. If "So What" had been a more fallible composition or performance, I might

11. Jason Rogers Titus, Miles Davis' "So What" as Modal Jazz Case Study (unpublished Ph.D. dissertation, University of Rochester) ("The piano chords at the beginning of the tune's head (the "a-men" or "response" in the "call and response" gesture) are one of the piece's most salient features. The innovative voicing of these chords became an identifiable marker of modal jazz in the 1960s.").

use even my limited knowledge of music theory to criticize the song or the way it was delivered. Instead, I simply use my knowledge to more thoroughly enjoy this music. When I listen to "So What," those two chords provide a familiar pattern, organizing the sounds, sort of like the meter of good poetry.

The syllogism, too, has a meter. If we study it a bit, we will hear it in the arguments lawyers make and the opinions judge write. The more we study it, the more it provides a familiar, identifiable pattern, organizing the facts and law, like the meter of good poetry. Lawyers would make more persuasive, carefully designed, even aesthetically pleasing legal arguments if they had a better understanding of some of the rules and language of formal logic and intentionally applied it to the design of their arguments. It would provide a new way of looking at argument. It would provide a new perspective for evaluating argument. It would enrich their understanding of why arguments are made, why arguments are appealing, and why arguments are good or bad. It would provide a new perspective for reading cases, writing opinions, designing briefs, telling stories, developing themes and theories. Even when confronted with an unexpected argument, unexpected witness testimony, that exhibit you have never seen before, or a citation to "a case just published by the court of appeals," the foundation of formal logic provides a simple, familiar tool for you to use to craft your response.

Last, since formal logic is foundational to legal argument, it is not only a tool for making convincing argument. "Although questions related to the formal validity of an argument may be only preliminary to an examination of the material desirability of the premises assumed, they are among the most important of preliminary questions."[12] Questions of logical integrity in legal argument are important because lawyers are engaged in the discipline of legal argument. Arguments should, at least, be logically sound.[13] Fallacious arguments are not compelling justifications for the conclusions they purport to support. Arguments based on fallacious logic do not further a principled judicial process or foster just results.

Lawyers who spot formal logical fallacies in their own or opponents' legal arguments are not only better arguers, they are engaged in a process designed to preserve the integrity of the discipline of legal argument. The more attentive lawyers are in evaluating the logic of their legal arguments, the more they contribute to the exchange of logically sound, consistent, disciplined arguments. Such arguments add value to the argumentative discourse in the courtroom, the more effective they become at evaluating competing legal arguments, and the more competently they are able to predict legal outcomes and advise clients.

Lawyers solve problems, in part, by working with raw materials that might be described as a chaotic universe of facts, disagreement, emotion, expectation, legal rules, indeterminacy, and ambiguity. They confront this chaotic assembly of raw

12. WASSERSTROM, *supra* note 3.
13. *Id.*

materials and organize them, crafting these disparate components into coherent arguments. They practice the craft of legal argument to solve their clients' problems by organizing the facts and law and resolving uncertainty with custom-made advice and solutions, identifying legal issues, and translating legal principles into explanations told in the language of the layperson. They solve judges' problems by ordering facts and law and resolving indeterminacy in legal rules and definitions with arguments to justify resolutions of indeterminacy. They solve jurors' problems by designing persuasive paths for them to understand the significance of and resolve conflicts in evidence.

Formal logic plays an important role at the heart of the craft of lawyering and the design of all of these solutions. My hope is that this book will provide you with some old tools for gaining new perspectives on making and evaluating legal argument: tools that will enrich your ability to make arguments that bring order to conflict, encourage just and consistent judicial decisions, and provide rich, thoughtful, sound, just solutions to the problems faced by the clients, judges, jurors, and justice system you serve.

12.6 Chapter Twelve in Review

- The arguments lawyers make are just one element within a complex system of legal reasoning and judicial decision-making.
- Formal logic provides a framework within which lawyers can design argument and assess foundational logical integrity of legal arguments.
- Formal logic provides a persuasive method for communicating both factual and legal arguments. The syllogism provides a structure for evaluating the persuasive power of argument and is especially effective for identifying logically fallacious arguments.
- Logic is not the only method of persuasion. Formal logic is not the only logical tool useful for persuasion. However, avoiding arguments that are formally fallacious should be a minimal requirement of any persuasive legal argument.
- Understanding formal logic and its place in legal argument helps lawyers craft persuasive arguments and provide a framework for engaging in argumentative dialog.
- Lawyers who master the logical framework of the arguments they make and respond to empower themselves to leverage logic to be more creative, to manage complex factual and legal problems, and to translate legal concepts into arguments that will be understood by and persuasive to the clients, judges, and jurors in their audience.

Appendices

Exercises: Solutions and Discussions

Appendix A

Chapter Five: *Breslin Real Estate Group, LLC d/b/a Breslin Real Estate Solutions v. Elderberry Software and Media, Inc.*

The fallacy of denying the antecedent term appears in paragraphs 10 and 11 of the Complaint. Paragraph 10 sets out a contractual provision which takes the form of a hypothetical proposition. Note that the proposition is stated in the negative ("In the event CUSTOMER fails to make full and complete payment"). The plaintiff pleading, in paragraph 11 negates this term ("Customer did not fail to make full and complete payment"). Additionally, the hallmark language of hypothetical argument, "if . . . then" language is missing, but the "in the event . . ." language has the same logical meaning. The argument might be arranged in the following syllogism:

> If the Customer fails to make full payment, then Developer is not obligated to complete the software.
>
> Customer did make full payment.
>
> Therefore, Developer is obligated to complete the software.

Because the argument in paragraphs 10 and 11 rests on denying the antecedent term in the syllogism, it commits the fallacy of denying the antecedent.

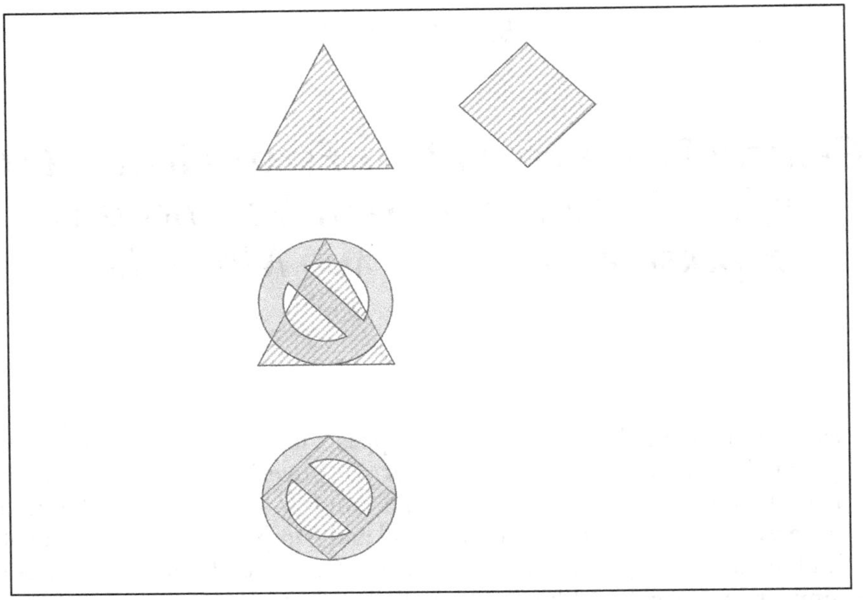

Figure 69. *The fallacious form of hypothetical syllogism called the fallacy of denying the antecedent.*

You get a sense that the complaint reveals only favorable facts (as plaintiffs frequently do in their complaints) and that there is "more to the story" here. This illustrates one of the problems with arguments that take the form of the fallacy of denying the antecedent. While failing to make a payment might be a basis for discontinuing development of the software, timely payment might not be the only obstacle to ensuring development of the software, and we would likely learn in the case that the defendant had a basis, other than nonpayment, that justified its refusal to develop Phase 3.

Appendix B

Chapter Six: *Annalise Forester v. Graham C. Hayes*

The form of defendant's argument is apparent in the conclusion of his brief. The sentence "where a jury verdict is the result of passion or prejudice, such a verdict must shock the conscience of the court" is a hypothetical premise. It is a little bit tricky to identify because it (like the exercise at the end of Chapter Five) does not include the "if . . . then" language so frequently used to identify hypothetical syllogisms. However, the "where" language has the same meaning.

Counsel is either using sloppy logic or is being downright logically disingenuous. The defendant does not like the jury verdict. He didn't like it at $150,000, and he would not have liked it at $100,000. The defendant might be concerned that even if he is successful in demonstrating that the verdict shocks the conscience of the court, the court might simply respond by reducing the amount of the jury's verdict from $150,000 to $100,000. Accordingly, the defendant would prefer to meet the "passion or prejudice" standard, get a new trial, and endeavor to obtain a better result, possibly, even a "no cause of action" verdict in favor of defendant.

The conclusion contains at least two syllogisms, but in a fallacy-based perspective on legal argument we only need to find one fallacious connection at a time. Further, identifying just one fallacious connection in a polysyllogistic argument is enough to defuse the logical force of the argument. In this argument, we can focus in on the argument that attempts to justify a conclusion that a new trial is required. That argument includes a premise derived from the facts: the defendant believes that this verdict shocks the conscience because it was more than the plaintiff asked for. That is not a bad argument. The defendant then uses that conclusion as a premise in a more problematic argument that commits the fallacy of affirming the consequent:

If a verdict is the result of passion or prejudice, then it shocks the conscience.

This verdict shocks the conscience.

Therefore the verdict is the result of passion or prejudice.

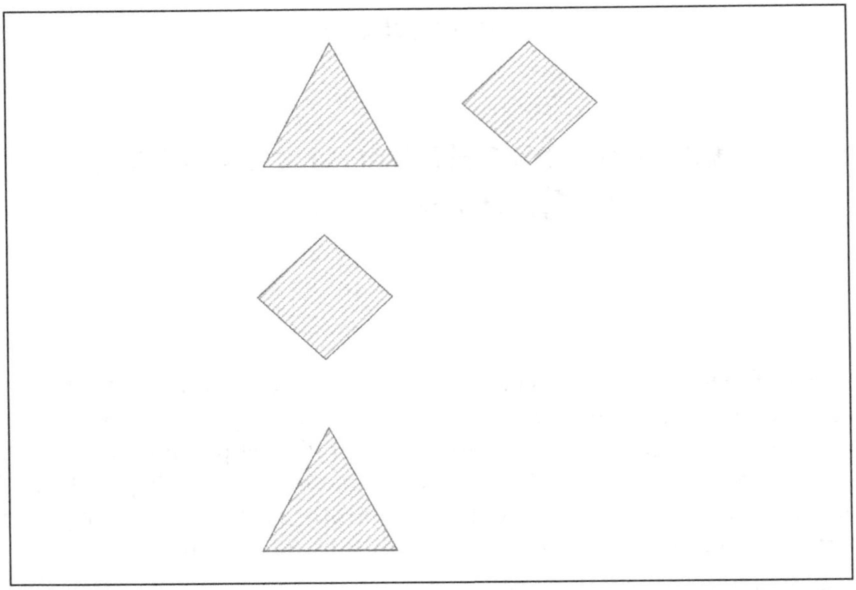

Figure 70. *The fallacious form of hypothetical syllogism called the fallacy of affirming the consequent.*

The conclusion contains yet another syllogism, reasoning that because the verdict was the result of passion or prejudice, a new trial is required. However, the problem with this polysyllogistic line of reasoning is in the middle syllogism described above. While it may be true that a verdict that is the result of passion or prejudice should shock the conscience (jurors are frequently counseled to simply apply the facts to the law and not to be swayed by passion or prejudice), not all verdicts that shock the conscience are the result of passion or prejudice. A jury might just make a mathematical error, for example. This is not to say that defendant cannot establish that the verdict was the result of passion or prejudice; he will just have to find some other logically sound argument to support such a conclusion. His argument misstates the order and inference of the relationship between verdicts based on passion and prejudice and verdicts that shock the conscience.

Appendix C

Chapter Seven: *Mack Bryce v. Eastern Ohio College*

The problem presents an issue that might be described primarily as an issue of fact: is there any evidence that the person driving the golf cart was an agent of the defendant?

> Some EOC agents were persons wearing EOC apparel on the date of the accident.
>
> The driver of the golf cart that injured the plaintiff was a person wearing EOC apparel on the date of the accident.
>
> Therefore, the driver of the golf cart that injured the plaintiff was an EOC agent.

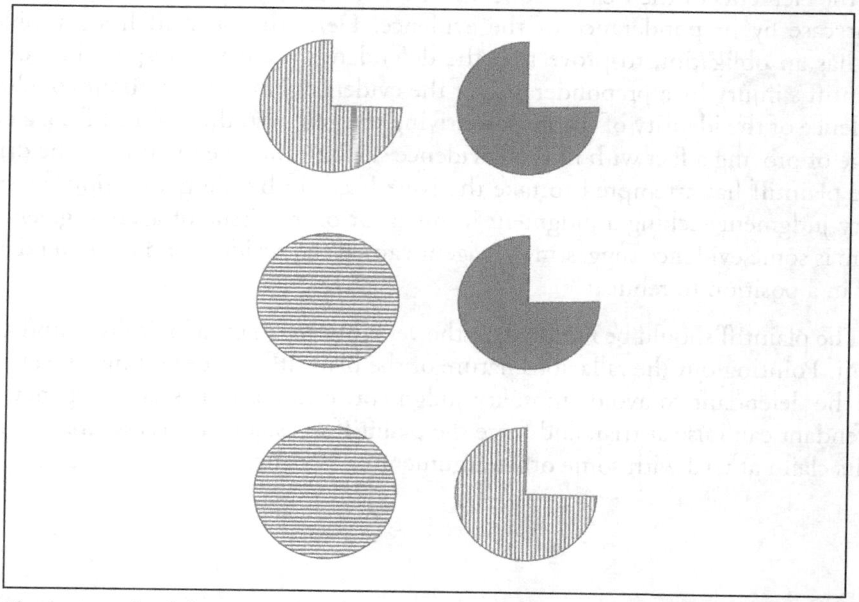

Figure 71. *The fallacious form of a categorical syllogism called the fallacy of the undistributed middle term.*

The focus here moves to the middle term: "persons wearing EOC apparel on the date of the accident." The middle term appears in the major premise first. The major premise does not distribute the term there, since the premise is in the form of a particular affirmative proposition. We know from this proposition that some of the persons wearing EOC apparel on the date of the accident were EOC agents. Of course, the event is a home college football game, and we would expect that most of the people wearing EOC apparel on such a day are simply fans of the team and the school, and not necessarily employees of EOC. This is the primary problem with the argument. The next instance of the middle term, in the minor premise, does not help solve this problem either. It takes the form of a universal affirmative proposition. This tells us something about the entire class of the driver of the golf cart that hit the plaintiff. However, the middle term is still undistributed here. The driver is just one of many people wearing EOC apparel.

Accordingly, since neither instance of the middle term (the term that allows us to justify a relationship between the terms in the conclusion) is distributed, the syllogism fails to reach a reliable conclusion. It commits the fallacy of the undistributed middle.

The problem provides another opportunity to see a deductive logic argument in a legal context. Of course, in a civil case, plaintiffs do not have the burden of proving the elements of their claim conclusively. Ordinarily, they only need to establish their case by preponderance of the evidence. Here, the plaintiff has a problem. He has an obligation to prove that the defendant's agent was responsible for the plaintiff's injury by a preponderance of the evidence. However, without conclusive evidence of the identity of the person driving the golf cart, the plaintiff faces a challenge of proving a fact with limited evidence surrounding the identity of the driver. The plaintiff has attempted to take the issue head-on by filing a motion for summary judgment seeking a judgment in his favor on the issue of agency, given that there is some evidence suggesting an agent caused the accident and the defendant is not in a position to rebut it.

The plaintiff should be required, at the very least, to make a logically sound argument. Pointing out the fallacious nature of the plaintiff's argument may be enough for the defendant to avoid summary judgment, create a fact issue on agency that defendant can raise at trial, and force the plaintiff to establish this essential element of its claim at trial with some other argument or evidence.

APPENDIX D

CHAPTER EIGHT: *SQUAREBARRELL SOLUTIONS, LLC* v. *INTERIOR DIAMETER, INC.*

The argument made by movant can be described as committing the fallacy of the illicit process. As the note preceding the problem invites you to assume, there are cases where a 30(b)(6) witness is produced for a deposition but cannot provide answers to all of the questions posed to them. In some of those cases, the failure to provide answers is not sanctionable.[1] The brief submitted by movant only focuses on the cases where the failings of a 30(b)(6) witness merited sanctions. One way to describe the movant's effort to reach a legal conclusion about all of the cases regarding 30(b)(6) witnesses who cannot answer all of the questions at their deposition is to say it commits the fallacy of the illicit process. When the brief claims, "Accordingly, parties who fail to produce knowledgeable witnesses for 30(b)(6) depositions are without substantial justification for their failure to comply with discovery rules," it is making a universal claim about all such parties. However, the premise offered to justify such a conclusion is not distributed. The movant offers only a sample of the cases dealing with 30(b)(6) witness testimony in its brief.

Of course, if the respondent does not do their homework and find some cases that make clear that other 30(b)(6) witness failures are not sanctionable, the undistributed nature of movant's premise might not be patent. However, once the premise is disclosed as only speaking to some, not all, failures, the respondent has accomplished something important: the movant's argument is logically fallacious, and if movant is going to win their motion, they will have to do better. At the very least,

1. *See, e.g.*, Wilson v. Lakner, 228 F.R.D. 524, 528–29 n. 7 (D. Md. 2005) ("[o]bviously a rule of reason applies. There is no obligation to produce witnesses who know every single fact, only those that are relevant and material to the incident or incidents that underlie the suit." Also stating, "absolute perfection in preparation is not required"); Henrik Klinge Retained Trust v. Triumph Apparel Corp., No. 1:09-CV-1812, 2012 U.S. Dist. LEXIS 10194, at *18, (M.D. Pa. Jan. 27, 2012) ("[W]here [the Rule 30(b)(6) representative] represented that he did not know the answer to a particular question . . . we do not find his conduct during the deposition to have been evasive, misleading, obstructionist, or false."); Costa v. County of Burlington, No. 07-CV-904, 2008 U.S. Dist. LEXIS 56266, at *10-11, (D.N.J. June 27, 2008) ("Simply because defendant's witness could not answer every question posed to him does not equate to the fact that defendant did not satisfy its obligation to prepare its 30(b)(6) witness."); Courtney v. Ivanov, No. CV 3:13-227, 2016 U.S. Dist. LEXIS 46519, at *22 (W.D. Pa. Apr. 6, 2016) ("The fact that [plaintiff's] 30(b)(6) representatives did not have answers to every question that [defendant's] posed at the depositions does not warrant a continuation of the depositions.").

respondent has placed themselves in a posture where they can make a competing argument that the facts of the case fit into the same category of cases where sanctions were not imposed.

Breaking the argument down into a syllogism might look like this:

> Some cases involving a party's failure produce knowledgeable witnesses for 30(b)(6) depositions are cases where the court found the party's discovery conduct to be not substantially justified.
>
> [Four cited] cases where a party's failure to comply with discovery rules is not substantially justified required imposition of discovery sanctions.
>
> Therefore, cases of parties who fail to produce knowledgeable witnesses for 30(b)(6) depositions are cases that require imposition of discovery sanctions.[2]

2. You may also have identified another fallacy in the brief: the fallacy of the undistributed middle term. This formulation of the argument attempts to arrive at a conclusion based on a middle term ("cases where a party's failure to comply with discovery rules is not substantially justified") that is not distributed in either of the premises.

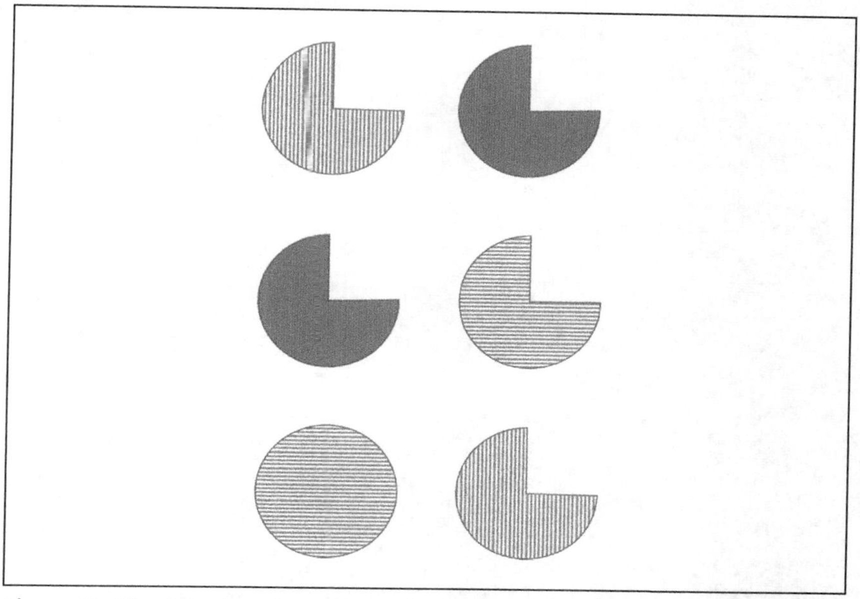

Figure 72. *The fallacious form of a categorical syllogism called the fallacy of the illicit minor term.*

The conclusion takes the form of a universal affirmative, distributing the minor term ("cases of parties who fail to produce knowledgeable witnesses for 30(b)(6) depositions"). The minor term is undistributed in the minor premise because the movant only cites four cases; there are other cases of unknowledgeable 30(b)(6) witnesses. Because the conclusion attempts to assert something about all such cases, while the premise only refers to a few of those cases, the argument commits the fallacy of the illicit minor term.

Appendix E

Chapter Nine: *Toy-Vo, Inc. d/b/a Toypocalypse v. Collin Lewis*

The fallacy of the negative premise is found in the plaintiff's counsel's line of cross-examination. Of course, the questions themselves are not necessarily an argument, nor are they fallacious. The conclusion counsel suggests, however, fits into a pattern of fallacious argument. The gist of counsel's argument is that the absence of a causative factor, like management, employees, or business model, requires a conclusion that the new location of the business was the cause of the plaintiff's lost profits. That is, the plaintiff's argument is that the absence of one factor as the cause of lost profits requires the conclusion that some other factor did cause the lost profits. This is the hallmark of the fallacy of the negative premise. The syllogism might look something like this:

> The management team was not a cause of the plaintiff's lost profits.
>
> The new location of the business is not the management team.
>
> Therefore, the new location of the business is the cause of the plaintiff's lost profits.

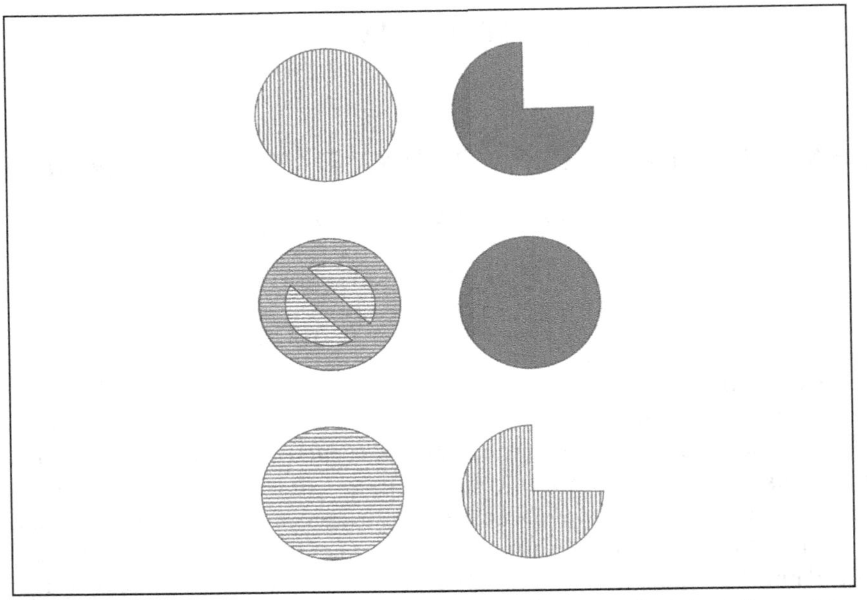

Figure 73. *The fallacious form of a categorical syllogism called the fallacy of the negative premise.*

In a complicated case of business losses, lawyers frequently argue about whether the defendant's actions caused the losses, or whether some other factor was the cause. Defendants in these cases typically point to some other potential cause and hope that the plaintiff is unable to carry the burden of proof in establishing that the defendant caused the damages. Because we can draw limited inferences from negative premises, logic has a place to play in evaluating the persuasive value of these kinds of arguments. Of course, this only takes us so far. In a case in which there are a finite number of causative factors, eliminating all but one factor is still logically persuasive. Such a technique effectively limits the choices to two disjuncts and validly asserts the truth of one disjunction from the denial of the other—a technique studied in Chapter Ten.

Appendix F

Chapter Ten: *Marathon Logistics III, Inc. v. Brule River Capital, LP*

The basis for a disjunctive premise that will be at issue on appeal should be apparent in the special interrogatory: "Do you find that Defendant acted in bad faith or has been stubbornly litigious?" Hidden in this disjunctive question is an ambiguous disjunction. Does the jury have to find that the defendant acted in bad faith but was not stubbornly litigious? Does the jury have to find that the defendant was stubbornly litigious, but not bad faith? Can the jury find that defendant was both acting in bad faith and stubbornly litigious? The context of the legal standard suggests that an inclusive disjunction is appropriate here. However, this is not express in the special interrogatory. Further, the space provided for a response does not prompt the jury as to the requested response. The jury could respond with a "yes" or a "no" or some other response. The jury responded by indicating a finding that one of the two disjuncts was present. The jury is silent regarding the other disjunct.

This would not ordinarily be a problem. Because a disjunction only requires one or the other, a finding of one is sufficient to end the inquiry and support an award of attorney fees. However, there was a problem with the instructions to the jury on bad faith, one that brings into question whether the defendant is properly liable for attorney fees. The jury was not correctly instructed on bad faith. The jury responded affirmatively only as to bad faith. We might anticipate the arguments of the parties as a result of the appellant court's decision regarding the errant instruction. The defendant will argue that because the jury only identified bad faith and the instruction on bad faith was wrong, the jury verdict must be read to require a reversal of the verdict on attorney fees and a remand and new trial on the issue of bad faith only. In a sense, the defendant will be making a logic argument. The jury confronted a disjunctive premise, leaving a choice between bad faith and stubbornly litigious. The jury affirmed bad faith. Therefore, the jury rejected stubbornly litigious.

The plaintiff might respond by suggesting such an argument is based on a logical fallacy. One cannot reach the decision that one disjunct did not exist from an affirmation that the other did exist. That would be the fallacy of affirming a disjunction. Accordingly, the plaintiff would argue that on remand the jury should assess the same question, preserving both disjuncts as potential bases for an award of attorney fees.

Figure 74. *The fallacious form of a categorical syllogism called the fallacy of affirming a disjunct.*

The problem raises as issue of whether formal logic is always the right tool for every task, a question explored in Chapter Eleven. Was the jury performing formal logic when it rendered a verdict and completed a special interrogatory? Probably not. Are the rules of formal logic always the best rules to apply when understanding a text, or contract, or statute, or special interrogatory form? Probably not. Could this problem have been avoided by anticipating the ambiguity in disjunction? Had the lawyers considered this potential problem, they might have provided a more detailed jury instruction, one that required that the jury answer questions relating to each of the two disjunctions.

INDEX